The Christian Century Reader

Representative Articles, Editorials, and Poems
Selected from More than Fifty Years of
The Christian Century

by

HAROLD E. FEY and MARGARET FRAKES

ASSOCIATION PRESS
New York

To Charles Clayton Morrison and Paul Hutchinson

Preface

In the past half-century American Christian thought has changed in important respects. A useful yardstick for measuring the scope of these changes is the fifty-three annual volumes of the weekly Christian Century. Here is recorded the swing from faith in progress, automatically ascending on the escalator of evolution, whose inventor was God, to the present dialectical realism; from a concept of the kingdom of God as something largely dependent on man's initiative to that of the kingdom as one in which the initiative lies with God, with man participating in God's redemptive activity; from the concern of the social gospel with the outward structure of justice to the inwardness of an ethic of culture in which the divine Spirit moves at every level in love and liberation. The movement in Europe from Ritschl to Barth has been paralleled in America by the swing from Rauschenbusch to Reinhold Niebuhr.

Today, as a new era dawns, God is using the power of ecumenical faith and experience to add a new dimension to churchmanship in Asia, Africa and Latin America, as well as in Europe and America. In the social order mighty new forces are loosed, for good as well as for evil. The development of these forces is also seen in these pages. The impact in the last half-century of nationalism on tribalism, of religion on politics, of church on state and state on church, of the Christian conscience on industry, agriculture and the professions can be traced here. The social responsibility of business, of science, of education, of medicine, of law and even of the arts begins to emerge. The great issues of peace and war, of race and class, of affluence in some societies and poverty in others, attain new insistence. The

7

cold war confrontation of democracy and communism, both armed with weapons of ultimate destruction, contributes an apocalyptic urgency as this half-century ends. All issues test the validity of the affirmations by which faith answers the great questions: What does God intend? Why are we here? How can we know and do his will? What can we do to be saved?

When The Christian Century reached its fiftieth year of publication in 1958, the idea emerged that we should make a selection of editorials, articles and poetry which would, in book form, distill the scope of these changes as they had been caught in this journal of Christian opinion. The task of selection was a formidable one; the annual volumes usually exceed 1,500 magazine pages, and a half-century of publication adds up to something more than a 20-foot shelf of large volumes. Time for working through something like 75,000 pages had to be worked into the schedules of persons actively involved in editing and publishing a weekly paper. But time was found, principally by Associate Editor Margaret Frakes, who spent an aggregate of several months at the task of selecting and organizing this material. Her great capacity for discernment and her discriminating judgment are seen in the representative quality of these selections.

Now our work is done, and we present this volume as one which attempts fairly to represent the scope and purpose of The Christian Century. In a larger sense, it also represents the direction, temper and understanding of Protestant Christianity in this century. While I am at present the editor of The Christian Century, the reader should know that the editorial minds which principally shaped this record belonged to Charles Clayton Morrison and Paul Hutchinson. Dr. Morrison "re-founded" The Christian Century in 1908 and was editor until 1947. The late Dr. Hutchinson, who became managing editor in 1924, was editor from 1947 until 1956, when I, who joined the staff in 1940, succeeded him.

Harold E. Fey, *Editor*
The Christian Century

Contents

Preface   7

I. INSTRUMENTS OF WITNESS

Has the Church Collapsed?
An Editorial   February 18, 1915   21

Our Secularized Civilization
Reinhold Niebuhr   April 22, 1926   22

End Missions Imperialism Now!
Hugh Vernon White   February 14, 1934   29

The Menace of the New Paganism
Arnold J. Toynbee   March 10, 1937   36

The Iona Idea
Editorial Correspondence by
Paul Hutchinson   September 11, 1946   42

The Church as Prophetic Critic
John C. Bennett   January 6, 1954   47

The New Look in American Piety
A. Roy Eckardt   November 17, 1954   53

The Church in Suburban Captivity
Gibson Winter   September 28, 1955   59

Harbinger of Hope
An Editorial   December 13, 1950   66

An Analysis of Revivalistic Method
An Editorial   July 1, 1909   70

Needed: Evangelism in Depth
Editorial Correspondence by
Cecil Northcott   June 26, 1957   74

II. FOUNDATIONS

At Henry Drummond's Grave
Charles Clayton Morrison   September 1, 1910   81

Honoring the Past
Robert E. Speer   May 26, 1910   87

The Changing World
An Editorial   September 28, 1911   88

The Sense of God's Reality
Harry Emerson Fosdick   November 6, 1919   90

God Lets Loose Karl Barth
Douglas Horton   February 16, 1928   96

A Letter from Karl Barth   December 31, 1958   102

Arrested Liberalism
An Editorial   October 26, 1938   105

Post-Fundamentalist Faith
Edward John Carnell   August 26, 1959   110

How My Mind Has Changed
1. A Liberal Bandaged but Unbowed
   Robert L. Calhoun   May 31, 1939   113

2. Beyond Religious Socialism
   Paul Tillich   June 15, 1949   123

3. Ordeal of a Happy Dilettante
   Albert C. Outler   February 3, 1960   128

III. THE WORLD ECUMENICAL CONFERENCES

The World Missionary Conference
Charles Clayton Morrison   July 7, 1910   139

The Conference at Stockholm
Lynn Harold Hough   September 24, 1925   148

The Rapprochement of the Churches
Peter Ainslie   September 22, 1927   156

Beginning at Jerusalem
Samuel McCrea Cavert   May 10, 1928   164

The Church Faces Its World
   Winfred Ernest Garrison   August 18, 1937   171

The Quest for Unity
   Charles Clayton Morrison   September 1, 1937   178

Appraising Amsterdam
   An Editorial   September 29, 1948   185

Evanston Retrospect
   An Editorial   September 22, 1954   189

IV. DAYS OF TRIAL

The End of War
   An Editorial   January 2, 1909   197

A Vicarious Nation
   An Editorial   December 28, 1911   198

A Christian's Duty in Wartime
   An Editorial   April 12, 1917   199

The Paramount Issue
   An Editorial   October 28, 1920   201

Father of the Pact
   An Editorial   February 12, 1941   204

Communism Knows There Is a Revolution!
   An Editorial   February 22, 1933   207

After Twenty Years
   George W. Norris   March 31, 1937   212

An Exchange Between Brothers
   1. The Grace of Doing Nothing
      H. Richard Niebuhr   March 23, 1932   216
   2. Must We Do Nothing?
      Reinhold Niebuhr   March 30, 1932   222
   3. The Only Way into the Kingdom of God
      Richard Niebuhr
      A Communication by   April 6, 1932   228

The German Church Says No!
   Harold E. Fey   September 1, 1937   231

If Russia Wins
John Haynes Holmes   July 30, 1941   240

An Unnecessary Necessity
An Editorial   December 17, 1941   245

Citizens or Subjects?
An Editorial   April 29, 1942   251

Gazing into the Pit
An Editorial   May 9, 1945   256

America's Atomic Atrocity
An Editorial   August 29, 1945   259

Fifteen Years in Hell Is Enough
An Editorial   August 3, 1960   265

V. Some Areas of Concern

Labor and the Federal Council of Churches
An Editorial   December 26, 1908   273

The Sacred Rights of Property
An Editorial   March 21, 1912   274

Hunger on the March
Paul Hutchinson   November 9, 1932   274

Another "Century of Dishonor"?
An Editorial   January 31, 1913   279

Ira Hayes—Our Accuser
Editorial Correspondence by
Harold E. Fey   February 9, 1955   280

The Triumph of Temperance
An Editorial   March 19, 1914   286

The Temperance Movement Today
Albion R. King   March 8, 1961   287

The Church Amid Racial Tensions
Alan Paton   March 31, 1954   293

What Does the South Want?
James McBride Dabbs   September 19, 1956   297

Non-Violence and Racial Justice
Martin Luther King, Jr.   February 6, 1957   302

VI. NATIONAL SCENE

In God We Trust
  Henry J. Cadbury | July 7, 1954 | 311

Why Is the DAR?
  An Editorial | June 5, 1946 | 313

We Shall Not Sign
  An Editorial | June 10, 1953 | 314

High, Wide and Ugly
  An Editorial | March 15, 1961 | 318 ᴱ

The Meaning of "Separation"
  An Editorial | November 26, 1947 | 321 ᴱ

Churches Should Pay Taxes!
  An Editorial | April 9, 1947 | 327

VII. PEOPLE AND PLACES

Amateur Dramatics at Dayton
  An Editorial | July 30, 1925 | 335 ᴱ

Sinclair Lewis' Sunday School Class
  Samuel Harkness | July 29, 1926 | 339 ᴱ

Einstein and the Red Flag
  Editorial Correspondence by
  Paul Hutchinson | August 28, 1929 | 343

Gandhi
  An Editorial | February 11, 1948 | 350

The Sage of Ballard Vale
  Philip M. Kelsey | January 15, 1958 | 353

Italy and the Pope
  Editorial Correspondence by
  Margaret Frakes | October 29, 1958 | 356

Sunday at Lambaréné
  Albert Schweitzer | March 18, 1931 | 359

The Sometime Holy Land
  Editorial Correspondence by
  Theodore A. Gill | October 10, 1956 | 366

The Tomb of the Chosen One
Editorial Correspondence by
Dean Peerman   August 23, 1961   374

VIII. OTHER VOICES

On the Religious Significance of Poetry
Marietta Neff   January 2, 1909   383

Pasternak: Poet of Humanity
Amiya Chakravarty   July 6, 1960   384

Jazz at the Altar?
Elwyn A. Wienandt   March 23, 1960   388

The Bible Against Itself
An Editorial   October 28, 1959   394

The "Western"—A Theological Note
Alexander Miller   November 27, 1957   398

The Play that Carries a Plague
Tom F. Driver   September 7, 1960   404

IX. ALONG THE WAY

My First Communion
Edward A. Steiner   February 21, 1924   415

The Altar of Automobility
Editorial Correspondence by
Martin E. Marty   January 22, 1958   417

Three Columnists
1. Safed the Sage: The Sins
   I Have Saved   March 10, 1927   423
2. Quintus Quiz: The Per-
   fect Ending   September 29, 1937   424
3. Simeon Stylites: Appoint-
   ment for the Prophet
   Amos   April 30, 1958   426

Poems
God's Dreams
Thomas Curtis Clark   November 8, 1923   429

Non-Employment in Heaven
  Elinor Lennen   October 16, 1929   430

Prayer
  Amos N. Wilder   July 24, 1935   431

War Relics
  Tertius van Dyke   November 9, 1938   431

Spring Offensive
  Edwin McNeill Poteat   March 27, 1940   432

Luther
  W. H. Auden   October 2, 1940   433

To a Japanese Warrior
  Hargis Westerfield   January 30, 1946   434

Towards Gethsemane
  Warren Lane Molton   February 22, 1956   434

Portrait of a High Court Judge
  Winifred Rawlins   September 4, 1957   435

Ruach
  Pierre Henri Delattre   July 16, 1958   436

Journey to the Holy Land
  Edith Lovejoy Pierce   December 23, 1959   437

Atonement
  Tony Stoneburner   May 11, 1960   438

Afternoon Coming
  Betsy Feagan Colquitt   November 2, 1960   439

Tautology
  William I. Elliott   December 21, 1960   440

At a Grave on Easter
  Stanley J. Rowland, Jr.   March 29, 1961   441

Index   443

The Christian Century Reader

I

Instruments of Witness

OPTIMISM: faith in the church's survival.

February 18, 1915

Has the Church Collapsed?

AN EDITORIAL

An article in the January number of the Century Magazine affirms that the church has collapsed, that it is gradually losing its hold upon the community and sinking into helplessness in the face of the complex interests of modern life.

There has never been a time since the apostolic age when an observant critic could not make the same charge against the Christian society. The church has always been a gradually changing organism, and change to many minds implies decay. To see customs, practices and beliefs once held venerable and authoritative gradually losing their hold alike upon the church and its environment is no doubt disquieting to those who regard such things as a part of the fixed order of Christianity.

And just such lamentations have been voiced through all the centuries since the Master was among his people in the flesh. And such changes will always be experienced. They are as necessary in the church as in nature. The trees put away bark and leaves when they have served their purpose. Birds and beasts understand the laws of change and the discarding of outworn and useless belongings. These are signs, not of decay, but of growth.

We believe the church in the present generation is facing more difficult problems than ever before in its history. We believe that it is recognizing the futility of many of its former occupations and pronouncements. But that which is interpreted by some of its critics as disintegration is merely the attempt which good and wise Christians make to adjust themselves to a changing social order and to discard useless materials in the

21

effort. We believe that the church has some distance yet to go in this seemingly destructive process. But it is only to make way for a more efficient response to the world's need. The only discouraging sign of the times is the refusal of some parts of the church to meet the demands of the changed conditions. Wherever the church depends upon ancient forms and formulas for its influence over society, it must fail. It is only a genuine and timely contact with the living needs of the world today that can give it the influence it craves.

The best proof of the vitality of Christianity is its constant readjustment to the most outstanding needs of the time. The astonishing thing about the church today is its new activities, easily planned to touch the social order at the points most critical and needed. It is the mark of a living organism that it thus adjusts itself to new conditions and puts forth new organs when there is need. Never was this so true of the church as today, and in spite of all deficiencies, which are numerous enough, the church was never rendering a more timely and effective service than at the present moment.

PASTOR OF A DETROIT CHURCH and one of the Century's then contributing editors, the man who later was to become world famed as a theologian and as an analyst of the social and political order warned in 1926 against ecclesiastical and cultural shortcomings which a generation later were to be widely and ruefully acknowledged.

April 22, 1926

Our Secularized Civilization

REINHOLD NIEBUHR

Unqualified optimism on the present state or future prospect of religion in modern civilization can emanate only from a very superficial analysis of modern life. In America such optimism is justified by the undeniable prestige of the church in the popular mind and the vitality of the institutions of religion. In Europe optimism is not even supported by these facts. Yet America is in many respects more pagan than Europe, which means that the vitality of the institutions of religion is not in itself a proof of authentic religious life. The fact is that we are living in a completely secularized civilization which has lost the art of bringing its dominant motives under any kind of moral control.

Recent events in Europe reveal what unrepentant tribalists Western people are and how little they have learned from the great tragedy. They seem to lack both the imagination to realize the folly of their ways and the humility to conceive of their folly as sin. While we in America affect to pity Europe, the sense of moral superiority, which is always the root of pity, is based on illusion. We are no more moral than Europe, but our tremendous wealth and our comparative geographic isolation save us from suffering any immediate consequences of our moral follies. However active the institutions of religion may be in our national life, there is no trace of ethical motive in our national conduct. To the world we appear, what we really are, a fabulously wealthy nation, intent upon producing more wealth and seemingly oblivious to the consequences which unrestrained lust of power and lust of gain must inevitably have on both personal morality and international harmony.

The fact is that the social life of the Western world is almost completely outside of ethical control. A political leader of Gandhi's type would be unthinkable in the Western world. While it may be true that all groups are naturally predatory and have never been effectually restrained by moral scruples, yet there is a measure of indifference to and defiance of moral law in our modern world which compares unfavorably with the best in either our own or oriental history. The fact is that we are living in a completely secularized civilization.

The secularization of modern civilization is partly due to our inability to adjust the ethical and spiritual interests of mankind to the rapid advance of the physical sciences. However much optimists may insist that science cannot ultimately destroy religion, the fact remains that the general tendency of scientific discovery has been to weaken not only religious but ethical values. Humanism as well as religion has been engulfed in the naturalism of our day. Our obsession with the physical sciences and with the physical world has enthroned the brute and blind forces of nature, and we follow the God of the earthquake and the fire rather than the God of the still small voice. The morals of the man in the street, who may not be able to catch the full implications of pure science, are corrupted by the ethical consequences of the civilization which applied science has built. While pure science enthroned nature in the imagination, applied science armed nature in fact.

It is a part of the moral obfuscation of our day to imagine that we have conquered nature when in reality applied science has done little more than debase one part of humanity to become purely physical instruments of secular purpose and to cause the other part to be obsessed with pride in the physical instruments of life. The physical sciences armed nature—the nature in us—and lured us into a state where physical comfort is confused with true happiness and tempted us to indulge our lust for power at the expense of our desire for spiritual peace. We imagine we can escape life's moral problems merely because machines have enlarged our bodies, sublimated our physical forces and given us a sense of mastery. The mastery of nature is vainly believed to be an adequate substitute for self-mastery. So a generation of men is being bred who in their youth subsist on physical thrills, in their maturity glory in physical power and in their old age desire nothing more than physical comfort.

Vaguely conscious of the moral inadequacy of such an existence, men try to sublimate it by restraining their individual lusts in favor of the community in which they live. Thus nationalism becomes the dominant religion of the day and individual lusts are restrained only to issue in group lusts more grievous and more destructive than those of individuals. Nationalism is simply one of the effective ways in which the

modern man escapes life's ethical problems. Delegating his
vices to larger and larger groups, he imagines himself virtuous;
the larger the group the more difficult it is to fix moral responsibility for unethical action.

It would have been too much to expect of religion that it
find an immediate antidote for the naturalism and secularism
which the modern scientific world view has created. It was
inevitable that the natural world, neglected for centuries,
should take vengeance upon the human spirit by making itself
an obsession of the human mind. But it cannot be said that
religion has been particularly wise in the strategy it developed
in opposition to naturalism. Religion tried to save itself by the
simple expedient of insisting that evolution was not mechanistic but creative, by discovering God in the evolutionary process. Insofar as this means that there is room for freedom and
purpose in the evolutionary process, no quarrel is possible
with the defenders of the faith. But there is, after all, little
freedom or purpose in the evolutionary process—in short, little
morality; so that if we can find God only as he is revealed in
nature we have no moral God.

It would be foolish to claim that the defense of a morally
adequate theism in the modern world is an easy task; but it is
not an impossible one. Yet most modernists have evaded it.
Modernism on the whole has taken refuge in various kinds
of pantheism, and pantheism is always destructive of moral
values. To identify God with automatic processes is to destroy
the God of conscience; the God of the real is never the God
of the ideal. One of the vainest delusions to which religionists
give themselves is to suppose that religion is inevitably a support of morality. There are both supramoral and submoral
factors in religion. Professor Santayana makes the discrimination between two instincts in religion, the instinct of piety
and the instinct of spirituality, the one seeking to hallow the
necessary limitations of life and the other seeking to overcome
them. Pantheism inevitably strengthens those forces in religion
which tend to sanctify the real rather than to inspire the ideal.

That is why modernism, which has sloughed off many of
religion's antimoral tendencies but has involved itself in

philosophic monism and religious pantheism more grievously than orthodoxy ever did, has been so slight a moral gain for mankind. Liberal religion is symbolizing a totality of facts under the term God which orthodoxy, with a truer moral instinct, could comprehend under no less than two terms, God and the devil. It would be better to defy nature's immoralities in the name of a robust humanism than to take the path which most modern religion has chosen and play truant to the distinctive needs of the human spirit by reading humanity into the essentially inhuman processes of nature. There is little to choose between the despair to which pure naturalism tempts us when we survey the human scene and the easy optimism which most modern religion encourages. What we need is both the spirit of repentance and the spirit of hope, which can be inspired only by a theism which knows how to discover sin by subjecting man to absolute standards and how to save him from despair by its trust in absolute values.

The secularization of modern life is partly due to the advance of science, but also to the moral inadequacies of Protestantism. If liberal Protestantism is too pantheistic, traditional Protestantism is too quietistic to meet the moral problems of a socially complex age. Protestantism, as Professor Whitehead in his *Science and the Modern World* has with rare insight pointed out, has no understanding of the social forces and factors which impinge on and condition human personality. It believes that righteousness can be created in a vacuum. It produces no sense of tension between the soul and its environment. The conversions of which it boasts may create moral purpose, but that moral purpose is applied to a very limited field of motives where application is more or less automatic. It helps men to master those sins which are easily discovered because they represent divergence from accepted moral customs: the sins of dishonesty, sexual incontinence and intemperance.

No religion is more effective than Protestantism against the major social sins of our day, economic greed and race hatred. In a recent trial of Negroes, growing out of a race riot in one of our metropolitan centers, the defense lawyer shrewdly manipulated the selection of the jury so that there would be at least a minority of Jews and Catholics in the jury box, and it is reported that their votes were for the defense when the jury failed to reach a decision. No real progress can be made against the secularization of modern life until Protestantism overcomes its pride and complacency and realizes that it has itself connived with the secularists. By giving men a sense of moral victory because they have mastered one or two lusts, while their lust for power and their lust for gain remain undisciplined, it is simply aggravating those lusts which are the primary perils of modern civilization.

Protestantism reacted against the dualism in Roman Catholic ethics which produces asceticism on the one hand and an easy-going connivance with human weakness on the other. It is true that there is a dualism in Roman Catholic ethics, which can develop, let us say, a Cardinal O'Connell on the one hand and a Cardinal Mercier on the other. But Protestantism has a dualism equally grievous, which produces a Cardinal O'Connell and a Cardinal Mercier in the same skin, a pagan and a puritan in one person, whose puritanism becomes an effective anodyne for a conscience not altogether easy in the sins of paganism. If a choice is to be made between monastic and quietistic ethics, surely monastic ethics must be termed the most Christian, for it is better that the world shall be feared than that it be embraced with a good conscience.

How a fretful anxiety about a number of lustful temptations can develop a perfect complacency in regard to other temptations may be seen by the fact that the church is not now so conscious of some of the sins of modern civilization as some of our most thoroughgoing realists. If Scott Nearing had the ear of New York he could convict it of sin more surely than Bishop Manning can. The *Nation* prompts its readers to a consciousness of social sin more effectively than does, say, the *Watchman-Examiner*. It is significant, too, that the very part of the country in which the churches insist upon "regenerate membership" and recruit such a membership by persistent revivals is most grievously corrupted by the sin of race hatred. Protestantism—and insofar as Roman Catholicism has departed from the best medievalism, Catholicism, too—has no understanding of the complex factors of environment out of which personality emerges. It is always "saving" individuals, but not saving them from the greed and the hatred into which they are tempted by the society in which they live. Protestantism, it might be said, does not seem to know that the soul lives in a body, and that the body is part of a world in which the laws of the jungle still prevail.

Perhaps it might not be irrelevant to add that its failure to understand the relation between the physical and the spiritual not only tempts Protestantism to create righteousness in a vacuum but to develop piety without adequate symbol. That is why the church services of extreme Protestant sects tend to become secularized once the first naive spontaneity departs from their religious life. In Europe nonconformist Protestants tend more and more to embrace the once despised beauty of symbol and dignity of form in order to save worship from dullness and futility. In America nonconformist Protestantism, with less cultural background, tries to avert dullness by vulgar theatricality. The Quakers alone escape this fate because their exclusion of symbol is so rigorous that silence itself becomes symbol. If worship is to serve man's ethical as well as religious needs, it must give him a sense of humble submission to the absolute. Humility is lacking in Protestant worship as it is missing in Protestant civilization. If this humility is medievalism, we cannot save civilization without medievalism.

THE FINDINGS *of the Laymen's Missionary Inquiry led missions leaders to re-examine previous aims and methods. The fruits of that re-examination were apparent in many articles and editorials through the thirties, and are reflected today in the theology of missions as well as in program emphases. The author of this article was for many years an official of the American Board of Commissioners for Foreign Missions.*

February 14, 1934

End Missions Imperialism Now!
HUGH VERNON WHITE

The missionary movement has arrived at maturity, and there is urgent need that the churches as well as the missionaries take account of it. It is not that we are wiser than our fathers, but that developments of recent times have revealed the true nature of the forces which play upon the life of man. The church has expended much time and energy and more than once fought battles in the realms of belief and conduct. But all this has taken place within the limits of Christian tradition whose main features have been generally accepted, thus leaving the struggle and dispute to secondary things. But today it is those main features of the Christian faith which find themselves confronted by really challenging forces; it is the fundamental issues that are now joined, and the time has come when Christianity must become aware of its own intrinsic nature and the part it should play in the stress of elemental forces.

Missions shares this struggle with the whole Christian fellowship; but there are certain points at which it is more immediate and concrete for the missionary, and for that reason the consciousness of the church is focused in his efforts. Three such issues have emerged today and demand the mature and responsible thought of the churches: (1) the relation of Christianity to other religions, (2) the relation of Christianity to the national state and (3) the relation of Christianity to the economic order.

A century ago the missionary went out with a Christian ethic of personal and social life which was so clearly superior to many prevailing practices in non-Christian lands that those practices had to yield. Polygamy, suttee, foot-binding (I wish I could add slavery) and the cruder superstitions were evils which Christian missionaries could assail with full confidence and for which they had the remedy. But alas, today the missionary has to face ethical and intellectual demands for which there is no ready answer. Christianity must work out its strategy while it fights; it must determine its true ends and principles in the midst of struggle. The larger issues are no longer concealed behind lesser ones with only the prophetic eye to see them.

Everybody is aware of a marked change on the part of missionary leaders toward other faiths. This new attitude found expression at the Jerusalem meeting: "We rejoice to think that just because in Jesus Christ the light that lighteth every man shone forth in its full splendor, we find rays of that same light where he is unknown or even is rejected. We welcome every noble quality in non-Christian persons or systems as further proof that the Father, who sent his Son into the world, has nowhere left himself without a witness." There are tremendous implications in this frank statement; we cannot stop with it, but must go on to develop its meanings and applications. Religious bodies are prone to rest their case with verbal formulas, sometimes intentionally ambiguous in meaning, and resist any efforts to carry through to valid interpretations and application of them.

One virtue of the report of the Laymen's Foreign Missions Inquiry is that it tries to work out explicitly the implications of this statement in both theory and practice. It may have taken the right line or it may not, but in any case it does define a meaning. It is a case of the lay mind versus the professional, the latter seeking a formula which means different things to different groups, as a basis of common action; the former saying that common action now calls for a more precise definition of principles. If anyone should seek to make such a definition authoritative, it would destroy co-operation, but to admit the need and to work with open mind toward it ought to produce far more real and deep-going unity of effort.

At any rate it is now plain that the new rapprochement between diverse religions makes it important that the church find a way to understand and even co-operate with other religious groups and individuals that will not be ambiguous and will preserve due respect for the distinctive things in Christianity. It is not mere politeness that we need, but candor and mutual respect as regards real differences.

The rise of nationalism makes acute the right relation of Christianity to the national estate. The church is confronted with the necessity of finding what that relation is and then seeking to realize it. The Holy Roman Empire and the Protestant theocracies identified Christianity with the state. Until recently the doctrine of the separation of church and state has been a fairly satisfactory one so far as the institutions of politics and religion are concerned. But beneath this formal separation has remained the fact that it is the same people, at least in part, who constitute the citizenship and the church membership. Or, more important still, religion and government both claim supreme authority over the same persons, and the Christian citizen as an individual and in fellowship with other Christians must find the principle for the adjustment of these two authorities.

Now one of the objectives of Christian missions today is the development of an "indigenous" Christianity in each country. As expressed by Kagawa, "We want Jesus Christ to take out his first and second naturalization papers in Japan." Great satisfaction has been found by missionary leaders in the national Christian churches in the orient. Yet Christianity is a universal religion; that is one of the basic reasons for the world-wide mission. Indigenous Japanese Christianity and indigenous Chinese and Indian Christianity, while being expressed in the forms of thought and culture that are Japanese and Chinese and Indian, must be something more; and so it is with American Christianity. What is that "something more," and what does it imply as to tension between the Christian fellowship and the state? An American Christianity that is not consciously something more than American cannot give any help to the younger Christian groups which are being tossed and buffeted by the surge of nationalism in Japan, China and India.

The spread of communism has forced another issue which had already begun to trouble the consciences of sensitive Christians, although we cannot say that the church as a whole has even yet taken any serious account of it. Just now Christianity is in danger of being identified with capitalism in its opposition to communism. When we are told that "communism and Christianity are in actual fact two competing systems offering to reconstruct China . . . they are two antithetic and contrasted systems, either of which will affect the whole political, social and spiritual life of the people," the question at once arises: What are the Christian correlates to the communist economic system and social practice? For communism is not only a faith and a philosophy; it is a detailed system covering all the social and economic arrangements of life. If we seek for the corresponding aspects of a Christian "system," an examination of the practices of Christian people and groups would have to answer in terms of the dominant capitalism, for it is under that system that most Christians live.

It must be said with frankness and finality that such an answer is intolerable. Capitalism is not Christianity. The opposition of Christianity to communism is not unqualified and complete. Christianity has far more affinity for some of the basic principles of communism than for the corresponding principles of capitalism. It is very easy to refute the materialistic philosophy of communism and to oppose its atheism. But a truly Christian judgment will condemn even more severely the practical atheism and materialism of a capitalistic order.

Christianity is not an economic system, but it has a faith and ideal which puts upon any system the demand that it honor rather than exploit human personality, that it operate as a technique to provide for the material well-being of all the people and not for the exploitation of the weak by the strong. We urgently need an interpretation of Christianity that will cut across both capitalism and communism and press for practical embodiment of its own reverence for personality. More important by far than an assault upon the theory of communism is the vigorous working out of Christianity's criticism of capitalism and the development among Christian people of a Christian judgment and conscience in economics. Tomorrow on the mission field will be a happier day if this is done.

Both churches and mission forces need to see more clearly what they are primarily out to do in the work of missions. Increasingly the various boards are working together, forming common programs and uniting institutions. The list of union schools, hospitals and seminaries is already long and is growing longer. Closer consultation and co-operative planning, partly forced by the economic conditions but really expressing a trend of purpose, are making it possible to speak of a Christian world movement.

Now this does not mean agreement in theology. Such agreement does not exist, and probably never will. The co-operative effort in modern missions is significant precisely because it does bring together in common action groups which hold different doctrinal positions. From the standpoint of such co-operation the only heresy is the denial of the right of others to hold to their beliefs and share in the common task. Those who do share in it have thereby renounced that heresy.

But it does mean that there is agreement of purpose, at least in some major part of the purpose of Christian missions. What that purpose is, it is not hard to determine. Jesus reiterated it, and the life of every truly Christian missionary exhibits it. As man himself is the object of God's love, so all things are instrumental to the service of man. Even the Sabbath, which epitomizes institutional religion, "was made for man and not man for the Sabbath." Peter's ardent declaration of love for Jesus was thrice turned toward human service: "Feed my sheep." The final criterion of judgment is: "Inasmuch as you did it [or did it not] to these my brethren, you

did it [or did it not] to me." And this goes even for those
who do not consider themselves his followers. Here is the bold-
ness of the Jerusalem message: "We find rays of that same
light where he is unknown or even rejected." The first Epistle
of John sounds the same note: "If a man say, I love God and
hateth his brother he is a liar; for he that loveth not his
brother whom he hath seen, cannot love God whom he hath
not seen." It is not necessary to multiply instances of the clear
expression of this dominant principle of Christianity, but it
is important to see clearly its relation to Christian missions.

It means that the central aim and purpose of missions is to
serve men. All other things are accessory and instrumental to
this end. The church was made for man and not man for
the church; doctrine was made for man (and by man) and
not man for doctrine; Jesus held himself to be the one who
came to minister and not to be ministered to. The great and
familiar verse John 3:16 declares the order of things in the
mind of God to be the same: "For God so loved the world
that he gave his only begotten son." The only mission that
has a place in the world today is the mission chiefly intent
upon serving men. This does not settle questions of method
or theology, but it does provide a regulative principle and
affirms that all the developments of church order and doctrine, as well as forms of educational and other service, are
means and not ends and might be modified or abandoned
without giving up the central aim of the Christian mission.

The Christian churches and missions, by adopting such an
objective, will thereby renounce all exploitation of the peoples
of the world in the interests of a religious system, church or
doctrine and completely free themselves from the charge of
religious imperialism. Such a purpose is really the unifying
agreement which has been drawing together the various denominational groups; it now needs to be clearly held and announced, and the churches should throw their full and enthusiastic support back of the programs which seek to embody
it.

Maturity of the missionary movement calls for an adult
mind on the part of the churches in their attitude toward

missionary work and results. If the indigenous church in each land means anything it means that there are likely to emerge forms and expressions of Christianity which we would not recognize as such. Are we prepared to welcome this? Can we summon devotion and enthusiasm for a sowing of the seed of Christian faith and life in other lands which does not guarantee a fruitage of doctrine, forms of worship and practical outworkings like our own? It is such a challenge that is given to our Christianity today. We must mean deeply what we say about indigenous Christianity and have a faith in the inherent power of the spirit of Christ and in the people of other lands that will prompt the most hearty support of a movement which will, when it becomes fully autonomous, produce new and differing results.

And it also means that we must throw away the time schedule. It will take centuries, not decades, to get the Christian gospel deeply into the mind and heart of China and India and Japan, as well as Africa and other parts of the world. The kind of results we want are not going to come until that gospel has found its way into the deepest springs of thought and action and has had time to grow its own forms of conscience and culture, a process which is by no means complete in our own country. We must stop asking for statistical proofs that the Christian mission is succeeding and even be a little suspicious of such proofs. We must be neither too much elated by apparent success nor depressed by apparent failure, but steadfastly seek the clearest line of human service in the spirit of Christ and the most sincere testimony to Christ himself and leave it to God to give the increase.

*THE DISTINGUISHED British author of A Study of History
contributed as an Anglican layman to a series of articles an-
ticipating the 1937 ecumenical conference on Life and Work,
held at Oxford.*

March 10, 1937

The Menace of the New Paganism
ARNOLD J. TOYNBEE

The adversary who is challenging Christianity today is a rival
religion—a *single* rival religion. True, this anti-Christian faith
is coming into action under different names in different parts
of the world; but the more these alternative versions of the
postwar paganism insist upon their points of difference—the
more they abuse and attack one another—the more clearly
they betray their kinship with one another to the eyes of the
Christian observer. And this element in each of them which is
common to all of them is just the thing that makes them, all
alike, incompatible with Christianity.

Let us begin by looking for a moment at the success which,
in their own spheres, these new faiths achieve. Fascism and
communism can dare to ask, and can be fairly sure of receiving,
from their followers today a response which Christianity now
hardly dares to ask, because it cannot longer be sure of its
hold upon the people who call themselves Christians. It is by
making these large demands on human nature, and not by
offering people the license to do as they like and live at their
ease, that the postwar paganism has been winning its masses
of converts. This means that it is indeed a formidable spiritual
force. And we shall not think it any the less formidable when
we discover the secret of its success.

I think one can see two reasons for the fascination which
the postwar paganism undoubtedly does exert upon the rising
generation. It not only appeals, like Christianity, to the im-

pulse toward self-denial and self-sacrifice—an impulse which can, of course, be enlisted in a bad as well as in a good cause. The postwar paganism also gives its converts directions for their conduct in practical life; and these directions are of the kind which human nature craves for: they are simple, clear, concrete and confident. A believing Fascist or Communist can probably get more definite instructions than a believing Christian about how he is to behave here and now: whom to love, whom (in his case) to hate, what to fight for, what to worship. On a long view, this extreme concreteness may turn out to be one of the weak points of this paganism; but on a short view its plain answers to plain questions are a tower of strength. And on any view this exaggeration of what is surely a virtue in itself makes the postwar paganism an adversary which has to be taken very seriously by Christianity.

In its own estimation, this postwar paganism is indeed nothing less than Christianity's supplanter and successor. "Christianity," say the Fascist and Communist missionaries, "is an old religion which has had its chance and has failed to make use of it." Christianity, they say, has been in the world for ages and has not succeeded in making any appreciable difference to human life. If the spirit and teaching and practice of Christianity were really the way of salvation, they would surely have saved the world by this time. So today, they tell us, Christianity stands condemned by the verdict of history. It is, therefore, high time for Christianity to retire from the stage and yield the floor to a new religion which claims to have a better understanding of human nature, and believes for that reason that it can produce results where Christianity has nothing more substantial to its credit than a scrap-heap of unfulfilled and unfulfillable ideals. "Fascism and communism," say their preachers, "stand for pagan performance as opposed to Christian promise; they stand for deeds in place of dreams."

This attack on Christianity is made by the postwar pagans in good faith. It is just this belief in their own program that is their strength. Yet this overweening pagan claim calls down upon itself a shattering Christian answer. The answer can be put in three points. In the first place, the really new thing in the world is not paganism but Christianity. In the second place, if there are any new features in the postwar paganism, they are features which this paganism has borrowed from Christianity. In the third place, the core of the postwar paganism, under its Christian varnish, is something as old as the hills— an ancient error which Christianity has fought and conquered not once but many times already. Let me try to put each of these points to you very briefly.

First, Christianity is not old but young. In thinking of Christianity as old, our modern pagans are unconsciously looking at history in the short perspective of a prescientific age. If you bear in mind the fact that the human race has been in existence not for mere thousands but for hundreds of thousands of years, and then think of the life of mankind on earth up to date in terms of the life of a single human being, you will see that 37 A.D. is no farther off from 1937 A.D. than yesterday is from today in your life or in mine. And in this really very brief period of less than two thousand years Christianity has in fact produced greater spiritual effects in the world than have been produced in a comparable space of time by any other spiritual movement that we know of in history.

Christianity promises to inspire men and women to lead a new life and to teach them how to do it, and this promise has already been fulfilled in the lives of the saints. These lives are an earnest of a life that may be lived one day by all the members of the church on earth, for sainthood is not some half-legendary grace of the early church which died out within a few centuries of the church's foundation. It is a spiritual power in Christianity which has broken out again and again wherever and whenever the church has been challenged by the world, as it is being challenged today. There was an outbreak of sainthood in sixteenth-century Italy in answer to the challenge of the Renaissance, and another in nineteenth-century France in answer to the challenge of the Revolution. And if Christianity rises to the present challenge from the postwar paganism, the appearance on earth of another batch of saints will no doubt be one of the practical concrete ways in which the church will be given the strength to deal with its present adversary.

The second point in our Christian reply to the pretensions of the paganism of today was, you will remember, that, so far as one can find anything new in the twentieth-century paganism, this new thing is something that has been borrowed by paganism from Christianity itself. I do see one new thing in this latter-day paganism which is, I am certain, of Christian origin, and that is its wholeheartedness. Christianity has put into the spiritual life of man on earth an intensity which was never given to it by any older religion—not even by Zoroastrianism and Judaism, which were Christianity's two forerunners. Christianity has done this by giving us a new insight into God's purpose in the world, and into man's part in that purpose—an insight which shows us the immensity of the importance of our conduct here and now. Christianity places our conduct in this life on earth in its gigantic setting of infinity and eternity, and by opening our eyes to this vast spiritual vision it calls out our deepest spiritual energies.

Now I fancy that the present post-Christian form of paganism has succeeded to some extent in "stealing the thunder" of Christianity (to borrow a phrase from the vocabulary of primitive religion). This post-Christian paganism has succeeded in capturing, for its own trivial and narrow ends, some of that wholehearted Christian devotion which ought to be given to God alone. And if this has really happened it should be taken deeply to heart by Christians for two reasons. For one thing, this pagan practice of a Christian virtue shows up the lukewarmness and indecisiveness which have paralyzed so much of the Christianity of the modern age, for if the church had remained true to herself she would not have seen her children transferring their allegiance elsewhere and laying their Christian spirit of devotion at the feet of false gods. And then, again, there is nothing so dangerous and so destructive as a wholehearted devotion that has been diverted from the service of God to the service of some lower object. The spiritual driving-force drawn from Christianity has given the new paganism a daemonic power which the old paganism never wielded, and this power is—let us frankly admit it—tremendously formidable. If Christianity is to conquer a paganism that has been allowed to equip itself with the church's own weapons, the church will have perhaps greater need of God's grace than it has ever had before.

And now I come to the last of my three points. That is that, apart from the new Christian intensity with which our postwar paganism has managed to arm itself, this paganism which is challenging Christianity once more today is not a new thing in the world, as Christianity itself is, but, on the contrary, is something very old—as old, perhaps, as human nature. Our postwar paganism is, in fact, in one form or another, simply the idolatry which used to hold the field in the ages before Christianity appeared in the world, and which Christianity has always been struggling to weed out of people's hearts. In speaking of fascism and communism as idolatry, I am not just hurling a term of abuse at them. By "idolatry" I mean something which is, I think, quite definite and clear, and which is also, I think, written large on the face of both these two latter-day pagan movements. By "idolatry" I mean a religion which either does not know, or else refuses to recognize, that there is no god but God, and which therefore worships the creature instead of worshiping the creator.

As the works of God's creation are infinite, idolatry has taken a great variety of forms. One form is the worship of organized human power. This organization of power may be local and sectional, or again it may attempt to embrace the whole of mankind; and either the local tribe or humanity at large may be, and has been, erected into an object of idolatrous worship. Each of these two ancient idols has now been set up on its pedestal again by the new paganism. The tribe is the idol of fascism; humanity is the idol of communism.

The high priests of tribalism preach to their devotees that the whole duty of man is comprised in the service of the local tribe into which a man happens to have been born. The tribesman's tribe is to be the tribesman's god. This tribal god is to have an exclusive claim upon the tribesman's allegiance and devotion. And this idolatrous worship necessarily debars the tribe-worshiper both from worshiping the one true God and from being his own human brother's keeper outside this one tribe's narrow limits. This tribe-worshiping form of idolatry is the religion of Ishmael, whose "hand will be against every man, and every man's hand against him." It was also the religion of Sparta, and of the other city states of ancient Greece with whom the Spartans were perpetually at war. And these ancient city states came to the bad end which in our day is threatening to overtake the national states into which Christendom has broken up in modern times. Sparta and the rest of them met the fate of the Kilkenny cats. They fought each other to extinction, and on their ruins was established that Roman Empire which became an object of idolatrous worship in its turn.

In the Roman Empire, a generation which had become disillusioned with tribe-worship found a new idol which, in contrast to Sparta and Athens, stood for the whole of mankind, and not just for one section of it.

The idolatrous worship of organized human power is the fatal error which is common to all the varieties of our postwar paganism. The error is so profound that the triumph of this paganism could spell nothing but disaster for mankind. But to say that human society is not a proper object for religious worship does not, of course, mean that the tribe or the state or the nation or the world empire are evil in themselves. No doubt they have their place in human life, since man has been created as a social creature. But the function of these man-made social organizations is certainly not to usurp the throne of God. Their function—and it is an honorable though a humble one—is to serve as stepping-stones on the way toward the only society in which man can find a true satisfaction for his social nature; that is, a society which, so far from usurping the place of God, has God himself for its principal member. The true home of man is the *Civitas Dei*, the "City of God" in which the common fatherhood of God creates a brotherhood between all the human citizens of the divine commonwealth —a brotherhood which cannot be established by any bond of which God himself is not the maker.

AS SOON AS round-the-world travel—of a sort—was possible for civilians after World War II ended, the then managing editor of the Century set out to discover to what extent religion had managed to survive the stresses of the tragic years just past. From some quarters he transmitted pessimistic reports—but not from the isle of Iona, off Scotland's rugged western coast.

September 11, 1946

The Iona Idea

EDITORIAL CORRESPONDENCE

Oban, Scotland, August 20

One comes away from the Iona Community believing that here is living seed being planted in the worn soil of Scotland's spiritual life. In this company of ministers and artisans who have gathered to rebuild the ruined abbey on St. Columba's island on the edges of the Hebrides, one finds the promise of a revival that will really revive the Scottish churches. There is nothing sensational to point to yet in the way of results. In fact, the community is still suffering from the shortage of recruits caused by the emptying of Scotland's theological colleges by the war. But there is the one thing that counts, the one thing for which one comes to look most ceaselessly in all Europe's religious communities—there is life.

Scotland desperately needs a revival. The land is full of churches; the ministry remains an honored profession; the academic standards of the theological colleges at Edinburgh and Glasgow and St. Andrews and Aberdeen are as high as any in the world. But the mass of the people have drifted away from any save the most formal contacts with the church. It is estimated that 75 per cent of the Scotch people no longer attend services even at the high festivals of the Christian year. With the country gripped by one of the most intense industrial struggles under way anywhere on the globe, and with a stridently secularistic communism and extreme left-wing socialism growing by leaps and bounds, the churches too often seem to be in a state of suspension in a remote dogmatic vacuum.

Iona is a desperate attempt to turn that vacuum into a spiritual battlefield. Ten years ago its founder and leader, George F. MacLeod, resigned the pulpit of the famous Govan Old Parish Church of Glasgow to gather a group that would adopt a rule of living as severe as that of a monastic order and, under that rule, would launch a crusade to make the Christian gospel of the Incarnation vital in every aspect of Scottish life. Most of the Christian world now knows of the way in which, summer after summer, this group, in which ministers live and work side by side with masons and carpenters, has labored at the rebuilding of the ruins of the old Iona abbey. But the rebuilding of the abbey is only a symbol of what Dr. MacLeod and his comrades hope to do in building the Christian enterprise back into the whole structure of Scottish life.

Each year, after the three summer months of work with trowel and mortar on Iona are over, the members of the community move back to the mainland for nine months of tremendously hard work at reviving the churches. Some of them go, two by two, to minister to remote highland communities where the ministry of the Word has fallen on meager days. Some go into churches in the slums, or in the vast housing developments that are springing up around every industrial center, to arouse and train the laity for a program much like the visitation evangelism now being tried in American churches. Some go into the dockyard areas, or into factories, where they may work as regular laborers while trying to arouse their fellows to a new sense of the relevance of Christian truth. Some go into the Iona Youth Trust, with its community house in a Glasgow slum section and its innumerable other enterprises to win the loyalty of Scottish youth. All are pledged to daily hours of personal devotion and Bible study, and to an exact accounting of the use made of every hour of the day. Most of them have voluntarily undertaken to live on the scant income which government statistics say represents the national average.

I have just spent almost a week at Iona, but I despair of giving any adequate impression of the pulsing life and hope I found there. The plans are too many and varied, and the personality of the man who launches most of them is too overwhelming, to be caught in a single letter. But let's start with the man—George F. MacLeod. Descendant of a long line of famous Scottish preachers, George MacLeod went from a First World War captaincy in the Argyll and Sutherland Highlanders to a chaplaincy in lumber camps in British Columbia and directly from there to Edinburgh's most fashionable church —St. Cuthbert's, at the lower end of the famous Princes Street gardens, under the shadow of the castle. After four years of that he moved to the Govan Church in a Glasgow slum area. But after eight years there he could be confined to the parish ministry no longer. The Iona Community was the result.

The world can contain few men with the physical vitality, the mental brilliance, the limitless itch for adventure, the bubbling humor, the devotional depth and the farseeing vision of George MacLeod. On Iona he is the center of every hour's activity, whether that is work on the walls or worship in the restored abbey church. Three miles from Iona, on the island of Mull, he has established at Camus a fishing camp for high school boys, and though he gets to Camus only once or twice a week he is the dynamo there, too. (The boys carry on a regular fishery, selling their catch in the commercial market; Dr. MacLeod is, among a dozen other things, a licensed fishmonger.) Throughout the winter he roams Scotland, preaching the Iona gospel to all who will listen and keeping heart in the Iona missioners.

When I landed in Iona after a three-hour voyage by steamer from Oban, the port at the rail-end, I had visions of being handed a trowel and set to work laying stone. But a three-minute conversation must have afforded Dr. MacLeod all the knowledge he needed of my abilities as a craftsman, for I promptly landed in the potato-peeling squad. As potatoes are basic to the Iona diet, that meant more than two hours a day at that form of k.p. But, like everyone else, I was proving my right by the work of my hands to join in the worship and the discussions which fit the members of the community for their service on the mainland.

The first worship service in the abbey church comes every

morning immediately after breakfast. There is another, candle-lit, just before the lights go out at night. Sometimes there is still another in mid-afternoon. Over the week end when I was there, there were services Saturday evening, three Sunday morn-ing and one at six on Sunday evening, all broadcast by the BBC. Perhaps the one which moved me most deeply was the service that only about twenty of us participated in one night, while MacLeod and most of the community were away presenting a concert to raise funds for the Iona visiting nurses' service. As we sat there, the rain poured down on the abbey roof and the candles flickered in the gusts of wind that found their way in-side the ancient walls. At the benediction I found myself say-ing, "While memory lasts, I will remember this hour."

But there was a realism about the symbolism of the first Sunday morning service I never will forget. It began, after the community leader, in his Glasgow doctor's robes, had taken his stand behind the communion table, with the singing of the metrical version of the 43rd Psalm, continued through the sermon and reached its climax when, with the singing of Psalm 24—

> Ye gates, lift up your heads on high;
>   ye doors that last for aye,
> Be lifted up, so that the King
>   of glory enter may—

the minister, accompanied by a procession of elders, bore the communion elements through the congregation to the altar. For the bread was brought in great loaves of home-baked whole wheat; it was the bread which the communicants had raised by their labor and baked in their own kitchens that was conse-crated and broken to them as the sacramental loaf.

And that, symbolically, is really the essence of the Iona idea. The Incarnation must be experienced in every aspect of the everyday life of Scotland. Or, as Nathaniel Micklem put it when it was objected that MacLeod and his associates are at-tempting to involve the church in issues which are none of the church's business: "The Iona movement is all of a piece: the rebuilding of the old ruins, the coupling of intellectual work with manual, the bringing of the common loaves to church, the fishing nets round about the Holy Table [at Camus], the direct prayers which are about slates needed for the roof or about John Doe, who is working away in Glasgow at his boys' club, the insistence that politics and craftsmanship and economics and drama and home and religion are not to be separated, the holy indignation that the church has become to some considerable extent a coterie, out of touch with life, a Sunday affair, a self-contained and separate bit of the national life."

"Far from this social concern blunting the personal question, it only serves to sharpen it," MacLeod himself insists. "In effect it does not mean that we become more interested in economics than in our Bibles; more concerned to visit factories than to pray; more concerned with public meetings than with public worship, with circulars than with the sacraments. The actual experience is precisely opposite. When once we see that it is the bodies of Christ's brothers that lay entangled on the wire of the Italian and the eastern front, because men will not distribute bread in the abundance that God has given; when once we see that it is that which can become the Body of Christ which is sold in the wheat markets of the world, and that is 'in short supply'; and when we see dozens of our most socially sensitive youth—the sons of Christian homes—by reason of our seeming indifference regretfully turning away from the church of their fathers to embrace a creed of conflict, then the personal challenge of the Christ becomes more stark than ever it was before in our lives; the problems of prayer become more intense, the understanding of our Bibles more urgent, public worship more essential and the sacraments more desperately needed for our souls and the ingrafting of our children."

I wish that I could take space to tell a few of the many stories that have already given the rebuilding of Iona an almost legendary quality. The story of the way stones were found for the walls after the owner of the island had refused to permit its stones to be used, of the way water was found for the workers after permission to tap the island's water resources had been denied, of the way the sea cast up timbers for a roof after war restrictions had cut off all lumber—these and many others almost fall into the category of the miraculous. But I must forego the temptation to pass on such tales.

At the moment, as I said in the beginning, the aftermath of the war is holding activities on the island to a minimum. Dr. MacLeod even refers to the rebuilding as at present a "blazing bluff." But no one connected with Iona doubts that within a year or so the community will again be in full stride. Just this month Archibald Craig is resigning his post as secretary of the British Council of Churches to join the Iona forces. As the theological colleges begin to graduate their normal numbers, it is believed, there will be no lack of recruits for the stern "rule" of the community. And if all other sources of replenishment were to fail, the elemental drive in George MacLeod himself would promise a healthy future. St. Columba put Iona on the map of Scottish history. It is not beyond the bounds of possibility that MacLeod and his Iona Community will put it on the map of the world church.

Paul Hutchinson

MOUNTING CRITICISM of the church's role as critic of the prevailing order brought from the professor of Christian theology and ethics at Union Theological Seminary a spirited defense of that role and a challenge to the church to serve not only as healer but also as prophet.

January 6, 1954

The Church as Prophetic Critic

JOHN C. BENNETT

The role of the church as the prophetic critic of society is neglected today; instead, the chief emphasis is on the healing ministry of the church, on Christianity as the antidote for anxiety, on the gospel's promise of peace of mind. There is a prophetic No which still needs to be said, but there is a tend-

ency to omit it, in part because of our preoccupation with the
"positive" message and in part because in the nation's present
state of mind prophetic criticism is more than usually misunder-
stood or resented.

I am not suggesting a one-sided return to what I call here
prophetic criticism. My only concern is to call attention to the
fact that things are now out of balance. Is it not of the essence
of the Christian gospel that healing and judgment belong together? The deepest source of healing is the forgiveness that
follows confession. At the heart of our faith is the cross, which
is at the same time the demonstration of the consequences of
sin and the revelation of God's forgiveness. In the light of the
message entrusted to it the church is called to act as prophet,
pastor and priest at the same time for the same people. There
was a strong negative note in almost all the prophets of Israel;
and, while Jesus showed only compassion toward all who recognized their weakness and need, his words to the hard and self-
righteous were as negative as anything that we find in the
prophets.

There are two good reasons for shrinking from the role of
negative critic. One is that the prophet who assumes this role
easily becomes self-righteous and unlovely. Prophets who emphasize the negative side of their message often become single-
track and very poor guides. They are inclined to identify their
own convictions, even on difficult political issues, with the will
of God. There are in the Christian faith correctives for these
tendencies, but only too often they do not take effect. The
prophets should realize that they also are under judgment, that
they have their own special temptations. Most often confession
with the people rather than denunciation of the people should
be the way in which the prophet speaks. I have in mind here
the church and its representatives in their prophetic role.

The deeper reason for shrinking from this role today is that
we realize the real difficulty in relating negative judgments,
which create in people a sense of guilt, with the healing of their
souls. The emphasis on the destructive effects of guilt feelings
and anxiety seems to point the church away from stressing
negative criticism. We may admit that most guilt feelings

which disturb the deeper level of the soul are misplaced, that they are a holdover in mature life from experiences in childhood which are irrelevant to the moral experience of the adult. The warning of psychiatrists and educators against instilling in children feelings of guilt which can have these later disturbing effects is much needed. But this does not mean that there is no place for the kind of moral judgment that is relevant to mature experience and that makes men uneasy, more fully aware of the consequences of their decisions, more sensitive to the dark side of their culture. The appropriateness of such moral judgment is merely the other side of the reality of moral obligation and of human freedom.

There are three conditions in our country today which make it difficult, but all the more necessary, for the church to give emphasis now to the negative or critical elements in its message.

First is our national tendency to develop a shell to protect us as a nation against criticism. It is imperative for the church to break through this shell. Recently I became vividly aware of this problem when I was in a group of about a dozen churchmen who were trying to agree on something to say together on social problems. Two of those present objected to a simple statement to the effect that our responsibility to God rises above all other claims and responsibilities. Their reason for objecting to this idea was that it might make room for treason.

The first thing to say about this is that Christians can expect at times to be regarded by some people as taking positions which are treasonable. Ever since the first apostles said "We must obey God rather than men" this has been a possibility. The Christian, when he so acts, is trying to be loyal to what he believes is God's purpose for his country and to his country's true welfare.

One view of this fear of treason is that Americans have received such a shock because of the revelation of actual cases of Communist-inspired treason that they are now a wounded people and need to be dealt with very gently. There is some truth in that contention, and the church should take it into account. The other side of the picture, and at the moment the far more important side, is that, while there have been real wounds, there are today powerful men in our country who specialize in reopening those wounds, not to help them to heal more completely, but for quite other purposes—to gain a partisan political advantage or to secure personal publicity; but most often in order to discredit by insinuation, if not by direct charges, all who believe in some changes in the economic order. These men use the conflict in faith between Christianity and communism to give a Christian sanction to the most conservative interpretation of the American way of life.

There is so much activity of this kind that, while some consideration should be given to the sense of having been wounded in the past, our greatest emphasis should be on the new wounds that are being inflicted in the name of national security, in the name of anticommunism, in the name of patriotism. Our country has almost lost the capacity for self-criticism or for listening to criticism from others. The church is the one voice in our national life and in our local communities that is under no American authority. Its duty today is to seek to counteract the fog of fear and defensiveness which envelops our national life.

The second factor in our culture which makes it difficult, but extremely important, to give more emphasis to the church's role as prophetic critic is the habit of viewing most things from the standpoint of "public relations." Now responsible and honest public relations are a necessary instrument in our complicated society, and there is no institution that does not need to make use of this instrument in order to communicate to the public the things it stands for and the reasons for supporting its work.

There is, however, a false type of public relations in America which is the result of the attempt to apply to human groups and institutions the methods of advertising which may be suitable in selling soap or automobiles. There may be kinds of soap which are 99 or 100 per cent pure; there may be automobiles which are mechanically almost perfect; and claims for either the soap or the automobiles may not be exaggerated. I pass over the insinuations of superiority to all other products, which often are less than honest.

But "public relations" becomes absurd when we apply the

same kind of advertising and promotional techniques alike to the American economic system, to business in general, to labor, to a political party or candidate, to the policies of a government, to a public utility, to a book, to a church. All these things are very human and very mixed, and there is always another side that is carefully suppressed. We Americans have formed the habit of selling things to each other in this way. I often wonder how far people discount what others say when they remember what they have themselves said or left unsaid on another occasion. It often seems that people who are otherwise discerning believe their own propaganda. I have had the privilege of meeting with representatives of business and labor and various agricultural groups and have often noticed how very sensitive each group is to any criticism. They like to draw pretty pictures of themselves which are too good to be true.

This tendency is quite different in origin from the defensive shell which we develop because of fear of communism. It has independent roots in our habit of selling things, which is so large a part of our life. But it has the effect of reinforcing the defensiveness which is due to fear. Together these two factors exaggerate perennial tendencies among men to resist self-criticism and to concentrate on the beam in the brother's eye.

Surely within the church there must be a definite attempt to counteract this tendency to deceive others and ourselves, and especially to oppose the use of the Christian religion as a means of commending ourselves, our policies and our institutions to ourselves and to the world. The use of our religion as a sanction for what we ourselves desire most to preserve leads easily to American forms of idolatry which may be more treacherous enemies of Christian faith than explicit denials of it.

The third factor which is both obstacle to and reason for giving new emphasis to the neglected function of the church as critic grows out of the fact that the churches reflect the assumptions and attitudes of particular communities, often of a particular social class or residential area. The democratic structure of many of our denominations suggests that the church should do no more than echo the attitudes and convictions of its members. Some denominations are more inclined than others to suggest that Christian truth is established by majority vote.

To speak of majority vote in this way may be an unfair carica-ture, but it does call attention to a real problem in Protestant-ism. Even our denominations which are most democratic in their form of government and which stress as much participa-tion as possible by all their members must recognize that, if a church is Christian, it is confronted by a revelation of God's truth which it did not create and which no majority vote can cancel. It is confronted by a word of judgment from beyond the desires, expectations and ideals of its members. The preaching of the Word of God is one method by which the church pro-vides for the hearing of this judgment. It is often very difficult for the church to accept this judgment when it concerns the social institutions with which the church lives and the culture which surrounds it and almost saturates it.

The freedom of the pulpit is freedom to be responsible to the revelation of God in Christ and not to any national or socially dominant ideas concerning what is good. Like other forms of freedom it is easily abused, and the interpretation which individuals give to the revelation needs to be checked by various forms of corporate prophetic teaching. One of the finest examples of such corporate teaching in the church was the letter from John Mackay and the General Council of the Presbyterian Church in the U.S.A. to the ministers of that church. For-tunately, while this letter was addressed to the church, the world was allowed to read it, for it was published in full in the *New York Times.*

This letter brought a Christian judgment to bear on the greatest moral threats to our national life and on our favorite self-deceptions. It dealt chiefly with the false ways in which we respond to the menace of communism. It dealt very force-fully with the disregard of human rights in the current inquisi-tions and then spoke of the fanatical negativism without any constructive program of action which is leading the American mind into a "spiritual vacuum." It said: "Our national house, cleansed of one demon, would invite by its very emptiness the entrance of seven others. In the case of a national crisis this emptiness could in the high-sounding name of security, be occupied with ease by a fascist tyranny."

In calling attention to the present lack of balance in the message of the church and, perhaps even more, in the current popular interpretations of Christianity, I want to emphasize something more than the need of preserving both the prophetic role of the church and its role as healer of the soul. Criticism or the prophetic No should always be in the context of the total gospel so that men will not be afraid to hear it or defend themselves against it. Only as people are helped, even while the No is being spoken, to see beyond it to God's love for them and for the world can they really receive the word of criticism. Let the positive word come first, so that the gospel may undercut the fears which cause men to harden their minds and hearts against any criticism; but then the word of judgment is needed to prevent all that is positive in the gospel from creating false peace of mind in personal life or complacency about our national culture.

PERCEPTIVE ANALYSIS of movements commending religion as peace-of-mind insurance and God as the ever-ready "Man Upstairs"—by a member of the Lehigh University Faculty.

November 17, 1954

The New Look in American Piety

A. ROY ECKARDT

When the Apostle Paul visited the Athenians he perceived that in every way they were very religious. Paul would probably make a similar observation about this country at mid-twentieth-century. "Religion," Ralph Sockman recently pointed out, "seems to have become the vogue in America."

Piety is more and more diffusing itself among our people, particularly in ways that supplement the regular ministry of the churches. A nationally circulated "slick" magazine carries a page on which a well-known clergyman dispenses "peace-of mind" religion to people writing in with spiritual problems. Religious books continue to lead best-seller lists. Popular song writers profitably emphasize religious themes. Radio stations pause not simply for the usual station breaks but for recommended moments of meditation. The movie-makers know that few productions can out-box-office religious extravaganzas. The new piety has successfully invaded the halls of government. Attendance at prayer breakfasts is quite the thing for politicians these days. Ostensibly, even cabinet meetings can function better after a "word of prayer." And the pledge of allegiance is given the new religious look by the addition of the words "under God."

The divergent voices of American culture religion are one in the faith that God is an exceedingly handy fellow to have around.

It is hardly fair to condemn out of hand revivals of religion. There is doubtless sincerity of motive in much of the new piety. Besides, God is able to use not alone the wrath but also the foibles of men to praise him. For St. Paul the thing that counted was that Christ was preached, whether in pretense or in truth. The extent to which a reawakening religion may be born of the Spirit and may indicate genuine religious devotion is immeasurable.

It hardly follows that the new piety is to be accepted uncritically. There is nothing in the Bible to support the view that religion is necessarily a good thing. Scripture has no ax to grind for religion; on the contrary, it is highly suspicious of much that passes for religion. The lamentable thing about the current revival is the failure of many people to make discriminating judgments of differing religious outlooks. The truth is that a given brand of piety may represent nothing more than nice, virile idol worship.

Consider three aspects of the new piety which should cause Christians concern.

1. The cult of "peace of mind." The Christian church speaks in the name of the Great Physician who makes whole minds,

souls and bodies. Were we to turn away those who hunger and thirst for spiritual peace, we would betray part of our pastoral function. That this cult has spread so phenomenally may well represent a divine judgment upon our ministry.

The fact remains that the peace-of-mind cult readily turns into religious narcissism. The individual and his psycho-spiritual state occupy the center of the religious stage. Here is piety concentrating on its own navel. The Christian gospel, we must object, is in its redemptive wholeness a challenge to men to surrender themselves for the sake of Christ with the result that their hearts will go out to their brethren. The New Testament forcibly reminds them that in this world they have tribulation. They are to be of good cheer, but only because Christ has overcome the world. The shadow of his cross may indeed fall across their own lives.

The peace-of-mind movement is deficient morally and empirically. It has no grasp of the deep paradox that "whoever would save his life will lose it, and whoever loses his life for [Christ's] sake will find it." Lasting peace of mind is impossible apart from peace with God; yet enduring peace with God comes only when a man is ready to surrender his own peace of mind.

This new cult counsels "personal adjustment." But adjustment to what? New Testament Christianity is hardly adjusted to its environment. It makes us seriously wonder, in fact, how much the social order is worth adjusting to. The gospel urges us to nonconformity: "Do not be conformed to this world but be transformed."

An evil aspect of peace-of-mind religion is its acceptance, by default, of the social status quo. An unannounced assumption is that the present condition of the social order is irrelevant to one's true needs and outside the scope of one's obligations. In truth, to limit religion to "spiritual" concerns is to abdicate responsibility in the struggle against man's inhumanity to man. The tragedy is that the peace-of-mind cult unwittingly furthers the rise of radical politico-economic movements which step in to fill the void left by the absence of a social gospel.

A final irony is that peace-of-mind religion fails to address itself to the very cultural crisis which helps produce more distraught souls than the practitioners could ever handle. But its greatest sin lies in using God as a means for human ends. This is blasphemous. The Bible tells us that God uses us for *his* ends. "Woe to those who are at ease in Zion, and to those who feel secure on the mountain of Samaria."

2. The cult of the "Man Upstairs." A rhapsodic inquiry greets us from the TV screen and the radio: "Have you talked to the Man Upstairs?" God is a friendly neighbor who dwells in the apartment just above. Call on him any time, especially if you are feeling a little blue. He does not get upset over your little faults. He understands. We have been assured by no less a theologian than Jane Russell that the Lord is a "livin' Doll," a right nice guy. Thus is the citizenry guided to divine-human chumminess.

This view of religion is not wholly unlike the one just considered. However—to borrow William James' terminology—the peace-of-mind cult makes more of an appeal to the "sick soul" religionist, while the cult of the Man Upstairs attracts more the "healthy-minded" type. The latter individual is not so much weighed down by fears and complexes. On the surface at least, he is well adjusted. The appeal of religion is that it can make him get even more pleasure out of life. Fellowship with the Lord is, so to say, an extra emotional jag that keeps him happy. The "gospel" makes him "feel real good."

In this cult religion verges on entertainment, perhaps merges with it. Thus "gospel boogie," replete with masters of ceremonies, gospel quartets, popcorn and soda pop, is able to play to jam-packed audiences in many cities. The financial take from the paid admissions is considerable.

Those whose God is the Friendly Neighbor would not dream of hearing him say, "For three transgressions of America, yea for four, I will not turn my wrath away." Our new culture religion is helping to mold us into a people possessed of the certainty that the Lord is squarely on our side. Whatever we think and do can be carried on in good conscience.

The stern fact remains that to behave as if man as man were not anxious with himself in the presence of his fellows and, especially, of God, is to dull the moral sense. It is to destroy man's dignity as a free being. He is dehumanized. His life is reduced, as Will Herberg says, "to the level of subhuman creation which knows neither sin nor guilt." The moral and spiritual life is buried in triviality.

The Christian whose norm is Scripture must always have a particularly uneasy conscience. He recognizes the gulf between the quality of his life and the sacrifice of God's only Son on the cross. He knows the love that came down on Calvary. He knows the judgment too. And he knows that the love cannot be separated from the judgment.

The Man Upstairs is a foolish idol fabricated from out of the proud imaginations of the human spirit, a childish projection of granddaddy. The real God is the relentless One who pursues us and gives us no peace until our religiosity is transformed by repentance. In the very hour that the gospel quartet soothes with the universalist-hedonist refrain, "Everybody's gonna have a wonderful time up there," the sheep and the goats are being sorted out. "It is a fearful thing to fall into the hands of the living God." Old Testament scary stuff? No, the Epistle to the Hebrews. The adjective in the phrase "livin' Doll" is precisely what causes us so much trouble. The real God is the Hound of Heaven. We wish he would go and live somewhere else. But the Lord refuses to move, no matter how we try to take the threat out of him by reducing him to a friendly neighbor. The cult of the Man Upstairs meets its nemesis before the Holy Presence.

3. The cult of "we" versus "they." This cult is more tangibly sinister than the other two. It is just a short step from a god who is the Great Adjuster and/or the Friendly Neighbor to the god who fights on the side of his chosen people, supporting their racial, economic or national interests. The crucial point is that the first two cults have already stimulated and endorsed powerful human emotions. The obvious outcome is that it is un-American to be unreligious. We are the good spiritual people. The God of judgment has died.

Yet it is perverse to conclude that our cause is God's cause. To equate the two is to be in for a shock before the transcendent justice of God. The dangers in the "we" versus "they" cult are especially evident today in relations between this country and the rest of the world. The nation that best fulfills its God-given responsibilities is not necessarily the nation that displays the most religiosity. A country possessed of the might of the United States might do better to go into its closet and pray to its Father in secret rather than standing on the street corners parading its piety before men. The piety of individuals stands a relatively better chance of inducing repentance than does the public piety of nations. The temptation is just about irresistible for a powerful nation to rely on its religiosity as proof of its own virtue. Thus is threatened the possibility of sober and responsible political action.

Against all human idolatries we may set the peace of Christ which passes all understanding. We have not earned his peace. It is a gift we have received. It does not center in the self or the group. It centers in the cross and the empty tomb. It provides an ultimate vantage point from which the whole drama of life may be viewed. It is the peace of a disturbing forgiveness. God ceases to be fashioned in our image; we are made over into his. We are granted not a short-cut or trivial solution to our anxieties but the grace to laugh and to know that our anxieties are of no ultimate consequence. The peace of Christ comes, mysteriously, when we forget all about our peace, when we prostrate ourselves before the holiness of God, and when we discern the source of evil not in "them" but in our own hearts. What is more humiliating than to be forgiven by the Lord of heaven and earth, to be accepted just as we are—petty and full of pride?

The peace of Christ issues in the nonchalance of faith and service. The gospel meets the desperate human need of which the cults are an ominous symptom. It does so in the very act of defeating idolatry.

WHEN HE WROTE this article the author was at work in the Episcopal experiment in church renewal centering on the Parishfield Community in Michigan; now he pursues his advocacy of renewal as assistant professor of ethics and society at the University of Chicago divinity school.

September 28, 1955

The Church in Suburban Captivity

GIBSON WINTER

Suburbia is now a dominant social group in American life. This group has been dramatized in recent novels by J. P. Marquand, who has turned his searching eye from the Boston aristocrat to the suburban competitor. Although suburbia is generally considered a place, suburban places vary considerably. They form a single group by reason of their state of mind rather than by their geographical similarity. What is this suburban state of mind and what does it mean for our churches?

In one generation there has been a swing of power to suburbia which is touching all aspects of American life, and the churches are no exception. In fact it can be said that suburban church life has become the controlling force in American Christianity. The numerical, financial and plant concentration of the churches is more and more to be found in the suburbs. The leadership of most church boards is drawn from suburbia, even when these leaders continue their membership in an urban church to which they commute. The clergy of most churches also have been recruited from suburbia in the past fifteen years. Is this the same old leadership living in a different place? Or are there special characteristics of suburban leadership which are now becoming manifest in the churches?

Suburbia has two aspects, the geographical and the mental. The growth of residential areas outside the commercial districts of large cities has created a geographical suburbia. This spatial suburbia ranges from lower middle income groupings to top-salary residential areas. Its structure and location are thus highly differentiated. Its common element is a state of mind. This is the real suburbia, no matter what geographical form it may take. Let us look at this state of mind which has captured or is capturing the leadership of the churches.

Advancement in life is a keynote of the suburban mind. Whether he is a wage-earner or a manager, the suburbanite views work as a means of advancement, along with pay increases—from production worker to foreman, from assistant superintendent to superintendent. And it remains a vehicle of advancement even when he has been many years on the same rung of the ladder with no hope of further ascent. Success for him is not defined in terms of service or skill. Success equals advancement with a pay raise, and this is the real meaning of work.

The management or employer view of work permeates suburbia. Even the dwellers in lower suburbia see work in terms of production needs, cost problems and profit drives. These are management people, even though they may share in profits to a smaller degree than many of the skilled wage-earners. To be sure, some foremen may not have this mentality, and some production workers may have it. But on the whole suburbia has a managerial mind, although most suburbanites lack top management's prestige and pocketbook.

Mobility is another characteristic of suburbia. The actual mobility of this group varies with its advancement up the economic ladder, but the suburbanite never sees himself as rooted, anchored, placed. He may have lived in one place for twelve years, but his whole attitude suggests temporary friends and provisional organizational commitments. And if the sense of mobility eases a little with arrival in super-upper suburbia, much of this disquiet is transferred to summer and winter vacation trips.

The fragmentation of commitments that inevitably accompanies advancement and mobility is a further characteristic of the suburban mind, and a source of much distress. The suburbanite is the superactivist. His need to get acquainted in each new area on the way up the ladder leads to innumerable activities. Since he lacks the sense of security that comes from established relationships, he finds himself unable to refuse organizational obligations and so overextends his activities. Suburbia is the most time-conscious and pressure-conscious segment of our society. The suburbanite and his family are spread all over the map in activities, one of these being the church.

Movement from the lower to the upper rungs usually means thickening insulation from new ideas and growing dependence for opinions and actions on advice from fellow climbers. Competition and tension increase rather than decrease with progress upwards, because at each stage more is at stake and fewer can be rewarded. Furthermore, position in suburbia depends entirely on current income, since the advancement plan forces climbers to live up to the maximum of their income or beyond it all the way along. Retirement early or late usually means banishment to outer darkness; hence tension increases with the height of ascent. In this regard upper suburbia should be clearly distinguished from America's rapidly disappearing upper crust, who operate on inherited wealth and family position.

The suburban mind, then, is characterized by the urge for advancement, the management point of view, and a sense of mobility, accompanied by overactivity and constant tension. This, of course, is a generalized picture, not a photograph of any particular section of America.

We come now to the effect of this mentality on the life and thinking of Christianity in America. Will we recognize the gospel as mediated by suburbia? We live and work with a church through which God has promised to speak and act. What kind of vehicle is the suburban mind for this speaking and acting?

There are two kinds of strength in that mind which have already affected the churches. First, suburbanites are very active in organizations, and notable numbers of them are now active in churches. Suburban churches with their endless round of activity reflect this group's tendency to overextend itself organizationally. Moreover, the suburbanites are often the ones who carry the organizational load in the urban churches to which they commute. Membership is simply no problem in a go-getter suburban congregation. Whatever one's estimate of their Christian insight and commitment, these people are rallying around. The activism of the suburban mind has poured energy and leadership into church programs.

Second, amid the tension of his competitive life what little sense of security the suburbanite has focuses on his family. He is interested in "the kids." In many respects the suburban family is one of the most fragmented types in our society, but it is moved by a real concern to have the best of everything for "the kids." This concern gives the churches a leverage to get parents into church with their children for the sake of the children, and at the same time generates pressure on the churches to develop family-centered worship and programs. The move to re-establish Christian training in the family, which has been spreading through the churches, is for the most part a result of this pressure from suburbia. Despite its largely feminine character, there is a real potential in a congregational life which is giving serious attention to the family unit.

When we compare American and European church life, there is no question but what membership and activity tip the balance favorably toward America. Here is active, competent leadership voluntarily enlisted. Converted or unconverted, the congregation is in evidence. Furthermore, the members will make almost any sacrifices in the interests of the kind of family life they seek but seldom experience. Able leadership in family units is no small asset in a day when churches throughout the world are fighting for survival.

Why should domination by suburbia be called captivity when suburbia has brought numbers, leadership and prosperity to the churches? Because despite the strength it has produced this domination is a threat to the church's witness to Christ's lordship.

Suburbia has introduced its concept of success into the very center of church life. Advancement, monetary and numerical extension of power—these are the criteria by which suburbia measures all things. Most church programs are now burdened with endless haphazard activity in the service of success so defined. The task of the churches as witnesses to Christ's lordship and to the power of the cross has been submerged. Clergy and laity alike are infected with the advancement ideology out of which they have grown. The test of every parish enterprise is whether it will bring monetary and numerical progress.

Any remnant of corporate thinking which still existed in the Christianity of our century has been lost in this suburban encounter. Suburbia has been developed out of the industrial scramble with its pushing competition and its distributive rewards. Some arrive, some get left—that is life! Is this not also true of Christianity? Suburbia is the prime representative of individualistic thinking. The church's captivity to it is the death blow to recovery of the biblical view of corporate life, corporate sin and corporate salvation. Suburban Christianity consists of a series of ladders from parish house to heaven—one for each individual strong enough to climb. The ideal of such a religion is the confident, peaceable, energetic and successful individual.

"Salvation" and "redemption" are disturbing to suburbia. These words disturb everyone, of course, but suburbia sees them as representing sticky, nonactive, old-fashioned Christianity. Prayer in fellowship and shared reading of the Bible are threatening to suburbia even more than to other segments of society. Why? It is hard to say. Possibly emotional repression and control are necessary qualifications for advancement in our society, and therefore emotional frigidity especially characterizes the suburban mind. Whatever the reason, the biblical faith is rarely met with in suburbia despite growing church membership and activity.

Strange as it may sound, numbers are also a problem in this milieu. Families are joining "active" churches faster than any staff of clergy or nucleus lay fellowship can train and assimilate them. Despite a nominal church background, this is an unconverted, untrained mass of people who make the problem of church membership comparable to what it was in the time of Constantine, when Christianity became a recognized institution of Roman society. The leadership and control of the churches have been captured by a suburbia which at best is only partly cognizant of the gist of the Christian message. These leaders are competent in business, but only a few have any true understanding of Christianity. Moreover, they and their clergy are too busy to stop to hear the gospel.

Finally, suburbia has nailed up an impenetrable layer of insulation between the churches and the world of work, community, politics, housing and daily bread. This isolation of church life from everyday life has been a characteristic development of industrial society. Suburbia has been shaped in a parallel drive to remove family life and neighborhood from places of business and labor. The human toll that industry takes and the derelicts it spews out are left behind in the cities and ignored in most suburban churches. It is easier to ignore things from which we are removed. Work, political struggle, racial tension—all those unpleasant things take place there in the nasty city where we earn money. Here in suburbia we talk about our children, our God and our many social obligations. If those people in the city had gumption they'd move out. In short, by removal to suburbia the witness of the churches in the world is being translated to an ethereal, spiritual level.

The church's insulation from the world was not created by suburbia; it has simply found its consummation there. In a sense, suburbia expresses most fully the secularization of life which has accompanied industrialism. It represents the final step in the secularization of the church and in the isolation of Christianity from man's struggle for bread.

The emphasis on success, the highly individualistic ideology, the hyperactivity, the deep gulf between this "religion" and daily life—these are anti-Christian forces dominating the leadership introduced into the churches by the suburban captivity. They far offset the numerical and financial gains.

This characterization of the suburban mind has grown out of the writer's experience—a rearing in suburbia and parochial work there, together with a sociological estimate of America in an industrial age and attempts in the Parishfield Community to train Christian men and women for witness in the world. From each vantage point, suburbia looms as a controlling factor in American church life. This is a secular captivity of the churches. Nevertheless, Christ has worked with his church in times of lesser and greater disobedience. Our task is to be honest in confessing our disobedience and to trust him to forgive us, change us and work through us. Yet our confidence in Christ's mercy and promise is no excuse for overlooking the fact that we have all connived, albeit unwittingly, at selling the churches into a suburban captivity.

The captivity of the church is a national tragedy of the first order, for it occurs at a time when America's position of world leadership requires a prophetic church at home. Suburban leadership is the antithesis of the prophetic note in the gospel. No one welcomes this prophetic note; to take it seriously is to make the initial, radical break with the suburban mind in which all of us share.

Suburban domination may well be God's word of judgment upon us as his church. For our trespasses and complacency we have been delivered to Babylon. Yet the gospel is a word of hope and deliverance that can still open up and transform hearts bent on advancement and individual success. Such a conversion of suburban leadership would be the beginning of a new Christian era. If and when it comes, it will be by the impact of Christ's judgment and grace and not by more activity. May this word be heard in the churches!

FORMATION of the National Council of Churches was advocated in many Christian Century editorials and articles, and when the council was finally created, in 1950, it was hailed in a special issue of the magazine. The choice of title of this editorial was influenced by realization of the despair widely felt over China's entrance into the Korean war just then, in a particularly dark hour.

December 13, 1950

Harbinger of Hope
AN EDITORIAL

The brightest and only enduring star of hope in the darkness of global night is the sovereign reality of the merciful God. Man's distracted mind is gratefully recalled to this polar star when the Christian community is united in deeper solidarity at the very moment when the world community seems again to be breaking up. Here is evidence in the midst of time that the eternal is not left without a witness. Here is a reminder that man's destiny is not necessarily doom and catastrophe, blind, senseless and utterly callous; but that it may be fulfillment, fellowship in a community of faith, joy in an unmerited but nevertheless unbelievably real redemption. Here in the midst of despair is a harbinger of hope.

Two and one-half years ago the World Council of Churches was formed in war-shattered Europe. Long before that continent had achieved even the first small beginnings of political reintegration which are visible today, the churches proclaimed their oneness in Christ. The new council brought together from all over the earth and from nearly every country over 150 denominations of Protestant and Eastern Orthodox Christians and joined them in a fellowship of faith in which they affirmed that "we are responsible for one another." Its influence has already reached out beyond its original boundaries and brought in other churches. It has even managed to hold Christians together in spite of the polarization of mankind into two warring communities.

Now, by an even greater miracle of grace, two-thirds of the members of American Protestant denominations have united to form the National Council of Churches of Christ in the United States of America. The twenty-five Protestant and four Eastern Orthodox denominations forming the council have a combined communicant membership of over thirty-one million. If their membership were stated in the terms used by the Roman Catholic Church—i.e., counting all baptized and inactive members—it would be far over forty million. That this should happen in America, where the scandal of sectarianism has grown to dimensions unequaled in any other land, is an answer to the prayers of millions of faithful church members and an event unsurpassed in modern Christian history.

It has been charged that the ecumenical principle is something that flourishes best when it is embodied in abstract conceptions and far-away organizations. Where, say the skeptics, is ecumenical Christianity in Sauk Center, Minnesota, or Millville, New Jersey? Where is it in Redwood City or Danbury, in Emporia or Plymouth? Where is it in Uvalde or Bennington, in Corvallis or Mobile? Doesn't it there become so thin that its very existence is in doubt? If it lacks the capacity for local expression, is its universality of much consequence?

There is an answer to such questions, as those churchmen know who have the capacity to sense the stirring of spirit which is going on in the churches of every American community. That ferment is finding expression at every level of human fellowship. At Cleveland it brought into existence an instrument of Christian communication across the broad plane of our national life. There is, in spite of conflicting forces, an American community. Now, at its very heart, a Christian community has emerged which is equipping itself to speak in Christian terms to "this nation under God." The emergence in Cleveland of this community into concrete and visible form on November 29, 1950, makes that day one which will live forever in the annals of great events in the spiritual pilgrimage of American Christianity.

The National Council is a council of churches, not an organic union of denominations. It is not a superchurch. It has no authority to coerce its members, or to bind them against their will. It has no intention of growing into such authority, for the important reason that the conception of the nature of the church which penetrates its every branch is alien to such authoritarianism. It is a voluntary association which will remain voluntary. It has come into existence because "in the providence of God, the time has come when it seems fitting more fully to manifest the essential oneness of the Christian churches of the United States of America in Jesus Christ as their divine Lord and Savior by the creation of an inclusive co-operative agency."

It is essential that from the beginning the objects of the National Council be kept in mind, for it is certain to be attacked and misrepresented, if for no other reason than that it cannot be ignored. These objects, as stated in the constitution which was drafted by representatives of the churches and adopted at Cleveland, are: "(1) To manifest the essential oneness of the co-operating churches in spirit and purpose for the furtherance of their common mission in the world. (2) To carry on such work of the churches as they desire to be done in co-operation. (3) To continue and extend the work of the interdenominational agencies named in the preamble, together with such additional objects and purposes as may from time to time be agreed upon. (4) To encourage devotional fellowship and mutual counsel concerning the spiritual life and religious activities of the churches. (5) To foster and encourage co-operation between two or more communions. (6) To promote co-operation among local churches and to further the development of councils of churches in communities, states or larger territorial units. (7) To establish consultative relationships with National Councils of Churches in other countries of North America. (8) To maintain fellowship and co-operation with similar councils in other areas of the world. (9) To maintain fellowship and co-operation with the World Council of Churches and with other international Christian organizations."

This statement of objects, it is necessary to repeat, defines the terms on which the churches themselves have agreed to co-operate. They wrote it. They agreed to it. But this does not complete the picture. At Cleveland they defined the broad areas in which they intend to co-operate. These are not peripheral areas, but include the most essential functions of the churches. Among them are Christian education, home missions, foreign missions and the relation of church to community life. Not all or even the majority of the activities of the churches in these fields will find expression through the council, but in each of the essential ministries of the churches there is a core of common endeavor, and it will be co-operatively occupied. In addition, the churches have declared that through the National Council they will increasingly undertake together their great ministries of evangelism, of missionary education, of stewardship. Organizations of churchmen and churchwomen will channel the common concerns of the denominations in their respective fields. Social and industrial relations, race relations, international justice and good will, family life, Christian vocations and the field of the relations between town and country churches will be co-operatively explored. Unitedly the churches will plan and work together in the fields of religious radio and television, in publication, in planning for church building and providing architectural services, in carrying their voice to America through press and other channels of mass communication.

All this was not created anew at Cleveland. Instead, the co-operation has been developing through the past half-century or more. It has grown through the manifold ministries of the interchurch organizations which were merged in a creative new synthesis at Cleveland. In each of these fields, vital enterprises of Christian co-operation are already at work. At Cleveland the churches did not blueprint something that must yet be created. They brought together the separate living elements of their common life and made them one. Henceforth the high central mission of the churches will be embodied in an organization whose unified purpose will proclaim that mission more effectively than it has ever yet been proclaimed.

But the "new council," as Dean Luther A. Weigle, chairman of the planning committee, pointed out in the convention newspaper, "should be regarded not only as a more effective instrument for common tasks, but as something more significant. It is the outward manifestation of a deepening sense of our spiritual unity in our Lord Jesus Christ as the one Head of the church. It is a forward movement in the direction of a greater Christian unity while at the same time we preserve the Christian liberty which is our precious heritage."

THE EVANGELISTIC REVIVALS of the early 1900's had their counterparts a half-century later. Selections from the Century files testify that the more some phases of church life change, the more others remain the same.

July 1, 1909

An Analysis of Revivalistic Method
AN EDITORIAL

There are richer possibilities in Christianity than the modern church is expressing.

What the church today most lacks is a vital consciousness of the sources of power and character with which the soul of Christ the Master had such open and intimate connection.

Our revivalistic method, the method by which we are most of us brought into the church and which we mostly use to bring others into the church, is responsible for the low order of spiritual life which obtains in our churches.

Modern revivalism produces an inferior order of Christian experience, and the continued use of the revivalistic method renders the church incapable of utilizing or even of perceiving a method by which a higher order of Christian experience might be produced.

It sets up false standards. It gets results by artificial means. It manipulates, but it does not instruct.

And it cannot instruct, for the state of mind which its characteristic work induces is not one of thoughtfulness.

The power of the revivalistic method lies in the situation it organizes, not in the individual soul's perception of vital truth.

What distinguishes the revivalist from the pastor? Is he superior to the pastor in the culture and grasp of his mind? Not at all. Is the revivalist a more spiritually minded man than the pastor? Certainly no one will claim for him any such preeminence.

Is he, then, a more lucid interpreter of the truth than the pastor? Is he a better teacher? No.

Does he hold up a more inspiring ideal of life than the pastor is accustomed to present? By no means.

What is it, then, that distinguishes the revivalist from the pastor?

This: the successful revivalist has learned the art of controlling a congregation as a whole. The unit with which he deals is the crowd, not the individual soul.

And the crowd has a soul of its own just as an individual has a soul of his own. The methods by which a "master of assemblies" can get at this crowd-soul, to move it, are just as definite as the methods by which one can get at the individual soul.

The revivalist is a man who has found the way to the soul of the crowd. The average pastor either does not know the way or else, knowing it, knows also that the Christianity of Christ has no business there.

The revivalist may not be conscious of his method; he may proceed instinctively and, perhaps, be all the more successful for not being aware of just what he is doing. But that his distinction from the pastor lies in his possession of the power of controlling men *en masse*, an analysis of any revival meeting will reveal.

Take for example the revivalistic device of voting the people up and down on this question and on that. "Stand up if you will accept Christ." "Stand up if you have any desire at all in your heart for salvation." "Stand up if you want us to pray for you." "All who want to go to heaven, stand up."

The result of this crowd movement in whatever direction the preacher may determine is to set up a form of crowd-hypnotism with the preacher in control and the ordinary inhibitions of the individual broken down. The instinctive rebellion of the intelligent man to such a practice is overborne by his sense of embarrassment in case he does not yield, and so he commits himself to the will of the preacher.

Or take again the device of leading the individual from one slight step to succeeding steps of increasing importance. It is a method ofttimes adopted when the evangelist's patience has been exhausted in an effort to get converts outright.

The appeal goes forth from the pulpit for those who wish to be prayed for to raise their hands. A number of unsuspecting hands go up. Immediately they are noted by the "personal workers" who go to them and engage earnestly in conversation.

A second request is made for those who raised their hands to stand up before the prayer in their behalf is offered. Once upon their feet they are invited to come forward and, with the assistance of the personal workers, many of them are brought to the front seat where they are given cards to sign stating that they purpose to live the Christian life. Whereupon the public confession of faith is taken by the evangelist.

Another method often used by the revivalist to get at the soul of the crowd is to adopt at the opening of his meeting a policy of abuse in preaching. The evangelist abuses everybody in general and in particular. It may be the church members or the ministers or the "sects" or polite society, so-called, or the city administration. He wins at once a reputation for bravery, nerve.

This, of course, is the trick of every demagogue and charlatan, the trick adopted with such amazing success by the late Dr. Dowie, who won his power by his pastmastership in the art of abuse. People like it. It excites curiosity and it always results, if it is cleverly executed, in winning the soul of the crowd.

The use of the so-called personal workers' organization in the typical revival illuminates the essential method of such meetings. There is hardly a successful evangelist at work today who does not depend mainly upon this personal work during the singing of the invitation songs.

No leader deceives himself with the idea that, amid the confusion and excitement of the hour, these personal workers could possibly sink an intelligible idea in any unsaved soul. The evangelist does not use personal workers as persons to seek and save the souls of other persons. He uses them as a factor in de-individualizing (it is an outlandish word!) the people and creating the crowd-soul.

What the evangelist wants is to get the situation broken up. He wants confusion, movement, a swaying of the crowd, excitement and curiosity and a sense of expectancy, lifting the crowd to a tiptoe of feeling, while he the while, above the buzz and roar and chatter, is wildly swinging his arms and shouting his perspiring exhortation to the throng.

The effect is to work chaos in the mind of each person similar to that exhibited by the crowd as a whole. Ideas are confused, logical connection is broken down, the sense of reality is lost, natural inhibitions are overcome, a certain feeling of detachment is induced and the individual finds himself caught up by the powerful currents of social feeling.

He is out and out, momentarily, a victim of a hypnotized social situation, and the simplest thing in the world, the almost inevitable thing for him is to go forward or stand up or do whatever the leader suggests.

But all this means the temporary breaking down of the structure of his own personality, the invasion of his personal right as a man to do his own thinking about God and his soul upon the basis of his own intelligence.

No informed evangelist who genuinely loves men as individuals and seeks to open up a well of living water in their inner souls will be the instrument of creating this hypnotic situation in the name of Christ.

If he is interested in building up a church, he might be deluded into the notion that this kind of success really builds up the church.

If he expects large donations at the close of his meetings, there is no surer way to get them than to start in the people the habit of yielding to crowd suggestion.

But if he is genuinely and sincerely trying to make the

highest type of men and to put them into the control of Jesus Christ, he will indignantly eschew all such methods. He will see that they work through an uncanny, hypnotic and un-spiritual principle and cannot advance far the kingdom of God.

June 26, 1957

Needed: Evangelism in Depth

EDITORIAL CORRESPONDENCE

London, England

How does Billy Graham look now from London, two years after his campaign here? What permanent effects remain in Britain following his campaigns? What are the results in the parishes, in the churches, in the Christian life of Britain? Is Graham the prelude to religious revival?

None of these questions permits of a simple answer. This is an old land, conditioned and indoctrinated by generations of Christian living, dominated by a state church, obedient still to the outward conventions of Christianity and responsive to the personal presentation of religion, particularly by some-one as attractive as Graham.

Graham is wise enough to know that the Christian faith is not just a private emotion. Thus his London and Glasgow campaigns were linked with "organized Christianity." He was out to give the churches new life and help restock them with vital Christians. How well did he succeed?

Eight months after the Harringay campaign, the *London Evening Standard* conducted a study on "Where Are the Billy Graham Converts?" Twenty vicars of large London parishes were asked what had happened to the converts who were re-ported to them by the Graham card system. These 20 parishes had a population of 420,216 souls. A total of 336 individuals were reported to them. Of these 226 were old churchgoers, 110 "outsiders." The vicars reported that 45 of the outsiders were still coming to church. Since 36,000 were reported as converts in this campaign, the investigator assumed as a result of this sample test that 24,000 were "old faithfuls," and of the other 12,000 fewer than 4,000 were still in the churches. These figures have not been seriously challenged.

Did Graham break through to the unchurched, the non-religious, the "tele-mass"? The answer by and large is No. But a No with qualifications. While he was operating in London, Graham put religion into the news, made people talk religion in the streets, clubs and pubs. His "mass assault" softened up the crusty overlay under which the British keep their personal emotions and beliefs.

That in itself was an achievement, and it is a permanent achievement from which the Christian faith in Britain is still benefiting. Take, for instance, the flow of candidates to the ministry. All denominations report that many of the young men now coming forward owe some of their decision to the Graham impact. What made many of them decide for the ministry was either a Graham meeting or the relayed power of the movement generated by the evangelist. Whether it is good for the Christian ministry to be led by young ministers bearing the recognizable stamp of the "gospel according to Graham" is a matter for debate. I am merely reporting a fact.

Another fact to be noted is the rising tempo of a powerful evangelical drive developing independently of the churches. This evangelicalism bears the expected marks of Bible faithfulness, a certain unctuous piety, and an aggressive power for personal salvation. This movement tends to by-pass the denominations and even suggests that "those who are not with us" are not red-hot for the Christian religion and not concerned about winning souls. Graham himself kept free from this strident, critical note and was always appreciative of the churches' continuous battle against the world, the flesh and the devil.

Another effect of the "Graham impact" in Britain is the

subtle suggestion that this method of "personality evangelism" is the only method fit to practice in the modern world.
Consequently a number of "lesser Grahams" are entering the
field of personal evangelism supported by the light of publicity
which throws into a gray shadow the more prosaic life of the
churches.

In colleges and universities the "Graham impact" has given
power and prestige to the more conservative groups of students. It is said that science students in particular accept
the "word from Graham" as the one which points to the final
authority of the Bible, the inerrancy of Scriptures, and the
infallible court of judgment which is available to man in the
printed word of God.

During the summer of 1956 one of the big vacation camp
organizations handed over its place on the Yorkshire coast at
Filey to an evangelistic organization. Over 3,000 people paid
for a week's vacation with forty hours of evangelistic addresses
thrown in, plus an introductory recorded address by Graham.
This move into the vacation world with evangelism is a new
one for Britain.

It is admitted on all sides that there is no revival of religion
in Britain. The deeply laid secular spirit which views the
competence of men as equal to every need is at the moment
triumphant. Graham did a great deal to expose the shallowness
of this claim by his exposure of the bitterness of the human
heart and the deep longing of men and women for inner
peace. But he was unable to penetrate to the ills which produce this state of mind. His emphasis on the personal response
in the Christian faith is of course fundamental and he is
sufficient master of communication to know that the "tele-
mass" society is only capable of absorbing a reiterated message. He had little or no insight however into the conditions
of a society which now dominates the individual and in which
millions of people are prisoners, incapable of free decisions
and chained to the routine and techniques of the mass.

It is no criticism of Graham to note that as an evangelist
he is not living in the twentieth century. His techniques are
certainly contemporary and his organization knows all the

tricks of the advertiser's trade. But his research methods have evidently not led him to see modern man as the prisoner of his own created world from which he cannot leap at a single bound.

The twentieth century in Britain still awaits its evangelist. Perhaps it will never get him because the task of the world's redemption lies with the total Body of Christ through the travail of its corporate life. New methods of giving that life increased power and vigor are needed, and Graham and his allies are among them. But it must not be presumed that the kingdom of God belongs to them only.

Evangelism in the modern world must probe much deeper than the swift, immediately personal method of a revived traditional approach. It must speak to the entangled situations of life and conduct in which men are involved whatever their overnight "decision for Christ" may be. The methods of "personal evangelism," rewarding and dramatic as they often appear to be, are no substitute for the long and painful evangelism of our common life in industry, trade unions, employer groups and economic organizations. The Christian Church is prone to sail off on the elated tide of evangelistic campaigns and neglect the far tougher job of evangelizing the pagan ways that involve even converted Christians.

"Evangelism in depth" is a cry heard at every conference dealing with the world mission of the church. That means claiming not only a personal dedication from individuals but also a dedication of their community, family and industrial relationships. Begin with the individual? Yes. But don't end there. The Bible is worthy of a far deeper response than merely my own personal emotional response. The church is more than an organization looking for a few additional recruits from an evangelistic campaign. It is the very Body of Christ engaged in the unending warfare of her crucified and risen Lord. Billy Graham himself, I believe, would subscribe to all this. But does the vast movement of "personal evangelism" and "personal evangelizers" he has let loose see it this way?

Cecil Northcott

II

Foundations

IN SCOTLAND to attend the World Missionary Conference of 1910, young Editor Morrison chanced upon a name on a tombstone that led him to recall his questionings at a critical point in his own growth toward spiritual and intellectual maturity.

September 1, 1910

At Henry Drummond's Grave

CHARLES CLAYTON MORRISON

Our trip through the Trossachs and the beautiful Scottish lake region, made famous to readers of English literature in Scott's story of Rob Roy, brought us toward evening to Stirling, where we were planning to spend the night, going on in the morning to Edinburgh in time for the opening session of the Missionary Conference that afternoon. Stirling proved to be an intensely interesting place. The long twilight in Scotland at this time of year would give us until after ten o'clock to look about the town. We made first of all for the old castle at the top of the long steep hill on the side of which the town is builded. Whether because of its intrinsic points of interest, or because it was the first castle we had visited, or simply because the guide was one of the best we had met with in all our trip, the impression remains with us that Stirling was by far the most interesting of the score of venerable castles we visited throughout England and Scotland.

Here was the coveted point of vantage held alternately by the Scotch and English in the intermittent warfare of the days before both kingdoms passed under a single crown. In its broad esplanade stands a grand statue of Robert Bruce, and from the wall one can see the field of Bannockburn where Bruce in 1311 gained his decisive victory over the forces of England. The far-stretching plain, clothed as it was that evening in the golden glow of a wonderful sunset, and backed

81

up in the distance by mighty Ben Lomond, Ben Venue, Ben
Ledi and Ben Vorlich, left on our minds a landscape impression least likely to be effaced of all the glorious views of our
trip.

Leaving the castle we gained admission to the old Grey-
friar's church a little way down the hill. Coming out, we
strolled each according to his own whim through the park-like
cemetery stretching up the hill almost to the castle. I had no
notion of finding any grave of particular interest and was re-
maining in the place more for the enjoyment of the landscape
than for communion with the spirits of the great dead. Moving toward the church in the direction of the exit gate I
happened to descry the name DRUMMOND on a stone and,
looking carefully, made out that it was a simple monument
to none other than the world-beloved author of *The Greatest
Thing in the World*.

A hush fell upon my soul. I was more grateful to see this
simple slab than the heroic statue of Bruce or the great
monument to William Wallace yonder on another hill, more
grateful to behold this spot of earth than the landscape which
had fascinated my eyes for the past two hours. For this man
more than any other stood to me as the symbol of my spiritual experience in the most strategic period of my life. The
past twenty years stood before me in vivid panorama. My early
ministry, dealing, as I see it now, with an aspect of life too
far beyond the reach of my callow experience to be real, was
fertilized by his exposition of the thirteenth of First Corin-
thians. How my hand inevitably reached for *Natural Law in
the Spiritual World* when the early sermon-making process
went hard! It seems to me now that what life, what flesh
and blood, my early sermons had, they got from these two
books more than from the Bible. For, I must confess, the
Bible was not revealed to me as a book of life until some
years later. I thought of it as a book of law, divided into
"dispensations," and I defended its authority and "inspiration"
with much ambitious logic. Only as life deepened and I came
to feel the need of the Bible in my own soul did I come to
realize that it was my business as a preacher to communicate

to others the life I myself was able to draw from the Scriptures. So I always think that Drummond saved me in those embryonic years from a wholly lifeless ministry.

But perhaps I exaggerate. One is prone to be unjust to one's earlier self and it may be so in my case. There was one point, however, at which the mind of Henry Drummond had touched my own with an influence so vivid and gracious that, as I stood there at his recent grave among those weather-worn tombstones, I recalled it with indisputable clearness.

After two years of preaching I entered college a sub-freshman. I brought with me a fair intellectual stock, consisting mainly of a thorough knowledge of the Disciples' theology and a finished system of the universe! During my entire college course I preached on Sundays in a town not far away. It was the custom of the churches of that county to hold a "basket meeting" at the county seat sometime in the early fall, and in my sophomore year I was asked to preach the Sunday evening sermon on this annual occasion.

I carefully prepared a sermon on the "Dignity of Man," taking my text from the first chapter of Genesis. It must have occupied a good hour in its delivery, and more than half of the time I spent on a single one of the divisions of the sermon, viz., the dignity of man's *origin*. I was delivering a diatribe against the evolutionary theory of man's origin and defending, as I conceived it, the notion of the divine origin. The Scriptures, of course, I arrayed against Darwin, and sought to show that evolution robbed man of his essential dignity.

Next day, on returning to the college, I met my best friend on the campus, a man who is today one of the most efficient pastors and preachers among the Disciples, and, as our Monday custom was, we exchanged our preaching experiences of the day before. After I had set forth the outline of my sermon and had dwelt at some length on the section which had mainly occupied me in the evening's presentation he asked, rather irrelevantly, I thought,

"By the way, Morrison, have you ever read much on evolution?"

"O yes," I replied, confidently.

"What have you read?"

"Well, I've read—" but for the life of me I could not think of any significant book or treatise on the subject I had ever read. He interrupted my reflection.

"Have you ever read *Origin of Species* or *Descent of Man?*"

"No," I admitted, "I have not." And yet I had said quite a bit about these books in my sermon, all in condemnation, of course.

"Have you read Fiske on the *Dignity of Man?*"

"N-no," I replied, and I felt that a book of that title would have aided me greatly in the preparation of a sermon on the same theme. My friend was not ungentle with me. Yet, in a tactful way, he got me to confess that I had never read anything authoritative on evolution, but had simply formed my judgment on the basis of religious newspapers I had read and sermons I had heard and a certain book on "Christian evidences" we had used together as a text book.

"Now, look here," he said finally, "you ought not preach that kind of a sermon without reading at least one book on the other side. It isn't candid, not to say honest."

"But the case against evolution is closed," I said, "and I do not wish to waste my time in reading atheistic books."

"You have no right to pronounce them atheistic until you have given them a fair reading," was his reply. He overcame my doggedness and won my consent to read the book he would select for me. Next day he brought me Professor Drummond's *The Ascent of Man.* It had only recently been printed and was at the moment being widely discussed by preachers and the newspapers.

I took the book home and devoured it in three days. I neglected my lessons during that time. The book opened a new world to me. It presented to me the possibility of believing in the scientific doctrine of evolution and in God, too —a possibility I had not entertained before. It brought me many problems. It started my mind on a course of thought which was accompanied by much pain for a year or more, but which ended in a new faith, deeper and firmer, as it was

richer, for having found God in his work and world without
losing him from his word.

The anguish of that year I can never tell. I used to lie awake
at night wondering if I should become an "infidel," or if not
an "infidel" a Unitarian. I read everything I could get my
hands on bearing upon the modern view of the world. I was
much impressed with Benjamin Kidd's *Social Evolution*, a
"critical" review of which I wrote for a club to which I belonged. I came upon the withered manuscript of it before
leaving home for Edinburgh and it revived the struggle of
that period of my college life. But there were two things that
saved me to my evangelical faith.

One was my Sunday appointment to preach. I didn't want
to preach. My mind was in chaos. I used to look with envy
at the students who had enough money to go to school without working. I had none. It was preach or give up college. I
am glad now I had to preach. I tried to be honest, but I kept
my doubts in the background. Nobody knew I was struggling.
Fortunately, there was a newly founded Unitarian church in
the town. Involuntarily I found myself taking a critical view
of the doctrines of this church. I preached much against them.
And when they would charge us with standing for the more
crass doctrines of orthodoxy, I found my chance to deny that
these crass views were essential to Christianity. So a constructive process was going on in my mind. With the Unitarians as a foil I was rebuilding my own faith and, perhaps,
liberating my church from some of its traditions. I feel quite
sure that if the Unitarians hadn't been there my ministry
would have been destructive and whining. I would have
talked more about my doubts than my faith.

I have often thanked God for that one Unitarian church, at
least!

The other saving influence in my experience was Drummond
himself. He had introduced me to the new world, and he
made my faith feel at home there. I came back to his books
again and again. The two principles in his *The Ascent of Man*
that were full of spiritual suggestion to me were the struggle
for the life of others which he found in nature as well as the

struggle for life, and the idea of *in*volution with which he met the charge that evolution was atheistic. There is nothing evolved that is not first *in*volved, he said. And if all this world of beauty and love and self-sacrifice and moral ideals has been evolved it was first of all folded into the cosmic order by some rational and spiritual being. If I had the book by me now I should like to set down in this, my travel journal, a great paragraph or two which sent a shaft of light into my unaccustomed mind.

But quite as much as what he said in his books, Drummond's own personal faith was my stay and support when arguments failed. It is strange how much our faith is based upon somebody else's faith. Henry Drummond always seemed to me a holy man. He was my ideal Christian before I knew him as a "heretic." I had known his life-story, his wonderful evangelistic power, his great love for the sinful, his illimitable faith in men's possibilities of recovery with the help of Christ. And when my faith wavered before some argument, my heart would say, "But there's Drummond; he believes!" and somehow I could not get my consent to make denial.

It seems a long time since then. Much water has flowed under the bridges since *The Ascent of Man* was published. I have come to think of evolution not so much in terms of biology as of logic, now. This scientific conception of the world dominates all modern thinking. Children in the lower grades are being trained to think in the terms of development, of evolution, and so are the youth in the university. Happily those scholars who stand in a relation to troubled young men similar to that in which Drummond stood to me are a great host. I suppose that Drummond will not be written down in the impartial history of thought as a philosopher of the first rank. But in the history of *my* thought he is first, for he did in me what Copernicus did in the solar system and Kant in psychology—he turned the world inside out, which is to say he turned it right side out and right side in.

AN EARLY THEOLOGICAL EMPHASIS: *For freer minds, rooted in but not enslaved by the past.*

May 26, 1910

Honoring the Past

ROBERT E. SPEER

It is no enmity to our past to believe that it did not exhaust God. I do not see any disloyalty to the past in believing that God means the future to be better than it. Unless the past has made ready for a better future, the past was a bad past. Only those things are good that make ready for better things to come after them, and those men are disloyal to the past, not who believe that it made preparation for greater things, but who believe that all the great things are in a golden age gone by. The worst disloyalty to the past is to mistake it for the future. Very great and glorious that past has been, but that past will have failed to teach its lesson for us, that past will have failed to fulfill its mission in the will of God, if it binds men forever in the chains of its institutional forms, if it has not made them ready for larger and completer things, and led them on to such a unity as Christ himself, we must believe, longed for while he was here and waits for now where he is gone.

September 28, 1911

The Changing World

AN EDITORIAL

It is commonly affirmed that theological convictions yield more slowly than any other sort to the pressure of advancing experience. This is partly true, because they represent the most valuable possessions of life. Yet in a changing world even these are modified, much more effectively than their partisans would concede. And it is because the alert and questioning spirit of the age is satisfied only when reality is attained. Contentment with bodies, shapes, appearances is impossible.

The religious discussions of the last century are meaningless today. Who of the younger generation in Presbyterian or Methodist churches could state intelligently the historic issues between Calvinism and Arminianism? In simple truth they no longer have significance.

Which of the younger men even in the ministry of the Disciples and Baptists could define with accuracy the direction and carrying power of the arguments, once so freely hurled, concerning the relation of baptism to the remission of sins, the work of the Spirit of God in conversion, the content and priority of faith and repentance, or the function of the Word in the creation of the new life? Few would even know on which side of the dividing line they ought to stand.

The discussions regarding miracle and the supernatural have ceased to interest our generation, confronted as it is with deeper-going questions; former theories of inspiration and infallibility as applied to the Bible seem remote from the values which our age finds in the sacred records; the classical speculations regarding the person of our Lord have the appearance of medieval subtleties in the presence of the big, stressful questions with which the modern man is confronted; the millenarian dreams of the theologies of despair seem futile and childish in the presence of the larger faith which our day is finding; and church rites, rituals, ordinances and orders are given a truer value as incidentals, not essentials of the religious life.

What is the duty of the church in a changing world? Manifestly to accept the law of change as fundamental and inevitable; to adapt itself to the changes with high sensitiveness to the fact that therein lies its only opportunity to fashion the moving mass into some resemblance to the ideal world of its hopes; and above all, to select for its supreme and persistent emphasis the things that abide.

The cardinal mistake of the historic church is its perpetual and petty concern with matters of ephemeral value. It would almost seem as if the great facts of religion were consciously permitted to take a secondary place, lest they should divert attention from cherished holding of doctrine, liturgy or organization. But the great things remain, and the little things fade out.

And the great things are evermore God and character and service. God, the Father-life of the world, the embodiment of being, the Soul of the universe, the Creator and Lover of mankind, revealed and brought near to humanity in Jesus; character, the only ultimate value, the consummation of life, the superb and convincing factor in the life of Jesus, who thus becomes the divine exemplar of the race; and service, the application of being and character to the realization of the divine program for the world. In a changing world these supreme values must be the joy and the reward of the sons of God.

THE STIRRING EVENTS in the career of one of the most eminent and often controversial of the preachers of the half-century were sympathetically chronicled in news story and special comment on many a Century page. In this early passage, as in many others, he spoke for himself.

November 6, 1919

The Sense of God's Reality

HARRY EMERSON FOSDICK

Our modern world is headed straight for some gigantic disappointments. Never were such splendid plans afoot in human history before; never were there so many men and women of high hope and far-seeing expectancy at work on schemes for human betterment so vast in scope and so promising in outlook. Statesmen dare to plan for organized international cooperation; workingmen dare to expect within this generation the launching of industrial democracy; churchmen plot campaigns that marshal millions into a united force.

Nothing is more clear, however, in the light of history, than this: new political, economic and ecclesiastical machinery does not alone solve problems; it creates problems, and, above all, it puts a strain on moral foundations, on spiritual resources, that must successfully be met or the best-laid plans come down in ruin. You cannot build a new forty-story business block on the old three-story foundations. With every expansion of the structure, with every elevation in the plans, the underlying bases become not less but more important. It takes far more brotherly spirit to run a League of Nations than to run a village; it takes far more personal unselfishness and reliability to make industrial democracy a success than it does to conduct the present order; and if the extensive Christian plans now afoot are to achieve their aims, the Christian faith in God must grow accordingly.

Amid all the creak and clatter of our far-flung Christian plans, therefore—the commissions, committees, campaigns, surveys, federations and budgets—all thoughtful Christians who are interested to avoid the disillusionment which the failure of so much splendid effort would inevitably cause will bear down hard upon the central matter: *the achievement of a deeper sense of God's reality*. That is the foundation of all our building. If that weakens, the excellence of the superstructure does not matter. That is the dynamic. If that fails, the skillful workmanship of the engine is effort thrown away.

Now, the sense of God's reality is a different experience from belief that God exists. All men believe that natural beauty exists, but some men feel it vividly, rejoice in it heartily, while others are never moved by it at all. From the chords of one man's heart every sound and sight and scent on an autumn day will draw music like a symphony. He knows what Keats meant when he sang:

> Oh, what a wild and harmonious tune
> My spirit struck from all the beautiful!

But here is another man who does not vividly perceive in nature any beauty whatsoever. He wishes that he did. He reads Wordsworth to see if he can find the secret, but it continually eludes him. He reads radiant descriptions of sunsets in the poets where the sun rides the western sea like a "golden galleon" or

> Throws his weary arms far up the sky,
> And with vermillion-tinted fingers
> Toys with the long tresses of the Evening Star.

Then *he* goes out to see a sunset, and he does not see anything like that at all.

That is the contrasting experience of men with reference to God, which is, of all others, most baffling. Atheism is not our greatest danger, but a shadowy sense of God's reality. We do not disbelieve that God exists, but we often lack a penetrating and convincing consciousness that we are dealing with him and he with us. This is the inner problem of prayer. And it

cannot be amiss for any man or woman, concerned with the
movements of the churches, to consider with what insights
he can surround and penetrate his praying, so that in it all
a vital consciousness of the divine presence shall make glory
at the center.

The troubles of our generation which so urgently demand
of us a fresh consciousness of God can help us to the very
experience for which they cry. For God is like water—the
intense reality of it is never appreciated by one who has not
known thirst. So God's unreality to us in part is due to our
easy-going way of taking him for granted, with little sense of
dire and dreadful need. Before the war, how many of us, conventionally religious, were dealing with God so! Then the war
broke out, and who could light-heartedly take God for granted
any more! We needed him too vitally to take him for
granted. This world was a wilder place than we had used to
think. Its boisterous currents showed bewildering power when
they had overflowed their banks, and all our little human pre-
ventions were washed away like piles of sand that children
raise against the onset of the tides.

Even now dismal possibilities lie ahead—upheaval, anarchy,
violence; it may be the League of Nations spoiled by opposition, apathy or treachery, and the whole world going on with
this military business, using all inventive genius for destructive
ends and making a worse hell of it all than the Stone Age a
thousand times over. Or, on the other side, what glorious possibilities! What hopes worth praying, toiling, fighting for! If
only this world were meant to enshrine a better order; if only
creation were moral to the core; if only—God! For if creation
is not basally moral, no God at all, and we with unaided
human fingers are trying to make an ethical oasis in a spiritual
desert, where no oasis was ever meant to be, then we are beaten
at the start. Soon or later the desert will heave its burning
sands against us and hurl its blistering winds across us, and
all that we have dreamed and done will come to naught.

Tremendously, we need God! For tasks inward and outward, personal and international, against sins deep-seated, in-
veterate and malign, we need God. Let the need, like thirst,

make its own satisfaction real! Let the beatitude on those athirst and hungry be fulfilled! For until a man comes to God in such a mood there is no possibility of reality in prayer.

The great social needs and the projected social crusades of our days, which so depend on faith in God, may well themselves create the atmosphere in which we find God. It is a grievous misinterpretation to suppose that God's reality dawned on men, like the Old Testament prophets, in mystical aloofness from the social needs and social movements of their time.

Moses came face to face with the Eternal in the Wilderness? To be sure, but the journey that so ended in a lonesome place before the face of God did not start in solitude at all. It began in Egypt amid a suffering people. He heard whips whistling over the backs of the Hebrews until he winced. He saw women staggering under the loads of bricks to build Pharaoh's treasure cities, until he could tolerate the infamy no longer. One day his scorching indignation burst all bonds. A brute of an Egyptian laying the knout upon a Hebrew! Furiously the son of Pharaoh's daughter ripped his dignities and titles off. Only one thing mattered—just *one* thing: Israel must be free! There, in a high hour of social passion and sacrifice, began the road that, leading out from fury to wisdom, brought him at last to God.

No pathway into the consciousness of God's reality has been trodden by nobler men than this road of social devotion and sacrifice. God's greatest souls have often started like Elijah, determined that at whatever cost he would denounce and defeat the tyranny of Ahab, and they have ended like Elijah, on the mountainside, listening to the still small voice of God. They have started like Dante, with a passion to save Italy from chaos, and they have ended like Dante, standing with Beatrice before the Great White Throne. They have started like Lincoln, vowing that if ever he had a chance to hit slavery, he would hit it hard, and they have ended like Lincoln, saying, "Many times I have been driven to my knees by the overwhelming conviction that I had nowhere else to go."

Such an open road to the vivid sense of God's reality is

waiting for every eager and prophetic heart today. The needs of men, the sins that must be blasted with concerted indignation, the causes that invite our ardent championship—these are not alien from the problem of prayer. They are a blazed trail into the secrets of prayer. The great prophets of God have moved along this path into a vivid sense of God's reality. Sacrifice for social weal unveiled the face of the Eternal.

The sense of God's reality is a vital experience, and like every other vital experience we don't so much learn it, or achieve it, or clamber up to it; we catch it by contagion. Some things never can be taught, no matter with what skilled witchery of words the case is stated and the lessons analyzed. Courage, for example! There doubtless is a theory of courage, but no careful learning of it would make anyone courageous. Indeed, in any situation, like the front line trenches at the zero hour, when courage is an absolute necessity and every man with all his heart is ardently desiring all of it that he can get, the one intolerable thing would be to talk about it.

But an *example* of it—how welcome and contagious! Bravery is fire; it kindles a kindred conflagration in every heart that has tinder in it. We not only learn what courage is by its incarnations, but we are set ablaze by it ourselves, and all the courage that we ever had we neither generated nor achieved; we caught it.

When men in trouble seek for fortitude, they will not find it in an exhortation. But some Bunyan, writing *Pilgrim's Progress* in a prison where it was so damp that, as he cried, "The moss did verily grow upon mine eyebrows"; some Kernahan, born without arms and legs, but by sheer grit fighting his way up until he sat in the House of Commons; some Henry M. Stanley, born in a workhouse and buried in Westminster Abbey; some Dante, his Beatrice dead, he himself an exile from the city of his love, distilling all his agony into a song that became the "voice of ten silent centuries"; or some more obscure and humble life close at hand where handicaps have been mastered, griefs have been built into character, disappointments have been turned into trellises, not left a bare, unsightly thing—such incarnations of fortitude and faith have infectious power. We win fortitude by falling in love with it. We are not taught it. We catch it.

Let a man in his thinking use such reasonable ways of conceiving God that he may help and not hinder his growing sense of God's reality. There was a time when God's immediate presence in our lives was not readily pictured. When men argued about God they said that the world was like a watch. It presupposed somebody who made it. That is, God was a mechanician; he had made this watch of a world and had gone off and left it to run by its own mainspring. God was a carpenter. He had built this house of a world and had left it to stand by its own laws. God was an engineer. He had thrown open the throttle of this world, had leaped the cab, and now the locomotive of itself goes thundering down the rails. Where is God? Back there somewhere!

We have no right to hold such a caricature of God. God is no man in the moon. God is in this world as we are in our bodies. Where are you? Is your hand you? Your eye? Is any part of your body you? We cannot see without our eyes, but we are not our eyes. We cannot see without the optic nerve, but we are not the optic nerve. We cannot see without the temporal lobe of the brain, but we are not the lobe of the brain. Where are we? All through our bodies we seem to be; yet nowhere in our bodies can we locate ourselves.

"God is a spirit," we read, and the mystery of it seems very great. But man is a spirit. Manifestly man is here; the evidence of his presence is on every side; nothing are we more certain of than that man is here—yet we cannot find man anywhere. Bring the scalpel and dissect; where is he? Bring the microscope and look; where is he? As truly about man as about God, could one cry, "Oh, that I knew where I might find him!"

As we are in our bodies, but not of them, so is God in his world. And the greatest event in man's life is the vital apprehension of that not as theory but as experience. A man perceives at last that he is like an aeolian harp. Fit the harp's frame to the window ever so carefully, yet it is not at all fitted—not until the invisible winds make music on its strings.

So man fits his body to the framework of this physical world, fits nerves to comfortable circumstances and mind to information, but the whole man is not so adjusted. Conscience, love, ideals, thoughts that "break through language and escape," faiths and hopes that make us men indeed—not till the invisible so makes music in us are we completely fitted to this world.

And the longer a man lives the more it becomes clear that all other adjustments are for the sake of this highest adjustment. This *is* a spiritual world, then, at its center. God *is* here, playing upon our lives. After that vision, clearly seen, one does not go out to seek God again. Shall man sally forth to hasten the sunrise? What has he to do with that? Let him go home and cleanse the windows. The sun is rising. It will find him out even in his little home and make him radiant if the way is clear. Shall a man go out to make the tides come in? What power has he? Let him rather take the sands away from the harbor's mouth. The tides are rising. They will come in if there is a way.

This, indeed, is the conclusion of the whole matter. *God is seeking us.* We do not need to search for him. He is the shepherd; we are the sheep. We need to let him find us.

THE TRANSLATOR *of the Swiss theologian's early works in a full-dress introduction to an American public just becoming aware of a new giant on the theological scene.*

February 16, 1928

God Lets Loose Karl Barth

DOUGLAS HORTON

"BEWARE," warns Emerson, "when the great God lets loose a thinker in this planet. Then all things are at risk. It is as when a conflagration has broken out in a great city and no man knows what is safe or where it will end." Nothing less than conflagration appears to have broken out in the religious thought of Europe. Many incendiaries may be pointed to, but there is one whose torch seems to have burned more brightly and to have been applied more effectively than that of any of the others.

Five years ago one began to hear, at the tables of the student clubs and restaurants of Germany, the name of Karl Barth. A young theologian recently called from Switzerland had made an amazingly impressive debut at the University of Göttingen. His chair—that of Reformed or Calvinistic theology—was subsidized in part by American Presbyterians, and was not in itself sufficiently exalted to catch the eye of Lutheran Germany. This circumstance made only the more significant the number of students who soon crowded his lecture hall, and the number of students, professors and townspeople who filled and overflowed any church where he had been advertised to preach.

He was remembered by many as having been himself a student in Tübingen and Berlin little more than twelve years before. Even then he had been marked as a man of unusual, if not wholly conventional, vitality. Born in Basel, in 1886, he had returned at the end of his university career to be the minister of the church in the little town of Protestant Aargau, north of Lucerne; and there, during the war period, he had preached on Sunday mornings before the good peasant folk, to the antiphonal booming of guns in near-by Alsace. The sombre thought of guns and of the stricken and perplexed Europe, governed then by guns, gave him long hours in his study. He studied, dreamed and wrote, until, almost simultaneously with the armistice, was announced the publication of his commentary on the Epistle of St. Paul to the Romans. It was this which elicited his call to Germany.

Of all the commentaries which have appeared since the birth of bibilical criticism, this is the weirdest. It is in reality 500 pages of pithy sermons upon the verses of the epistle taken in order. Of learned exegesis it is innocent, though not contemptuous. Of mighty feuilletons of etymology and textual apparatus there is no trace. It is a veritable Koran for paradox and want of sequence. But by the scholarly and lay world alike it was found fascinating. For four years, until his departure for his present eminent position at Münster, Professor Barth remained at Göttingen, and during that time he saw his theology, set forth in further books and in lectures and addresses, sweep through the universities of Germany, and today there seem to be hardly more than two classes of religious thinkers in the country, Barthians and anti-Barthians.

It is little wonder that Barth has been called by Count Keyserling the man who saved Protestantism in Germany. In the year that he took his seat on the faculty at Göttingen, no less than 246,302 nominal Lutherans, under the new laws of the support of the churches by taxation, professed atheism. Whether or not the work of Barth and his friends Gogarten, Thurneysen and others directly affected the drift of popular opinion in the republic, it is nonetheless true that the turn of the tide back toward the churches was almost synchronous with the beginning of the Barthian movement.

As for the world of thought, the very furor the young theologian has aroused in academic Protestant circles proclaims him a portent of the first magnitude. Harnack, the Zeus of the historical critics, has broken the seclusion his years would seem rightly to permit him to indite a series of essays against the new movement. Professor Troeltsch—whose too-early death is lamented on every hand—and Professor Jülicher, two other Olympians of the last great generation, have treated Barth with seriousness and apprehension. For every critical Oliver, the Barthian theology has an admiring Roland. Young Germany hears the new gospel gladly. And Professor Lange, whose painstaking researches in Reformation and post-Reformation history make his utterance authoritative, does not hesitate to call Barth "the greatest man since Schleiermacher." Among Roman Catholic writers are found almost as many eager friends of the new thought as among Lutherans and Calvinists. In general they seem to accept it as far more cousinly to their own doctrines than anything else Protestantism has produced since the days of the Reformation.

But the crowning tribute to the man Barth is the almost universal acknowledgment of religious debt which even his critics have made to him. The acrimonious words which are likely to flash from any debate, and which have not been wholly absent from this, are smothered beneath the expressions of generous gratitude with which opponent after opponent prefaces his discussion.

One of the secrets of the swift access the new theology has found into the life of the Continent is that it takes its beginning from the scene in the local church rather than in the university library. Barth, like Schleiermacher, and unlike many of the book-theologians of the last decades, has enjoyed the inestimable advantage of a pastoral contact with real people. His approach to the problem of life and the beginnings of his "theology of crisis" were made when as a minister he first realized the utter impossibility of communicating to his hearers the faith by which he himself was animated.

According to Barth, man is safe upon the sea that lies between God and the world as we know it because the sea is God's and he made it, but he persistently tries for the Godward shore, and is usually either expecting to reach it or deluding himself that he has already done so. Security is his aim and illusion—economic security, religious security, moral security, intellectual security. But there is no way from man to God.

For man to attempt to know God and to solve the problem of life is to set sail upon this infinite sea. His best hope will be to beat back and forth into the wind, but what can it profit him? Philosophy is only an endless oscillation, a dialectic never finished.

Professor Barth's ethics are such as to delight the realist without disturbing the idealist, the search for the morally right being a form of hopelessness, but a thoroughly sanguine form. Its object is always attainable but never attained. Here Professor Barth is the embodiment of the continental reaction to associating Christianity with a particular social movement, whether it be "kultur," pacifism, socialism or anything else. His part of Switzerland had been heavily under the influence of Ragaz of Zurich, the blazing prophet of social Christianity who, like his friend Walter Rauschenbusch, saw in the labor movement the greatest single contemporary salient of the advancing kingdom of God. Barth gathers the questionings of his friends into one gigantic interrogation point, and flings down to ethical theory the demand that it base itself not upon the conscious will of man but on the uncertainly, though actually, felt will of God. The truest rallying cry that can be used by any leader, he would say, is that suggested by Carlyle for Margaret Fuller, "I don't know where I am going; follow me!"

There is a trend in morality which corresponds to the dogmatic movement in thought. We become superior, and if we are honest with ourselves we will recognize our superiority—but the shorter name for conscious superiority is pride.

Pride being the hatefullest of the virtues, the human spirit now turns away from this certain-sure morality, though it has nothing else in particular to turn to. It begins to ride loose to all current ethical forms. It loses squeamishness about the decencies. It extols freedom as an end in itself. It becomes emancipated. It bobs its conscience. It blows ideals as smoke rings. It hates Eighteenth Amendments because they are constitutional. It will maintain its emotional integrity. It will follow its own desire. But no mood is more perfectly unsatisfactory to the morally in earnest. They do not wish to follow their own desire; they wish to follow God's.

There is nothing left but to fall back on paradox—to seek God's will zealously with the conclusion foregone that God's will cannot be found—to join the contemporary crusades for righteousness with the conviction that they will be one day proved, like the great Crusades, to have been ill advised and wrong! This is not discovering God's will, but it is, after all, acknowledging it.

Professor Barth's animadversions upon worship are the very dissidence of dissent. To him the ordinary service of the church is the maddest of all man's efforts to reach God. One can expect from it only an unedifying oscillation between fictitious spiritual tranquility and honest skepticism.

Shall one then enjoy God in worship, when the naked essence of such worship is a selfish self-hypnosis?—or shall one, in want of any certainty, eschew the life of prayer entirely? The paradox, once more, is our refuge: let a man realize at once his infinite need for finding God, and the infinite futility of his search, and in the clash of those two infinities within his soul, the God of the infinities will be adumbrated—but only adumbrated.

Many of his critics have harassed the young professor of Münster for what they name his desperate pessimism. "There is no way from man to God." They forget his other theme: "There is a way from God to man." It is in this thought that his paradoxes are ultimately resolved; since any attempt to use God, even for purposes of describing him to others, throws us into dilemma, we must allow him to use us.

"There is a way to come into relation with the righteousness of God. This way we enter not by speech, nor reflection, nor reason, but by being still." God, in a word, takes the initiative and reveals himself. Allow him then to do so, preaches Barth. It is only when you are agonizedly aware of the failure of your own effort that God begins to move upon you.

Karl Barth, in a word, is a reincarnation of John Calvin. His message, *in nuce*, is the Sinaitic sovereignty of God. Only when you ultimately confess the poverty of your own thought, only when you acknowledge yourself a bewildered sinner in his sight, only when you know yourself, even at the gate of death, to be the shadow of a breath, will the vast Transcendence make you miraculously aware of himself in you. He will come to you as strange content of reality, rather than form, for form is only your manner of adopting him. Give him form, and his presence shrinks back into a hint. Add nothing to him, and he will remain to you the dreadful Perfect.

To the German people, stunned by the war and the consequences of defeat, their former optimism shattered and spent, shuddering to contemplate the debt-darkened years of the future, Barth in the phase of his dreadful insight into the futility of all search for security must seem a veritable Jeremiah, and his teaching an evilly perfect rationalization of their indigence and perplexity. But in the phase of his harking back to the perfect sovereignty of the ruler of this world and all worlds, his words must seem an embodiment of their one hope.

Professor Barth has recently been introduced personally to a paradox which he is not the first man in history to have discovered: he now knows that the people stone their prophets. On the occasion of his being called to succeed the venerable Doctor Lüdemann in the chair of systematic theology in Bern, such a storm of protest arose from an articulate group of Bernese churchmen as would have dismayed the doughtiest. There is "culture-Protestantism" elsewhere than in America. Its devotees in Switzerland do not relish this theologian's suggestion that the modern worship of the state or even of the family, instead of God, has the same effect as the worship of the "beast of the bottomless pit" or of some "voracious idol." They join with others in their own country and in Germany in condemning his thought as "desperado-theology." To Barth, being such a one as saith among the trumpets, Ha Ha! the very protest must have made the call more tempting; but he declined.

As an immense counterblast in his behalf, the voice of the friends of the new viewpoint was lifted up throughout the German-speaking world. There is a vast company of folk in stations high and low who find his paradoxes singularly satisfying and alive. They feel in them a hint of "Reality"—of a Reality which we cannot reach but which can reach us. Among this company many of our English poets and thinkers would, I am persuaded, have numbered themselves. This is hardly strange in view of the long-standing influence of Calvin among us.

. . . and thirty years later:
December 31, 1958

A Letter from Karl Barth

Dear Editor: Your friendly letter of July 23—for which I thank you heartily—caused me real embarrassment. I opened it expecting that it would be an invitation to take part in a third series, to be published in 1959, on the theme "How My Mind Has Changed"; and to this I would (perhaps!) have contributed with pleasure, as I did to the 1939 and 1949 series. But it appears that you want something altogether different for 1959; namely, a preview of the future—a statement of what tasks and problems I would set myself if, in the light of my past experience, I were now beginning my work as theological teacher and writer. I gather from your letter that you have sent the same invitation to other well-known theologians of my generation, and that you intend to publish our assembled remarks on this theme in book form, for the benefit of today's younger theologians.

What will these contemporaries of mine have to say to this invitation and this plan? I cannot speak for them. But I must say that for my own part this project of yours leaves me nonplused, and so, however gladly I would serve you, I cannot agree to contribute to it.

To the best of my memory, at no stage in my theological career did I ever plan more than the immediate next steps. And these next steps grew inevitably out of the steps I had already taken, and out of my impressions of the needs and possibilities latent in every new day and every new situation. As I see it now, my career has been a "succession of present moments." I found myself—the man I had become up to that time, equipped with whatever knowledge I fancied I had acquired—always set suddenly before some biblical or historical or academic complex, some theme thrust upon me from outside, some immediate problem (for example a political one); in short, some new thing that I did not look for but that claimed me. Then I tried to stand up to this new thing as best I could. That was difficult enough, and so I never could think about tomorrow or the day after tomorrow. I have hardly ever had or carried out anything in the nature of a program. Rather my thinking and writing and speaking issued from my encounters with people, events and conditions that flowed toward me with their questions and riddles. I discovered them—at first, the liberalism and socialism of the beginning of the century; or later, the text of the letter to the Romans; or still later, the theological tradition of the ancient and the Reformed church; or the German situation after 1933 or the Swiss situation after 1939. I discovered them; which is to say, these people, events, conditions burst upon me; they spoke to me, engaged my interest or compelled me to say something about them. I never planned to be, do or say this or that; I was, did or said this or that as the time for it came.

That is the way it has been with me—for twenty-five years now, and especially in working out the *Church Dogmatics*: from one semester to another, from one week to another. So with my other books, lectures, sermons. They are, as it were, trees of all kinds, big and little, that sprang up, grew and spread before me. Their existence did not depend on me; rather I had to watch over their development with all my attention. Or I might say that I feel like a man in a boat that I must row and steer diligently; but it swims in a stream I do not control. It glides along between ever new and often totally strange shores, carrying me toward the goals set for me, goals that I see and choose only when I approach them.

Whether God in the inscrutable wisdom of his providence destined and created me to be so unsystematic a theologian, or whether in my human confusion I have made myself such, who shall say? But one thing is sure: if you, dear sir, are of the opinion that (as you say in your letter) I have helped to bring about today's theological situation and continue to shape it, then you must reckon with the fact that this is the manner in which I have lived as a theologian up to this day, this the manner in which I have made my contribution to contemporary theology. I prayed for my daily bread, received it and ate it, and let the next day take care of itself. I do not think that at this time of life I shall change my ways. And I do not think that anyone can expect of me more than I can accomplish in my own way during the years yet left me.

And now you will surely understand and not take it amiss that I cannot play along in the "symphony of the future" you plan—not with the first or second violins, nor with the flutes or the double basses, nor as the able man who presides over the great kettle drum. Why not? Certainly not because the future of theology in general (and so also of my own theology) does not interest me; otherwise I would not continue working, as I would like to do so long as time and strength are granted me. But because now as in the past the present makes such claims on me that I can indulge in picturing the future only in passing dreams if at all—and because as concerns the future itself (if I did not prefer to remain silent) I should have something serious to say only when that future had become the present.

Respectfully and expectantly I look forward to what the other members of the company of elders you have called on will spread out before us in the way of prognoses, programs and prospectuses. And I should rejoice if their comments proved of benefit to the young people who are coming into the field today. But I would have to be a different person, with a different way of life, if I were to produce even thirty—not to speak of 3,000!—sensible and useful words in this matter. All that I can really contribute to your enterprise is three English words—unoriginal and banal but responsibly uttered: Wait and see!

With kindest regards and greetings,

Karl Barth

THE IMPACT on "liberal" faith of widening change in theo-logical orientation was subjected to frequent survey and synthe-sis in the Century's pages—as in this editorial of the late thirties.

October 26, 1938

Arrested Liberalism
AN EDITORIAL

All writers on religion today are having trouble with the term "liberalism." A new orientation of Christian theology is taking place, and those who formerly were proud to be called liberals are the leaders in it. They are conscious that their minds are turning away from many of the major conclusions which the liberals of the late nineteenth and the early twentieth centuries set up as the "assured results" of liberal thought. Certain doctrines and facts which were either denied or held as irrelevant are now seen as both true and important. Other problems wholly invisible then are now seen as decisive for Christian faith. Under the spell of this new awareness, these erstwhile liberals are seized with a sense of disillusionment in respect to their former intellectual affiliation and look back upon it with regret and even with self-reproach because of their blindness.

Most of these writers have adopted a tone of scorn toward liberalism. Liberalism was unrealistic, they say; it was superficial and shallow; it rested upon optimistic presuppositions which a deeper insight into reality now shows to have been naive. These presuppositions included a certain optimistic belief in the inherent goodness of man, accompanied by a distinct relaxing of the conception of sin and of man's moral progress in history as an inevitable process eventuating in a utopian kingdom of God on earth, thus continuing and consummating the upward climb of biological evolution which science had disclosed; a monistic metaphysic in which man and God were so closely interfused that one of two consequences followed: either God guaranteed man's spiritual destiny (quietism), or man must assume full responsibility for his own destiny (humanism); a moralistic conception of the person of Jesus which held him to be a great teacher and exemplar in the moral life of man, but relegated the concept of his saviorhood to such categories as allegory or myth or drama.

These presuppositions, which underlay the most influential thinking of the period now closing, are now being subjected to the most radical and drastic criticism by Christian thinkers. And it is the fashion for this criticism to center its attack upon liberalism itself as the source and cause of so great a departure from the historic Christian faith. Over against liberalism these critics place what they call "realism," with the implication that liberalism is not, has not been, and cannot be realistic. We must abandon liberalism, it is now the fashion to say, in order to deal realistically with the facts of human nature and man's relation to God which have been, historically, the substantive elements of the Christian revelation.

More is involved here than a verbal problem. It was, perhaps, natural enough for the initial critics of "liberal theology" to vent their sense of disillusionment not merely upon the "theology" but upon the "liberalism" under whose spirit it had taken form. Moreover it seemed, for the moment at least, good strategy to stigmatize the whole movement of thought which had come to be labeled liberal. Liberal scholarship had become complacent with respect to its attainments. It needed to be shocked. Its particular views had become so fully identified with liberalism that the quickest way to get attention riveted upon their superficiality was, perhaps, to condemn liberalism itself as superficial. But this stratagem may prove, in the long run, to have been too costly.

Certainly it will prove to be too costly if it allows Christian people to fall back into the position from which liberalism rescued them. It is a great mistake to define liberalism in terms of any particular doctrine or set of doctrines which thinkers working in its spirit may at a given time hold. The spirit of liberal thought is one of the most precious gifts to modern man which have come out of the intellectual struggle of past centuries. To hold it in disdain, to stigmatize it as incompatible with true Christianity, to set it over against realism, to proclaim its bankruptcy, is hardly less than a wanton act. The cure of the errors of liberalism will be found, not in something other than liberalism, but in a fresh attack by liberalism itself upon its own findings in the light of new evidence and insight.

The truth of the matter is that if any specific doctrines are relevant to a definition of liberalism at a given time, such doctrines are those against which liberalism is at that time in revolt, rather than the doctrines which it positively espouses. Certainly this was the case in the past generation. The free spirit of liberalism having become pretty well established in other spheres—notably in science, history and politics—finally entered the religious scene. It began its operations by questioning the truth of certain conceptions held by Christian people—particularly the literal inerrancy of the Bible, the obscurantist dogma concerning the origin of the Christian revelation, and a cosmological view of the origin of the universe and of man. The issue involved here was so sharp that, among the orthodox, the favorite characterization of liberalism was that of "destructive criticism."

In that period, liberalism could with some justice be defined negatively in terms of the doctrines which it was actually engaged in undermining, because these doctrines were held in a spirit which was the opposite of liberalism. But it could not justly be defined in terms of the doctrines which were set up in place of them. For upon the ruins of the old foundations all kinds of doctrines were set up—stretching all the way from mysticism to atheism. Certainly not all of these could be identified as liberalism, for they represent incompatibilities and contradictions.

It is therefore erroneous and unjust to identify liberalism with the set of doctrines enumerated in a preceding paragraph, and to condemn liberalism under the guise of attacking these particular doctrines. Why are these doctrines under attack? Why are they widely felt to be an inadequate expression of the Christian faith? Is it because their critics have decided to return to and reoccupy the fort from which the liberal spirit of free inquiry drove them out a generation ago? This certainly is not the reason. There is in evidence no such reactionary movement on the part of the critics of the late nineteenth- and early twentieth-century theology. Its critics do not attack it in the name of a literal Bible, or the Genesis cosmology, or an obscurantist dogma of the origin of the Christian revelation.

Even Karl Barth (to take as an example the most conspicuous "conservative" figure in the new movement) is hospitable to the most advanced form of higher criticism. He has no quarrel with the doctrine of evolution or any other position of science, as such. And while his critics charge him with obscurantist dogmatism, he defends his position in terms of sophisticated intelligence and on a plane that makes discussion possible and profitable. This was not the case with the conservatism of a generation ago, or with such vestiges of it as still survive. Conservatism moved in one plane and liberalism in another, and these planes hardly touched each other, to say nothing of over-lapping.

The true spirit of liberalism cannot crystallize around specific doctrines and affirm them as final. It sees that in every doctrinal position which our finite intelligence can take there are both a Yes and a No—what it is now the fashion to call a dialectic. No attainment of thought and no achievement of the moral will is final or secure. Neither human intelligence nor human purpose has here any continuing city. Once a position is attained and occupied, it is bound to be infested with perils which require that we move on to another position in order to resist and escape them.

What is this thing called dialectic if not the very essence of liberalism? Yet those who use this concept as a regulative principle in their thinking are those who affect to despise liberalism. And those who cling to liberalism in terms of its achievements of yesterday scorn so-called dialectical thinking. But what Barth and Tillich and Niebuhr are telling us in the name of dialectic is essentially the same thing that liberals told the orthodox of yesterday: namely, that human thought is dynamic, not static; that it is a movement, not a position; that Christian theology grows with the growth of life, and changes when life presents it with new and unanticipated situations. This preachment was constantly on the lips of all the old-fashioned liberals. They exhorted their conservative brethren to open their minds to the new truth which, as they liked to say, was breaking forth from God's word and world.

The same exhortation must now be addressed to liberals themselves. They must not be allowed to become conservative, to dry up the springs of fresh revelation. They must not become the victims of arrested liberalism. A die-hard liberal is no better than a die-hard conservative. In this day when the truth of the gospel is presenting itself with fresh significance and power, in forms both new and old, to a generation which, under the very eye of the liberalism of yesterday, has wandered farther from the Christian faith than any generation since Christianity became the religion of the West—in such a day it is important

above all else that Christian thinking should not be divided by
mere verbalisms.

Two attitudes constitute a true liberal: one is his everlasting
expectancy of the unexpected; the other is his determination
to see the unexpected when it occurs and take account of it
with an open and a faithful mind. But these two attitudes also
constitute a true realist. Realism and liberalism are one. They
should not be put asunder either by those who speak in the
name of a realism which sees truth where the liberalism of yesterday did not see it, or by those who speak in the name of a
liberalism which finds its glory chiefly in its past.

ANALYSIS of certain right-wing positions in the theological
spectrum, by a professor at Fuller Theological Seminary.

August 26, 1959

Post-Fundamentalist Faith

EDWARD JOHN CARNELL

Let me say a word about that anxious breed of younger men
who are conservative in theology but are less than happy when
they are called "fundamentalists." These men are both the
cause and the effect of a radical atmospheric change within
American orthodoxy.

The fundamentalist movement was organized shortly after
the turn of the present century. It served as a rallying point for
a host of gifted and not-so-gifted conservatives, who rushed to
do battle with modernism. The charge was that modernism had
surrendered the gospel to German higher criticism and to ex-
travagant social philosophies patterned after biological evolution. Subsequent events, such as the disintegration of modernism and the return to biblical theology, show that the fundamentalist movement was not tilting against windmills.

But if such is the case, why did the movement fall into general disrepute? The answer is quite within reach. Through a series of subtle internal changes, fundamentalism shifted from an affirmation to a negation. The result was a cunning pharisaism that confused possession of truth with possession of virtue. Fundamentalism stood in the temple of God, thankful that it was not like modernism. Status by negation, not a humble reliance on the grace of God, served as the base for Christian security.

Having exempted itself from the scrutiny of divine righteousness, fundamentalism often took on the mannerisms of a pugnacious cult. The test of Christian discipleship was no longer "works done in love." The test was "assent to the fundamentals of the faith." In this way the foolishness of the cross was obscured by the foolishness of those who came in the name of the cross. Assent to doctrine is no match for demonic pretense, for even the devil can pass a course in Christian theology.

But fundamentalism made its crowning error when it enlisted the doctrine of the church in its quest for negative status. While the doctrine purported to come from Scripture, scrutiny showed that it derived from the conviction that possession of truth is the same thing as possession of virtue. And since only fundamentalists were in possession of truth, they alone were virtuous enough to form the body of Christ. All other elements in the Christian community were apostate.

It was by a discovery of this pompous theological error that I awoke from dogmatic slumber. I now realize, though once I did not, that the nature of the church is *never* measured by the doctrinal maturity of those who profess Christ. Doctrine clarifies the plan of salvation, but a sinner is justified by faith and repentance, not by assent to doctrine. Believers, in some cases, must overcome deeply embedded prejudices before they can appreciate either the scope or the relevance of Christian doctrine. But this deficiency, other things being equal, is no mark against the person. The want of doctrinal maturity, like the want of subjective holiness, is remedied by sanctification, not justification. When fundamentalism confined the body of Christ to those who received the system of revealed doctrine, it obscured the distinction between justification and sanctification. It returned, in effect, to the ethos of Roman Catholicism.

I know that much of this will sound elementary to outsiders. But to one reared in the tyrannical legalism of fundamentalism, the recovery of a genuine theology of grace is no insignificant feat. The feat calls for a generous outlay of intellectual honesty and personal integrity.

Since a goodly company of younger conservatives are trying to restore the classical lines of orthodoxy, philosophy of religion ought to reserve the term "fundamentalist" for the person who confuses possession of truth with possession of virtue or who defends a separatist view of the church. Unlike fundamentalism, orthodoxy does not affect a monopoly on truth. It rejects the cultic quest for negative status; it is ready to entertain friendly conversation with the church universal.

The term "orthodoxy," of course, is freighted with unfortunate connotations of its own. It often suggests either a sterile confessionalism or a provincial stand against progress. Still, it is a useful term, for it denotes the conservative tradition in Christian theology. I call myself orthodox because I cordially assent to the great doctrines of the faith. But I do not for one moment suppose that assent to doctrine is either the instrumental cause of justification or the touchstone of Christian fellowship. Were I to do so I would be reverting to fundamentalism.

It is too bad, in a way, that we have to use labels at all. In Antioch they were content to be called Christians. But all is not lost. By using carefully selected labels, we at least clarify our position in the theological spectrum. And once we are done with the business of semantics, we can turn to the really exciting item on the agenda of faith: sharing fellowship with all who love Jesus Christ and who are willing to test and correct their partial insights by the full insight of God's Word.

HOW MY MIND HAS CHANGED

IN 1939 Dr. Morrison's thirtieth anniversary as editor of The Christian Century was marked by a series of articles in which leading theologians of the day, both at home and abroad, revealed how their thinking had changed during the decade just past. Ten years later a second series on the same theme appeared; twenty years later, still another; ten years thence, another may be expected. Herewith, one contribution from each decennial series.

May 31, 1939

A Liberal Bandaged but Unbowed
ROBERT L. CALHOUN

When Dr. Morrison's thirty years of editorial service through The Christian Century began, I was in the eighth grade. During a full half of these thirty years, his mind has been a salutary factor among the many which have been reshaping mine. It is with an acknowledgment of debt, therefore, that I try to set down here some account of what has been going on in me during a part of this time.

Not that it matters much, to any but the few people who have to get along with me at close range. What matters most to them, moreover, is how I actually behave, not what I have been thinking and why. But only on the latter point is there anything to say here. And there is little assurance that even this can be reported accurately, for ten years back. In the absence of a written record there are only afterthoughts to offer, and afterthoughts in these matters are of course tidied up to suit one's present mood and the public gaze. What follows, then, should be regarded with suspicion. Especially if it should fit in too neatly with what everybody else says in this series. For that will mean that instead of reporting an individual course of events, I shall have slipped into a current fashion, and simply retailed that.

In any case it seems necessary to start by trying to say what there was of me when the decade began. My mind, or whatever it is, has always been a rather messy jumble of strains never properly sorted out. One of them is an incurably sentimental, Pollyannish one that has to be snubbed continually, and at times is highly embarrassing. Another seems to be a more legitimate sort of emotional irritability that makes for weeping, glowering or wall-banging on various provocations. This sometimes boils over quite suddenly. Another is a combination of indolence, timidity and like ingredients that seem to go along with a distressingly slow basic tempo and chronic tardiness of response in all sorts of situations. Still another, late to appear but seemingly as durable as the rest, is a kind of profane delight in logical clarity and "hard facts." This strain was a dominant one in my lawyer father, but he died before I knew him as a distinct person at all. It probably was strong also in his father and grandfather, both southern Presbyterian preachers who pioneered in Minnesota from territorial days. I have a marked-up copy of Jonathan Edwards' works that belonged to the former, and another of Calvin's Institutes that belonged to the latter, and in both it is the hardier passages that are underscored.

This strain of realism cropped out first in my younger brother, who until his death in 1927 was studying medicine and preparing for research in pathology. I slowly learned to prize it in him, and in other medical friends and relatives-by-marriage among whom it has been necessary for me to keep some sort of footing for upward of twenty years. The scientific temper and habits of mind concretely embodied in these half-dozen chemists and medical people have been for two decades a part of my household air. Without being able to match them, I have liked their straightforward thinking, and have come to rejoice at finding similar straightforwardness in certain philosophers and theologians from Plato onward.

This relatively late discovery of what "science" means to a

scientist was superimposed for me on a small-town, middle-class, midwestern upbringing and a liberal college and seminary course. Both upbringing and education were absorbed like so much milk and eggs, with entire docility and without any intellectual misgivings. There were plenty of emotional headaches, such as a verbally precocious and otherwise immature youngster has to put up with in school and college. But there were no mental or spiritual upheavals, no serious disillusionments, and no fundamental doubts of any sort. Throughout a rather sickly, sheltered, happy boyhood and a more independent but never obstreperous youth, an ingrained confidence in people—especially older people—and a naive trust in God never wavered. These were most of all my mother's gift to me, and she was a person of no lukewarm kind.

With minor though growing disturbances, this outlook of mine had lasted through college, through six years of further study at home and in England during the war and the early "peace," and then through six years of teaching in college and seminary. A decade ago, between 1926 and 1929, for reasons that do not matter here, the whole structure was demolished. Naive trust was gone, and first numbness, then corrosive doubt, took its place. Doubt that there is any God, and that the world's noise means anything. Doubt that human beings —even older people—are fit to run their affairs without such tutelage as they plainly do not have. Doubt that I, in particular, had ever been or would ever be more than a kind of glib, walking lie, made of shiny words. The collapse, long overdue, was thorough.

All these doubts have persisted, and I presume will persist. But their deadly paralyzing force seems to be gone. After the first few months of chaos, a new foundation of confidence began to take shape in me, far below the word-level. At first tenuous and elusive as cobweb, it gradually became a fabric of such strength that neither criticism (which I have courted) nor shock has since broken it. It seems to be one sort of faith in God. But it is so undramatic and matter-of-fact, so lacking in thrills and moral splendor, that if anyone should say he has a better name for it, I am quite ready to listen. I know it is not the outcome of a deliberate "will to believe," nor of an articulate thought process. Of "unconscious wishes," naturally, one can speak with less assurance, but at least I am not wholly unacquainted with the better-known theories about these also, and have tried to take them into account. In any event, the faith I am talking about is something come upon me, not something I consciously produced. Both I and others have tried to break it down by critical analysis, thus far without success.

This new confidence was first prompted, unless memory at this point is all wrong, by two very hard facts: the invincibility of a clear-headed medical student dying of cancer, and the impassive bulk of the Rockies above timber line, which I saw for the first time four months later. To them was added almost at once the departure of another young doctor, my closest friend, for the Rockefeller yellow fever work in Africa, from which he did not return. I worked over his diary later, and read with a layman's eye the papers in which he had summed up his part of the co-operative research. What even I could see in his mind and in my brother's, a kind of quiet ruthlessness and candor in search of truth, stood up well alongside the rock masses of the continental divide. It was reassuring beyond words to find that sort of strength so unostentatiously embodied, so close by. It was no less reassuring to realize that the actual world they had faced—the world of mountains and microbes—though it had brought death to their bodies had first yielded up some of its secrets to their minds, for other men to use. It was not simply a nightmare world, then. At least in some respects it made sense.

How far it might make sense I do not know. Some of the easier parts of Whitehead, then Plato, then a whole series of thinkers lighted up by these two, helped me to glimpse a few of the simpler presuppositions that scientific men take for granted in their work, and encouraged me to look further. Next it became evident that workmanship of all sorts, from the humblest to the most exalted, calls for similar presuppositions. Little by little the notion grew on me that all of these slow-coming, painfully obvious insights of mine were, without exception, elaborations of the inarticulate confidence which had itself been growing in me all the while. My faith in God, then, born or reborn out of the ruin of thirty years' attempts at thinking, was slowly taking shape in the midst of close companionship with working scientists, a little of whose temper I may have caught. It was guided by philosophic arguments, a little of whose drift I have understood. And it grew and became interwoven into an everyday working life which has called for so much more than all my resources that I am never caught up.

That tells about where things were and how they were going ten years ago. The personal theology in which these tendencies were trying to articulate themselves was liberalism of a familiar sort. My thinking ranged between the romantic immanentism of Schleiermacher, at one extreme, and the science-minded, sharp-edged theism of Tennant, at the other. Kant was presupposed in both, and Plato (especially in his later dialogues) seemed to me to have laid foundations for them all. Platonism became a growing enthusiasm and "rational theology" a kind of passion.

Along with this went a simple sort of social liberalism: the outlook of a sheltered, small-town person of mild habits, very slightly aware of the more savage forces that operate in the economic and political arenas. Except at one point. The peace treaties and the postwar flood of prewar documents had driven me to a pretty thoroughly disillusioned pacifism, as regards modern war. I knew then a good deal less than everybody knows now about international politics, the forces that underlie it, and the diversity of its problem situations. The detailed pattern of my pacifism, therefore, has changed, like any empirical conviction, in the light of new data, mainly in the direction of pessimism for the immediate future. The tangle of political and economic conflicts is so much worse than I realized ten years ago, and the apparent resources of human intelligence so much less, that I no longer hope confidently for "peace in our time." But the basic conviction has grown stronger, not weaker, with every year that nothing men can do to mankind is worse than the totalitarian war of our era.

This is not to call war "absolute evil," nor to say, "there

never was a bad peace." Nothing human is absolute evil, not even war; and Versailles and Munich—those "open covenants, openly arrived at"—cry to heaven how bad a peace can be. The point is simply that however bad the alternative, a general war is almost certain to be worse. Moreover, if and when general war comes again, there will be need for a much larger minority than there was in 1914 to resist the inevitable war hysteria, the orthodox dehumanizing of the enemy, and the making of another nationalistic peace. I am still a pacifist, then, set against war—most of all against expeditionary war in defense of democracy, peace, freedom, religion, or anything else high and noble. Even wars for self-defense, legally justifiable and pulse-stirring as they are, seem in most cases to retard rather than to advance the labored struggle of mankind toward humane living. In some cases it may be otherwise. I do not see how one can know in advance, unless one can get very clear answers to the questions: "What precisely is to be defended? Is it likely to survive mobilization of industry and the public mind for war? What other methods have been tried, and are still to be tried?" But trying to answer these questions is likely to bring into the foreground problems of quite another sort, though it took me a good while to see it.

If the aftermath of 1919 ruined my taste for war, it was the aftermath of 1929 that has ruined my complacency about our kind of peace. Before the Coolidge bull market I took American capitalism for granted. Worse than that—and my ears redden at the memory—I was more than a little dazzled by the noisy prosperity of 1928-29, and mistook it for boisterous, if somewhat immoral, good health. Economic crises were to me only vague words, and economic morality chiefly a matter of individual honesty and good will. Mea culpa. It took three years of growing disillusionment and anxiety to cure me of that particular blindness. But the cure promises to be lasting. I read some samples of Veblen and then of Marx and Lenin and various lesser image-smashers, trying hard for the first time to see what they were driving at. This was not easy for an economic illiterate, but it seemed all the more necessary for that reason. At the same time, it seemed necessary also to try for some notion of what more orthodox economists were saying; so I tried to read a little of Moulton, Slichter and Keynes as well.

Keynes' *The Economic Consequences of the Peace* had dropped at my feet like a meteorite back in 1920, and stirred me to a fine moral indignation, but it had been an isolated impact. Now, with the predictions of that book being visibly fulfilled on all sides, I began to sense in some living fashion a really concrete relation between ethics and economics. For the first time it began to dawn on me in what sense moral values may be recognized as interwoven with, and "dialectically" exemplified by, the massive order of economic facts. Instead of seeing moral obligations simply as individual and social ideals externally related to the factual order of life and physical reality, I began to see them as demands on human life no less intrinsically real than gravitation. Familiar words about God in history, and a moral order of the world, were becoming concrete for me as I struggled to come to terms with economic determinism, both as theory and as an increasingly evident and momentous fact.

Not, however, as the most ultimate nor the most important kind of fact. The still more ultimate world of mountains and microbes and the uneasy animals we call men, once established in my thinking, remained unforgettable even for a little while. Human nature, in the sense of man's basic physical, emotional, impulsive and intellectual constitution, somehow moral at the core, seemed plainly more fundamental than any particular sort of human behavior, even economic; and human nature itself emerges in a world order far more ancient and more fundamental still. Against that background, dogmatic collectivism has seemed only a little less shallow than naive individualism. Less shallow because it recognizes at least that the individual is not master of his fate and cannot live for himself alone, but still shallow in supposing that the human group—class, race or species—can do so.

There is no particular elation, but there is a grim sort of reassurance, in seeing men's latest collective efforts in Russia and Germany to seize for themselves by violence a kingdom of heaven, colliding once more with stubborn nature and human nature. Whether the totalitarian governments collapse or change their ways and whether the change comes soon or late, the epidemic of purges and the spreading disaffection of once enthusiastic followers reinforce the old lesson that power in itself is no cure for man's ills, and that human institutions are not equal to the task of assuring human salvation. Man himself is still more important than any of his actions or institutions, and much more difficult to make over. For that very reason, man is less important even to himself than the God whose world has brought mankind to birth, and who must save it if it is to be saved.

Concerning both of these more basic matters, man and God, my thought has moved from a primarily philosophic toward a more definitely theological orientation. Ten years ago I scarcely distinguished these terms, except as regards their scope. Theology seemed to me essentially a more specialized kind of religious philosophy. Eight years ago my first serious encounter with Barthian thought, embodied in Visser 't Hooft, Pierre Maury and Hanns Lilje, left me puzzled and combative, and I fear not much enlightened. But Richard Niebuhr's patient, resourceful flank attacks were already making me see that something was there which could not be ignored, something which makes theology a discipline more clearly distinguishable from philosophy than I had suspected.

Six years ago began in earnest my post-graduate theological education: six years of continuous hammering by the more "dialectical" members of a theological discussion group which still retains the fire, if not the innocence, of its younger days. The vigorous impacts of these men—Richard and Reinhold Niebuhr, Wilhelm Pauck, John Mackay, and later Paul Tillich and Emil Brunner, are some of them—have beaten upon me not only during semiannual week-end sessions, but day in and day out, through their writings and through my vivid, ever present memories of their minds (and bodies) in action. It has been drastic discipline, not always easy to take, but invaluable; the more because of lively counter-disturbances emanating from Edwin Aubrey, John Bennett, George Thomas and other sound liberals whose heads, like mine, are bandaged but unbowed.

It has become more and more plain that I am no fit material for a good Barthian, nor for any kind of theologian except some obstinate sort of liberal. The more extreme kind of revelation-theology, whether Barthian or other, seems to me all too likely to slip into the very subjectivism it deplores. Special revelations—the only sort recognized by this kind of theology—have always needed to be checked by some more general frame of reference: the written Scriptures coolly and historically studied, the tradition and common experience of the church, and the still more general experiences and tested beliefs of mankind. I cannot see any reason to suppose that this need for objective criticism of immediate insights is less today than it was in St. Paul's time, or in Luther's and Calvin's. Nor can I see that a single test, least of all a simple reference to the Bible as understood by the recipient of the special revelation, is now or ever will be a sufficient safeguard against the vagaries to which intensely sincere minds are sometimes even more liable than those whose convictions are less fiercely one-sided. In short, I see no way in which theology can get on safely without history, philosophy and common sense.

In principle, most if not all the members of the group just mentioned would agree, though in detail we are still healthily far from agreement. Such agreement and disagreement, with mutual understanding and respect, is the essence, I take it, of the liberal tradition in its broad sense, from the beginning of Christianity until now.

On the other hand, I have been driven, willy-nilly, to recognize that theology cannot get on without special revelations, either. Indeed, I have been convinced that it must start from such revelations, above all from those which center about Jesus Christ, and the faith which they evoke. This amounts to a Copernican change in my orientation. With it has come a new sense of the special significance—long obvious enough to others, but to me unsuspected—of the Bible, the creeds, theological tradition and the Christian Church. For years I tried to resolve these simply into illustrations of familiar logical formulas, the while overlooking or apologizing for their more refractory aspects. Now, with the sort of relief that comes when one moves from thin ice onto solid ground, I find myself taking them still more simply as concrete instances of living give-and-take among men, and between God and man, which both demand and resist logical inquiry. That they resist it is no reason to adjourn the effort to get them into rational perspectives. On the other hand, in their presence our logic seems clearly to have neither the first nor the last word.

I have been compelled, in short, to recognize that for theology two foundations are equally necessary: specific revelations of reality both divine and non-divine, and the principle of relevance or coherence which is basic to all rational living. Without the former, there would be no data for theology. Without the latter, all data would be meaningless, and none of them could be construed as revelations of God. *Fides quaerens intellectum* would more nearly describe my thinking today than at any prior time in these ten years.

The rise of the more blatant neo-paganisms has reinforced my conviction of the need for both these factors. If human decency is ever to be won, more plainly than ever it must be in part through the widening and deepening of the rational insights against which the cults of blood and soil are in revolt. But whatever hope I now have for such growth of man toward rational decency is rooted in faith that Jesus Christ has given us men our best clue to the natures of both man and God. If that be true, the Herods and the Caesars will not have their way.

June 15, 1949

Beyond Religious Socialism

PAUL TILLICH

It was not a dramatic change of mind that I experienced during the past decade—such a change is hardly to be expected in the sixth decade of one's life—but a slow, often unconscious, always effective transformation in various respects. One of these changes arose from the fact that the past ten years belong to the fifteen that I have lived in this country and that they were consequently years of continuing adaptation to the ways and thoughts of America.

The summer of 1948, when I returned to Germany for the first time since 1933, gave me a clear test of the amount of adaptation I have undergone. The change has been first of all a change in my mode of expression. The English language has worked on me what my German friends and former students considered a miracle: it has made me understandable. No Anglicisms occurred in the innumerable speeches I delivered, but the spirit of the English language dominated every sentence—the spirit of clarity, soberness and concreteness. This forced itself upon me, often against my natural inclinations. It taught me to avoid the accumulation of substantives to which German is prone and to use verbs instead. It forbade the ambiguities in which, because of its origin in medieval mystical literature, German philosophical language so often indulges. It prohibited the use of logically unsharp or incomplete propositions. It pricked my conscience when I dwelt too long in abstractions. All this was very well received by my German audiences and was felt as my most impressive change of mind.

Reporting in Germany on the state of theology in the

U.S.A. I said that America, while still following Europe's lead
in historical and systematic theology, is far ahead of it in
ethics. I could say this because I had become increasingly
aware that ethics is an integral element of systematic theology,
and that I had much to learn in social as well as individual
ethics from American thought and reality. In social ethics I
was partly prepared by my work as a "religious socialist" in
Germany. But only slowly did I realize the central importance
social ethics has in American theology and come to appreciate
the abundant and advanced treatment it has received.

While in my first years in the United States I was surprised and worried by the tremendous emphasis put on the
question of pacifism—a question that seemed to me of minor
importance and often the result of confused thinking—I
presently discovered that all theological problems were implicit in this problem. When therefore, in the years before,
during and after the Second World War, the pacifist ideology
was shattered in large numbers of people, I understood that
this was an indication of a new attitude toward the doctrine
of man and toward the whole of Christianity. And this change
in the mind of others made it easier for me to feel at home in
the theological work of this country.

When I first came to America, in 1933, I was labeled a "neo-
orthodox" or a "neo-supernaturalist." This was certainly in-
correct, but I must admit that some of my early utterances before American audiences could have created such an impression.
My task in the thirties was to give my students and other listeners an account of my theological, philosophical and political
ideas as they had developed during the critical years from 1914
to 1933. I brought with me from Germany the "theology of
crisis," the "philosophy of existence" and "religious socialism,"
and I tried to interpret these to my classes and readers. In all
three of these fields—the theological, the philosophical and the
political—my thinking has undergone changes, partly because
of personal experiences and insights, partly because of the social
and cultural transformations these years have witnessed.

Most obvious of the changes on the world stage is the political one—from the uncertainties of the thirties to the establish-

ment in the forties of a world-splitting dualism, in reality as well as in ideology. While before the Second World War there was some ground for hope that the religious-socialist spirit penetrating into East and West alike, though in different forms, would mitigate the contrast and prevent the conflict between them, no such hope has a foundation today. The expectation we had cherished after the First World War that a *kairos*, a "fulfillment of time," was at hand, has been twice shaken, first by the victory of fascism and then by the situation after its military defeat.

I do not doubt that the basic conceptions of religious socialism are valid, that they point to the political and cultural way of life by which alone Europe can be built up. But I am not sure that the adoption of religious-socialist principles is a possibility in any foreseeable future. Instead of a creative *kairos*, I see a vacuum which can be made creative only if it is accepted and endured and, rejecting all kinds of premature solutions, is transformed into a deepening "sacred void" of waiting. This view naturally implies a decrease of my participation in political activities. My change of mind in this connection was also influenced by the complete breakdown of a serious political attempt I made during the war to bridge the gap between East and West with respect to the organization of postwar Germany.

It has been said that the repudiation of civil liberties and the rights of man in the Communist-dominated countries means the disillusionment of liberals all over the world. This is certainly true of those who had more illusions than my religious-socialist understanding of man ever allowed me to entertain. But it cannot be denied that this widespread repudiation of human rights had a depressing effect also on those who, like myself, without being utopian, saw the dawn of a new creative era in a moment which actually presaged a deeper darkness.

To turn now to philosophy: "Existentialism" was familiar to me long before the name came into general use. The reading of Kierkegaard in my student years, the thorough study of Schelling's later works, the passionate devotion to Nietzsche during the First World War, the encounter with Marx (especially with his early philosophical writings), and finally my own religious-socialist attempts at an existential interpretation of history —all had prepared me for more recent existential philosophy as developed by Heidegger, Jaspers and Sartre. In spite of the fact that existentialism has become fashionable and has been dangerously popularized, I have been confirmed in my conviction of its basic truth and its adequacy to our present condition. The basic truth of this philosophy, as I see it, is its perception of the "finite freedom" of man, and conseqently of his situation as always perilous, ambiguous and tragic. Existentialism gains its special significance for our time from its insight into the immense increase in anxiety, danger and conflict produced in personal and social life by the present "destructive structure" of human affairs.

On this point existential philosophy has allied itself with therapeutic or depth psychology. Only through the late war and its aftermath has it become manifest that psychic illness—the inability to use one's finite freedom creatively—is more widespread in this country than any other disease. At the same time depth psychology has removed what remnants of the nineteenth-century mechanistic world view still remained, and has come to understand the sociological, ontological and even theological implications of phenomena like anxiety, guilt and compulsion neurosis. Out of this new co-operation of ontology and psychology (including social psychology) a doctrine of man has developed which has already exercised considerable influence in all cultural realms, especially in theology.

It was partly under this influence that I elaborated my theological system (I am not afraid of that word) during the past decade. Continuous thinking about the possibility of uniting the religious power of so-called neo-orthodox theology with the duty of every theology to address itself to the contemporary mind has resulted in the conception of a "method of correlation"—correlation, that is, between existential questions and theological answers. The human situation, as interpreted in existential philosophy and the psychology and sociology related to it, posits the question; the divine revelation, as interpreted in the symbols of classical theology, gives the answer. The answer, of course, must be reinterpreted in the light of the question, as the question must be formulated in the light of the answer.

In this way, it seems to me, it is possible to avoid two contradictory errors in theology, the supernaturalistic and the naturalistic. The first makes revelation a rock falling into history from above, to be accepted obediently without preparation or adequacy to human nature. The second replaces revelation by a structure of rational thought derived from and judged by human nature. The method of correlation, by overcoming the conflict of supernaturalism and naturalism, shows a way out of the blind alley in which the discussion between fundamentalism or neo-orthodoxy on the one hand, and theological humanism or liberalism on the other, is caught.

In the course of this mediating attempt it became increasingly clear to me that one achievement of so-called liberal theology has to be defended with great religious, ethical and scientific passion; namely, the right and duty of philological-historical criticism of the biblical literature without any condition except integrity of research and scientific honesty. Any dogmatic interference with this work would drive us into new or old superstitions—myths and symbols not understood as myths and symbols—and, since this cannot be done without the unconscious suppression of sounder knowledge, to fanaticism. The power of this neo-biblicism is obvious in continental Europe, but it can already be felt in this country also, and even among old-fashioned liberals.

Looking at the past decade of my life I see no dramatic changes of mind but a slow development of my convictions in the direction of greater clarity and certainty. Above all I have come to realize that a few great and lasting things are decisive for the human mind, and that to cling to them is more important than to look for dramatic changes.

February 3, 1960

Ordeal of a Happy Dilettante*

ALBERT C. OUTLER

Quite a lot has happened, both in the world and in my mind, in the last ten years. That we—the world and my mind —have come through them even partially intact is cause for earnest gratitude, for the odds often seemed stacked against us. It has been a demented time, a cliff-hanging time, a time of portents and marvels.

In it I have tried to be as relevant as possible—especially when I could tell for certain what that meant and where I could distinguish between the really relevant and the merely novel. I have nothing but scorn for the dogmatists who stubbornly insist that they already have the truth in a handbasket, that they have had it all along and need only to proclaim it to have it heard by the elect. And I have sought sincerely to hear the new sounds and sights of the *avant garde*—and their theological chaplains.

My assignment in this series, however, forced me to probe behind the frenzied calendar I have tried to keep this past decade and ask myself what it is that I have really been doing and trying to do. The answer, as far as I have come to one, seems to be that while I have been as busy and as discontent as Martha ever was the one thing needful in my theological career thus far has not been to keep up but to catch up.

For a long time now I have been convinced that one of the hidden causes of our current confusion is the often unrecognized hiatus in our consciousness between the Christian present and the Christian past. The Enlightenment and its theology caused a deep, near-fatal breach of continuity between contemporary Christianity and historic Christianity.

The consequences of this are all around us, in the unhistorical and sometimes antihistorical developments in Christian thought. How can this breach be healed? How can a man be a modern Christian, one who has assimilated the theological impact of the nineteenth century, and still claim his full share of the whole of the Christian heritage? I have been puzzling over these questions a long time. Alongside a hundred practical ventures of one sort or another the one constant and continuing project I can see in my distracted labors has been the effort to recouple the past and the present—and to persuade others that it must be done or at the very least attempted. To explain how I got started on such a project and what has happened to it in the past decade I have to go back to the beginning of my theological career.

Speaking in terms of atmospheres rather than dates, I was born and reared in the eighteenth century—in a parsonage-home of warm, vital piety and in a college still devoted to a classical curriculum. My years at seminary and in the pastorate (1928-35) marked a brief but exciting passage into and through the nineteenth century. My conversion to liberalism came in the years of the Great Depression—at the very time when the first effective critiques of liberal theology were being noticed in this country. It now seems long ago and far away, but that conversion left with me two significant residues that I still cherish: the liberal temper and the social gospel.

It was not until my years in the Yale graduate school (1935-38) that I was thrust boldly into the twentieth century—this in the course of a degree in historical theology. There I first read Barth and Irenaeus, concurrently. I was "all shook up" by A. J. Ayer's *Language, Truth and Logic*, Reinhold Niebuhr's *Moral Man and Immoral Society* and T. S. Eliot's "The Wasteland." At Yale, I first heard of Kierkegaard and existentialism, and I actually *met* Paul Tillich. I took seminars in the Institute of Human Relations and wrote a dissertation on Origen that was passed by Robert Calhoun, Roland Bainton and Erwin

* This article is reprinted from *How My Mind Has Changed*, a Living Age book published by Meridian Books, the World Publishing Co. It originally appeared in The Christian Century.

Goodenough. What a jumble it all was—and what an adventure! If I spread too wide and too thin at least I gained a range of insights and outlook that I would not even now exchange for a narrower specialization.

In this swift journey through three "centuries" I discovered for myself the radical tension between the Enlightenment and the relatively continuous Christian tradition down to the end of the eighteenth century. The nineteenth century stood—and still stands—as a sort of gap between my own theological childhood and maturity. I had pondered the previous breaks in the history of the church—the transplantation from Jewish to Greek soil, the transition from an illicit to an established religion, the passage from the ancient to the medieval world, the upheaval of the Reformation and so on. In each of these instances the further development of Christianity depended on the way the transition was handled or mishandled. It seemed to follow, therefore, that one of the specific and fundamental tasks of twentieth-century Christianity was to deal with the nineteenth century. As a matter of fact, this has been the strongest impulse in those theologies which have dominated this century thus far. In Barth, Niebuhr and others I saw a variegated pattern of *protest* and assimilation; in others such as Tillich and Bultmann there was an equally variegated pattern of *assimilation* and protest. Similar configurations appear in the new biblical theology and in the theological work of the ecumenical movement.

In the field of church history and the history of doctrine, however, no such progress is apparent. Contemporary Christian historians have been caught in a bind between their historiography and their theology. Time was when the first Christian historian, Eusebius, could follow the simple maxim that history was the stage on which the struggle between God and the devil was being acted out. But it has now come to pass that the modern historian is committed to the contrary maxim: God does not intervene in history—no appeal to divine action or causality will serve as an historical explanation. But what happens to *church* history when God is left out of it?

And yet we cannot escape our own church history, whatever

it is. We do not do so even if we attempt a leap of faith directly from the present moment to the New Testament—seeking to hear God's Word, so to say, from out of time. The fact is that we hear what we hear with the apperception produced by our own histories, and these affect what we hear and what we do in response. Nor is it better to select one or another segment of Christian history, such as the first or the fifth or the sixteenth century, and make that the norm for our own. Both these approaches ignore the question of the identity and the continuity of the Christian community and its message throughout the total historical experience of that community. But this is the question that has to be solved if we are to deal with any major instance of discontinuity.

Grandiose as it may be, and ill equipped for it as I am, I came to believe that this inquiry into the continuity of historic Christianity in contemporary Christianity was my theological vocation. This has meant a double effort to comprehend the Christian tradition in its historic continuity and the modern world in its intellectual and spiritual ambiguities. I have of course sought to merit the respect of my fellow historians and to speak to the condition of my fellow moderns. But I've had no illusions that I could master such a job, even by my own standards of excellence. It was bound to make a man a dilettante. A perfectionist in my shoes would have gone down in despair. But a *happy* dilettante is like a dog walking on his hind legs: rather pleased with himself that he can manage it at all!

The master image of the nineteenth century—man redeeming himself and his society—has been shattered beyond easy repair. Zealous as I was in that iconoclasm I have come to think that we must now attend to the other face of Christian man—his original *righteousness* and the basic health that God sustains even in his rebellious and sinful children. This idea has shaped my work on the relations between psychotherapy and the Christian message. But every shift in anthropology entails a readjustment in soteriology—and this means that we must have a new Christology: a modern doctrine of the Savior of modern sinners. Again, if a modern man is to witness to

Jesus Christ as *his* Lord and Savior, what sort of language, derived from what noetic categories, can he rightly use to celebrate his new life with God in Christ? Finally, how can he learn to think of himself in real relation with all other Christians "in this world and the next"? These are some of the "new" questions which I have seen emerging in the last few years and which I expect to see influencing the shape of theological things to come. At any rate they are the questions which have exercised my mind for the past decade, accounting for whatever changes have occurred.

In 1949 I was on the faculty at Yale and pastor of the Methodist church at Wallingford, Connecticut. It was an arduous and vastly stimulating situation. It signified that I wanted to be in close touch with the life of the church, to fill out my understanding of the Christian tradition and the contemporary world, and to work out a systematic theology on historical foundations. Presumably I could have done this as well at Yale as anywhere else. But like many another southerner who "left home" I was feeling a strong pull to go back—to help with the development of theological education in a region where Protestantism was still vigorous and to work directly with the churches through a university set down in their midst. The call to Southern Methodist University in 1951 seemed to provide such an opportunity. So we moved, though not without a few backward glances in the course of the early years. On the whole it has turned out rather as we had hoped.

In this new setting I have become a more loyal churchman than I was before without ceasing to love *academia* one whit the less. I think I am as critical as ever of the churches' failures —of nerve, of wisdom, of vision. Certainly I am still distressed at the stale, flat and unprofitable business that often goes by the name of Christianity in all too many places. But I have also found an opportunity to work for something different and better within the churches themselves and to help with the training of ministers furnished for the future with the resources of the past. Moreover I have discovered more authentic life and power in the churches themselves than even the pious cynics ever see. The residence of the Holy Spirit among the people of God is still a reality—and this has given both promise and hope, even in the midst of discontent.

This closer involvement in denominational affairs has had the effect of strengthening my commitment to the cause of ecumenical Christianity. I know now that the way to unity does not lie in the aggressive reassertion of our respective virtues or the recombination of the separated members of Christ's body. If it comes at all it will be through the mutual discovery and affirmation within the separated churches of that common Christian history which we share as Christians. If we are able to do this, however, we must also prepare our peoples for the mutations in form and policy that are bound to follow.

I have already mentioned the fact that Christology has come to confront us again as if it were almost a new question. Along with many others I have spent the past ten years exploring this maze and mystery—trying to rehearse its history and reformulate its import in modern terms. The gist of my conclusions thus far can be scantily summarized in five theses: (1) the definition of Chalcedon, understood in context, is still the basic text for a valid, modern Christology; (2) since Chalcedon, "orthodox" Christology—East and West—has failed to maintain a proper doctrine of the full and real humanity of Jesus Christ; (3) the Protestant stress on the work and corresponding de-emphasis on the person of Christ is a misunderstanding; (4) Enlightenment Christology was the function of Enlightenment anthropology and hence is now as archaic as its scholastic counterpart; (5) modern personality theory is a major new resource for the interpretation of the biblical and Chalcedonian witnesses to the Man of God's own choosing. I would like to see a modern restatement of the two-natures doctrine that would move from our knowledge of the agent of our salvation to an understanding of the act of our salvation, to that faith-acting-in-love which is the Christian life.

Ten years ago, as I can see by my lecture notes, I was still laboring traditional phrases—rational and irrational, natural and supernatural, transcendent and immanent, finite and infinite—as metaphors about God and the world. Aided by biblical theologians I have come to see that this split-level language does not ring true in terms of the Bible or Christian experience. I have come to believe that it is better to begin with the fact that God is *always* present and acting, whether "known" or not. Then one can speak of the two different ways that he is present: either in his mystery or his manifestation. God-Mysterious is utterly ineffable; God-Manifest is actually knowable, but only when, where and as he chooses to reveal himself. We are aware of God-Mysterious—and this awareness is as primitive as our awareness of motion, causality or self. We are also grasped by the presence of God-Manifest, and this supplies the data of religious knowledge. In neither case is God at our disposal.

Thus faith and reason are not two different ramps to two different levels of reality. Rather, they are two different responses to the two different modes of God's presence and action. Faith cannot verify itself; reason cannot originate its data. Our language-games—of worship and theology—must reflect these two dimensions of experience. The language of worship adores God-Mysterious, confesses God-Manifest, and speaks of repentance, forgiveness and new being. It is therefore essentially doxological and confessional. It confesses, without rational proof, that the supreme manifestation of God-Mysterious is Jesus Christ—in manifest fullness and not merely as symbol.

The language of theology is both like and unlike the language of worship. Theology is reflection upon the reality of worship and an explication of it. As such it is a rational affair —receiving its data as given, testing its methodology, trying to make sense—faith seeking to understand. The function of theology is to guide the dialogue between faith and understanding and to prevent either from excluding the other. Significantly new and somewhat unexpected resources for developing these notions are being provided for us in the work of those linguistic analysts who are exploring the meaning of theological explanations.

The happy dilettante, who believes in justification by faith *and* hope, prays to be judged by his intention as well as by his performance. He is as much concerned with what he can see as needful as with what he himself can provide. If I could choose my own epitaph I would want it to speak of one who was sustained in a rather strenuous career by the vision of a Christian theology that gives history its full due; that makes way for the future without having to murder the past; that begins and ends with the self-manifestation of God's Mystery in our flesh and our history; that binds itself to Scripture but also claims scriptural authority for a rational hermeneutics; that opposes human pride and speaks of God's healing grace without despising or exalting the creature; that unites justice and mercy without resorting either to legalism or to antinomianism; that organizes the Christian life by the power of grace and the means of grace; that celebrates our redemption by the invincible love of God which is in Christ Jesus our Lord—in sum, a theology that does justice to the reality it reflects upon. It is enough for any man to believe that he has been called to labor in some such task as this, for he cannot doubt that whether it is given him to plant, to water or to harvest, God will give the increase.

III

The World Ecumenical Conferences

ADVOCACY OF CHRISTIAN UNITY *and exploration of moves designed to bring it about animated the Century's pages from the start. One evidence of that concern: the paper's on-the-spot coverage of all the great world conferences that helped build the various ecumenical gropings into concrete witness. Herewith, selections from the wide coverage of each of those conferences: Edinburgh 1910, by Editor* MORRISON; *Stockholm 1925, by* LYNN HAROLD HOUGH, *Methodist clergyman and at that time a contributing editor; Lausanne 1927, by* PETER AINSLIE, *minister of the Christian Temple, Baltimore, and former president of the Association for the Promotion of Christian Unity; Jerusalem 1928, by* SAMUEL MCCRAE CAVERT, *Presbyterian minister later to serve as an executive of the Federal, National and World councils of churches; Oxford 1937, by* WINFRED ERNEST GARRISON, *church historian and for over three decades literary editor of the paper; Edinburgh 1937, by* DR. MORRISON; *Amsterdam 1948, by* HAROLD E. FEY, *then managing editor; Evanston 1954, by the entire staff.*

July 7, 1910

The World Missionary Conference

CHARLES CLAYTON MORRISON

Edinburgh, June 20

"About the biggest thing that ever struck Scotland," said my Edinburgh host as we sat together in his drawing room talking over the conference which had brought me to his city, and on account of which a thousand Edinburgh homes have been thrown open to entertain delegates from all parts of the earth.

Yes, and more than that, was the Archbishop of Canterbury's response at the session that evening, for, said he, "if men be weighed rather than counted this assemblage has, I suppose, no parallel in the history either of this or other lands."

This assessment of the strategic and prophetic character of the World Missionary Conference is the common judgment of the entire body of 1,200 delegates. Everyone feels the presence in the conference of a power not ourselves, deeper than our own devices, which is making for a triumphant advance of Christianity abroad. And not less are the delegates thrilled by

139

the sense that the conference foreshadows a new era for the church at home.

Indeed one is safe in saying that there is no home problem which the church is today facing which is not forced to the foreground in the consideration of missionary expansion. And it is coming home to many with the force and surprise of a revelation that these home problems—the problem of Christian union, the problem of Christian education, the problem of a socialized Christianity, and even the academic problems of criticism and theology—wait for their solution until they are carried into the white light of missionary passion.

But I must not indulge in this kind of writing now. There will be time enough later on for these reflections. The readers of The Christian Century wish to see the conference itself, and I will try to set it forth as well as I can with my pencil, in a forenoon of self-denying absence from a most tempting session.

The Assembly Hall of the United Free Church is the meeting place. It is not the largest hall in Edinburgh, but it is admirably adapted to the purposes of this conference. It must be remembered that this is a *conference*. It is not the same sort of a missionary meeting as that held in Chicago in May when 5,000 men gathered to hear great missionary addresses. The purpose of that Laymen's Congress was to quicken missionary enthusiasm, to develop a missionary conscience, to make the church feel her duty to carry the gospel to the ends of the earth.

This meeting in Edinburgh is a gathering of missionary specialists, in the main, who come together to exchange views on the ways and means of executing the Lord's command to preach the gospel to the whole creation. The missionary conscience is assumed here. The church's duty is taken for granted. Every delegate is already an ardent missionary believer.

But the past hundred years of missionary campaigning has brought to light an almost endless number of problems and difficulties about which these missionary workers—both those at the front and those administering the enterprise at home—have good reasons to hold divergent opinions. These problems form the subject matter for the discussions of the conference. A large hall like the Museum in Edinburgh or the

Auditorium in Chicago is too vast for effective discussion of problems. Hence this Assembly Hall, seating the 1,200 delegates on the main floor, with galleries on four sides for wives of delegates and representative visitors, especially missionaries, is just suited to the purpose.

Let us go in at 9:45 some morning and observe and listen.

They are singing "Crown Him with Many Crowns" as we enter, and then a prayer is offered by Bishop Charles H. Brent of the Philippine Islands. He speaks with God in the simple speech of a child, and one knows whence is the secret of the great faith and enthusiasm that has called him to give his life to the establishment of pure Christianity in America's new possession in the Orient.

The chairman is Mr. John R. Mott. Of course we should now say "Dr." Mott, since he was thus decorated last Tuesday by the University of Edinburgh. The vice-chancellor characterized his name as one "honored and revered in all the universities and seats of learning throughout the world, for it is the name of a dauntless crusader who has found his mission in the advancement of the spiritual side of university life, of a great leader who has for years exercised an extraordinary ascendancy over the students of all countries." Dr. Mott was elected as the chairman of the conference in committee, which means that he is the real executive chairman of the gathering, governing its sessions from day to day.

Yonder among the delegates to the left is Lord Balfour, former secretary for Scotland in the British Cabinet and a leader in church and state. He is the president of the conference and has led in the two years' preparation for the great gathering. His presidential address on Tuesday evening sounded a great note for the unity of the church. "The hope has sprung up in my mind," he said, "that unity if it begins on the mission field will not find its ending there. It is a thought not without its grandeur that a unity begun on the mission field may extend its influence and react upon us at home and throughout the older civilizations. Surely there is much more that should unite us than keep us apart."

In a seat halfway down the aisle there sits the Archbishop of

Canterbury, the head of the Church of England, in his knee breeches and gaiters, democratically taking his place beside a Methodist missionary from Korea. Across the aisle is Professor E.C. Moore of Harvard, whom a daily paper this morning described as "the very antithesis of the typical Yankee," and behind him Lord William Gascoyne-Cecil, son of the late Lord Salisbury.

That eager-looking, bold-browed man on the other side of the area watching the speaker and listening to him with an intentness bordering on fascination, is the Hon. William J. Bryan of the United States. He spoke yesterday on the significance of the educational ideal in mission work. People were glad to hear him. He spoke well—splendidly, indeed. He said that Christianity's character was nowhere better revealed than in its willingness to run the risk of educating the inferior people of the world. Our religion does not fear the light. Mr. Bryan is speaking many times in Edinburgh. He is announced to speak in Glasgow in a day or two and will visit other cities, bearing the inspiration of this great meeting to those who have not been able to attend it.

Just two more rows in front of us is the Hon. Seth Low, former mayor of New York City and formerly president of Columbia University. He is highly regarded in the conference. Sitting beside President A. McLean of the Disciples' Foreign Missionary Society is Missions-Inspector Pastor J. Warneck of Germany, world-wide authority on the animistic religions. Behind Editor J.H. Garrison of St. Louis is Dr. Robert E. Speer, Presbyterian missionary secretary in the United States, whom the University of Edinburgh honored with the degree of D.D. last Tuesday, in company with the Archbishop of Canterbury and President T. Harada of the great Christian Doshisha University, in Japan, who is sitting near the front.

There is George Sherwood Eddy, a young man of wealth who is supporting himself in mission work in India, speaking as effective a message to this conference as he did to the Chicago Laymen's Congress a few weeks ago. The familiar face of S.B. Capen, president of the American Board, calls our attention to Dr. J.M. Buckley, "the bishop of Methodist bishops,"

S.M. Zwemer, Presbyterian missionary to Arabia, Bishop W.H. Tottie of the Church of Sweden and President W. Douglas MacKenzie of Hartford Seminary, who sit in a row.

To the right of that post, a bit under the gallery, sits Bishop Anderson of Chicago, and two seats away is the saintly face of the Rev. Alexander Whyte of First St. George's Church, Edinburgh, whom more American preachers love than any other living pulpiteer.

It is a great assemblage of the church's greatest men. But all are on the same level. Germans, French, Americans, Englishmen, Scandinavians, Japanese, Chinese, Hindus, Africans—all are here and mingle together in an easy equality. Missionaries, preachers, teachers, editors, statesmen, business men—all come into the hall and sit where they happen to find a place, with no scale of precedence arranged for. It is an unparalleled confluence of the big men of the kingdom of God.

The most admirable feature of the conference is the thoroughness of the preparation that has been made by its leaders. A vast deal of thinking was done before the delegates assembled. You will note that many of the members hold in their hands a rather unwieldy document as the president rises to announce the work of the day. That document is the proof-sheet report of a commission of experts who have been at work for two years gathering materials on the problem which is to be the subject of discussion today.

There are eight of these commissions. To each of them the conference devotes one day, taking as the basis for its discussions the report prepared by the commission, the proof sheets of which were put into the hands of some of the delegates some time before they left their homes for Edinburgh. Note the subjects with which the commissions deal: "Carrying the Gospel to All the Non-Christian World"; "The Church in the Mission Field"; "Education in Religion to the Christianization of National Life"; "The Missionary Message in Relation to Non-Christian Religions"; "The Preparation of Missionaries"; "The Home Base of Missions"; "Missions and Governments"; "Co-operation and the Promotion of Unity."

The very titles show the vastness and sweep of the missionary enterprise. And some conception of the work of these commissions may be gained if we look at the report of one of them in some detail as revealing and illustrating the character and method of the other seven. Commission I, under the chairmanship of Dr. John R. Mott, has as its subject the evangelization of the world. Dr. Robson of the United Free Church of Scotland and Dr. Julius Richter are vice-chairmen. Associated with them are missionary experts such as Dr. Dennis of New York, Dr. Eugene Stock of London, and Bishop Montgomery, secretary of the Society for the Propagation of the Gospel of the Church of England. In addition to these are missionaries in active service and representatives of the British and Foreign Bible Society, the Student Missionary Movement and the YMCA.

Three sections of this commission have been at work—one in London, one in New York, one on the Continent. After agreement upon certain questions dealing with vital missionary problems, these questions were sent to over two hundred representative missionaries and leading native Christians all over the world for their deliberate replies. So large was the response to these that for this one commission thirty clerks were kept busy for three weeks in order that one set of replies might be sent to each member of the commission. Each member reported to the chairman, who had a draft report of the whole prepared and sent for revision to the sections of the commission sitting in Great Britain and America and on the Continent. After full and careful criticism the draft report has been revised, and it is this carefully prepared report which is now published as a paper of the conference.

Let us assume that we are visiting the conference on Saturday. The subject for the day's consideration is "The Missionary Message in Relation to Non-Christian Religions." It is a live question to every missionary. And since the science of comparative religion has grown up in the past quarter-century, it is a live question to every thoughtful person. We will hear some interesting talking. Let us hope that it may lead to fuller light!

Seven minutes is the limit for a speech. Chairman Mott is inexorable in enforcing the rule. Professor D.S. Cairns of the

University of Aberdeen, chairman of the commission dealing with this subject, opens the discussion by calling attention to the salient features of the report. What attitude shall the messenger of Christianity take toward the religion of the people with whom he works? That is the point of the whole problem. Concluding, he says that the situation which the non-Christian nations present at the present moment is something like the spiritual situation which confronted Israel in the days of the rise of the great prophets. Israel had been getting on comfortably enough with the traditional religion and the inherited faith, until suddenly a shadow fell upon the whole Israelitish life. It was instinctively felt by her spiritual leaders that in the traditional religion there must be more than they had already attained, a reserve spiritual force which would enable the nation to meet the new and formidable emergency which had risen; and in the long and illustrious succession of Hebrew prophecy they saw the endeavor of the spiritual leaders to meet that new emergency by the broadening and intensifying of the nation's sense of the living God. Did not the evidence disclose that today the Christian Church was face to face with a formidable situation? As one read the reports one seemed to be looking into the great workshop of history. One saw the forces that were making nations, that were making religions, and those who had eyes to see saw the forming of something very vast, very formidable, and full of promise. The inevitable question arose: Is the church at this moment fit and spiritually ready for this great emergency? Is it equal to the providential calling?

Pricked by this question, delegates from all over the house sent up their cards to the chairman, asking to speak.

The first group of speakers talk on the animistic religions, the backward and childlike sort of religion possessed by such peoples as those who inhabit parts of Africa. Dr. Wardlaw Thompson, missionary to Africa, contrasts the attitude of high-caste, cultured Hindus toward the missionary with that of the primitive or barbarous peoples, where the missionary is admittedly one of a "superior" race. This docility of the "inferior" race is at once the missionary's opportunity and peril.

As an illustration of the diverse ways in which the animistic peoples approach Christianity, a speaker tells of one who became a Christian, moved at first by the desire to secure a decent burial for his body. All the speakers make vivid, however, what the gospel means to the animistic tribes—that it breaks for them the spell of terror and introduces them to a life which is a jubilee of liberty and joy.

From the animistic the conference goes with a leap to the problem of Chinese religions. There the life of the nation has been molded by ancestor-worship to a cohesion which has outlived the changes of 5,000 years; and Christianity, when it demands that a man surrender that, demands that he become an outlaw from his own nation.

Dong King-en, a Chinaman in picturesque, flowing native garb, urges the necessity of Christianity's making itself more indigenous to China by making its converts study their own language and literature. This theme—the necessity of Christianity's making its contact with a heathen people at such points as to insure its becoming an indigenous religion and not just an accidental importation—becomes the thesis of the day.

A striking contribution is made by Dr. K. Chatterji, a converted Hindu. With his patriarchal gray beard, a benign expression and a complexion which might be of the West, he states in beautiful and soft English what difficulties a Hindu experiences in becoming a Christian. He had long stumbled at the doctrine of Atonement. The Hindus have a vivid sense of punishment due each individual for his wrongdoing, and it is inconceivable to them that another should suffer for their sins. At a previous session a speaker had called for the preaching of the "old-fashioned gospel in the old-fashioned way." Dr. Chatterji gives the effective reply. He makes the conference realize the great harm done by unethical representations of the doctrine of the Atonement, and how pathetically missionaries are handicapped who do not appreciate the inner life of the people whose religion they wish to supplant.

Dr. Campbell Gibson, Presbyterian missionary to China, a master spirit in the conference, testifies to the responsiveness of the Chinese mind to spiritual truth. The Rev. Mr. Lloyd of Foochow gives it as his opinion that the idea of God as Father presented the most natural point of contact with the Chinese mind because filial piety was the highest of all the graces in China.

Dr. Mackichan, principal of the Wilson College, Bombay, emphasizes the importance of approaching the mind of India along the avenues of its own thought. This does not mean that they are to adapt the content of their message to suit Indian thought. Their philosophy is based on metaphysical thinking of the highest order, yet it has not reached a saving conclusion. They have had to tell the Indians that they sympathize with their failure, and that Christ satisfies their unfulfilled longings.

So the discussion runs on during the whole day. Probably forty persons speak. Yet Chairman Mott announces at the end that he had in his hand forty-two names which time would not permit him to call upon. Dr. Robert E. Speer is given fifteen minutes to make the closing speech, as vice-chairman of the commission. He fearlessly counsels the frankest comparison of Christianity with other religions. This because we are sure —absolutely sure—that such a comparison can result only in the enhancement of the glory of our holy faith.

Many other things are said. What I can write is but a sip of the overflowing cup of good things. The theme of Christian unity is running through the whole conference like a subterranean stream. It breaks through the ground of any subject the conference may be considering, and bubbles on the surface for a time. It is almost the exception for a speaker to sit down without deploring our divisions. The missionaries are literally plaintive in their appeal that the church of Christ reestablish her long lost unity. But tomorrow is to be given over to a discussion of the whole subject, and my heart thrills with expectancy and eagerness to hear the great words that I cannot doubt will surely be spoken.

And my first impulse, of course, will be to tell The Christian Century readers all about it.

September 24, 1925

The Conference at Stockholm

LYNN HAROLD HOUGH

"Christianity is the name of a number of different religions," says the cynic. And indeed there are times when the differences between the groups within the Christian Church seem quite as great as those which divide the groups outside. There are men who believe that Christianity is an immutable body of absolute truth. There are those who believe that Christianity is a growing and evolving organism. There are men who believe that Christianity is essentially a mystic fellowship of the soul with God. There are those who believe that Christianity is essentially a productive social passion. There are those who believe that Christianity is a lovely ritual, an organism of sacraments, the essential and perfect vehicle of the divine grace. There are those who believe that Christianity is essentially a voice, a flashing of inspired thought from mind to mind, a perpetuation of the fire of prophecy. Can these and all the others meet in some deep and understanding unity of spirit? Can the contradictions be forgotten in the presence of the living Lord? Can the many religious groups stand together as one religion in the face of the need of the world? The reply to all these questions is that in a measure at least all of these things have been done in this year of grace 1925 at the beautiful city of Stockholm, when seven hundred delegates from all about the world met to consider the problems of life and work which confront the Christian Church.

It was a gathering full of the pageantry which captures the eye. The stately processional in the cathedral, the brilliant reception by the king and the queen in the royal palace, the fairly glittering banquet when about twenty-five hundred people were guests of the city of Stockholm in the magnificent town hall—these and many another event gave a kind of purple richness to the conference. All that grace and dignity and graciousness could do to give the gathering a noble setting was done by the king, the people and the city. It was rather remarkable to see the crown prince at almost every session of the conference listening intently to all the addresses. The patriarchs from oriental churches gave a touch of remote and baffling color to the scene. And as the days wore on they seemed more and more at home with their brethren of the West. The requiem service in memory of the Russian patriarch Tikhon was a grave and memorable ritual set all about words of wise and gracious appreciation of a brave spirit.

The three languages used were English, French and German. In the case of many of the addresses copies in two of these languages were scattered through the assembly while the speaker used the third. In other cases a translator gave a brief summary. It was all done with great skill, and the daily paper *Life and Work* kept the delegates in close contact with every detail of the program. Reports of commissions which had been considering the great themes of the conference were ready for the perusal of all.

If you looked out from the speakers' platform, to the right sat a group of Germans. At the front were the Orientals. Back of them from right to left were the Americans and the British, and to the far left the French and other Europeans. The galleries held spectators whose forms, leaning forward, would indicate moments of tense interest and dramatic quality.

Such moments indeed there were. To be sure, matters of Faith and Order were carefully ruled out, but every question regarding the practical application of Christianity came in for frank and free discussion. And there was no attempt to disguise those disagreements which emerged as the discussions wore on. God's purposes for the world, economic and industrial problems, social and moral problems, international relations, Christian education and plans and methods of co-operation were all discussed from almost every conceivable point of view. At the king's formal opening of the conference in the royal palace there was a hint of the fashion in which varied attitudes were meeting. His Majesty in a few wise and thoughtful words had opened the assembly. The patriarch and pope of Alexandria in a brief address in graceful French quoted the apostle Peter as placing the king in the world "first after God" (la première place après Dieu). It was rather a relief when Dr. Brown followed with words of appreciation for "Your Majesty's welcome on behalf of the people of Sweden." No finer act of courtesy characterized the whole gathering than the sentence in the Lord Bishop of Winchester's address to the king: "We represent the free churches, the Presbyterian churches and the Anglican communion both in Britain and in the various parts of our empire." That placing of the free churches first by an Anglican prelate will not be forgotten. And here it must be said that the opening sermon by the Bishop of Winchester in the cathedral was a noble and fearless call for that deep and fruitful change of mind which would enable the church to face its responsibilities in the world.

From the first address by "Seine Magnifizenz der Landes-bischof von Sachsen" (Dr. Ihmels) it was evident that the German delegation represented what to the Anglo-Saxon groups was a strange and baffling point of view. There was moral vigor and spiritual depth, and often the very greatest intellectual subtlety and dialectical ability in these German addresses. But the sense of social Christianity as men have dreamed of it and worked for it in England and America since the days of Maurice and Kingsley, of Josiah Strong and Walter Rauschenbusch was entirely absent. It was as if the original inwardness of the Lutheran position, driven to even profounder depths by the pain and passion and tragedy following the war, had become the defining element of the Christian faith to these men and women. They could speak with astounding insight of the life within. They stood with what seemed at times a bitterly cynical anger in the presence of the sanctions of an interpretation essentially social. That the sword had deeply entered their souls was evident enough. Even when a gallant Frenchman with a gift for the sort of passionate oratory which reaches the heart stretched his hands toward the German group and cried,

"We want to love you," there was not a movement of applause from the Teutonic section. Now and then a flaming word torn from the heart of some German speaker revealed the intenseness of his loyalty to the lost cause, and one began to understand a little the temper which in extreme cases believes that the whole matter of the rights and wrongs of the war must yet be investigated but that only Germans possess the scientific qualities of mind necessary for an adequate investigation.

That there was a minority in the German delegation we learned to be true, but the delegation always acted as a unit and the minority did not find a voice. But the spiritual temper of the conference was such that it was not anger which this group aroused. Even the one tense moment, when a speaker authoritatively stated that if certain things were done the German delegation must leave the conference, passed safely. The psychology of a defeated nation is always a tale of sad and baffled inward turning, and the conference never forgot that these men and women, so many of them with somber faces and all of them with such sad and bitter and baffled thoughts, were brothers and sisters who must receive the fullest consideration, the most gracious and understanding sympathy. Perhaps some members of the English group went farthest in the attempt to enter into the very meaning of the experience of the German group. And in individual cases there resulted a deep and hearty fellowship full of promise for the future.

The French group was characterized by a bright and winged clarity of speech. There was often a sympathy for groups outside the immediate circle of organized Christianity which expressed itself with an almost lyric eagerness. Oratory of a very high and authentic quality characterized some of the French utterances. But all the while in the background there was a lurking fear, a sense of the need of "security," a sense of living where earthquakes shake the ground, which made one feel how full of danger is a future built upon the life of peoples in whose hearts anxious suspicion dwells. One evening at Skansen a distinguished member of the French delegation dined with a little group of us. As we looked out over the water with the fascination of gay bright lights playing upon our eyes, he talked with complete and disarming frankness. He admitted the presence of a military group in France. It was evident that with his simple and sincere purpose of good will this was a party to be repudiated. But all the while we felt that the word "security" was a deep and abiding watchword with him. World-wide good will? Yes, surely. But first of all security for torn and bleeding France. One went back to the great conference thinking deep and serious thoughts. How can these suspicions be quieted? How can peace really be brought to the minds and hearts of men?

The British group carried itself with great urbanity. There was constant intercourse between its leaders and members of the American group. It became clear that the great debt which the British are facing so heroically was weighing most heavily upon the men who were so ready to meet as intimate friends their American associates. Perhaps it would be putting the matter too strongly to say that there was an unexpressed bitterness. But one did come to the end of long and intimate conversations with the feeling that there are matters of fact which need most careful consideration as we come to the heartiest understanding with our British friends. Once and again the statement was made, in groups which were discussing these matters informally, that the whole amount borrowed by Britain from the United States had been used not by Britain but by her allies, so that the debt under which she is staggering is entirely a debt incurred for other nations. If my memory serves me, this is essentially the statement made by Lord Balfour a little while ago and almost summarily contradicted by a high official at Washington. It ought not to be too hard to get at the facts, and no one would welcome them, in whichever direction they weigh, more than our British friends.

Of course all this is incidental in respect of the larger matter that no British Christian leader really understands the aloofness of the United States in an hour when the world is staggering under an almost unbearable burden, and when the matter is put in this fashion the memory that Britain adopted just such an attitude of aloofness after the Napoleonic wars does not really constitute a defense of our position. Whatever can be

said from the standpoint of the give-and-take of cool and cynical diplomacy, it can scarcely be urged that at this point we
are on Christian ground. But these things cannot be said in
any deep way to have interfered with the fellowship of British
and American delegates. No end of the most intimate sort of
friendships cross lines which separate the English-speaking peoples. Personally I was never happier at Stockholm than when
off for a walk with some English friend, and the very proof of
the depth and reality of the friendship was that it stood the
test of the frankest sort of talk.

In the conference itself differences of position between the
groups of delegates of various communions and nations came
to sharp expression, oddly enough first in respect of the matter
of birth control. It was an American who in a keen and passionate address threw down the gauntlet in favor of this reform. And there was something strangely naïve about the reply
of the lady from Germany who with obvious and hearty sincerity declared that girls should be brought up to think of
bringing children into the world with joyous anticipation and
to trust the good Lord for the future of the children when
they had come. It is to be feared that the wife of a drunkard
looking forward to another arrival in a home already bitterly
pinched by poverty would not find much comfort in these glowing words.

The second matter of open difference had to do with prohibition. And here one must refer to the strange and difficult
address of Lord Salveson. As a distinguished jurist, as a representative of that British fair play which is colloquially expressed
in the splendid word "cricket," one felt that one had a right
to expect not only the frank and honest expression of the attitude of a man who did not believe in prohibition, but a certain noble courtesy toward those whose position he was attacking, and a certain special care not to misstate their attitude
or any matters with respect to their action. Very reluctantly one
is driven to say that his address was an expression of tempera-
ment rather than the statement of a poised and careful mind,
and that his misstatements in respect of matters of fact were
particularly baffling in a man who holds the high and demand-

ing position of a judge. It is not strange that a group of Americans issued a protest not against his lordship's position but in respect of the misstatements which his address contained.

In respect of the matter of the attitude of the church toward war there was of course a deep and honest difference of opinion. And there was a clear and unhesitating expression of this difference. The hatred of war was definite and perhaps one may say universal. But opinion varied from the absolutist position to the view that war is a necessity in the present situation in the life of the world. The very discussion, however, cleared the air and the net result was surely to give propulsion to all those forces set in battle array against war itself.

The really remarkable thing about the conference was just that with these and other differences of opinion fellowship was never broken. The message sent out at last was inevitably a sort of "common for all" which by no means reflects the moral and spiritual altitudes reached by the conference. The message represents a point from which we will move forward. The noblest individual utterances represent the heights to which we must climb.

The sense of the underprivileged, of the lot of the poor, of the need of social and economic readjustment, of the yeast moving with insurgent power in the life of youth, of the physical basis for full living in adequate housing, of the necessity of steady employment and at a wage which leaves a margin for recreation and culture, the sense of the world as an organism and the commanding hope of humanity as a vast fraternity of good will—a league of friendly minds—moved in and out of the thought of the conference, found a place in its conscience, and at last for many became a shining and alluring ideal to whose realization there must be given a supreme consecration and a passionate loyalty.

Individual men made superb contributions. The Archbishop of Upsala was indefatigable in his labors. Dr. Henry Atkinson embodied the genius of efficient organization and hearty good will. Dr. Adams Brown was a quiet influence making for amity between international groups. Bishop Brent struck a deep chord which vibrated through the whole conference. Principal

Garvie was all the while touching varied groups with a kindly intellectual sympathy which had its own secrets of power. Dr. Worth Tippy made his influence felt in a far-reaching way in the consideration of economic problems in committee and before the conference. Pasteur Wilfred Monod put a passionate social and religious sympathy into the very heart of the conference at its beginning. Men like Dr. S. Parkes Cadman and Dean Shailer Mathews made their presence and influence felt in manifold ways. And so one might go on and on.

The informal meeting of groups which crossed the national lines was one of the happiest features of the conference. And the presence of capable and able religious journalists like Mr. Porritt of the *Christian World* and Dr. Lynch of *Christian Work*, and of understanding interpreters like Edward Shillito of London, who is to edit the volume which will report the conference, meant an enriching of the life of the gathering as well as a profoundly understanding setting forth of its activities through the religious press.

Of course there were some personal actions which one is sorry to remember. The American who wrote to Stockholm suggesting that he be entertained by the crown prince scarcely represented our best tradition. But altogether the gathering was swept by too large a purpose and too noble a passion for the frequent emergence of these unlovely personal attitudes. Sometimes a moment of lofty intellectual perspective was reached, as when Dr. Carnegie Simpson brought the discipline of a highly articulated mind to the analysis of the meaning of personality. So in informal discussion, in public address and debate, in the work of committee and commission, the delegates met together day after day. And all the while the meaning of a Christendom organized for justice and fraternity, for the piety which enfranchises the individual and liberates society, was unfolding before their eyes. Men at the conference often thought and spoke of Nicaea. It is not impossible that in a millennium and a half men may think and speak of Stockholm.

September 22, 1927

The Rapprochement of the Churches

PETER AINSLIE

The Lausanne Conference was the opening door toward wider Christian fellowship. It registered the fact that there is a movement in the whole church for the unity of Christendom which the love of our separate communions will not be able to suppress. We appear to have gone the limit in our divisions. Any other divisions in the church will likely be of minor consequence. The tide has definitely turned toward unity. The Lausanne conference had two main roots—one in the World Missionary Conference in Edinburgh in the spring of 1910, which revealed how widely on the foreign missionary fields the spirit of federation and unity was operating, and the other in the General Convention of the Protestant Episcopal Church in the fall of 1910, which called for a commission on a world conference on Faith and Order, having to do with the whole church, at home and abroad. Other communions in America, notably the Disciples and Congregationalists, took similar action in their general conventions at the same time, as did the Eastern Orthodox in their general synod in Constantinople.

During these seventeen years the churches began to rephrase their thinking and slowly to readjust their attitudes. The Protestant Episcopal Church organized an interdenominational commission, which made approaches practically to the whole church. Most of the non-Roman Catholic communions, representing about one-half of the Christian world, responded by the appointment of commissions to co-operate in preparation for the conference. The Roman Catholic half declined co-operation, to our regret, but the pope has taken a friendly interest, and Roman Catholic publications have recently had many articles bearing on unity. Two of their priests—one from Austria and the other from Breslau—sat throughout the conference as unofficial observers.

Such a conference is at once entangled with difficulties. To begin with, there are the linguistic barriers. Translations do not always convey the same meaning. Then there are the results of denominational isolation, by which traditional impressions have been handed down from generation to generation without revision, so that a person of one communion thinks of a person of another communion as being something which he is not. Denominationalism sets up hard and fast prejudices and creates an unbrotherly atmosphere through which it is difficult to discover that which is real in others.

All denominationalism, whether Eastern Orthodox, Roman Catholic, Anglican or Protestant, has about it an unwholesome atmosphere, not Christian at all but pagan, especially where there is sharp isolation such as has obtained between many of the Christian communions. In the conference the Eastern Orthodox delegates explicitly claimed infallibility for their church, and a like claim of infallibility was more or less present in the minds of many delegates of other churches. At the same time it is well to remember that all the churches are under the ban of excommunication. The Eastern Orthodox excommunicated the Roman Catholics; the Roman Catholics excommunicated the Eastern Orthodox and, a few hundred years later, the Protestants and Anglicans; and these, in turn, continued the same policy of excommunication, until today every communion is under the ban—either it went out on the threat of excommunication, or was put out. This, of course, would be childish if it were not so tragic. It reveals how completely the church has been ruled by the pride and opinion of men rather than by the Holy Spirit.

Up to this time there has been little indication of penitence on the part either of the excommunicator or the excommunicated. Out of all this historical tangle and the scramble for orthodoxy, infallibility and spiritual superiority there was, of course, not much place for humility and penitence. The distinctive denominational claims of all—catholic and protestant

—have grown less spiritual with the years and therefore more foreign to the religion of Christ, so that the world has judged the religion thus set forth as in large part fictitious, and from it the multitudes are slowly turning away.

The Lausanne conference came at an opportune time. Both the church and the world are weary—the church weary in its unnatural and unspiritual struggle, the world weary for God whom the church has eclipsed with its denominational rivalries. Inevitably the past would project itself into the conference—too much so—but it was unavoidable with groups as conservative as were the delegations from so many churches. They were mostly officials, sensitive to upholding the communions from which they came. There was a marked concern for the institution at home, which our forebears founded and which we are still building. It is not too much to say that most of the delegates who spoke looked backward. However, in their back-gate look there was usually a tolerance and forbearance, sometimes a pathos, all of which indicated that vast changes were already under way.

The personnel of the conference was of unusual interest. There were representatives from all the continents and from many of the islands of the sea—England, Scotland, Wales, Ireland, Norway, Sweden, Denmark, Holland, Belgium, France, Germany, Switzerland, Poland, Russia, Romania, Bulgaria, Serbia, Hungary, Czechoslovakia, Estonia, Latvia, Slovakia, Greece, Armenia, Egypt, South Africa, Australia, New Zealand, Tasmania, India, China, Japan, South America, Canada, United States and elsewhere. There were patriarchs from Jerusalem, Antioch and Alexandria; archbishops from the Eastern Orthodox, Anglican and Lutheran communions; bishops from these communions and from the Old Catholics, Methodists and Moravians; members of the supreme courts of Germany and Scotland; deans, canons, professors, executives, editors, ministers, priests, missionaries—and seven women! It was a fine company of Christian people, many of whom had traveled thousands of miles to confer on the great task of a united Christendom.

The mere fact of such a conference was a vast achievement.

The addresses revealed the depth of earnestness in the hearts of the delegates as they sat through the sessions from the beginning to the close. A wide variety of views crowded every day's discussion, but a most commendable spirit prevailed. This was due largely to the chairman, Bishop Charles H. Brent, and to the deputy chairman, Dr. A. E. Garvie. With three languages—English, German and French—as channels of expression in every session and with traditional misunderstandings and sectarian prejudices, there would be, of necessity, some critical moments, but the chairmen always so wisely steered the conference out of troubled waters that those instances which did occur were of trifling consequence by the side of the spirit of gracious fellowship which pervaded the delegates both in the conference sessions and in the university halls and hotel lobbies. All these experiences tend to make friendships, and friendship, after all, is the highway to a united church.

Bishop Brent's opening sermon in the cathedral was the call of a prophet. He was calm and courageous, but, out of several hundred speakers, perhaps not more than two dozen followed in his prophetic path. He was not afraid to say that "the hundred missionary societies in China today are as suicidal for Christianity as the civil divisions are to the national peace and prosperity." Missionary appeals are losing their power through our sectarianism, being resented by the natives among whom missionaries work and, at home, falling upon the indifferent ears of a denominational church. It is far more important to the cause of Christianity that the missionary boards in the homelands should get together and form definite plans for co-operation than to encourage the growing protest from the foreign missionary fields against imposing upon them a denominational Christianity. A few men on missionary boards would lose their positions by taking such a stand, but they would hasten the unity of the church and the conversion of the world. Which is more important?

The conference discussions divided into six subjects, each being considered for an entire day, beginning with two thirty-minute addresses, followed by four or five fifteen- and ten-minute addresses, and the rest of the day being given to open discussion. The subjects were: "The Church's Message to the World—the Gospel," "The Nature of the Church," "The Church's Common Confession of Faith," "The Church's Ministry," "The Church's Sacraments" and "The Unity of Christendom and the Relation Thereto of Existing Churches." Then the conference was divided into small groups of twenty or twenty-five, so that everyone had an opportunity to contribute to the discussion, which enriched the findings that came out of these discussions, representing, as far as possible, the general mind of the gathering. These findings were received and will be sent to the various churches represented. Upon the action of the churches the continuation committee will consider plans for another conference, for Lausanne is only the beginning. As to how many conferences will be necessary, that depends upon how fast the churches travel toward unity.

The report on the church's message was received with the support of the whole conference. The Eastern Orthodox delegation asked to be excused from voting on the other reports; but they heartily supported this one, which affirmed that the message of the church to the world must always remain the gospel of Jesus Christ—the gift of a new word from God to this old world of sin and death, being the prophetic call to sinful men to turn to God as the only way by which humanity can escape from those class and race hatreds which devastate society, and fulfill humanity's longing for intellectual sincerity, social justice and spiritual inspiration.

The report on the nature of the church was a little more difficult. It affirmed that the church is constituted by the will of God, not by the will or consent or beliefs of men, whether as individuals or societies. God is its creator, Jesus Christ its head and the Holy Spirit the source of its continuous life. The church is the communion of true believers in Christ Jesus, according to the New Testament, built upon the foundation of apostles and prophets, Jesus Christ himself being the chief cornerstone. Recognizing various views as to the nature of the church, the report expressed sorrow in consequence of our divisions and urged the unity of the church.

The report on the church's common confession of faith

brought to the front the creedal controversy. The majority of the communions represented hold to the Nicene and Apostles' creeds; others, such as Baptists, Congregationalists and Disciples, recognize these as witnesses in past generations, but do not hold them in the same reverence, emphasizing instead a personal faith in the living God through the living Christ. The report sought, with much difficulty, to cover both of these positions, recognizing, as it affirmed, that the creeds are our common heritage from the ancient church and, at the same time, leaving on record the unanimous testimony that no external and written standards can suffice without an inward and personal experience of union with God in Christ.

The report on the ministry was one of the longest of all the reports. It affirmed that the ministry is a gift of God through Christ to his church, and is essential to the being and well-being of the church, that men gifted for the work of the ministry, called by the Spirit and accepted by the church, are commissioned through an act of ordination by prayer and the laying on of hands. Various forms of ministry have grown up according to the circumstances of the several communions and their beliefs as to the mind of Christ and the guidance of the New Testament. These have been abundantly used by the Holy Spirit, but the differences which have arisen in regard to the authority and function of these various forms of ministry have been and are the occasion of manifold doubts, questions and misunderstandings to the distress and wounding of faithful souls. Consequently the provision of a ministry, acknowledged in every part of the church as possessing the sanction of the whole church, is an urgent need. The episcopal, presbyterial and congregational systems, being believed by many to be essential to the good order of the church, must have an appropriate place in the order of the reunited church. Each communion, recalling the abundant blessing of God vouchsafed to its ministry, should gladly bring to the common life of the united church its own spiritual treasures.

In the report on the sacraments it was agreed that they are of divine appointment and that the church ought thankfully to observe them as divine gifts, baptism being administered with water in the name of the Father, the Son and the Holy Spirit, for the remission of sins, not ignoring the difference in conception, interpretation and mode which exists among us, and the holy communion being the church's most sacred act of worship, in which the Lord's atoning death is commemorated and proclaimed. The report closed with a prayer that the differences which prevent full communion at the present time may be removed.

The report on the unity of Christendom and the relation of existing churches thereto was severely and unnecessarily attacked; nevertheless, it was a most satisfactory report, being divided into four sections: (1) fellowship in Life and Work, as expressed in the Stockholm conference of 1925; (2) fellowship in Faith and Order, as expressed in the Lausanne conference; (3) ways of approach emphasizing appreciation of each other, prayer for one another and working together; (4) completed fellowship, which would be realized by all God's children joining in communion at the Lord's table, closing with the prayer that God would give us wisdom and courage to do his will.

It was an admirable report with which to close the conference—cautious, practical and hopeful. It was prepared chiefly by the Archbishop of Upsala and the Archbishop of Armagh and reviewed by Bishop Brent, the Bishop of Gloucester, Canon Tatlow and others. It ought to have passed with an enthusiastic vote. Inasmuch as all the findings had to pass the conference unanimously, this report was referred to the continuation committee. It furnished another instance of a sectarian outburst, which must be expected so long as sectarian attitudes hold priority over penitence in a divided church. In this instance the protest came from the Anglo-Catholics. It might have come from any other, for many Christians regulate their interest in Christian unity upon whether it comes their way. The Anglo-Catholics are not alone in this by any means, but their cause was greatly discounted by such an unreasonable protest, which looked as if it was the last chance, coming at the close of the conference, and they wanted to make use of that chance.

But the results of the conference exceeded the expectation of many. It is a great advance when men who differ widely can sit down together and discuss frankly and patiently their differences and arise with understanding and appreciation, if not agreements. This was the victory of Lausanne.

It would have been a still greater victory if the conference could have closed with the celebration of the Lord's Supper. It really lacked that seal of fellowship. And the fact that it could not be done left an ugly picture. But it could not be done, showing us how far we are from possessing the badge of Christian discipleship, which is love. Long ago for love the church substituted orthodoxy, which is very much less expensive. The council of Nicaea, in 325 A.D., confirmed the transfer. Orthodoxy is a word, however, which no dictionary can define, there being several hundred meanings, depending upon which communion one is a member of.

Out of this confusion has come sectarianism, which is the affirmation by one particular communion that it is right and all the others are wrong. It is common for the episcopal communions, such as the Eastern Orthodox, Roman Catholic and Anglican, to speak of themselves as the "church" and all the other communions as the "sects" or the milder term "denominations," which means the same thing. A somewhat similar position is taken by several Protestant communions. To affirm that the Roman Catholics or Anglicans are *the* church and that Presbyterians and Methodists are sects—that is to say, spiritually inferior to them, and outside of *the* church; or that one of the Protestant communions is *the* church and the Roman Catholics and Anglicans are sects, belongs in the same small business of excommunication. It shows how completely the pride and opinion of men, rather than the Holy Spirit, rule in the consciousness of Christian people. Would that all communions might stress penitence, rather than pride!

Lausanne marked the passing of uniformity and the coming of diversity within unity. Rebaptism and reordination must gradually fade out in any plan for unity. The equality of all Christians before God must find its embodiment in the ecclesiastical order. The next conference will go beyond this conference. If there could be a conference without officially appointed delegates and constituted of younger groups, the interpretations would go far in advance of our denominational conservatism. There is room in these times for adventurers, and the adventurers will come.

May 10, 1928

Beginning at Jerusalem

SAMUEL McCREA CAVERT

No one could have attended the meeting of the International Missionary Council at Jerusalem during the two weeks ending on Easter Day without discerning that momentous changes are taking place in foreign missions. To one whose eyes are riveted on the past or even on the present these changes may seem confusing; to one who looks down the future they must appear to be fraught with the richest promise. For him ceaseless change is no occasion for alarm but an evidence of vitality. Misgiving would rather be in order if missions remained static, uninfluenced by the new currents of life and thought that are flowing through the world.

For one thing, the Jerusalem meeting made it clear that the missionary enterprise is coming to be not something that we do for other peoples but something that we do with them. Gone was the note of condescending superiority.

As one sat day by day with great personalities from China, Japan, India, Africa, South America and other quarters of the earth, one realized that the final meaning of the missionary movement is the development of a world-wide fellowship in which every race will make its own indispensable contribution to the building of a Christian world. It was a high-water mark in the history of foreign missions when the council declared that the churches of the West need to receive Christian missionaries as well as send them.

In the second place, there was manifest at the Jerusalem meeting a greater desire to understand other religions sympathetically and to appreciate the things that high-minded non-Christians live by. Prior to the meeting a series of stimulating papers had been prepared by competent scholars, setting forth the values in Islam, in Hinduism, in Buddhism and in Confucianism. Criticism of some of the papers was heard on the ground that they were too extravagantly favorable in their estimate of non-Christian faiths, but the very fact that such an impression could be made shows how far missionary thinking has advanced since the days when all religions except Christianity were regarded as evil. At one point at least it was agreed at Jerusalem that other religions can be regarded as allies of Christianity quite as truly as rivals; for a new enemy of all religion, Christian or non-Christian alike, was recognized in the materialism now rampant in all lands. In the face of sheer secularism and atheism all religions, however inadequate as a final fulfillment of the quest of the soul, are at any rate an assertion of spiritual realities and of the value of those things which are unseen and eternal.

Joined with this new attitude of glad appreciation of non-Christian religions was an unshakable assurance of the uniqueness and universality of Jesus Christ. Indeed it was felt that the more clearly one discerns the value in other faiths, the more certainly will it be seen that Christ is the one overtowering personality in whom all those values, found elsewhere in partial and fragmentary form, come to such complete realization as to make him the Lord and Savior of all mankind. The message frankly admitted that in the past the missionary movement had not "sufficiently sought out the good and noble elements in the non-Christian beliefs," and in a generous spirit went on to call attention to some of the worthy things in non-Christian systems.

In the third place, the Jerusalem meeting furnished us most encouraging evidence that the Christianizing of our social relationships is coming to be regarded not as a mere by-product but as part and parcel of the missionary task. "Winning the world for Christ" was no longer synonymous with occupying all geographical areas with missions and churches; that there are vast unevangelized regions was beyond all dispute, but the missionary responsibility was equally seen to mean the bringing of all areas of human activity and social life under the sway of Christ. In thinking of medical missions, the emphasis was not upon the hospital as opening up channels for evangelism. Caring for the bodies of men was rather regarded as in itself a spiritual ministry, as in itself a form of Christian witness, revealing the spirit of Christ and indicating what a Christian society is like. No longer were "souls" thought of as entities that could be saved apart from their social environment. Man was treated as a unity, with his spiritual life related to all his surrounding conditions. Easily three-quarters of the agenda, as a result, was directly occupied with great social and international issues which found no more than incidental mention at even so recent a missionary gathering as the great world conference held in Edinburgh in 1910!

At Edinburgh who thought of economic and industrial problems as of more than peripheral interest to missions? At Jerusalem no topic was more prominent. At Edinburgh few perceived how close to the marrow of the missionary movement is the substitution of interracial understanding and good will for the prevailing prejudices and discriminations. At Jerusalem no one could get far away from this overshadowing concern. At Edinburgh it would have been regarded as a side issue to study the organization of the rural community. At Jerusalem even rather technical phases of the problem were of such urgency that a detailed survey had been made of rural life in one oriental country, Korea, and the council declared that "experts" on rural life must be included on missionary staffs. At Edinburgh the strongest accent was on evangelism; at Jerusalem the ideal was the same but a new emphasis had entered in, an emphasis on religious education as the great means for effecting the transformation both of personal character and of social life which the gospel demands.

In the discussion of industrial problems, the enlarging horizon of missions was disclosed most luminously. The report on this subject frankly acknowledged that "the missionary enterprise, coming as it does out of an economic order dominated almost entirely by the profit motive," has not been "so sensitive to those aspects of the Christian message as would have been necessary sensibly to mitigate the evils which advancing industrialization has brought in its train," and then proceeded to scrutinize mercilessly the exploitation of backward peoples as the result of the economic penetration of Africa and Asia by the West. Public loans for the development of undeveloped areas, it was declared, "should be made only with the knowledge and approval of a properly constituted international authority and subject to such conditions as it may prescribe," and "private investments should in no case carry with them the right of political control." (Somebody please page Nicaragua!) Concrete attention was given to the protection of the more primitive races from forced labor, the alienation of their land and other economic injustices. A set of industrial standards which missions should hold up before governments in their dealing with so-called backward peoples was adopted, paralleling in many ways the "social creed" of the American churches.

In order to make certain that such statements as these should have more than ephemeral significance, it was proposed that the International Missionary Council should establish, as a part of its organization, a "bureau of social and economic research and information" on problems arising from the contact between Western civilization and undeveloped countries. This plan for helping mission agencies to be more competent to meet the terrific problems confronting the peoples for whom the missionaries work was adopted only after warm debate, and not with entire unanimity. One member of the council was heard to remark to his neighbor, "If this is the kind of program that missionary councils are interested in, we had better withdraw from them and devote ourselves to spiritual work!" The fact that the proposal for a research bureau was definitely approved, subject to concurrence by the National Christian Councils of the various countries, is a noteworthy indication of progress.

In facing the baffling issues involved in the contacts between the races the council was relentlessly candid and honest, but the final report was somewhat disappointing to those who had hoped that the marvelous fellowship between the races throughout the fortnight on the Mount of Olives might eventuate in an epoch-making declaration. To be sure, there were many admirable statements confessing how far short the churches have fallen from measuring up to the Christian ideal and calling for equal treatment of all races in policies having to do with immigration, citizenship and economic opportunity. But the general effect was marred by the disposition of a handful of delegates to infer that intermarriage might somehow be implied in every reference to "social equality." As a matter of fact, no statement on intermarriage was at any time put before the council, but a sudden cautiousness laid hold of some of the white members at the point where the proposed report said:

In lands where the races live side by side the fullest participation of all in racial intermingling for social, cultural and above all religious fellowship, and the development of friendship which such intercourse engenders, is the natural expression of our common Christianity.

Even though the statement was not substantially modified as the result of the debate, one could not help feeling in some of the discussions an atmosphere too suggestive of half-hearted compromise. One member was heard to make the comment in private conversation that a favorable reference to anything that could be called "social equality" would cost his mission board $100,000. But surely the Christian cause would have derived an incalculable gain if, at the loss of even millions of dollars, it were to bring about a day when the bogey of intermarriage could no longer serve as an excuse for perpetuating our unjust social discrimination against our colored brothers.

In international affairs it was the question of using military or naval forces to protect missionaries that occupied the center of attention. It must be added that the interest in this issue, so far as the mission boards were concerned, seemed confined chiefly to the Americans, but they were re-enforced by the Orientals and the missionaries. An outspoken resolution which had been drafted, designed to put the council unequivocally on record as opposing any resort to military protection, was effectively shelved for a time by the protest of British delegates that their agencies had not yet given any consideration to the matter. Indeed, the council was on the very point of final adjournment without having taken any positive action. This eleventh hour sidetracking was prevented by the insistence of one American member. It is only simple justice to mention his name; it was Bishop Francis J. McConnell. E. Stanley Jones, of India, followed him by declaring: "If no action is taken on this matter, much of the rest of what we have said and done will be rendered fruitless." After the issue was thus squarely reopened, just as the clock was striking midnight and ushering in Easter Day, a clear-cut resolution was adopted which said, in part:

Inasmuch as the use or the threat of use of armed forces by the country from which they come for the protection of the missionary and missionary property not only creates widespread misunderstanding as to the underlying motive of missionary work, but also gravely hinders the acceptance of the Christian message, the International Missionary Council (1) places on record its conviction that the protection of missionaries should only be by such methods as will promote good will in personal and official relations and (2) urges on all missionary societies that they make no claim on their governments for the armed defense of their missionaries and their property.

From all the addresses and discussions, reports and resolutions of the two weeks' gathering one comes back with two impressions that overtop everything else like mountain peaks among low-lying ridges.

The first is the glorious realization that there exists today a Christian movement which has become really conscious of its world-wide character and able to function as a world-wide unit. To point out conditions that limit this universal fellowship would be easy—as, for example, the fact that the ancient Orthodox churches of the Near East are not included in it. In that respect, Stockholm and Lausanne were ahead of Jerusalem. Still, it remains true that in the International Missionary Council we have the most definitely organized and articulate world organization of Christian forces today. United in it, under its new constitution adopted at Jerusalem and under the far-seeing chairmanship of Dr. John R. Mott, are not only all the Protestant missionary forces of the West, but also the National Christian Councils which in recent years have come into being in China, Japan, India and many other parts of what is commonly called the missionary field. To have achieved even this measure of unity across our divisive national boundaries is a notable achievement for which no thoughtful person who feels deeply the inadequacies of a merely national Christianity can be too thankful. One hopes it may be a prophecy of an international council of churches which may soon bind together the total life and work of the churches throughout the world.

The second outstanding impression that one carries away from Jerusalem is the spiritual greatness and power of the foreign missionary movement. All the criticisms of it are dwarfed into pettiness in comparison with the majestic moral meaning of this enterprise of building a Christian world. The closing paragraph of the message adopted by the council is one that will long abide in the memory of those who were at Jerusalem and truly expresses the call which they heard to a fresh and courageous commitment to the world-wide cause of Christ:

We are persuaded that we and all Christian people must seek a more heroic practice of the gospel. It cannot be that our present complacency and moderation are a faithful expression of the mind of Christ and of the meaning of his cross in the midst of the wrong and want and sin of our modern world. As we contemplate the work which Christ has laid upon his church, we who are met here on the Mount of Olives, in sight of Calvary, would take up for ourselves and summon those from whom we come, and to whom we return, to take up with us the cross of Christ, and all that for which it stands, and to go forth into the world to live in the fellowship of his sufferings and by the power of his resurrection.

August 18, 1937

The Church Faces Its World
WINFRED ERNEST GARRISON

Oxford, July 27

At such a gathering as the World Conference on Church, Community and State—the title currently used almost to the exclusion of "Life and Work"—in such a place as Oxford, it requires a little time for the mid-American participant, even if he is not unfamiliar with the scene, to adjust his mind to the serious and urgent issues of the conference. Oxford always works magic on any visitor who is worthy of the privilege of being a visitor. Its beauty and its history conspire to weave a spell. And the personnel of the conference, though mostly clad in the common garments of international commerce and convention, has its sartorial highlights—Eastern Orthodox archbishops with flowing robes and patriarchal beards, Russian priests with towering headdresses, Anglican bishops in aprons and gaiters, Lutheran bishops who wear their gowns and pectoral crosses even at the breakfast table. It is well to have these visible symbols of the variety of cultures within the one church. They reveal the problem of making it effectively one as at once more difficult and more significant than it appears in a conference among those who wear identical clothes, have their hair cut in the same style and speak the same language.

Diversities of language are indeed a serious hindrance to mutual understanding. English, French and German were the official languages of the conference, and the interpreters were wonderfully competent in both translation and condensation. But a two-minute translation of a ten-minute speech comes under suspicion of incompleteness. The explanation that "we translate only the ideas, not all the words" is sometimes but not always adequate. Seldom was a speaker who understood the three languages quite satisfied with the version of his speech in the other two. But we must continue to pay for the presumption of the builders of Babel.

Languages may diverge in discussion, but they converge in worship. The services of devotion, held morning and evening in St. Mary's Church, have been a vital factor in the conference. There the *Una Sancta* becomes a reality. The three languages are used in rotation, without translation or the need of it. Even the Russian choir spoke intelligibly to all, though in an unknown tongue. In prayer and hymn the miracle of Pentecost is repeated, and each hears in the language in which he was born.

The range of concrete materials with which the conference deals is suggested by the titles of the five sections into which the delegates were divided for simultaneous sessions of intensive discussion: "The Church and the Community" (meaning by "community" what the Germans mean by *Volk*, society in its larger units viewed with reference to its cultural and racial coherence rather than its political organization); "Church and State"; "The Church and the Economic Order"; "Church, Community and State in Relation to Education"; "The Universal Church and the World of Nations." It is evident that these comprehensive categories could easily cover discussions and pronouncements upon every phase of the church's function and responsibility in relation to the modern world. They were indeed intended to do no less. It is equally evident that the treatment of these topics could not proceed without some critical scrutiny both of the social facts and of the past and present behavior of the church in relation to those facts as well as of the secular powers in relation to the church.

This is a very large order, even for four hundred learned delegates assisted by an equal number of no less learned associates, having the advantage of careful preliminary studies and giving undivided attention to the problems for a period of two weeks in the congenially contemplative atmosphere of Oxford. The difficulty of mobilizing the intellectual resources of such an assembly is very great. A new U. S. Congress does not get much done in the first two weeks, even with the advantages of a continuing organization, a body of guiding precedent, a fairly general mutual acquaintance and a single language. To ask the members of an ecumenical conference to give, within a fortnight, a diagnosis of the world's ills, an evaluation of the church's previous and present efforts to cure them, a statement of the rights and duties of the church in relation to political and cultural organizations, and a prospectus for future action which will satisfy the legitimate claims of both and promote the welfare of all mankind—that seems to be asking the impossible. Yet something like that was what was asked of the Oxford Conference; and something like that, it may be said subject to certain limitations, is what the conference accomplished. At least it made significant advance in that direction.

No achievement whatever would have been possible without the careful groundwork that had been done in advance—largely by Dr. Oldham, Dr. Shillito, Mr. Henriod and, for the American section, Dr. Leiper, and their colleagues too numerous to name—and without the technique of procedure that was chiefly in the hands of Dr. Mott. The preparatory work made possible findings which were studies rather than improvisations. The technique of the conference, while it had some steam-roller qualities, gave the maximum opportunity for the expression of the widest variety of opinions, kept the business moving and brought the discussions within the necessary limits of time. Doubtless many a delegate is leaving Oxford with undelivered speeches curdling within him. Doubtless most of these would have been good speeches. But let those who thought the chairman cruel remember the U. S. Senate and reflect upon the horrors of unlimited debate.

The complexity of the problem faced by the conference is not fully stated when mention has been made of the range and magnitude of its topics. There is the added fact that to every important question there were two contrasting lines of approach. They may be called the dogmatic and the pragmatic; or the *a priori* and the empirical; or the theological and the sociological; or, as one speaker defined them, a dogmatism which makes an absolute separation between the world and God and refuses to let the church be held responsible for anything that happens in the world, and a "pseudo-religious activism" which would make the church the servant of every benevolent or reforming impulse.

Let us suppose that some phase of the relation of church and state is to be considered. One approach insists upon beginning with definitions and general concepts. What is the chief end of man? What is the essential nature of the church? Is the state a gift of God or a human instrument? It tends to answer these questions in terms of complete divine transcendence, a mystical and pre-existent church (*Una Sancta*) which can do no wrong though its human agents can and do, and a sinful world in which the only absolute duty is to choose the course that is least wrong. The other approach, considering church and state as concrete phenomena sufficiently defined by their observable characteristics, asks: How may their relations be adjusted so that human liberty may be safeguarded, social order may be preserved and religion may have its proper place in life?

I offer no commentary upon the relative merits of these two types of approach, but it can scarcely be denied that the attempt to satisfy the demands of both of them at once was the source of no little difficulty in the discussions and of some confusion in the reported findings. But since both points of view exist within the churches which have here been trying to express and deepen their unity, a body of findings which ignored either would fatally misrepresent the situation.

In view of the conviction of so large an element—including all the Eastern Orthodox and most of the Continentals and Anglicans—that the relation of the church to the world, or of the Christian man to society, can be profitably discussed only after a sound theological foundation has been laid, it is doubtless wise that steps should be taken toward the merging of "Life and Work" and "Faith and Order" in a permanent organization which shall constitute a single ecumenical federation of churches. Such steps were taken at Oxford by the appointment of seven representatives to confer with an equal number who, it is hoped, will be appointed at Edinburgh.

Any attempted summary, in a few paragraphs, of the findings of the Oxford Conference in its five fields of study would be too fragmentary to be serviceable. Only a few detached and striking items can be mentioned.

The relationship of men in communities and races was viewed as a gift of God; but the elevation of Volk into an object of supreme devotion and the claim of superiority for one race over another and discriminations on the ground of race or color were declared to be contrary to the spirit of Christ. (A Dutch delegate from South Africa said that the denunciation of racial discriminations would give great offense to his people, but his protest fell on deaf ears.) Anti-Semitism was specifically repudiated.

Any totalitarian program for the state was declared to be hostile to the liberty of the church and, what is more, hostile to the liberty of human personality. The church is under no less obligation to protest when the rights of others are invaded by the state than when its own rights are denied. An attempt was made to secure the adoption of a clear-cut statement that the church has no rights for which it can properly demand recognition by the state except such as can be stated in terms of the rights of citizens to freedom of thought, expression, assembly and organization; but the idea of special rights for the church as a divine institution was too strongly entrenched. It was declared that the church has a right to demand from the state "freedom to determine the nature of its government and the qualifications of its ministers and members, so far as it desires." Even this guarded statement, as amended by the addition of the final clause, was held by a Swedish Lutheran delegate to be a demand for what is impossible in an established church. He may be right. It is an inescapable fact that when free-church men and established-church men undertake to frame a joint statement about the relations of church and state, they can come to agreement only by a studied ambiguity or by a cautious avoidance of controversial aspects of the question. There was not much ambiguity in the statement as adopted, but there was plenty of avoidance.

The absence of the German delegates was deeply regretted. A message of sympathy was adopted and a delegation was authorized to convey this message in person and carry a report of the conference. The spirit which prompted this action is above criticism, but it may reasonably be doubted whether the coming of such a deputation from Oxford to visit those who were not permitted to go to Oxford will not exasperate the German government and provoke reprisals.

But there were German delegates at Oxford—three representing the federation of evangelical free churches. On the platform of the conference Methodist Bishop Melle testified to the gratitude of the free churches of Germany for the "full liberty" which they enjoyed; following the injunction of St. Paul they pray for all who are in authority, and they are grateful "that God in his providence has sent a Leader" who was able to "banish the danger of Bolshevism in Germany and to rescue a nation of from sixty to seventy millions from the abyss of despair to which it had been led by the World War and the Treaty of Versailles and its wretched consequences, and to give this nation a new faith in its mission and in its future." Before this speech there had been whispered rumors that if these free-church delegates spoke their sentiments they might not be permitted to return to Germany. After it, there seemed no reason to doubt the cordiality of their reception by the department of propaganda upon their return.

The declaration on war was eagerly awaited. It did not fail to declare war is "a particular demonstration of the power of sin in this world," but it did not say that any specific war is a sin or that participation in it is sinful. Man is "caught in a sinful situation," in which "the best that is possible falls far short of the glory of God and is, in that sense, sinful." Avoiding commitment as to any specific attitude which the church and Christian men ought to adopt toward war when war comes, the conference report contented itself with exhibiting the various views which Christians actually hold on that subject and with saying that while the church could neither affirm that any one of these was right and the others wrong nor acquiesce in the permanent continuance of these differences, it should promote the study of the problem with a view to a better understanding of the purpose of God.

From the pacifist standpoint, this was a pretty weak outcome of the deliberations. It represents no advance. "Dick" Sheppard, Canon of St. Paul's, was quite willing to be quoted as saying that, whether considered as the statement of a Christian attitude toward war, as an announcement to governments of the church's judgment upon war or as a guide for Christians in deciding what their own course should be in case of war, it is a total loss. When asked what he and his fellow pacifists would do about it, he replied, with characteristic smiling earnestness: "Blow it up! In a debonair manner, of course."

One cannot but feel that on this as on many other points the theologians considered the doctrine of original sin as a very present help in trouble. "To all human institutions clings the taint of sin." "Each man must bear his share of the corporate sin which has rendered impossible any better course." "Some . . . believe that in a sinful world the state has the duty, under God, to use force when law and order are threatened." The apology for doing un-Christian things for the defense of Christian principles in a sinful world is called being "realistic." But the sections on international relations contain also many strong affirmations of the duty and opportunity of the church to serve as a unifying force among the nations and as an advocate of those principles of justice and liberty which, if generally observed, would prevent the clash of arms.

Limitations of space do not permit adequate comment on the findings of the commission on "The Church and the Social Order." It should be read in full, and there will be early opportunity to read it. It contains much enlightened and liberal social doctrine, and countenances no complacency with things as they are. It warns against being "deceived by the utopian promises of new social faiths," for "because of the sinfulness of the human heart and the complexities of social life none of the programs for the reconstruction of the economic order can be trusted without qualifications." The report as prepared by the commission and adopted by the conference has the appearance of having been written by men who, rather radical themselves, were aware that it would have to be adopted, if at all, by the votes of those less so.

A list of the pioneer leaders whose faith and vision created the first conference on Life and Work and paved the way for this second was presented in a memorial. To these deserving names I venture to add another the absence of which leaves a wide gap in the record—the name of Peter Ainslie. He was neither patriarch nor archbishop, and it is not always easy for those who direct the affairs of assemblies involving high ecclesiastical dignitaries to estimate adequately the services of those who have been the prophets rather than the high priests of such a movement.

The conference has closed, leaving in the mind of every member a more vivid sense of the ecumenical character of the church even now, in spite of its divisions. "Our unity in Christ is not a theme for aspiration," says the closing message; "it is an experienced fact." There is a large measure of truth in these words. There was no unseemly argument about a joint communion service, as in the final days at Lausanne. It was avoided by the expedient of having an Anglican service, conducted by Anglican ministers, to which "all baptized believers" were invited. This is something less than perfect "unity in Christ." Non-Anglicans were present as guests, rather than as members of the family. It was an act of gracious hospitality, duly appreciated as such; but it was a symbol of the separateness of churches as well as of the unity of Christians. There are important aspects of unity which are still a theme for aspiration.

September 1, 1937

The Quest for Unity

CHARLES CLAYTON MORRISON

Edinburgh, August 12
The Conference on Faith and Order which has been in session in this city since August 3 seems, in outward appearance, like an adjourned sitting of the Oxford Conference on Church,

Community and State. I would guess that more than one-half of the personnel is the same. The vice-chairmen, representing, as well as four men can be said to do so, the larger units of world Christianity—Orthodox, Anglican, Presbyterian and Free Churches—are the same. The chairmanship alone is different. At Oxford, the presiding officer was the Archbishop of Canterbury, but after the opening formalities he relinquished his duties to Dr. John R. Mott, who managed the deliberations of the conference and directed its procedure. Here in Edinburgh this function is discharged by the Archbishop of York (Dr. William Temple), who presides at all sessions. But there is the same picturesqueness of dress and tonsorial adornment (?) which made the Oxford assemblage a happy hunting ground for photographers.

There is, however, an inward difference between the two gatherings. This difference has to do with the subject matter of the conferences. At Oxford the church was considered in its relations with the secular order—the nation, the state, the economic system and the educational process. At Edinburgh our problem is found within the church itself. It arises out of the fact of the church's disunity. We stand at the end of a long era whose most conspicuous feature has been the proliferation of schisms. But the world is too strong for a divided church. The church cannot perform the task envisaged at Oxford unless it can recover its lost unity. Yet how can such diverse elements, ranging all the way from the Eastern Orthodox to the Congregationalists—not to mention the Quakers—join together in anything worthy to be called one church? At first blush it seems like a hopeless undertaking. But there is a conscience in the churches which refuses to allow appearances to decide the possibilities. It is determined to explore below the surface of our variety and see if there are not great stretches of agreement sufficiently fundamental to afford a foundation for a genuine and a visible unity.

In this conscience the Edinburgh Conference has its roots. Twenty-seven years ago—in 1910—by a coincidence so singular that many of us regard it as a providence—three American denominations, the Protestant Episcopal, the Disciples of Christ and the Congregationalists, in the same month, in two instances on the same day, in their respective general assemblies, without advance knowledge of one another's purpose, proclaimed that the hour was come to do something on a wide scale to recover the lost unity of Christendom. The Episcopalian manifesto was the most definite. It called for a world conference on the subject of Christian unity. Certain of its leaders, notably the late Bishop Charles H. Brent, were set apart to undertake plans for such a conference. This movement materialized in 1927 as the Conference on Faith and Order held at Lausanne. The outcome was none too encouraging. Indeed there were elements of unhappiness in the aftermath of that gathering. Other churchmen had meantime come to believe that the approach to unity through faith and order was a wrong approach. They held that a more promising approach was through the church's life and work. Led by Archbishop Nathan Soderblöm of Sweden, a conference had been held, in 1925, at Stockholm, from whose deliberations the matters of creed, sacraments and orders were excluded. The deliberations centered upon the practical questions of interchurch co-operation in life and work. The results of this effort were none too inspiring. A general mood of discouragement set in, and though both Lausanne and Stockholm were kept alive by means of continuation committees, there was little enthusiasm among the churches.

Within the past three years, however, a wholly new mood has been defining itself throughout Christendom. With a suddenness which is unprecedented in Christian history the whole body of Christian believers in every part of the Western world has awakened to the consciousness that the entire secular order of the modern world, instead of moving steadily toward the acceptance of Christianity, has been for centuries moving steadily away from it. The whole domain of Western culture, in its political, economic, intellectual and ethical aspects, is seen as ruled by ideologies which have no affinity with the Christian faith. Our most realistic minds have become aware of the fact that the church has been giving away both itself and its treasures in its compromises with secular philosophies. Others have seen this surrender as due mainly to the preoccupation of the divided churches with their fractional apprehension of Christian truth, which left each sect an easy prey to the encroachment of an aggressive secularism.

In the preparations for the Oxford Conference, which has just been held, the Faith and Order movement took on new life. It became clear that the church could not assume a functional responsibility of the magnitude envisaged at Oxford while its faith and order were broken into sectarian compartments. Christianity could not presume to speak an authoritative word to a broken and dismembered civilization if its own body was dismembered. A sectarian church could not mend the sectarianism of society. Thus the world situation forced home to the Christian intelligence the anomaly and sin of a divided church. The lonely prophets of Christian unity whose voices have cried in the wilderness of our sectarian complacency for many decades now began to be heeded. The forthcoming Conference on Faith and Order thus took on a more realistic character in the minds of those engaged in preparing for it. But even so, there was a general disposition to discount the significance and promise of the Edinburgh Conference which was to open one week after the adjournment at Oxford.

With deep gratitude I am able to say that the doubts and misgivings which many of us took to Edinburgh have entirely vanished. The Conference on Faith and Order is proving to be in no respect second to the Oxford gathering in significance and promise. Instead of eclipsing Edinburgh, Oxford has vitalized it. By defining the task of the church in terms of Christianity's social responsibility, Oxford has turned the church's mind inward upon its own condition. Edinburgh sees the Christian Church as a chaos of regional and sectarian provincialism. Such a church is not only impotent in the face of a civilization which worships the many gods of humanistic secularism, but its own life is threatened. Again and again this note of desperation is being struck. The Bishop of Lichfield in his sermon at St. Giles last Sunday said plainly that the Christian Church has its back to the wall. Its divisions have weakened its character. They render it susceptible to the seductions of secularism on the one hand, or push it into a sterile pietism or hollow formalism on

the other. The situation was described in the opening address
of the conference by the Archbishop of York. He said:

How can the church call men to the worship of one God, if it
calls them to rival shrines? How can it claim to bridge the divisions in human society—divisions between Greek and barbarian,
bond and free, between white and black, Aryan and non-Aryan,
employer and employed—if, when men are drawn into it, they
find that another division has been added to the old ones—a division of Catholic from Evangelical, or Episcopalian from Presbyterian or Independent? A church divided in its manifestation to
the world cannot render its due service to God or to man.

Dr. Temple went on to admit for himself that he belongs to a
church which still maintains a barrier against completeness of
union at the Table of the Lord. "But I know," he said, "that our
division at this point is the greatest of all scandals in the face of
the world. I know that we can only consent to it or maintain it
without the guilt of unfaithfulness to the unity of the gospel and
of God himself, if it is a source to us of spiritual pain, and if
we are striving to the utmost to remove the occasions which
now bind us, as we think, to that perpetuation of disunion."

It should be "horrible" to us, he concluded, to speak or think
of any fellow Christian as "not in communion with us." "God
grant that we may feel the pain of it and under that impulsion
strive the more earnestly to remove all that now hinders us from
receiving together the one Body of the One Lord that in him we
may become One Body—the organ and vehicle of the One
Spirit."

I quote at length from the Archbishop of York because of the
penetrating insight which his words disclose, and also because
he announced the theme or motif which has run through the
entire conference up to this hour. There is no squeamishness
here about the phrase "organic unity." That specifically and
confessedly is the goal to which this conference is oriented.
Nothing will satisfy the spirit of Edinburgh short of a visibly
united church. This does not mean that co-operation or federation of our denominations is unesteemed, but all such measures
are seen as way-stations toward a unity that is both spiritual and
structural.

What Edinburgh is seeking for is ecumenical faith and the ecumenical body. This word "ecumenical," and its substantive, "ecumenicity," are on all our lips. We are an "ecumenical movement"; both Oxford and Edinburgh are its expression. It is an old ecclesiastical word, of course, used commonly by the Roman and Orthodox churches, but new in the ordinary nomenclature of Protestantism. It represents the very opposite of Protestantism, which has been an expression of centrifugal and separatist rather than centripetal and unitive impulses. "Ecumenical" means about the same as "catholic," and I suppose has gained popular usage as descriptive of the present movement because it is free of the ambiguity attaching to the word "catholic" which, besides being a description of the whole body of Christ, is also the name of a particular branch of the church.

The use of this word "ecumenical" gives a measure of the magnitude of the task which the church of our time confronts. We are in search of the ecumenical or catholic church. Some say it already exists and only needs to be made manifest. Others say that it has been broken by our divisions and must be recreated. I incline to the latter conception. But my view has few supporters here. Edinburgh is under the spell of the idealistic philosophy which is able to treat ideals as actual existences. The question is not important, however, at this stage, and it would be both academic and pedantic to make a point of it. The important thing is that the church shall become conscious of its unity and build a structure which shall embody that unity. This Edinburgh is striving to do.

As at Oxford, it was difficult to choose one's section, because the subject matter of every section was so intriguing. Take the first section, for example. Its specific theme was "The Grace of Our Lord Jesus Christ." This was the title under which the basic faith of the church was to be expounded. Here was a new approach to the ecumenical faith. I am aware that the category of grace was held to be fundamental at the Lausanne Conference ten years ago, but it was not put forward as the comprehensive concept presumed to contain the essentials of the Christian revelation as we have it here in Edinburgh.

The more I reflect upon it, the more am I convinced that the whole of our gospel is involved in this concept of divine grace, that it plumbs the depths of Christian truth and leaves out nothing that is truly ecumenical in Christian belief. True, the historic creeds—Apostles' and Nicene—are presupposed in all our discussions, but there is profound significance in the fact that when a modern ecumenical conference goes in search of a conception which will set forth the essential content of historic Christianity, it does not expect to find it in a philosophical speculation about God, but in a revelation of his character and his disposition toward man. God's grace revealed in Jesus Christ—can you imagine anything more fundamental and all-inclusive? I hear that section number one has been able to reach a unanimous formulation, and that it adjourned its final session last night by singing, "Now thank we all our God"!

So much for "faith." One hardly dares to hope that there will be such unanimity or such progress toward unity when it comes to "order." This involves the conception of the church itself, its ministry and its sacraments. It is here that the really acute issues arise. Yet I believe that my own section is in process of making a distinct contribution, and I hear that section two is drawing the two wings of catholicity and evangelicalism together in a statement concerning the church. There is a vast gulf to be bridged between Western Protestantism and the rest of Christianity on the question of the church. Our American conception is local and pragmatic, for the most part, and its representatives feel modest and unaggressive in the presence of the scholarship of the Orthodox and Anglican communions. Besides, we know in our hearts that our ultra-congregational conceptions are totally inadequate both as a reflection of historic Christian reality and as a basis of competency in face of the world situation. There is a kind of wistfulness in the minds of leaders of the so-called free churches, and a disillusionment with respect to their irresponsible independency. This keeps them from putting forward their "system" as a possible basis for the ecumenical church.

September 29, 1948

Appraising Amsterdam

AN EDITORIAL

Two things must be kept distinct in any fair appraisal of the Amsterdam conference. One is the thing that was done there; the other is the things that were said there. The things that were said are of great importance, but they are of secondary importance as compared with the thing done. It was made emphatically clear that even the reports of the four sections were only "received" by the plenary body and "commended to the churches for study and consideration." No creed was adopted at Amsterdam, and no commitments were made in the fields of theology or evangelism or economics or international order, which commit any church or any Christian. The things said represented only the speaker who said them or, in the case of the formal documents, a consensus of judgment; and where no consensus could be achieved the disagreements were frankly set forth.

The whole body of pronouncements is thus open to critical examination by any church or any Christian. There will be differences of opinion on this point or on that, and these differences should not be repressed. But it will be a misfortune if those who were at Amsterdam return home so preoccupied with and perhaps irritated by these differences about the things said that they allow their appraisal of the conference to be determined by them rather than by their appreciation of the massive significance of the thing done.

The thing done at Amsterdam was the thing the churches sent their delegates there to do, namely, to bring into existence a new entity in Christendom, to be called the World Council of Churches. The 151 churches (denominations) represented there had previously accepted as the basis of their participation the single creedal formula of "Jesus Christ as God and Saviour." On this rock it was believed that the separated churches of non-Roman Christendom could erect a structure which would not only symbolize their common faith, but provide for co-operative action to meet the crying needs of our disordered world. To do this thing the churches sent 351 delegates and an equal number of participating alternates to Amsterdam. They did what they were sent to do, and left behind them an achievement which in itself is monumental and whose potentialities for the kingdom of God are beyond the wisdom of man to measure or discern. In doing this they believed that they were led by the Spirit of God whose guidance was sought with instant prayer and supplication at every step of the way.

Nothing must be allowed to eclipse this achievement, or to confuse the mind of the churches or the public mind as to its unique significance. The World Council of Churches is a new emergent in Christian history. Not since the Protestant Reformation has an event of such importance to the Christian faith occurred. Its importance can be appraised from many angles. But its deepest significance lies in the fact that it marks a reversal of the direction in which the current of non-Roman Christianity has been flowing ever since the Reformation. For four centuries the trend in Protestantism has been marked by the multiplication of sectarian divisions. No longer ago than two generations these divisions were accepted and even gloried in as a Protestant virtue. They afforded a special kind of church for every national tradition, every belief, every kind of liturgy, every social affinity, and even every taste. That there could be any wrong in thus dividing the church of Christ was hardly perceived.

The first gleam of insight came when the churches began to sense the great economic waste involved in maintaining these divisions. The second came when the missionaries overseas returned home to point out the absurdity of exporting denominationalism to non-Christian lands and to plead for permission to present only an ecumenical Christianity. The third insight came when the Christian conscience was confronted with its responsibility for the character of the social order. Undertaking to do something about it, the divided churches were made to realize their impotence before the massive blocs of secular power which they were unable to penetrate. But all these "practical" considerations, though their combined influence produced definite results in federations and other forms of association and appreciably dulled the edges of sectarian pride and self-sufficiency, did not get to the root of sectarianism.

It remained for Amsterdam to speak with prophetic clarity to the conscience of a divided Christendom and to call its divisions by their right name. Here from the ends of the earth was assembled the widest and most responsible representation of Christian leadership known in history, and with one voice, in every session, from beginning to end, our divisions were branded as *sin*. No hint or whisper of dissent was heard. One spirit permeated the whole body—it was a spirit of contrition and penitence for the sin that lay at the root of our "unhappy divisions."

This, of course, was not the first time that our divisions were branded as sin. Prophets have arisen from time to time in the past who have called upon the church to look not only at the "practical" handicaps which denominationalism lays upon the cause of Christ, but to see the sinfulness inherent in these divisions. Also there has been a cumulative trend in the ecumenical movement itself in this direction. But at Amsterdam this movement of the Christian conscience became collectively articulate and voiced itself in a solemn and oft-repeated call to penitence and a clear recognition that only a corporately united church is competent to possess for itself and to manifest to the world the riches of the Christian faith.

All this, however, does not mean that the World Council conceives of itself as the embodiment of this ideal. On the contrary, it accepts Christendom "as is," with its great array of "churches," and offers itself as a meeting point and an instrument for their co-operation. It emphatically disavows any pretension to be a "super-church" or even to foster organic union among the separated bodies. Its function is more modest. Some may have expected a united Christendom to emerge at Amsterdam, and because it did not emerge, they are likely to appraise the event in terms of disappointment. Any appraisal based upon such an expectation will be unfair and will mislead the churches and the general public.

Certain publications have already slanted their reports and comments in this mistaken direction. Because Amsterdam was no Pentecost, because no "tongues of flame" sat upon the heads of its members, the conference is interpreted as a purely businesslike deliberation, moved by anxiety, caution and practicality. This, we believe, is a distortion of the reality. No one should have expected a Pentecost nor, in truth, desired one. Pentecost was the birthday of a new religion. Amsterdam proceeded on the major premise that the world does not need a new religion, but that the faith which first became articulate at Pentecost is still the saving faith for mankind. This faith is smothered and choked by the sin of those who profess it, and it is hard to imagine a more profound corporate penitence for this sin than that which became the solemn undertone in prayer and testimony at Amsterdam.

Though the World Council disavows any claim for itself as the fulfillment of the dream of a united Christendom, it does cherish the dream. We have only to turn from our consideration of the thing done to the things said at Amsterdam to discover that this dream takes form as the paramount matter upon which the whole assemblage was in unmistakable accord. When one studies the documents wrought out by the conference's four sections, it will be seen how insistently the sin of division was condemned and the need of corporate unity proclaimed. This should provide positive encouragement to every movement now afoot in the United States and Canada to reduce the number of denominations by mergers, and to the more comprehensive undertaking that would bring together in one body those denominations which already "recognize one another's ministries and sacraments."

If any American Protestant went to Amsterdam with anxiety lest the thing done there would drain off interest in these movements nearer home, his apprehension may now be set at rest. In the light of the things said, there is little danger that the World Council will be used as a compensatory device to relieve the nascent conscience on Christian unity which has been slowly forming in our own churches and moving into action. These undertakings, however, will proceed outside the jurisdiction or orbit of the World Council as the free and independent action of the churches concerned. Though such movements may not be fostered by the World Council, they will plainly have its blessing. Instead, therefore, of draining off the interest and devotion that have already been generated for a united Protestantism here at home, the thing done at Amsterdam, interpreted by the things said there, should pour a reinforcing stream of vitality into the centripetal movements now so hopefully under way.

Formation of the World Council of Churches marks the beginning of the end of an era and the opening of a new epoch in the history of our Christian faith. We must not assume that the thing done has been made permanently secure against the vicissitudes of the future. The World Council has only just been born. For some time it may have to live precariously. It is the responsibility of the churches, the clergy, the philanthropists, the theologians and the rank-and-file Christian to steady it with their support in these days of its infancy. No thoughtful Christian will allow any disagreement with anything said at Amsterdam to discount in his mind the monumental importance, in the providence of God, of the thing that was done there.

September 22, 1954

Evanston Retrospect

AN EDITORIAL

For what will the Evanston assembly of the World Council be remembered? Amsterdam, of course, will be remembered as the place and time of the council's birth. Its historical importance was fixed before it ever was called to order. Other things happened there, such as the tense debate between John Foster Dulles and Josef Hromadka on the relation of the churches to the communist challenge, or Sarah Chakko's dramatic defiance of Karl Barth's dogmatic attempt to make the Scriptures talk like a nineteenth-century German householder. With the passage of time, however, these things fade into obscurity. "Amsterdam 1948" means, and always will mean, just one thing—the birth of the World Council.

What, six years hence, will "Evanston 1954" mean? Prophecy is hazardous. Developments during the period to intervene before the Third Assembly could make Evanston remembered for unfortunate things—the disruption introduced by disputes about the Second Coming or by the collision over the conversion of the Jews; the cloud cast across the council's future by Archbishop Michael's flat repudiation of its whole approach to Christian unity. Yet these too are matters which, in the course of time, we expect to see gravitate toward the periphery. At least, we devoutly hope that this will prove so.

For the American public, and perhaps for many in other countries, the chances are that Evanston will be remembered principally for its size. It brought more people together; it commanded more newspaper space; it stirred up more kinds of hullabaloo than any non-Roman church gathering—the German Kirchentag perhaps excepted—in modern times. In this publicity-conscious age, when the comparative importance of events is too frequently measured in terms of number of inches in the newspapers or hours on the air, it is not wholly a bad thing to have held a WCC assembly which left this impression behind it. For the World Council *is* important, and what it represents is still more important. But no one would be happy today at a prospect that, years hence, Evanston might be mainly remembered for its size.

Among those who were there, one thing Evanston is sure to be remembered for is its friendliness. Visitors from abroad, it was reported at the meeting of the Central Committee which immediately followed the assembly, complained that they had no time to cultivate new or deep friendships. But certainly there was a pervasive atmosphere of personal good fellowship which made a pleasant contrast to the exploratory good form which ruled at Amsterdam. The men and women in the Evanston delegations might not be able to mingle at the Table of their Lord, but it was plain that they thoroughly enjoyed mingling with one another elsewhere. They will remember Evanston for that. And the churches at large can thank God for it.

But the attempt which is apparently being made in some quarters to project this personal camaraderie at Evanston into a foretaste and promise of coming Christian unity—the koinonia which is the third Greek recruit to the ecumenical vocabulary: "Now abideth Oikoumene, Agape and Koinonia"—does not have a great deal to go on. There were high moments at Evanston; moments when the assembly came very close indeed to being transformed into a unified and unifying fellowship of worshipers, a genuine koinonia. We will long remember the communion service conducted by the Church of South India and the hush over McGraw hall as Bishop Newbigin read the Message as the two closest approaches to such a genuine fellowship. Yet there was a considerable sector of the assembly which stayed away from the former for reasons of conscience, and the deep emotion stirred by the first hearing of the Message was quickly shattered when blocks of delegates rose to vote No.

Always at Evanston, and not far below the surface, there were grim disunities which the World Council may at limited times and to limited degrees transcend, but which it has hardly even begun to dissolve. The personal fellowship at Evanston, such as it was and grateful as the participants were and will continue to be for it, was not the kind of fellowship that can reach out beyond a meeting to bring divided congregations and denominations together. It will not have much if any effect on the scandal of denominational competition in our American towns. It will leave the Greek Evangelicals as insecure as ever. It will do little to end the bewilderment of African natives over the conflicting claims of various church ordinances. Evanston will not be remembered for having carried forward the cause of Christian unity. It might possibly (though we hope not) be remembered for having shown how far off and blocked-off the goal of unity is.

There will be, we expect, some negative remembrances of

Evanston. This 1954 assembly is likely to leave its mark in warning, if not in great achievement. The first sessions of the new Central Committee, we are told, were largely taken up by recalling aspects of the assembly which its participants had not liked. That was probably to be expected, and in some ways was a healthy sign. It is good to be assured thus early in the World Council's life that its assemblies retain the essential Protestant virtue of self-criticism. If Evanston 1954 should come to be remembered as the assembly where needless detours and dead-end streets were discovered and charted, that would be an outcome of some promise.

Evanston, we dare hope, could thus come to be remembered as the place where the World Council discovered how quickly the impulse to Christian unity in action could be sidetracked and reduced to impotence by a demand for prior theological agreement. The Christ who judged between sayers and doers would not be surprised to find that common Christian action is providing the community in which common Christian statements are being attempted. He would be glad, we believe, that the former has not been made to wait on the latter. But he could hardly be satisfied with the increasing lag of theology behind enterprise.

Evanston made the surprising disclosure that the social action which the church has been so nervous about lately, stepped forward confidently to save the day. And the theology which has recently been so sure of itself, got absolutely nowhere at all. Could it be that if the World Council studied its theology less dogmatically and more in action, from the saddle, so to speak— that the council would last longer and go farther? Certainly if it does not find a new manner, if four more assemblies handle theological or dogmatic themes as badly as this one did, the outlook is not encouraging. Give the World Council about four more such theological or dogmatic main themes—say, the nature of biblical authority in 1960, the nature of the church in 1966, the nature of salvation in 1972 and the creedal basis of the council's own being in 1978—and if the world itself hasn't blown up by that time the council almost certainly will.

Perhaps Evanston may also be remembered as the assembly where the demand for lay and pastoral representation began to come into the open. We add that "pastoral" gratuitously, for truth to tell it was only the laymen (and laywomen) who made their discontent heard at the Second Assembly. The reason probably was that there were some articulate laymen present, while if there were parish ministers they were lost in the crowd. But the World Council's future depends greatly on whether it can be brought into living relationship with the actual churches in which actual men and women try actually to worship and to serve God. That relationship will never be established while its assemblies are almost reserved for clerics, particularly titled clerics, and most of all for professorial clerics. If its assemblies are not something more than a projection of board rooms or seminars they will soon, so far as the "grass roots" are concerned, be nothing at all.

One positive discovery made at Evanston may, if sufficiently taken to heart, become the thing for which that gathering is longest remembered. That is the fact that the churches move most perceptibly toward unity and power as they seek to deal together with the issues which make life so bitter for so many. There was an arresting display of Christian leadership when Evanston tackled some of the dismaying social problems of our times. Some, not all. On the problem of atomic war, it must be conceded, Evanston showed no advance over Amsterdam. But on such a problem as race it was quite possible to envision new revelations of potential power if the churches represented at the assembly act on their findings.

In the light of Evanston we are more convinced than ever that working together is for the churches the road, and the only open road, to coming together. If the World Council exists to further Christian unity, the contrast shown at Evanston between the assembly milling about in its efforts to deal with theological conundrums and its relative confidence in defining Christian positions on social issues should persuade its leaders that what they most need to do now is to point to human tasks in which the member churches can work co-operatively. At Amsterdam, the delegates who voted in the First Assembly to form the council were largely influenced by the experience of watching their churches, during the ten years while the council was "in process of formation," reinforce one another in works of mercy and help of many kinds all over a war-ravaged world. By the time the Second Assembly met these co-operative tasks had dwindled to not much more than help for refugees. Reflection should show that a vigorous comradeship of the churches requires more common tasks.

In retrospect, Evanston 1954 will be remembered for its evidence that the ecumenical impulse, given concrete form only six years before, is still alive and still engages the hopes and dreams of multitudes of Christians in every part of the world. But Evanston also struck a note of warning that should not be ignored. That warning was wrapped up in the change which it was felt necessary to make in the Message. As first proposed it would have contained the electric words:

Six years ago our churches entered into a covenant to form this council, and affirmed their intention to stay together. We thank God for his blessing on our work and fellowship during these six years. We enter now upon a second stage. To stay together is not enough. We must grow together.

When the assembly finally adopted its Message those final words had been watered down to "We must go forward." It was a change big with warning.

IV

Days of Trial

*WHEN THE TWENTIETH CENTURY was young, tech-
nological and intellectual advances seemed to optimistic man
to have rendered any future war unthinkable.*

January 2, 1909

The End of War

AN EDITORIAL

While they are drawing up rules to govern active warfare in
London the Wrights are attaining new wonders in France with
their flying machine, and Octave Chanute, the first of recognized authorities on aerial navigation, says, "The end of war is
in sight." Count Zeppelin will soon be ready to demonstrate
anew the power of the solid dirigible to make long flights and
regular trips between designated places, while the *Scientific
American* talks about the possibility of vacuum envelopes after
the Zeppelin model, a type that would do away with many of the
weaknesses of a gas bag. Roy Knabenschue recently sailed about
over the city of Los Angeles at a great height and threw confetti
"bombs" enough to have effectually destroyed the city had they
been actual high-class explosives. At the same time he effectually answered the critics who claimed ineffectiveness for bom-
bardment by an airship of any kind because it would be impossible to drop bombs from it, thus lightening the load, and
maintain a navigable position in the air. True, the last Hague
Conference forbade the use of air vessels for dropping bombs,
but that has not the authority of international law until legally
enacted by the treaty-making powers of the several nations, and
there is no more reason for making such an enactment than
there is for ruling out shimose or lyddite or decreeing that the
dreadnaught is the finality in battleships. It would be tanta-
mount to a beginning of disarmament. Theoretically the Wright
aerodrome should easily arise to a height of two thousand feet,
sail eighty miles an hour, and remain aloft as long as the motor

would run. They have actually attained a height of over three hundred feet, sailed more than a mile a minute, and remained in the air nearly two hours, and they have never tempted fate by going to the apparent limit. No gun can be trained at sharp enough angle to reach even a comparatively low altitude, and if so could not be effectually aimed at a speck in the sky going a mile a minute. There only remains the battle above the clouds, a thing too horrible to be imagined and too expensive to be provided for. Meanwhile the moral sentiment against war increases mightily and is more powerful than deadly invention.

December 28, 1911

A Vicarious Nation

AN EDITORIAL

Great and luminous were the words spoken by Dr. J. H. Jowett in his Fifth Avenue Presbyterian pulpit the other day when, in a sermon on peace, the preacher flung a challenge into the conscience of our Christian nation. The congregation almost stopped breathing, we are told, while he made his plea that some nation should adopt Christ's principle of life and make itself a world savior by breaking its alliance with the carnal forces of militarism and risking its destiny in an alliance with reason and righteousness. Dr. Jowett had been showing that peace came to the individual soul because of the blood of Jesus Christ shed upon the cross. He then said: "And O I would that some great Christian nation would, in some time of crisis, make peace by the blood of its own cross, by some sublime act of glorious sacrificial magnanimity! I would that some Christian nation would disown the axiom that the law of nations is the law of the beasts, and 'laying aside every weapon of carnal warfare,' would rely for her continued existence upon the powers of reason, 'upon the service she would render to the world' and the testimony she would bear to Christ. You may deride the suggestion as ideal, but what am I here for but in the ministry of the ideal, and amid the fog of worldly compromises and expediencies to keep its radiant dignities in sight. And it may be, as a man of statesmanlike mind declared some years ago, 'it may be that a nation martyred for Christ's sake may be within the counsel of God'—a nation which sought to make peace by the blood of its own cross." The same challenge was uttered by Henry Sloane Coffin at the Edinburgh Conference, in an address which has hardly been commented upon, but which was one of the most masterful interpretations of Christianity at that historic council. This insight of Dr. Jowett's is the heart of Christ's message to our national life.

But then came World War I....
April 12, 1917

A Christian's Duty in Wartime

AN EDITORIAL

War does not take away our obligation to be Christian.

The witness of Christian conscience has been particularly strong against war in recent years. Now that we find ourselves involved in the greatest military struggle in Christian history, we ask ourselves in some perplexity what our duty is.

A man said the other day with regard to a personal altercation, "I would like to leave the church for thirty minutes and settle this thing in the old-fashioned way!" This was not a well-advised remark for a Christian to make. We shall be tempted in this war to put aside for a while our Christian idealism and revert to the more primitive attitudes of wartime. This would mean that after the war we would be poor morally and spiritually as well as financially.

On the other hand, there will be those who will insist that a Christian's duty in time of war is the same as in time of peace. Some will weaken the hand of the government by ill-advised utterances which will be intended to help on the cause of peace, but which by reason of their disloyalty will make the pacifist cause ridiculous in the eyes of patriots. If during the coming days of struggle we shall see the sacred cause of universal peace become identified with "copperheads" and cowards who use so-called "conscientious objections" as a cover for lack of courage, it will be a great misfortune to the world. War brings men duties.

World peace cannot be practiced by one nation only. This involves a national suicide that defeats its own ends. America has not wanted war. We have deliberated while those who have become our allies have been fighting our battles. At last the most peace-loving President of American history has been driven to declare for war. He is a Christian man. He has believed, as most of us believe, that though war is a mighty evil, there are some things worse.

A great temptation is now to be faced. It may seem to some that the dream of universal peace has been completely discredited. It is our duty to hold to our hope of universal peace, even in the midst of war. Perhaps this war is one step nearer the goal of a permanent peace. With the democracies of the world ranged in alliance against the outstanding exponent of militarism, we may even now be taking the first step in the program of a League to Enforce Peace. This program implies that the whole world will join in punishing the aggressor, this disturber of the peace. We must continue to hope, however, that beyond the stage of development when we must maintain peace by an international police force, we shall at last realize a peace that rests entirely upon moral feeling. To have war take away from us this fine faith would be to suffer an irreparable loss.

We shall be tempted in wartime to indulge in bitter and unreasonable hate. There are nicknames current in Europe now, such as "boche" and "hun." We heard a man say only yesterday, "Germans are like Indians; the only good German is a dead German." Such statements leave scars in our souls. The President has set us all a good example in discriminating between the German government and the German people. For the latter, he expresses his respect and good will, especially to those who are living in our own country. Civilization is deeply in the debt of the German people; it has many a score against the present German government.

Is it not time to quicken our faith in God? Not in a millenarian sense, we declare that the end of the age is at hand. Our earth will go on, but we are about to enter a new epoch in human history. It is in hours of crisis and reconstruction that we seem to need God most. From this day forward we should go to our tasks with a new consciousness of the presence of God. We are concerned that the will of God shall be done at last in our beloved America.

AN APPEAL for support of the League of Nations as carrying tentative promise of peace in future years. Just ending was a bitter political campaign in which the League had been made the pawn in a partisan tug-of-war.

October 28, 1920

The Paramount Issue

AN EDITORIAL

Out of the confusion and disillusionment which mark the present state of the public mind, one conviction is slowly gaining place. This is the feeling that the one great duty of the hour is the insistence upon some assured plan of bringing the tragic world situation to a close. Half of the people of the earth are starving; moral standards are being disregarded in an increasing tide of immorality; religion is losing its hold upon the nations of the old world, and competent witnesses make clear the fact that Protestantism is in actual peril of extinction in several of the European lands as the result of the war.

The one people that has the power to stay this flood of trouble and despair is our own. The United States went into the world conflict at a time so late that without severe suffering, such as came to the other contending nations, the glory of victory was achieved. What is the significance of the fact that our people suffered so little, and yet had a real experience of the war? Must it not be that we were thus prepared to understand and assist in the great task of reconstruction? No other people has the power to do this. The rest are broken and staggering under the burdens which the war has laid upon them.

Something has been done by the United States. We have given to a limited degree for relief work. We have done something to rehabilitate the stripped territories. But our moral support, which is far more in demand than any physical aid can be, we have deliberately withdrawn at the very moment when it was most required. We took to the nations of the earth the fairest program of co-operative protection against fresh wars and the old and sinister diplomacies that had ever been conceived. It was hailed by all as a solution of the world's most threatening difficulties. It was not a perfect plan, but it was a beginning. Furthermore it was safeguarded by provisions for its constant amendment and modification by the co-operation of a court and a council.

No document is perfect. The Constitution of the United States, of which much is spoken and written as if it were an unalterable and final utterance, has been in process of modification since the day it was formulated. And the end of the work of amendment is not yet in sight. We need not have expected a perfect instrument in the League of Nations. But we had one that was the best promise of international understanding that had ever been submitted. We ought to have been willing to begin with it, and change it as required.

But at once on its presentation to the people, the partisan spirit seized upon it and sought to make it the topic of party controversy. On the one side was a President who seemed incapable of working with other men, and insisted on having an unmodified covenant. On the other was a group of men intent on the political assassination of the President, and willing to make their attack upon the League the means of accomplishing their purpose. And in the impasse that followed, it was neither the President nor the Senate group that paid the heaviest price, but the nation.

In the thought of the world the United States descended from that high level of international solicitude where our boys in the service had placed us, and appeared to be concerned only to achieve the selfish ends of isolated and self-indulgent life. While the world is facing the tragedies of poverty, famine, moral degradation and the return of the ancient hatreds, we have waved an airy farewell to all concern for any but ourselves. The soul of the nation is in greater danger than are even the suffering peoples of Europe. We have shown to them the fair land of promise, and then by withdrawal from their aid we have prevented the consummation of their hopes.

There is just one moral issue before the nation in this campaign. That is the notification to the rest of the world that we have not forgotten our former friendships, nor abandoned the world to its ruin. Moral encouragement might still save the peoples from despair and mutual destruction. But there is not much time to lose. Among the candidates there is little choice. The politicians have made it difficult for citizens to exercise the right of the franchise with any satisfaction or enthusiasm. It is a sterile time so far as statesmanship goes. But one thing can be done. One can study the way to make his vote count for some sort of international agreement that will not leave the world comfortless. That agreement in its present estate is represented by the League of Nations. Something better may come out of later studies and formulations. But now is the moment of crisis. Tomorrow may be too late to save Europe and the Near East from the tragedy of an abandoned undoing. It is an issue above the skyline of partisanship. It is a great moral obligation.

WITH THE LEAGUE REJECTED by the United States, the Century's pages through the later 1920's were filled with reports on progress of movements to outlaw war. Editorial efforts centered first on Senator William E. Borah's campaign to incorporate outlawry of war into agreements establishing the world court. That campaign failing, Dr. Morrison in 1926 joined with Salmon O. Levinson, a Chicago lawyer, in a movement calling for renunciation of war and branding as a crime its use as an instrument of national policy. In 1928 the legal principle involved was finally recognized in the Pact of Paris, whose signing the editor was invited to witness. Though subsequent events rendered overoptimistic the cable he sent Mr. Levinson from Paris ("With my own eyes I have just seen your great dream come true"), Dr. Morrison continued to hope that the principle, still embedded in the flouted pact, might someday come alive again —and indeed it was invoked by Justice Robert Jackson as the basis for procedures at the Nuremberg trials of war criminals after World War II. From the mass of Century material covering the movement to outlaw war, one editorial—that written at the time of Mr. Levinson's death—has been chosen to convey the spirit and the aims of the entire endeavor.

February 12, 1941

Father of the Pact

AN EDITORIAL

Death overtook Salmon O. Levinson at the moment when his titanic labors for peace seemed most in vain. With all of Europe, most of Asia and much of Africa at war, and the rest of the world moving with hypnotic gaze toward that furnace of Moloch, one hears as echoes from a lost day the words of that pact of which he was justly called the father: "The high contracting parties agree that the settlement or solution of all disputes or conflicts, of whatever nature or of whatever origin they may be, which may arise among them, shall never be sought except by pacific means." His was the bitterness of knowing at the last that the pledges of governments on which he had relied had proved worthless in the day of testing.

But this does not mean that the contribution of Mr. Levinson to the world's future has been lost in the flouting of the Pact of Paris. A day will come when mankind, taught by its agony, will turn again to the building of a permanent structure of peace. When that day dawns the need for a codified international law will be acknowledged, and the cornerstone of any firm structure of world law will of necessity be the outlawry of war. Ultimately the insight which Mr. Levinson had, that war must be put beyond the pale, must be made criminal in legal as well as in moral status, will be accepted as the starting point for the building of a new world order. And in that day the service which that man rendered mankind's future will be universally recognized.

Few modern careers have better illustrated the achievement which is within the reach of one who believes passionately in his cause and will not be denied. Looking back on what this one man accomplished it is hard to believe that when he started his crusade for the outlawry of war he was almost unknown beyond the restricted circles of his professional practice, that he was without organizational support, political influence or journalistic representation. The Christian Century is proud to remember how early it found a place beside him in that struggle. It was a struggle marked by disappointments, setbacks, defeats—discouragements that would have broken the spirit or dimmed the hope of any lesser man. After the Pact of Paris had been signed came the greatest defeat of all, a defeat which persists to this hour. Yet this man would never acknowledge that ultimate victory was beyond attainment. He had a persistence, a resilience, a power of coming back undaunted to the fray surpassing that of any other man it has been our fortune to know.

It must not be thought that the extraordinary powers of his mind were restricted to the single cause of delegalizing the status of war. He worked ceaselessly at such intricate and technical problems as the liquidation of the war debts, the protection of American government from the harm wrought by political corruption, the safeguarding of the federal credit. At one moment he would offer a prize for the encouragement of American poets; at the next he would plunge into prodigious legal labors in behalf of friends or liberal enterprises caught in the tidal wave of the depression. An advocate who asked no quarter in the rough-and-tumble of public debate, he displayed a prodigal sympathy and generosity in the intimate circles of his personal friendships.

Our own parting from him was in keeping with his whole career. Sharing the anxieties of this paper as to the effect on democratic government if the pending lend-lease bill should be enacted, on the day before he died he marked and sent a passage which he had discovered in the speeches of Daniel Webster in order that its warning might be passed on, by this medium, to the American public. These are the solemn words of Webster to which he directed our attention:

Good intentions will always be pleaded for every assumption of [executive] power, but they cannot justify it, even if we were sure they existed. It is hardly too strong to say that the Constitution was made to guard the people against the dangers of good intentions, real or pretended. When bad intentions are boldly avowed, the people will promptly take care of themselves. On the other hand, they will always be asked why they should resist or question that exercise of power which is so fair in its object, so plausible and patriotic in appearance and which has the public good alone confessedly in view. . . . It may be very possible that good intentions do really sometimes exist when constitutional restraints are disregarded. There are men in all ages who mean to exercise power usefully; but they mean to exercise it. They mean to govern well; but they mean to govern. They promise to be kind masters; but they mean to be master. They think there need be but little restraint upon themselves. Their notion of the public interest is apt to be quite closely connected with their own exercise of authority. They may not, indeed, always understand their own motives. The love of power may sink too deep in their own hearts even for their own scrutiny, and may pass with themselves for mere patriotism and benevolence.

In that parting memorandum, which lies here before us as a solemn farewell, Mr. Levinson had underlined the closing ten lines. Constantly, through the years he had done that sort of thing—providing materials to assist the thinking of legislators, diplomatists, heads of state, journalists beyond number, all without thought of personal credit, eager only for the dissemination of the idea. The subject of this parting message showed how to

the very last he refused to lose himself in past issues but lived in
the very center of the world of his day.

Mr. Levinson did not accomplish all the purposes for which
the powers of his great mind and the hopes of his great heart had
nerved him to strive. But in his enunciation of a bedrock principle upon which to build a new and true system of international
law he accomplished more than it is given to most men to do.
May he rest in eternal peace.

AS COLONIAL BONDS ARE LOOSED, *new patterns of
domination, of conflict, arise. A 1933 editorial forecasts what
the challenge of communism in newly awakened areas was to
mean to Christianity in the days ahead.*

February 22, 1933

Communism Knows There Is a Revolution!

AN EDITORIAL

Christianity versus communism for the control of the future!
This, many voices are declaring, is the struggle which is coming
to an issue the world around. In communism they see much
more than a theory of social organization or a system of political
action. It is, to these interpreters, essentially a religion, a religion
with its own inspired word, its own saints, its own eschatology,
and—more important than all else—its own ability to inspire
devotion and sacrifice. In fact, it is this latter characteristic of
communism that really sets it aside from the dominantly in-
tellectualistic socialism that had, previous to the Russian revolution, resulted from the teaching of Marx.

As these observers see the contemporary world this new religion stands as an avowed challenger of Christianity. It is possibly the most aggressive and most plausible challenger that has
ever confronted Christianity. In the name of a complete anti-
religion it offers men not only the goals which, in its vision of a

kingdom of heaven on earth, Christianity has proclaimed, but likewise an opportunity and a method for the use of those resources of self-sacrifice and service in a common cause which modern man has failed to find elsewhere. Officially, communism attacks religion. Psychologically and actually, it offers another religion. The issue for the future hinges on its claim that this new religion actually releases greater spiritual values among those who embrace it than can any faith which is a heritage from the past.

Academic discussion as to this struggle between Christianity and communism can continue endlessly without either side in the argument convincing the other. At the moment, however, it would be well for Christians, who are in danger of entering on such a struggle under the influences of the illusions produced by the fact that their faith is almost twenty centuries old, to look with care at such actual situations as this struggle has already produced. Take, for example, the present state of affairs in China.

Despite the rupture between China and Japan, which is producing a political issue in the classic tradition in Manchuria, it is likely that the thing now happening in China which will have most influence on the future is the advance of communism across the interior. This advance has now reached a point where it has been seriously proposed, in certain Chinese quarters, that if the resources of the Nanking government should be pooled with those of the North China militarists to oppose the threatened Japanese advance southward from Jehol, control of the central Yangtze valley should be turned over to the Communists! Such a proposal is a counsel of despair, and could only be seriously entertained if the Nanking government were on the point of abdication.

But the fact is that the Communists are now in vigorous action in at least half of the eighteen provinces of China proper, and that they maintain skeleton governments in at least six of the provinces. Chiang Kai-shek, the Nanking generalissimo, has recently concluded the most ambitious of his campaigns against the reds with public assurance that their power has been broken. On the contrary, they have now launched a campaign against

Szechwan, largest and richest of Chinese provinces, and press reports indicate rapid red advances in the northern provinces of Shensi and Shansi. This, as a glance at a map will show, is a further pushing toward the northwest, where it is undoubtedly the design of the red leaders ultimately to link on with Mongolia, and so to complete a Communist bloc of territory that will run uninterruptedly from the vicinity of Canton to the Baltic Sea.

The conservative elements in China have opposed this Communist advance ever since 1927, with stern and at times ferocious measures. Yet it goes steadily forward: Chiang Kai-shek returns from "victory" over red armies only to discover the armies he claims to have defeated moving into possession of vast new territories. What is the explanation? The stock answer is, of course, Moscow. It is all a result of the sinister intrigues of Stalin. The clubs of the port cities listen endlessly to tales of Russian gold, Russian arms, Russian plots, Russian plotters. Nor is it our purpose to deny that the hand of Moscow can be discerned at work in the advance of Chinese communism. Stalin has no great amount of money to spend outside Russia, and his philosophy is opposed to the Trotskyite theory of world revolution. But Stalin undoubtedly regards China as the most fruitful field for missionary labor today, and it is reasonable to believe that such attention as is being given to the development of foreign Communist movements is being largely concentrated on that land.

However, only a naïve observer will be satisfied with the explanation that Russian machinations are responsible for all that is happening in central China. There has been too much human agony suffered, the Communist advance has been maintained too long and at too bitter a cost to make such an explanation convincing. The truth is that the regions which have seen Communist achievement are regions in which the common man, a farmer, has been ground down for generations under as brutal a form of peasantry as any civilized state has known. The Communist uprising in interior China is to be basically understood in terms of one issue—land control. It is the old hunger of the man with the hoe to own his own farm, to stand as a free man in the midst of a free man's fields. Essentially, the Communists are making headway in interior China because they have proclaimed a revolution in the ownership of land.

Now what is the relation of Christianity to what is actually taking place? Individual Christians, both missionaries and Chinese, have shown a comprehension of the actualities, and sympathy with the ends which the hitherto dispossessed peasants are seeking. But, in general terms, it is not too much to say that Christianity has recoiled with as much horror, as much antagonism from the excesses of the peasant revolt, as have the commercial interests in the ports. There has been as vociferous condemnation as could be contrived of the terrible excesses which the peasants have committed in their uprisings against the landlords; there has been next to nothing said about the system of landlordism itself and its ideal of a peon society. The brutalities of the Communists have appalled the Christians; it has not proved difficult for them to find justification for the brutalities resorted to in seeking to suppress the Communist activities. The antireligious slogans of the Communists have been answered by the adoption of anti-Communist attitudes which make both missionaries and Chinese Christian pastors habitually talk and act as though China were to be called on to choose between Christianity and a bourgeois order or communism and a peasant anarchy.

The tragic failure of Christianity to comprehend the actual issue in interior China is strikingly exhibited in the recent Laymen's Missions Inquiry. Here is a document that is supposed to be so radical that it is sending cold chills up and down the spines of most missionary executives and thousands of church leaders in the West. The appraisal commission, which spoke with sorrow of the "limited outlook" of the majority of missionaries, contained at least two agricultural experts and devotes a chapter of its report to agricultural missions. Yet it has failed utterly to see this struggle for the control of land. Or, if it saw it, it dared not put itself on record concerning it. It does, it is true, make a few gingerly suggestions as to easing the tension in "the struggle for lower rents and lower interest rates," but it hastens to add that "certain it is that he [the missionary] should not take sides in the heated controversies between landlord and tenant."

The total effect of the report, and of the speeches on the agricultural situation which have been made in the meetings held by the Laymen's Commission since its return, is to give the impression that, as Christianity sees it, the problem of the Chinese farmer is a problem of better methods of production so that he may learn, as the report puts it, that "once the basic needs of food, clothing and shelter have been provided, the ideals of the people, their mental and spiritual outlook, their appreciation of the beautiful, the attitude of members of the family toward each other and the personal relations of neighbors are more important than the things which money can buy." Think of holding that out as what Christianity has to offer to the man who has just begun to feel that serfdom need not be the eternal lot either for himself or for his sons!

The bald fact is that the comfortable, middle-class Protestantism of America has not yet begun to awake to the agony of millions of the world's hitherto dispossessed. Accordingly it cannot comprehend the impulse toward desperate action which is driving them. When it is brought out of the realm of abstract ideas and considered in terms of their actual relationship to present human actions, talk of a struggle between Christianity and communism is like talk of a contest between a nonagenarian sleep-walker and a youthful giant. In no real sense of the word does Christianity know that there is a world revolution under way. Until it awakes to that reality it will remain a marginal concern in the areas where the struggle has already grown intense, derided by some, opposed by many, and ignored by most.

A LOOK BACKWARD, by the great liberal senator from Nebraska.

March 31, 1937

After Twenty Years

GEORGE W. NORRIS

I am the only living man in the Senate who voted against the declaration of war with Germany. In my service of about thirty-five years in Congress I have undoubtedly made many mistakes, but my vote against the declaration of war was not one of them. On that April day twenty years ago when the joint resolution declaring war was under debate in the Senate, I said:

"We are taking a step today that is fraught with untold danger. We are going into war upon the command of gold; we are going to run the risk of sacrificing millions of our countrymen's lives in order that other countrymen may coin their life blood into money. And even if we do not cross the Atlantic and go into the trenches, we are going to pile up a debt that the toiling generations that come many generations after us will have to pay. Unborn millions will bend their necks in toil in order to pay for the terrible step we are now about to take. We are about to do the bidding of wealth's terrible mandate. By our act we will make millions of our countrymen suffer, and the consequences of it may well be that millions of our brethren must shed their life blood, millions of broken-hearted women must weep, millions of children must suffer with cold, and millions of babes must die from hunger, and all because we want to preserve the commercial right of American citizens to deliver the munitions of war to belligerent nations.

"I know that I am powerless to stop it. I know that this

war madness has taken possession of the financial and political powers of our country. I know that nothing I can say will stay the blow that is soon to fall. I feel that we are committing a sin against humanity and against our countrymen. I would like to say to this war god, You shall not coin into gold the life blood of my brethren. I would like to prevent this terrible catastrophe from falling upon my people. I would be willing to surrender my own life if I could cause this awful cup to pass. I charge no man here with wrong motives, but it seems to me that this war craze has robbed us of our judgment. I wish we might delay our action until reason could again be enthroned in the brain of man. I feel that we are about to put the dollar sign upon the American flag."

Is there any word in that speech which, in the light of all we know today, I shall recall? When I said we were about to put the dollar sign on the flag, I was severely condemned twenty years ago. Yet who can now doubt that we did so? The war hastened the process of concentrating the wealth of this country in the hands of the few; it is a process which has been going on at accelerated pace ever since.

How well do we know today, twenty years after, what some of us suspected on April 6, 1917. We know, for instance, that Germany did not "start the war," although she was culpable. But we know now that Russia, France and Great Britain had a hand in it, and were also culpable. We know that our allies came to us with hands outstretched and wet eyes, murmuring idealistic promises of a new order in the world. Justice was to be enthroned, and the Golden Rule was to supplant the old code of intrigue, deceit and distrust. And we know now that in their hands were rockets, while their own pockets were filled with secret treaties and plans for dividing the swag, which they carefully kept from us. We know this now.

For the thousands of our young men killed and maimed, for our billions spent, for the countless millions of heartaches, we have what? We have political corruption, such as was never dreamed of before. We have a new crop of millionaires such as the world has never before witnessed. We have a crime wave that staggers the imagination of the world. We have

214

gigantic, war-grown combinations of trade and money that are squeezing billions annually out of the people who gave till it hurt. We have a national avariciousness and a sense of grab, grab, grab that cannot be eradicated from the national consciousness for generations to come. This we have. Why? Because the war did what a few of us believed it would do —it stupefied and paralyzed the moral consciousness of the American people as nothing else could have done. And because it was a war of gigantic commercial interests from beginning to end.

We, with the balance of the world, are still suffering from that unjust and unnecessary struggle. The terrible condition we are now in and the terrible depression in which all classes of our people have suffered would affect us only in a minor degree if we had kept out of that war. It was a war where no victory was possible. The vanquished suffered no more than the victorious. It was a struggle where, so far as Europe was concerned, all parties to it were completely exhausted. We went into it with our allies, and, to a great extent through our efforts and our sacrifices, we were supposed to have obtained a victory. There was no victory. We are realizing every day that victory was only a name.

In that struggle, about one hundred thousand of our noblest and best gave up their lives. Many times that number are crippled and injured so that they are leading a life of suffering and misery. We know now that we will not get out from under the results of that struggle during our lives or during the lives of our children. Unborn generations will yet toil and suffer and sweat to pay for our participation in that catastrophe.

All wars are destructive. All wars are ruinous. But this war was more ruinous, more destructive than any which preceded it. For four years the largest armies ever known were engaged in the destruction not only of human life, but of property. Every student and every economist knows that the destruction of life and property must be paid for by humanity in toil and sacrifice.

I have always been and I am still an optimist. I believe that

better days will come; that honesty in government will regain
its foothold; that civilization will recover; and that men,
women and children will some day be relieved from the struggle and will have the necessities, the comforts and even some
of the luxuries of life. But before that day comes, we must
continue in our struggle and in our sacrifices, with earnestness
and with hope.

We went to war to end militarism, and there is more militarism today than ever before.

We went to war to make the world safe for democracy, and
there is less democracy today than ever before.

We went to war to dethrone autocracy and special privilege, and they thrive everywhere throughout the world today.

We went to war to win the friendship of the world, and
other nations hate us today.

We went to war to purify the soul of America, and instead
we only drugged it.

We went to war to awaken the American people to the
idealistic concepts of liberty, justice and fraternity, and instead
we awakened them only to the mad pursuit of money.

All this, and more, the war brought us. It is our harvest
from what we sowed.

AN EXCHANGE BETWEEN BROTHERS

ON MILITARY INTERVENTION *in the Sino-Japanese conflict of the early thirties: non-involvement vs. involvement, as debated by two famous brothers, both at that time professors of Christian ethics—H. Richard at Yale, Reinhold at Union.*

March 23, 1932

The Grace of Doing Nothing

H. RICHARD NIEBUHR

It may be that the greatest moral problems of the individual or of a society arise when there is nothing to be done. When we have begun a certain line of action or engaged in a conflict we cannot pause too long to decide which of various possible courses we ought to choose for the sake of the worthier result. Time rushes on and we must choose as best we can, entrusting the issue to the future. It is when we stand aside from the conflict, before we know what our relations to it really are, when we seem to be condemned to doing nothing, that our moral problems become greatest. How shall we do nothing?

The issue is brought home to us by the fighting in the East. We are chafing at the bit, we are eager to do something constructive; but there is nothing constructive, it seems, that we can do. We pass resolutions, aware that we are doing nothing; we summon up righteous indignation and still do nothing; we write letters to congressmen and secretaries, asking others to act while we do nothing. Yet is it really true that we are doing nothing? There are, after all, various ways of being inactive, and some kinds of inactivity, if not all, may be highly productive. It is not really possible to stand aside, to sit by the fire in this world of moving times; even Peter was doing something in the courtyard of the high-priest's house—if it was only something he was doing to himself. When we do nothing we are also affecting the course of history. The problem we face is often that of choice between various kinds of inactivity rather than of choice between action and inaction.

Our inactivity may be that of the pessimist who watches a world go to pieces. It is a meaningul inactivity for himself and for the world. His world, at all events, will go to pieces the more rapidly because of that inactivity. Or it may be the inactivity of the conservative believer in things as they are. He does nothing in the international crisis because he believes that the way of Japan is the way of all nations, that self-interest is the first and only law of life, and that out of the clash of national, as out of that of individual, self-interests the greater good will result. His inactivity is one of watchful waiting for the opportunity when, in precisely similar manner, though with less loss of life and fortune, if possible, he may rush to the protection of his own interests or promote them by taking advantage of the situation created by the strife of his competitors. This way of doing nothing is not unproductive. It encourages the self-asserters and it fills them with fear of the moment when the new competition will begin. It may be that they have been driven into their present conflict by the knowledge or suspicion that the watchful waiter is looking for his opportunity, perhaps unconsciously, and that they must be prepared for him.

The inactivity of frustration and moral indignation is of another order. It is the way of those who have renounced all violent methods of settling conflicts and have no other means at hand by which to deal with the situation. It is an angry inactivity like that of a man who is watching a neighborhood fight and is waiting for the police to arrive—for police who never come. He has renounced for himself the method of forcible interference, which would only increase the flow of blood and the hatred, but he knows of nothing else that he can do. He is forced to remain content on the sidelines, but with mounting anger he regards the bully who is beating the neighbor, and his wrath issues in words of exasperation and condemnation. Having tied his own hands he fights with his tongue and believes that he is not fighting because he inflicts only mental wounds. The bully is for him an outlaw, a person not to be trusted, unfair, selfish, one who cannot be redeemed save by restraint. The righteous indignation mounts and mounts, and must issue at last—as the police fail to arrive— either in his own forcible entry into the conflict, despite his scruples, or in apoplexy.

The diatribes against Japan which are appearing in the secular and religious press today have a distressing similarity to the righteously indignant utterances which preceded our conflicts with Spain and with Germany. China is Cuba and Belgium over again; it is the Negro race beaten by Simon Legree. And the pacifists who have no other program than that of abstention from the unrighteousness of war are likely to be placed in the same quandary in which their fellows were placed in 1860, 1898 and 1915, and—unless human attitudes have been regenerated in the interim—they are likely to share the same fate, which was not usually incarceration. Here is a situation which they did not foresee when they made their vow; may it not be necessary to have one more war to end all war? Righteous indignation not allowed to issue in action is a dangerous thing—as dangerous as any great emotion nurtured and repressed at the same time. It is the source of sudden explosions or the ground of long, bitter and ugly hatreds.

If this way of doing nothing must be rejected the Communists' way offers more hope. Theirs is the inactivity of those who see that there is indeed nothing constructive to be done in the present situation, but that, rightly understood, this situation is after all preliminary to a radical change which will eliminate the conditions of which the conflict is a product. It is the inactivity of a cynicism which expects no good from the present, evil world of capitalism, but also the inactivity of a boundless faith in the future. The Communists know that war and revolution are closely akin, that war breeds discontent and misery, and that out of misery and discontent new worlds may be born. This is an opportunity, then, not for direct entrance into the conflict, not for the watchful waiting of those who seek their self-interest, but for the slow laborious process of building up within the fighting groups those cells of communism which will be ready to inherit the new world and be able to build a classless international commonwealth on the ruins of capitalism and nationalism. Here is inactivity with a long vision, a steadfast hope and a realistic program of non-interfering action.

But there is yet another way of doing nothing. It appears to be highly impracticable because it rests on the well-nigh obsolete faith that there is a God—a real God. Those who follow this way share with communism the belief that the fact that men can do nothing constructive is no indication of the fact that nothing constructive is being done. Like the Communists they are assured that the actual processes of history will inevitably and really bring a different kind of world with lasting peace. They do not rely on human aspirations after ideals to accomplish this end, but on forces which often seem very impersonal—as impersonal as those which eliminated slavery in spite of abolitionists. The forces may be as impersonal and as actual as machine production, rapid transportation, the physical mixtures of races, etc., but as parts of the real world they are as much a part of the total divine process as are human thoughts and prayers.

From this point of view, naïvely affirming the meaningfulness of reality, the history of the world is the judgment of the world and also its redemption, and a conflict like the present one is—again as in communism—only the prelude both to greater judgment and to a new era. The world being what it is, these results are brought forth when the seeds of national or individual self-interest are planted; the actual structure of things is such that our wishes for a different result do not in the least affect the outcome. As a man soweth so shall he reap. This God of things as they are is inevitable and quite merciless. His mercy lies beyond, not this side of, judgment. This inactive Christianity shares with communism also the belief in the inevitably good outcome of the mundane process and the realistic insight that that good cannot be achieved by the slow accretion of better habits alone but more in consequence of a revolutionary change which will involve considerable destruction. While it does nothing it knows that something is being done, something which is divine both in its threat and in its promise.

This inactivity is like that of the early Christians whose millenarian mythology it replaces with the contemporary mythology of social forces. (Mythology is after all not fiction but a deep philosophy.) Like early Christianity and like communism today radical Christianity knows that nothing constructive can be done by interference, but that something very constructive can be done in preparation for the future. It also can build cells of those within each nation who, divorcing themselves from the program of nationalism and of capitalism, unite in a higher loyalty which transcends national and class lines of division and prepare for the future. There is no such Christian international today because radical Christianity has not arrived as yet at a program and a philosophy of history, but such little cells are forming. The First Christian international of Rome has had its day; the Second Christian international of Stockholm is likely to go the way of the Second Socialist international. There is need and opportunity for a Third Christian international.

While the similarities of a radically Christian program with the Communist program are striking, there are also great dissimilarities. There is a new element in the inactivity of radical Christianity which is lacking in communism. The Christian reflects upon the fact that his inability to do anything constructive in the crisis is the inability of one whose own faults are so apparent and so similar to those of the offender that any action on his part is not only likely to be misinterpreted but is also likely—in the nature of the case—to be really less than disinterested. He is like a father who, feeling a righteous indignation against a misbehaving child, remembers that that misbehavior is his fault as much as the child's and that indignation is the least helpful, the most dangerous of attitudes to take; it will solve nothing, though it may repress.

So the American Christian realizes that Japan is following the example of his own country and that it has little real ground for believing America to be a disinterested nation. He may see that his country, for which he bears his own responsibility as a citizen, is really not disinterested and that its righteous indignation is not wholly righteous. An inactivity then is demanded which will be profoundly active in rigid self-analysis. Such analysis is likely to reveal that there is an approach to the situation, indirect but far more effective than direct interference, for it is able to create the conditions under which a real reconstruction of habits is possible. It is the opposite approach from that of the irate father who believes that every false reaction on the part of his child may be cured by a verbal, physical or economic spanking.

This way of doing nothing the old Christians called repentance, but the word has become so reminiscent of emotional debauches in the feeling of guilt that it may be better to abandon it for a while. What is suggested is that the only effective approach to the problem of China and Japan lies in the sphere of an American self-analysis which is likely to result in some surprising discoveries as to the amount of renunciation of self-interest necessary on the part of this country and of individual Christians before anything effective can be done in the East.

The inactivity of radical Christianity is not the inactivity of those who call evil good; it is the inaction of those who do not judge their neighbors because they cannot fool themselves into a sense of superior righteousness. It is not the inactivity of a resigned patience, but of a patience that is full of hope and is based on faith. It is not the inactivity of the noncombatant, for it knows that there are no noncombatants, that everyone is involved, that China is being crucified (though the term is very inaccurate) by our sins and those of the whole world. It is not the inactivity of the merciless, for works of mercy must be performed though they are only palliatives to ease present pain while the process of healing depends on deeper, more actual and urgent forces.

But if there is no God, or if God is up in heaven and not in time itself, it is a very foolish inactivity.

A CRITIQUE of H. Richard Niebuhr's article, "The Grace of Doing Nothing," in the March 23 issue of The Christian Century.

March 30, 1932

Must We Do Nothing?

REINHOLD NIEBUHR

There is much in my brother's article, "The Grace of Doing Nothing," with which I agree. Except for the invitation of the editors of The Christian Century I would have preferred to defer voicing any disagreement with some of his final conclusions to some future occasion; for a casual article on a specific problem created by the contemporary international situation hardly does justice to his general position. I believe the problem upon which he is working—the problem of dissociating a rigorous gospel ethic of disinterestedness and love from the sentimental dilutions of that ethic which are current in liberal Christianity—is a tremendously important one. I owe so much to the penetrating thought which he has been giving this subject that I may be able to do some justice to his general position even though I do not share his conviction that a pure love ethic can ever be made the basis of a civilization.

He could not have done better than to choose the Sino-Japanese conflict, and the reactions of the world to it, in order to prove the difficulty, if not the futility, of dealing redemptively with a sinful nation or individual if we cannot exorcise the same sin from our own hearts. It is true that pacifists are in danger of stirring up hatred against Japan in their effort to stem the tide of Japanese imperialism. It is true that the very impotence of an individual who deals with a social situation which goes beyond his own powers tempts him to hide his

sense of futility behind a display of violent emotion. It is true
that we have helped to create the Japan which expresses itself
in terms of materialistic imperialism. The insult we offered
her in our immigration laws was a sin of spiritual aggression.
The white world has not only taught her the ways of imperialism, but has pre-empted enough of the yellow man's side of
the world to justify Japan's imperialism as a vent for pent-up
national energies.

It is also true that American concern over Japanese aggression is not wholly disinterested. It is national interest which
desires us to desire stronger action against Japan than France
and England are willing to take. It is true, in other words, that
every social sin is, at least partially, the fruit and consequence
of the sins of those who judge and condemn it, and that the
effort to eliminate it involves the critics and judges in new
social sin, the assertion of self-interest and the expression of
moral conceit and hypocrisy. If anyone would raise the objection to such an analysis that it finds every social action
falling short only because it measures the action against an
impossible ideal of disinterestedness, my brother could answer
that while the ideal may seem to be impossible the actual
social situation proves it to be necessary. It is literally true that
every recalcitrant nation, like every antisocial individual, is
created by the society which condemns it, and that redemptive
efforts which betray strong ulterior motives are always bound
to be less than fully redemptive.

My brother draws the conclusion from this logic that it is
better not to act at all than to act from motives which are
less than pure, and with the use of methods which are less
than critical (coercion). He believes in taking literally the
words of Jesus, "Let him who is without sin cast the first
stone." He believes, of course, that this kind of inaction would
not really be inaction; it would be, rather, the action of repentance. It would give every one involved in social sin the
chance to recognize how much he is involved in it and how
necessary it is to restrain his own greed, pride, hatred and lust
for power before the social sin is eliminated.

This is an important emphasis particularly for modern

Christianity with its lack of appreciation of the tragic character of life and with its easy assumption that the world will be saved by a little more adequate educational technique. Hypocrisy is an inevitable by-product of moral aspiration, and it is the business of true religion to destroy man's moral conceit, a task which modern religion has not been performing in any large degree. Its sentimentalities have tended to increase rather than to diminish moral conceit. A truly religious man ought to distinguish himself from the moral man by recognizing the fact that he is not moral, that he remains a sinner to the end. The sense of sin is more central to religion than is any other attitude.

All this does not prove, however, that we ought to apply the words of Jesus, "Let him who is without sin cast the first stone," literally. If we do we will never be able to act. There will never be a wholly disinterested nation. Pure disinterestedness is an ideal which even individuals cannot fully achieve, and human groups are bound always to express themselves in lower ethical forms than individuals. It follows that no nation can ever be good enough to save another nation purely by the power of love. The relation of nations and of economic groups can never be brought into terms of pure love. Justice is probably the highest ideal toward which human groups can aspire. And justice, with its goal of adjustment of right to right, inevitably involves the assertion of right against right and interest against interest until some kind of harmony is achieved. If a measure of humility and of love does not enter this conflict of interest it will of course degenerate into violence. A rational society will be able to develop a measure of the kind of imagination which knows how to appreciate the virtues of an opponent's position and the weakness in one's own. But the ethical and spiritual note of love and repentance can do no more than qualify the social struggle in history. It will never abolish it.

The hope of attaining an ethical goal for society by purely ethical means, that is, without coercion, and without the assertion of the interests of the underprivileged against the interests of the privileged, is an illusion which was spread chiefly among the comfortable classes of the past century. My brother does not make the mistake of assuming that this is possible in social terms. He is acutely aware of the fact that it is not possible to get a sufficient degree of pure disinterestedness and love among privileged classes and powerful nations to resolve the conflicts of history in that way. He understands the stubborn inertia which the ethical ideal meets in history. At this point his realistic interpretation of the facts of history comes in full conflict with his insistence upon a pure gospel ethic, upon a religiously inspired moral perfectionism, and he resolves the conflict by leaving the field of social theory entirely and resorting to eschatology. The Christian will try to achieve humility and disinterestedness not because enough Christians will be able to do so to change the course of history, but because this kind of spiritual attitude is a prayer to God for the coming of his kingdom.

I will not quarrel with this apocalyptic note, as such, though I suspect many Christian Century readers will. I believe that a proper eschatology is necessary to a vigorous ethic, and that the simple idea of progress is inimical to the highest ethic. The compound of pessimism and optimism which a vigorous ethical attitude requires can be expressed only in terms of religious eschatology. What makes my brother's eschatology impossible for me is that he identifies everything that is occurring in history (the drift toward disaster, another world war and possibly a revolution) with the counsels of God, and then suddenly, by a leap of faith, comes to the conclusion that the same God who uses brutalities and forces, against which man must maintain conscientious scruples, will finally establish an ideal society in which pure love will reign.

I have more than one difficulty with such a faith. I do not see how a revolution in which the disinterested express their anger and resentment, and assert their interests, can be an instrument of God, and yet at the same time an instrument which religious scruples forbid a man to use. I should think that it would be better to come to ethical terms with the forces of nature in history, and try to use ethically directed coercion in order that violence may be avoided. The hope that a kingdom of pure love will emerge out of the catastrophes of history is even less plausible than the Communist faith that an equalitarian society will eventually emerge from them. There is some warrant in history for the latter assumption, but very little for the former.

I find it impossible to envisage a society of pure love as long as man remains man. His natural limitations of reason and imagination will prevent him, even should he achieve a purely disinterested motive, from fully envisaging the needs of his fellow men or from determining his actions upon the basis of their interests. Inevitably these limitations of individuals will achieve cumulative effect in the life and actions of national, racial and economic groups. It is possible to envisage a more ethical society than we now have. It is possible to believe that such a society will be achieved partly by evolutionary process and partly by catastrophe in which an old order, which offers a too stubborn resistance to new forces, is finally destroyed.

It is plausible also to interpret both the evolutionary and the catastrophic elements in history in religious terms and to see the counsels of God in them. But it is hardly plausible to expect divine intervention to introduce something into history which is irrelevant to anything we find in history now. We may envisage a society in which human co-operation is possible with a minimum amount of coercion, but we cannot imagine one in which there is no coercion at all—unless, of course, human beings become quite different from what they now are. We may hope for a society in which self-interest is qualified by rigorous self-analysis and a stronger social impulse, but we cannot imagine a society totally without the assertion of self-interest and therefore without the conflict of opposing interests.

I realize quite well that my brother's position both in its ethical perfectionism and in its apocalyptic note is closer to the gospel than mine. In confessing that, I am forced to admit that I am unable to construct an adequate social ethic out of a pure love ethic. I cannot abandon the pure love ideal because anything which falls short of it is less than the ideal. But I cannot use it fully if I want to assume a responsible

attitude toward the problems of society. Religious perfectionism drives either to asceticism or apocalypticism. In the one
case the problem of society is given up entirely; in the other
individual perfection is regarded as the force which will release
the redemptive powers of God for society. I think the second
alternative is better than the first, and that both have elements
which must be retained for any adequate social ethic, lest it
become lost in the relativities of expediency. But as long as
the world of man remains a place where nature and God, the
real and the ideal, meet, human progress will depend upon the
judicious use of the forces of nature in the service of the ideal.

In practical, specific and contemporary terms, this means
that we must try to dissuade Japan from her military venture,
but must use coercion to frustrate her designs if necessary,
must reduce coercion to a minimum and prevent it from issu-
ing in violence, must engage in constant self-analysis in order
to reduce the moral conceit of Japan's critics and judges to
a minimum, and must try in every social situation to maximize
the ethical forces and yet not sacrifice the possibility of achiev-
ing an ethical goal because we are afraid to use any but purely
ethical means.

To say all this is really to confess that the history of mankind is a personal tragedy; for the highest ideals which the individual may project are ideals which he can never realize in
social and collective terms. If there is a law in our members
which wars against the law that is in our minds as individuals,
this is even more true when we think of society. Individuals set
the goal for society but society itself must achieve the goal,
and society is and will always remain sub-human. The goal
which a sensitive individual sets for society must therefore always be something which is a little outside and beyond history.
Love may qualify the social struggle of history but it will
never abolish it, and those who make the attempt to bring
society under the dominion of perfect love will die on the cross.
And those who behold the cross are quite right in seeing it as
a revelation of the divine, of what man ought to be and cannot be, at least not so long as he is enmeshed in the processes
of history.

Perhaps that is why it is inevitable that religious imagination should set goals beyond history. "Man's reach is beyond his grasp, or what's a heaven for." My brother does not like these goals above and beyond history. He wants religion and social idealism to deal with history. In that case he must not state his goal in absolute terms. There can be nothing absolute in history, no matter how frequently God may intervene in it. Man cannot live without a sense of the absolute, but neither can he achieve the absolute. He may resolve the tragic character of that fact by religious faith, by the experience of grace in which the unattainable is experienced in anticipatory terms, but he can never resolve in purely ethical terms the conflict between what is and what ought to be.

April 6, 1932

The Only Way into the Kingdom of God

A COMMUNICATION BY
H. RICHARD NIEBUHR

Editor The Christian Century

Sir: Since you have given me leave to fire one more shot in the fraternal war between my brother and me over the question of pacifism, I shall attempt to place it as well as I can, not for the purpose of demolishing my opponent's position—which our thirty years have shown me to be impossible—but for the sake of pointing as accurately as I can to the exact locus of the issue between us. It does not lie in the question of activity or inactivity, to which my too journalistic approach to the problem directed attention; we are speaking after all of two kinds of activity. The fundamental question seems to me to be whether "the history of mankind is a perennial tragedy" which can derive meaning only from a goal which lies beyond history, as my brother maintains, or whether the "eschatological" faith, to which I seek to adhere, is justifiable. In that faith tragedy is only the prelude to fulfilment, and a prelude which is necessary because of human nature; the kingdom of God comes inevitably, though whether we shall see it or not depends on our recognition of its presence and our acceptance of the only kind of life which will enable us to enter it, the life of repentance and forgiveness.

For my brother God is outside the historical processes, so much so that he charges me with faith in a miracle-working deity which interferes occasionally, sometimes brutally, sometimes redemptively, in this history. But God, I believe, is always in history; he is the structure in things, the source of all meaning, the "I am that I am," that which is that it is. He is the rock against which we beat in vain, that which bruises and overwhelms us when we seek to impose our wishes, contrary to his, upon him. That structure of the universe, that creative will, can no more be said to interfere brutally in history than the violated laws of my organism can be said to interfere brutally with my life if they make me pay the cost of my violation. That structure of the universe, that will of God, does bring war and depression upon us when we bring it upon ourselves, for we live in the kind of world which visits our iniquities upon us and our children, no matter how much we pray and desire that it be otherwise.

Self-interest acts destructively in this world; it calls forth counter-assertion; nationalism breeds nationalism; class assertion summons up counter-assertion on the part of exploited classes. The result is war, economic, military, verbal; and it is judgment. But this same structure in things which is our enemy is our redeemer; "it means intensely and it means good"—not the good which we desire, but the good which we would desire if we were good and really wise. History is not a perennial tragedy but a road to fulfilment and that fulfilment requires the tragic outcome of every self-assertion, for it is fulfilment which can only be designated as "love." It has created fellowship in atoms and organisms, at bitter cost to electrons and cells; and it is creating something better than human selfhood but at bitter cost to that selfhood. This is not a faith in progress, for evil grows as well as good, and every self-assertion must be eliminated somewhere and somehow— by innocence suffering for guilt, it seems.

If, however, history is no more than tragedy, if there is no fulfilment in it, then my brother is right. Then we must rest content with the clash of self-interested individuals, personal or social. But in that case I see no reason why we should qualify the clash of competition with a homeopathic dose of Christian "love."

The only harmony which can possibly result from the clash of interests is the harmony imposed by the rule of the strong or a parallelogram of social forces, whether we think of the interclass structure or the international world. To import any pacifism into this struggle is only to weaken the weaker self-asserters (India, China or the proletariat) or to provide the strong with a façade of "service" behind which they can operate with a salved conscience. (Pacifism, on the other hand, as a method of self-assertion is not pacifism at all but a different kind of war.)

The method which my brother recommends, that of qualifying the social struggle by means of some Christian love, seems to me to be only the old method of making Christian love an ambulance driver in the wars of interested and clashing parties. If it is more than that, it is a weakening of the forces whose success we think necessary for a juster social order. For me the question is one of "either-or"; either the Christian method, which is not the method of love but of repentance and forgiveness, or the method of self-assertion; either nationalism or Christianity, either capitalism-communism or Christianity. The attempt to qualify the one method by the other is hopeless compromise.

I think that to apply the terms "Christian perfectionism" or "Christian ideal" to my approach is rather misleading. I rather think that Dewey is quite right in his war on ideals; they always seem irrelevant to our situation and betray us into a dualistic morality. The society of love is an impossible human ideal, as the fellowship of the organism is an impossible ideal for the cell. It is not an ideal toward which we can strive, but an "emergent," a potentiality in our situation which remains unrealized so long as we try to impose our pattern, our wishes upon the divine creative process.

Man's task is not that of building utopias, but that of eliminating weeds and tilling the soil so that the kingdom of God can grow. His method is not one of striving for perfection or of acting perfectly, but of clearing the road by repentance and forgiveness. That this approach is valid for societies as well as for individuals and that the opposite approach will always involve us in the same one ceaseless cycle of assertion and counter-assertion is what I am concerned to emphasize.

H. Richard Niebuhr

AFTER VISITING GERMANY *during the time the Nazi regime was approaching its zenith, a future editor of the Century contributed a number of articles describing the darkening scene. At that time Dr. Fey was secretary of the Fellowship of Reconciliation.*

September 1, 1937

The German Church Says No!

HAROLD E. FEY

Suppose this had happened in America instead of Germany: Harry Emerson Fosdick stands in Riverside Church and preaches a sermon on "We ought to obey God rather than men." During the sermon he relates that on the Wednesday just passed G-men had broken into the locked church of Ernest Fremont Tittle in Evanston and arrested at the altar eight members of the Federal Council of Churches who were meeting there and had taken them away to some secret place. On Friday he himself had celebrated holy communion in his own church with nobody present except three young secret service men, "who have to inform upon the community of Jesus in their praying, in their singing and their teaching; young men who certainly were once baptized in the name of Jesus, and who certainly have pledged their faith to the Savior, who are now laying traps for his flock." Yesterday, he continues, at Philadelphia, six women and a trusted man of the Protestant churches were arrested for circulating a leaflet concerning the forthcoming forced church election which the government had decreed. Today, he says finally, the pulpits of scores of churches are empty because their pastors have been spirited away to unknown jails, together with many devoted laymen and women. "In the week beginning today the first prosecutions are to take place."

Change the name Fosdick to Martin Niemöller, change the other American names and places to German equivalents and make Riverside Church, New York, to read Dahlem Church, Berlin, and you have an inkling of how Niemöller's last sermon in Dahlem Church on June 27, 1937, sounded to German ears. At the midweek meeting the week before, Dahlem Church was so crowded that Niemöller spoke to two audiences. Dr. Wilhelm Frick, minister of the interior, had decreed it a crime to give money to the Confessional Synod. A wealthy layman of the church had just been arrested for violating this law. When Niemöller invited the hundreds of people present also to violate it by contributing to a collection to carry on the work of the Confessional Synod they responded generously and courageously. Then a wild clamor broke loose at the doors. A gang of Hitler Jugend were beating such collection takers as they could reach, yelling: "Cease collecting money for this club. It is forbidden." The pastor raised his hand and announced a hymn. Nobody who heard it will ever forget the impression created when high above the tumult at the entrances the majestic words rolled out:

> A mighty fortress is our God,
> A bulwark never failing . . .
>
> For still our ancient foe
> Doth seek to work us woe . . .

And though this world, with devils filled
Should threaten to undo us,
We will not fear for God hath willed
His truth to triumph through us.

A reporter who was present wrote: "Long after the Hitler youth demonstrators had gone their way, angry groups of citizens surrounded the church. The doors had been hurriedly locked, but groups in the street were shouting and gesticulating pro and con long after midnight." But on July 1 Niemöller, the last of the leaders of the Confessional Synod to keep his freedom, was also arrested, charged with "inciting to disobedience."

It is significant and encouraging to those of us who want to believe that the spirit of God still animates his church that the German totalitarian state has encountered its most doughty resistance among religious people. After the Nazis had crushed all political opposition including the powerful Social Democratic party; after they had liquidated the Communists, who polled six million votes just before the Nazis came into power; after they had regimented 168 well-disciplined and wealthy labor unions and an unknown number of employers' associations in one "labor front," after they had suppressed civic and women's and youth organizations without a struggle—they were forced unwillingly to reckon with the aroused Christian conscience. In spite of the return to Wotan by Ludendorff and his fellow neo-pagans and in defiance of the much more sinister nazification of Christianity by the German Christian movement, the church of Christ still lives in Germany. So the Nazis are compelled against their desires to enter into another *Kulturkampf* against Catholicism and Protestantism united in opposition to the state. Neither the National Socialists nor their opponents have forgotten that it was just such "cultural war" lasting eight years which brought Hitler's ruthless predecessor, Bismarck, to ignominious defeat in 1878. Already the struggle has aroused a quality of spirit which was thought to be dead in Germany.

On August 9 Pastor Niemöller was scheduled to come to trial. His people decided to meet in Dahlem Church to pray for him. When they arrived the doors had been locked by the Gestapo. A crowd gathered, for in these days prayer meetings as well as other religious gatherings are well attended in Germany. The police ordered the people to disband. They not only refused to go home, they staged a parade—the first open demonstration of opposition seen in Germany since the Nazis had consolidated their power. The frantic police pleaded with them to break up, and when they refused the officers brought vans and packed them with well-dressed men and women, taking more than a hundred to the police station. There they were required to register their names. When the police saw who their prisoners were, they immediately released most of them. For this was no ordinary crowd of rioters. Dahlem Church contains many of the nation's most influential economic leaders. Its congregations are dotted with the uniforms of high officials in the army and navy, and many other people important in German life attend regularly. For the first time in four years the police had faced a crowd which was completely unafraid of them. The government was appalled. The ban on the prayer meetings was lifted. The Reich minister suddenly decided to postpone the trial.

Contributing to this decision was undoubtedly the unexpected acquittal on August 7 of Dr. Friedrich Dibelius, former general supervisor of the United Church of Prussia. He had been charged by Dr. Hanns Kerrl, Reich church minister, with wilfully misrepresenting him in a letter. Dibelius had denounced the minister for having said that it was "absurd and trivial" to maintain that the only adequate foundation for the church is "recognition of Jesus as the Son of God." The court's surprisingly independent decision that Dibelius had adequate reason for his indictment created a profound impression, and put the Reich church ministry in a very bad light. Dr. Kerrl, who had scheduled the Niemöller trial almost immediately afterward, retreated in terror from the prospect of adding another such decision to feed the flames of church rebellion, and so called off the consideration of Pastor Niemöller's case, probably until after the annual Nazi party congress to be held in Nuremberg this month.

The temper of the opposition which the Nazis are facing is shown by these recent words of a leading German churchman: "Totalitarian states must learn that Christian churches are a reality. Toleration is not a luxury; it is a necessity. The church must therefore stand fast. Many want to yield, but we dare not. We must be ready every day to go to prison or concentration camp. If we do this for ten or fifteen years, the state will be compelled to acknowledge the reality of the church. Germans are strong in their respect for principle. Prison is not so awful as it seems before you are there. I have been there and I know. Our fathers by the help of God endured it and we by the help of the same God can do the same thing."

Whence come the extraordinary strength and courage which make the church struggle in Germany such a challenge to the rest of the Christian world? How does it happen that in "silent Germany" only the church has spoken out? What sure instinct has led these simple people to cut through the "network of lies" which has snared the intelligentsia of this nation whose scholarship and science have led the Western world?

Certainly it is not because the pastors have, in the easy phrase of a current lecturer, whittled their problems down to their own size before tackling them. Instead, they have discovered through the red illumination of bitter failure the strength that is made perfect through weakness. Niemöller recently declared that the Protestant church situation from any worldly point of view is hopeless. Its organization is gone. Its youth work is demoralized. Nobody knows who will be arrested next. Its financial resources have been seized by the state. "We have reached the end. We do not need to worry any more about church reform. These matters have been taken out of our hands. . . . But I assure you that the church is not at an end. When our intellects say that the church has reached the end of the road, God answers, 'No. It shall not be.'"

Neither does the church's strength come from fulfilling all the social demands which many of us in the American churches find in the gospel. Most of the pastors who have gone to prison because they refuse to preach at the behest of the totalitarian state that "Jesus is not a Jew" do not criticize the government for most of the aspects of its anti-Semitic campaign. Many of them will condemn its excesses but will not challenge the ethical basis of the government's attempt to segregate Jews in legal and cultural ghettos. Neither do they carry resistance to some actions of the totalitarian state to the point where they attempt on religious grounds to appraise the supreme goal and purpose of that state—war. Niemöller, who commanded submarines which sank thousands of tons of allied shipping during the war, is today almost as much of a navalist as President Roosevelt. According to his own statement, he is ready to resume his old vocation again if Germany is attacked. But nobody in the world can doubt that these men and women are living loyally and sacrificially up to the light they have.

One clue to the spiritual power which lies in the Confessional Church movement is found in its clarity of purpose. Within the limits of what it sees as Christian there can be no compromise. Niemöller said this summer that he and his associates "were standing on the point of a pin but if they fell they would crash thousands of feet." He meant by this that the form in which the issues of the church struggle arise seems trivial, but the questions of principle which are involved are of vast importance and may not be compromised. This is what the Confessional Church leaders emphasized on July 11 when they appealed to the government to make an honorable peace with the churches and then followed this appeal with an exhortation to all the churches "to preach the true faith and no other, to pray for the government that it render to God what is God's, and to pray for all who are in power." The government's answer, when Niemöller was that day released from Moabit prison on orders of the "investigating judge," was immediately to order his re-arrest by the secret police and his incarceration in the Alexanderplatz jail. A corollary of this clarification of purpose is that it has alienated from Confessional ranks all the half-hearted. Ambiguous neutrals have all found reasons for siding against them. Some of the present trouble arose when the pastors began to read from their pulpits the names of the scores of government officials and others who have resigned from the churches but who want still to make a "Christian appearance."

A second source of strength lies in the Confessional Church's rediscovery and reaffirmation of the totalitarian nature of the Christian faith. In the face of the all-inclusive claims of the German state it was compelled either to do this or to go over completely to the camp of the German Christians. Rosenberg, director of foreign affairs for the Nazi party, speaking on June 6 of this year, defined the scope of the state as follows: "National Socialism has not appealed to only a part of the German man or woman, but to the whole man and the whole woman, and therefore Germans accepted it wholly." In answer to this essentially religious claim, the Confessional Church does not equivocate. In the famous "instructions to pastors" issued just a week before Rosenberg's statement, it said: "The National Socialist ideology mobilizes all aspects of life within its sphere of activity and claims exclusive control. . . . The basis for all this is that National Socialism is itself the church. Accordingly all state activities assume a religious character. Politics is a divine mission. Service to the nation is a divine service. National Socialism therefore has a divine mission for which it claims the whole nation. Thus members of the German nation are made incapable of understanding their Christian mission and of fulfilling their Christian duties. The one-sided deification of racial and biological values and concrete accomplishment has created a hardheartedness regarding 'the inferior and the useless' which is a contradiction of neighborly love."

The important thing, however, is not that they have attained a true insight into the inner nature of National Socialism's claims, but that within their own experience the power and love of God have been richly reborn. They have reaffirmed the inclusive nature of the Christian faith at terrible cost to themselves, and in losing everything hundreds of men and women have had the amazing experience of suddenly finding themselves possessors of spiritual riches in comparison with which their former values of prestige, comfort, security and even physical freedom seem as worthless trash. The basis in experience for a new Philippian letter is being laid in Germany today, and the Confessional churchman is saying: "I count all things but loss for the excellency of the knowledge of Christ Jesus my Lord: for whom I have suffered the loss of all things and do count them but refuse, that I may win Christ and be found in him." It requires only a superficial knowledge of the history of the Christian Church to suggest what this rediscovery in the jails and concentration camps of Germany of the "righteousness which is of God by faith" may mean.

It is entirely possible that the Confessional movement, learning by what it suffers, may move on and take its stand on a much broader platform than the "head of a pin" to which Niemöller referred. Evidence that this is happening is found all through the instructions to pastors to which reference has just been made. This remarkable document is the most inclusive and open statement of opposition to the whole Nazi regime which has been issued in Germany since the Third Reich came into power. It accuses the state of taking over church activity in the fields of education, charity and recreation. It charges it with suppression of freedom of speech, assembly and the press. It indicts it for continual interference with the legitimate functions of religion and for setting itself up as a rival church. "The whole German nation is subjected to an ideological propaganda program which derides the Bible, the pastors, the church and Christianity generally. The state prohibits the church from fighting for the gospel under the conditions which its opponents enjoy. The battle for the gospel is pilloried as sedition." The document concludes with the announcement that the church "cannot abandon public teaching of the gospel through the published word" and calls upon all church members to aid in this activity.

So another source of strength which has been made available to the Confessional Church is the penetrating grasp of truth that comes when the rule of life is, "If any man will do his will he shall know. . . ." Following the above statement closely came another astonishing pronouncement from the Confessional leaders against the "complete and systematic de-Christianizing of the next generation of the German nation which is taking place. . . . We admonish all parents that they will be responsible to God for the Christian education of their children. . . . School instruction—even religious instruction in the schools—is largely influenced by a standpoint that rejects Jesus Christ's gospel. . . . Christian education is being undermined by the systematic schooling of educators and children in the meaning and purpose of the National Socialist ideology. . . . All youth, through the state youth organizations, is subjected to ideological schooling. In particular a considerable group of young people are being systematically and consciously de-Christianized in the Ordensburger, the student's schooling camps and the Fuehrer schools of the Hitler youth and the League of German Girls and are being trained solely in the religious attitude, mission and service idea of the National Socialist ideology. Christian schools are being transformed step by step into schools of racial ideology."

This completely uncompromising indictment of the anti-Christian character of National Socialism together with its call to Christian parents to resist Nazi youth leaders' work with their children constitutes a new high-water mark of courage. Its insight that the totalitarian state has become the anti-Christ against which men of faith everywhere are called to stand without flinching constitutes an invitation to daily prayer for the church of Christ in Germany. It also causes us to dwell with humility and foreboding on a Confessional leader's prophecy, made this summer: "Soon, within not more than ten or twenty years, you Americans will be called to face what we are going through."

*SUBSEQUENT EVENTS have proved that this early analysis
and forecast by the pastor of the Community Church of New
York City was indeed prophetic.*

July 30, 1941

If Russia Wins

JOHN HAYNES HOLMES

Russia is in the war. Naturally enough, most Americans
are rooting for Russia to win. But before we become emotion-
ally too involved, it would be well to consider what it might
mean to have Russia win this war, or her particular share
thereof. What would she get out of the struggle after it is all
over? We may be sure that Russia is not going to fight
through to victory for nothing. After she has scorched the
earth of uncounted miles of her territory, laid down the lives
of millions of her sons, seen her industries ruined, her cities
bombed, her treasure wasted and her dream of a Communist
utopia postponed for a hundred years, if not altogether ruined,
she is going to demand compensation in the settlement. Are
we sure we are prepared to grant her demands?

Let us turn away from the battle for a moment and look
into the future. Visualize the time when the fighting will be
done and peace must be made. What is Russia going to say
and do?

The peace table, wherever it may be set up, in Geneva,
or London, or Washington, will be an interesting spectacle.
There will be Churchill, Roosevelt, De Gaulle, Chiang Kai-
shek and the representatives of the governments in exile. And
there will be Joseph Stalin, smiling amiably through his mus-
tache as he smiled in that famous picture of Molotov and
Ribbentrop signing the Russo-German non-aggression pact,
and as he smiled again in what is destined to be that equally

famous picture of Molotov and Sir Stafford Cripps signing the Russo-British cobelligerency pact.

The Soviet dictator will sit along with the premiers, the presidents and the kings. His seat will be high up near the head of the table. For the action of Russia will have been crucial if the Allies win this war. When the peace conference meets, Stalin's decision to fight in 1941 will be regarded as vital to victory in this war, as Wilson's decision to fight in 1917 was regarded as central to victory in the last war. Stalin will be well able to say to his associates: "I won this war for you. I bore the heat and burden of the day when the struggle was most critical. Mine were the blood, the sweat and the tears. But I won this war not merely for you but for myself, for Russia quite as much as for Britain. I must be listened to. I'll sit here at Mr. Churchill's right."

First on the agenda of the conference, undoubtedly, will be President Roosevelt's "Four Freedoms," as first on the agenda of the Versailles conference were Woodrow Wilson's Fourteen Points. With this initial discussion Stalin will not be much concerned. He will sit there silently in his place, smiling his enigmatic smile, while the conferees debate how to establish the "four freedoms . . . everywhere in the world." Only when this question of "everywhere" comes to the fore will Stalin bestir himself. He will then say, in quiet tones, that these freedoms are interesting and undoubtedly important, but that, so far as Russia is concerned, they are not precisely . . . er . . . er . . . practicable. There will be other peoples excepted from their application, of course. Among these will be the 350 million people of India.

The four freedoms having been dealt with as satisfactorily as the Fourteen Points were dealt with at Versailles, there will next come the question of territorial settlements. Here Stalin will suddenly become alert and, before anybody has an opportunity to take the floor, will draw a slip of paper from his pocket and begin, "Gentlemen." Then he will proceed to lay down Russia's terms of peace. I venture to surmise that they will run something like the following:

1. Russia will annex Finland. In 1940, Stalin will explain,

Russia was very lenient with Finland. When Helsinki sued for peace after losing the inexcusable war of 1939-40, Moscow respected Finland's independence and took only certain strategic points necessary to Russia's military security. Then, when Hitler pounced without warning upon the Soviets, Finland followed suit, and Marshal Mannerheim led Finnish armies onto Russian soil. There must now be left no danger of any repetition of this offense, Stalin will affirm. Leningrad must be made safe!

2. Russia will annex Latvia, Lithuania and Estonia. Like Finland, these countries, Stalin will explain, were part of ancient Russia. The peasants and workers of these countries are entitled to enjoy the same proletarian emancipation that has been granted to the rest of the Russian people. Furthermore, these countries, like Finland, are necessary to Russia's military security. They are her bastions and bulwarks against the chaos of western Europe. So what was done at Versailles in 1919, and undone in 1940, must now be undone again, Stalin will say.

3. Russia will annex Poland, or at least that part of Poland which belonged to Russia before the war of 1914. It is true that the restoration of Poland was one of the noble fruits of the First World War. It is true that the new restoration of Poland, after the debacle of 1939 and the fourth partition of 1940, was one of the few perfectly distinct purposes of the Second World War. What did Britain go to war for if not to save Poland? In what hope did Paderewski and all his heroic countrymen live in those last months, and Paderewski himself die, if not in the hope that Poland should be born anew? But Stalin will explain that he shared in none of these promises. So far as the world knows, he gave no pledge to honor them when he joined the alliance with Britain. He has no sentiment about such things.

4. Russia will insist, under one form or another, on dominating the Balkans. Czechoslovakia, Hungary, Romania, Bulgaria, Yugoslavia, Greece will fall under her sway as they now lie under Germany's sway. What more natural fruit of a victory in arms over Germany? And to these, undoubtedly,

will be added the Dardanelles, as the key that turns the lock on all of eastern Europe.

5. Russia will probably demand East Prussia as her share of a dismembered Germany. Will Germany be dismembered? She certainly will, if this war is won by Britain and her allies. And in this division of the spoil, Russia will demand her ample portion.

6. After Europe, Asia! Here speculation is not so easy. But that Russia will openly and permanently take over Mongolia is probable, and that she will seize Manchukuo from Japan is not improbable. Russia's hunger for Manchuria is as insatiable as her hunger for the Dardanelles. And then there will be the settlement for all the aid she has given to China and the payment of Stalin's debt to the Communist armies in that divided country.

Such is the memorandum of demands which Joseph Stalin will quietly but firmly lay before a peace conference gathered some years hence to liquidate a victory which, if won, will be won largely by his arms. Just Stalin's little bill for services rendered! And that bill will be paid, be sure of that, to the very last farthing! When Churchill hailed Stalin as an ally and Roosevelt pledged to him support in this war, this indebtedness was acknowledged. When Britain signed the cobelligerency pact in Moscow, she signed a blank check to be filled in later by Russia. The outcome, if victory is won, is certain. After an immeasurably exhausting effort to destroy Nazi totalitarianism, the world will have succeeded only in putting in its place a more powerful, more widely extended, and therefore more formidable Communist totalitarianism.

Does this mean that I do not want Russia, and with her Britain, to win this war? That I desire a German victory? Not at all! I do not hope for an outcome of this war in terms of victory, but rather in the familiar Wilsonian terms of "peace without victory." Not otherwise, it seems to me, can the interests of humanity be served in contrast to the interests of nations and empires. As I clung to this formula when Britain was fighting alone against Germany, how much more do I now cling to it when Russia has become the possibly deciding factor in the fray. Her entrance makes it certain that, if victory comes to either side, the triumph of totalitarianism is inevitable. There is no solution to our problem of peace in any victory in this war. Only a "peace without victory" can last.

What has happened to our minds that we fail to see these plain implications? This is what war does to us. This is what happens when we loose the forces of violence and expect them to bring us salvation. Everything passes out of control. The worst turns to the best. All the high purposes and ideals with which we entered the fight become poisoned or lost. Our minds become palsied and our consciences dead. In the struggle to beat down the enemy, lest he beat us down, we resort to any means, however vile, that promise to be effective. We accept any ally, however disreputable or dangerous, who agrees to help us out. Before we know it we are crying with Satan, "Evil, be thou my good."

Stalin says that "our war for the freedom of our country will merge with the struggles of Europe and America for their independence, for their democratic liberties." "Democratic liberties"—that phrase is as blasphemous on the lips of Stalin as it would be on the lips of Hitler. Russia in alliance with Britain, as in alliance with Germany, remains what she was and is—a totalitarian dictatorship to be matched point by point with the dictatorship of the Reich. And now we find ourselves fighting against the latter to save the former! Where is democracy in such a fight?

This is the insane whirligig of war! Lift up the banner and draw the sword, and this is where we land. Our cause lost, our hope doomed, our integrity sacrificed, and all for nothing!

*FOR TWO DECADES the Century had championed every
move which seemed to promise an end to international conflict,
had counseled non-involvement by the United States. Then,
Pearl Harbor—and the "unnecessary necessity." Few editorials
ever brought in more heated response—unless it was the one
endorsing Franklin D. Roosevelt for re-election in 1936; after it
appeared, a special supplement had to be issued to care for the
flood of letters-to-the-editor. As to the "Unnecessary Necessity,"
some readers approved, many were disillusioned, most echoed
"what else could be said?"*

December 17, 1941

An Unnecessary Necessity

AN EDITORIAL

In justice to itself and to its public which has learned to expect from The Christian Century a candid and honest expression
of its opinion on whatever issue it touches, this paper is unable
lightly to change its tone of voice now that our own nation has
been caught in the clutches of war. Other organs and many patriotic leaders, facing the stark fact of war, seem able as a matter
of course to bury their past opinions, forget their misgivings
and in the name of patriotism rally exultantly to the support of
the government in the dark and grim undertaking which events
have forced upon us.

We, too, must accept the war. We see no other way at the
moment but the bloody war of slaughter and immeasurable sacrifice. Our government has taken a stand. It is our government. It
spoke for us as the voice of our national solidarity. It was our
voice. The President is our President, and all his official acts,
even those which we disapprove, are our acts. We are all bound
together in the bundle of a common national life. Those who
approved and encouraged the policy which has brought us to
this tragic hour and those who have resisted this policy whether
on moral or prudential grounds are one people. None of us can

escape the consequences of our government's acts. They were our acts even while we opposed them. Their consequences are on our heads even though we did all in our power to change the policy which has brought these consequences upon the nation.

We stand with our country. We cannot do otherwise. We see no alternative which does not involve national self-stultification. Our country is at war. Its life is at stake. We hate war. We opposed the course by which our government, in our name, was taking us into a war which was not our war. We proposed and expounded alternative courses which we believed and still believe would have precluded war and opened the way for an adjustment in the Pacific. Such an adjustment would not have satisfied the full demands of justice in a highly complex and intractable situation, but we believe that it would have been infinitely more just than any justice which war is likely to bring to the Far East.

The nation has chosen the hard way. It is the way of unimaginable cost and of doubtful morality. It has invited the attack upon itself by its adamantine assumption of responsibilities in the Pacific which were beyond our interests there, beyond our understanding of the situation which exists there, and if not beyond our power to discharge, will surely pile up a cost in suffering and sacrifice for ourselves and others which is incommensurable with any just ends we may hope a successful war will achieve.

This is not the time to review the course by which we have been brought to this tragic hour. Perhaps there will be no time for such a review until history takes its pen in hand. The negotiations at Washington will then come up for review. The terms addressed to Japan by our state department will be subjected to examination together with Japan's reply. It may then appear that our government's diplomacy was not conceived with the flexibility which the situation in the Far East demanded and in terms of America's interests and true responsibilities there. It may then appear that our government was thinking in the framework of Europe's war in which the United States is not a participating belligerent but whose outcome in the British interest it is pledged to insure.

Facts heavily stressed by the administration, such as the delivery of the Japanese reply one hour after hostilities had actually begun, may not appear so significant in the perspective of history. The terrific surprise attack on Pearl Harbor prior to a declaration of war, but following by many days the receipt of our government's ultimatum, may not in perspective merit the bitter characterization with which it is naturally stigmatized by a government which not only has to justify its course but must mobilize the nation's resources and harden its will for the struggle which that act precipitated. Even now, the reproaches which we heap upon Japan for opening fire before a declaration of war come back to mock us. History will record that the United States was itself at that moment engaged in an undeclared war.

That Japan's act was sheer treachery, that her negotiations at Washington were a decoy to divert attention while she prepared herself to strike, that she violated the rules of diplomacy and of international law, all this is true, and terrifyingly so in the light of her momentary success. But all war is filled with treachery. All war-making is accompanied by lying. The height of strategy is to catch the enemy when he is off guard. A thousand cynical commentators have recently been telling us that declarations of war are out of date. "Military necessity" makes its own rules and its own law.

Although the attack which has finally precipitated war in the Pacific came from Japan, thoughtful Americans will not enter it in any self-righteous mood. They will see it, rather, as an almost unrelieved tragedy—a tragedy which need never have happened and which would never have happened had it not been for sins of omission and commission on both sides. Not to dwell here on Japan's shortcomings, they will see many points in the past record at which the United States could have halted the destructive progress of the Japanese fire-eaters with little difficulty. To name but one instance, had the then existing neutrality law been invoked in 1937, when Japan attacked China, how quickly Japan's war machine would have been stalled for lack of vital materials! The reason then advanced for refusing to take that step was that to do so would deprive China of arms and the materials with which modern war is waged. Today, however, it is all too plain that China gained nothing of importance from the American decision while the Japanese militarists gained the petroleum products, the machine tools, the motors and scrap iron by which they have waged war for more than four years.

Most of all, in this bitter hour, there should be regret that during the years of opportunity nothing was done to afford positive help for Japan in wrestling with her terrible problem of providing a decent livelihood for her teeming population. It was this failure to offer help which, in the last analysis, threw Japan into the arms of the Axis. Years ago it became apparent that something must be done to provide more food for Japanese mouths, more opportunity for Japanese youth, or Japan would resort to desperate measures. Yet everywhere she turned she was met by prohibitions and moral lectures which, when translated into the thoughts of her hungry people, sounded altogether too much like "Go on being hungry." No large-scale proffer of adequate help ever came from the "have" nations with their empires, their high living standards, their complacent grip upon the earth's riches. It was this failure to do more than respond with words which induced Japan, so traditionally friendly to the United States, so lately an ally of Great Britain, to turn at last to the Axis in the wild hope that if Hitler should succeed in smashing the world order that has been, his Oriental ally might, in the resulting confusion, seize some prizes in Asia.

But all this is a subject for history, not for this moment. History will be more meticulous than those who are making history by waging war can be. America is at war—that gross fact eclipses all else and in the eyes of those who fight justifies the application of the vilest epithets to the enemy and the claim of purest virtue for ourselves. We shall get used to the psychology and the morality and the vocabulary of war because we are now engaged in war. Our skirts will be cleared of blame. The war was forced upon us. Japan struck. There is nothing for us to do but strike back, and with all our might. This will be the essence of our apologetic. And it will have its own truth. The war was indeed forced upon us by Japan's refusal of our demands backed by her treacherous attack upon our mid-ocean possession, killing our men, striking our ships and devastating our harbor city. Thus war came. Given the background of unyielding diplomacy, war was inevitable. It became a necessity.

Yet it was an unnecessary necessity. Herein lies its tragedy. As tragedy, the war has two aspects. There is the large-scale tragedy —of masses of men forced by their governments to butcher their brothers whom they have never seen and against whom, as men, they have neither hate nor reason to hate. And there is also the private tragedy in which the soul of every citizen is caught who reflects at all upon his implication as soldier or statesman or civilian in this unholy and bestial business. For such citizens the war is plainly a necessity—it is beyond their control. But in their hearts they know it is an unnecessary necessity. In this paradox is expressed the state of mind of multitudes of American citizens. They opposed their government's course and offered honorable alternative courses which would have brought not only peace but a higher order of justice than war can hope to attain. Such patriotic citizens cannot now—they literally cannot—allow the truth which they saw to be eclipsed by the dark fact of war. The catastrophic outcome which they clearly foresaw or reasonably feared has now become a reality. They cannot lightly forget or wave aside the fact that the war has come from a course of action which was neither necessary nor just. It is no dishonor to their patriotism that they cannot do so.

But the maintenance of their integrity creates for them a dilemma. Their dilemma is our dilemma. They are unable to support the war without seeming to approve the course that led to the war. But what they now confront is a condition, not a contingency. The condition presents them with a necessity. The course that led to it was not a necessity. But having taken that course the nation has no alternative now, with its cities and citizens under fire, save to fight. Those who disapproved that course and strove against their fellows and their leaders who were determined to take it are confronted no longer with arguments but with an event, with an event which commands a decision.

It is this kind of dilemma of which tragedy is made. And many of our fellow Americans are today wrestling in their souls with this tragic necessity. No doubt brave Jeannette Rankin, who cast

the only vote in Congress against the declaration of war, was
inwardly wrestling for release from the paradox of the necessity.
She had opposed every step of the government leading to the
European war and the government's policy leading to the
Japanese war. To vote now in support of a declaration of war
seemed to her like an approval of the government's course which
made war at last inevitable. This she could not do. Conquering
her tears she voted No. Who will say that her vote was wrong?
Only those who know nothing of the anguish with which the
Christian conscience of our time is wrenched and burdened by
the paradox into which it is thrust by the fact of war.

Others take the other way out of the dilemma. But they
will do so without exultation. They are not sure that they are
choosing the better part. They are torn with doubt, as Miss
Rankin would confess that her soul is torn with doubts. Regis-
tering her vote as a protest against the nation's policy which
brought on the war, she must be distressed by the fact that
she is unable to offer a national alternative in face of the
war as an accomplished fact. Likewise, those who choose the
other horn of the dilemma are torn with doubt lest, had they
refused to support their country in its struggle, they might
thereby have borne a witness which in the long run would
register for a revolution in the statecraft of the nation.

There is no easy way out of tragedy. And there is no easy
way out of this tragedy. For the starkest tragedy is that of an
unnecessary necessity. But there is no escape from the necessity of decision. The Christian Century goes into the war
with the consciousness of having to make a tragic choice, and
therefore with the haunting doubts and all the reservations
which this writing has suggested. Faced with our country's
struggle with a foe whose victory, now that the unnecessary
struggle is on, we cannot conceive otherwise than as a vast
destruction of the values of life which we hold dear, we choose
to stand with our country. In this choice communal instinct,
no doubt, plays a considerable part. It is a choice which has to
be made in that area which might be called the no-man's-
land of reason and ethics; a choice which faith must make in
the twilight zone of God's revealed will. We are not sure

that our judgment is sound. We are not sure that our choice is right. We are not sure but that our faith has faltered. We make no claim that we know the will of God or the mind of Christ. But with heart bowed in grief that ever such a choice had to be made, we shall keep an open mind and a listening ear for the truth and the right and the faith in which on some better day our conscience may find peace.

FROM THE FIRST shocking intimation that all Japanese-Americans on the west coast, no matter what the degree of their loyalty or the length of their residence in the U.S., were to be deported from their homes and means of livelihood and locked up in desert detention camps, the Century campaigned editorially against such travesty of justice, published many eye-witness accounts of the mass transfer and later confinement.

April 29, 1942

Citizens or Subjects?

AN EDITORIAL

When the war is over, Americans may discover that in the early months of the conflict democracy received its most staggering blows in their own country and not at Pearl Harbor or on Bataan. Actions taken under the guise of military necessity have already deprived numbers of the citizens of this democracy of their constitutionally guaranteed equality before the law. Essential democratic rights have been infringed and racial distinctions placed above law. A principle of discrimination has been invoked which will, if allowed to stand, divide our citizenship into classes and bring into question the basic presuppositions on which this nation was founded.

As this is written, more than one hundred thousand persons are being moved from their homes in the Pacific coast states to concentration camps in the interior. More than one half of this number are American citizens. They were born in this country and have never lived in any other. They owe allegiance to no other nation. They speak our language, have been educated in our schools, accept our customs, pay taxes, vote and render military service. Until recently there was never any question that they were entitled to the exercise of the full rights of citizenship under the Constitution. In its Fifth and its Fourteenth amendments, that Constitution provides that "no person may be deprived of life, liberty or property without due process of law."

Now, without resort to established legal procedures and without a proclamation of martial law which would suspend those processes, these citizens are being deprived of liberty and are suffering the loss of property. A presidential order authorizing military commanders to remove from defense areas any person whose presence is deemed by them inimical to defense has been used as authority for the compulsory evacuation of all persons of Japanese descent from a great zone running the length of the Pacific coast. No hearings or other procedure under the law are available to these tens of thousands of citizens to protect them from the loss of their liberty. They are being treated exactly as though they were enemy aliens. The speed of the evacuation and the cupidity of some of their white neighbors have caused them to suffer large losses of property. They have no means of redress. On the sole ground of their racial origin they have been deprived of the protection of the constitutional guarantees which have been set up as the inalienable safeguard of every citizen.

How far may this sort of thing be expected to go? What assurance is there that other classes of citizens may not on the same or some other basis have their rights suspended or canceled tomorrow? What happens to democracy when whole blocks of our population may summarily be thrown into segregated classes of citizenship?

The answer may not be as far to seek as we suppose. The establishment of classes of citizenship has already proceeded much further than is commonly recognized. We Americans, who have pointed with such scorn at the Nazis for their reduction of the Jews to a status of secondary citizenship in Germany, need to wake up to the fact that citizenship in this country has already been divided into four distinct classes, with a fifth in prospect.

The first class citizen of this nation, whose Declaration of Independence declared "that all men are created equal, that they are endowed by their Creator with certain inalienable rights," is the white whose economic status is such that he is free to vote no matter where he may happen to live. He is a citizen in the full democratic sense of the term. He participates in government in several ways and is, in theory at least, an unquestioned recipient of all the civil guarantees of the Bill of Rights. He holds these rights, not as a subject who owes fealty to an overhead power which is the modern counterpart of the feudal lord, but as a fully competent and equal member of a commonwealth which is governed by the will of the majority of its citizens.

The second class citizen of the United States is the white person who is denied the franchise by the imposition of the poll tax qualification on voting. In most of the southern states no white person is permitted to vote who has not paid in full the poll tax which is assessed against every adult. Since the tax is cumulative, a few years of non-payment confronts the prospective voter with an impossible problem. The dominant majority, who have a vested interest in keeping control of government in their own hands, oppose all efforts to remove the tax limitation on the exercise of the franchise. Consequently a large proportion of southern white tenant farmers have sunk to the status of second class citizens. They have no voice in the government. In a precise sense of the term, they are subjects, not citizens.

Color prejudice creates a third and a fourth class of citizenship. Although the Fifteenth amendment to the Constitution specifically states that "the right of the citizens of the United States to vote shall not be denied or abridged by the United States or by any state on account of race, color or previous condition of servitude," manipulation of the primary election laws and threats of violence to violators of racial taboos effectively bar Negroes from using their right to vote throughout the south. Southern Negroes therefore constitute a third class of citizenship. They are also subjected to other disabilities, being generally barred from jury service even where the interests of a member of their own race are concerned and suffering gross discrimination in educational and other rights.

The fourth class of citizenship has just been created. Solely on the ground of their race, thousands of citizens of Japanese descent are being confined to concentration camps. In spite of the fact that the federal government has assumed protective custody of farms and homes, they have suffered huge losses. No matter what conditions they find at the Owens Valley or other concentration points, for an indefinite future they will not have as much liberty as Indians confined on a reservation. Like Indians they must depend on the bounty of the government. What will happen to these fourth class citizens after the war is a matter of conjecture. Already there is a strong movement on the west coast to deny them the opportunity ever to return to their former homes. With other states refusing them admittance, there is grave danger that they may become our American pariahs, like the untouchables of India, occupying the lowest level in the caste stratification of what was once a democracy.

The possible emergence of still a fifth class of citizenship is threatened by the attempt of the department of justice to revoke the citizenship of naturalized citizens whose patriotism has become suspect since they were admitted to citizenship. The only basis allowed in law for revocation of naturalization —proof of fraud at the time of naturalization—is not being invoked. Instead a number of indictments have been obtained which amount to a prosecution for the expression of an opinion. By holding the threat of cancellation of citizenship over the heads of persons who express opinions which are not in accord with the views of the government which happens to be in power, these prosecutions will go far to intimidate a vast segment of our population under the belief that they stand in a different classification from the native-born, that their citizenship is held only tentatively and can be revoked at the pleasure of the powers that be. No group held in fear of such penalties can develop democratic vitality.

The meaning of this trend is clear. If this segmentation of our citizenship continues, it will produce for the nation as a whole a condition which already prevails in certain sections of the country. Minority rule, with all its concomitants of emotional exploitation, economic and educational discrimination, and its final dependence on terrorism, will succeed government which truly seeks to be of all the people, by all the people and for all the people. Inexorably we shall progress toward rule by a favored class, toward the extension and defense of the privileges of an elite, until the very claim that this is a democracy has been reduced to mockery.

That must not happen. We must not allow this United States of America, land of our devotion, to be split up into a miserable welter of divisions, with first class citizens looking down on seconds, second class sneering at thirds, and so on down the gradations of a caste system until the outcasts huddle at the bottom in their misery, like the Jews in Hitler's Reich. Wise citizens will therefore reject the counsels of those who have been frightened into such actions as have occurred on the west coast and cast about to see what can be done to remedy the situation while there is yet time. It is not too late to reverse this trend, and courageous action can do it.

If there are those who complacently assume that a stratified citizenship is desirable, whether democratic or not, let them read the second paragraph of the Declaration of Independence and tremble.

INEVITABLY, *some of the editorial material in a weekly maga-*
zine is penned at white heat in the brief period between the
breaking of a late news story and the locking up of pages for the
press. This piece was so written; it reflects the horror with which
the world read of the concentration camp atrocities as they were
revealed in the wake of the Nazi forces' retreat across Germany.

May 9, 1945

Gazing into the Pit

AN EDITORIAL

The horrors disclosed by the capture of the Nazi concentration camps at Buchenwald, Belsen, Limburg and a dozen
other places constitute one of those awful facts upon which
a paper such as this feels under obligation to comment, but
concerning which it is almost physically impossible to write.
What can be said that will not seem like tossing little words
up against a giant mountain of ineradicable evil? What human
emotion can measure up to such bestiality except a searing
anger which calls on heaven to witness that retribution shall
be swift and terrible and pitiless? How can men (and, it is
alleged, women) who have been capable of such deeds be
thought of or dealt with save as vicious brutes who must be
exterminated both to do justice and in mercy to the future of
the race?

We have found it hard to believe that the reports from the
Nazi concentration camps could be true. Almost desperately
we have tried to think that they must be wildly exaggerated.
Perhaps they were products of the fevered brains of prisoners
who were out for revenge. Or perhaps they were just more
atrocity-mongering, like the cadaver factory story of the last
war. But such puny barricades cannot stand up against the
terrible facts. The evidence is too conclusive. It will be a
long, long time before our eyes will cease to see those pictures

of naked corpses piled like firewood or of those mounds of carrion flesh and bones. It will be a long, long time before we can forget what scores of honorable, competent observers tell us they have seen with their own eyes. The thing is well-nigh incredible. But it happened.

What does it mean? That Germans are beyond the pale of humanity? That they are capable of a fiendish cruelty which sets them apart from all the rest of us? No, not that. For one thing, we read that a large portion of the victims in these concentration camps were Germans. We do not believe that the sort of Germans who were subjected to this torture under any conceivable circumstances would themselves have become torturers. For another thing, we have reason to know that mass cruelty in its most revolting forms has not been confined to Germany. We have seen photographs that missionaries smuggled out of raped Nanking. We have read the affidavits of men who escaped from the Baltic states and eastern Poland. We know what horrors writers like David Dallin and William Henry Chamberlin believe would be revealed if the prison camps in the Soviet Arctic were opened to the world's inspection. We know, too, the frightful things that have happened in this country when lynching mobs ran wild—things so horrible that they can only be told in whispers.

No, the horror of the Nazi concentration camps is the horror of humanity itself when it has surrendered to its capacity for evil. When we look at the pictures from Buchenwald we are looking, to be sure, at the frightful malignity of nazism, this perversion of all values which in its final extremity is actually intent, as Hitler himself has said, on reducing all European life to "ruin, rats and epidemics." But in the Nazis and beyond them we are looking into the very pit of hell which men disclose yawning within themselves when they reject the authority of the moral law, when they deny the sacredness of human personality, when they turn from the worship of the one true God to the worship of their own wills, their own states, their own lust for power.

Buchenwald and the other memorials of Nazi infamy reveal the depths to which humanity can sink, and has sunk, in these frightful years. They reveal the awful fate which may engulf all civilizations unless these devils of our pride and of our ruthlessness and of the cult of force are exorcised. And they reveal that the salvation of man, the attainment of peace, the healing of the nations is at the last a religious problem. The diplomats may mark out what boundary lines they please, the victorious armies may set up what zones of occupation they will, but if man continues this self-worship, the pit yawns for us all.

The foul stench of the concentration camps should burden the Christian conscience until Christian men cannot rest. The conventional ministry of past years is no ministry for these days when mankind totters on the brink of damnation. The puny plans which denominations have been making are so inadequate to this crisis that they are nearly irrelevant. Unless there is a great upsurge of testimony to the power of the Christian gospel to save men from the sin which is destroying them and their institutions, all the reconstitution of church paraphernalia now being planned will be so much building on sand. In this crisis the gospel cannot be preached dispassionately, tentatively or listlessly—not and save civilization from the pit. A time has come when the Christian must proclaim his gospel "like a dying man to dying men."

For we are dying men—dying, all of us and our institutions and our civilization, in the sins which have reached their appalling climax in the torture chambers of Europe's prison camps. Only faith in the God and Father of Jesus Christ, the God who sent his Son to reveal a common and all-inclusive brotherhood, can save us. Our contempt for the sacredness of life, our worship at the shrine of our own power, has gone so far that it has taken these horrors to shock us into awareness of the tragic fate toward which we are stumbling.

In God's providence, has not the World Council of Churches become a living hope for such a time as this? So far, progress toward the formation of the World Council has been cautious, following familiar patterns, a matter of negotiations and treaties among sovereign denominations. The goal has seemed largely to be the attainment of an organization. Is not the agony of mankind a call to the World Council to forget everything but the proclamation of the Christian evangel?

Should it not be the business of the World Council now to gather from all lands Christians who will go everywhere, pointing to the encroachments of human depravity which have been laid bare, proclaiming to men and nations, "Except ye repent, ye shall all likewise perish"? Let the council gather for this common task Niemöller and the Christian leaders with him who have withstood the Nazi scourge, as many of them as may emerge from imprisonment; let it gather Bishop Berggav and the noble pastors of Norway; let it gather every Christian in the world who sees the peril and knows the means of escape, and let it send them forth with such an evangel as has not stormed this sin-stricken world since the days of the first apostles. Buchenwald and the other concentration camps spell doom. But it is not simply the doom of the Nazis; it is the doom of man unless he can be brought to worship at the feet of the living God.

HIROSHIMA—and after.

August 29, 1945

America's Atomic Atrocity
AN EDITORIAL

Something like a moral earthquake has followed the dropping of atomic bombs on two Japanese cities. Its continued tremors throughout the world have diverted attention even from the military victory itself. Its effect in America is expressed in the letters which came spontaneously to The Christian Century following the publication of the facts concerning the extinction of Hiroshima and Nagasaki. None of these letters was elicited by any comment in these pages on the moral implications of the use of the atomic bomb by our forces. These writers speak for themselves. Their letters underline the horror and revulsion, the sense of guilt and shame, the profound foreboding with which the impetuous adoption of this incredibly inhuman instrument has been greeted in this country. It is our belief that the use made of the atomic bomb has placed our nation in an indefensible moral position.

We do not propose to debate the issue of military necessity, though the facts are clearly on one side of this issue. The atomic bomb was used at a time when Japan's navy was sunk, her air force virtually destroyed, her homeland surrounded, her supplies cut off, and our forces poised for the final stroke. Recognition of her imminent defeat could be read between the lines of every Japanese communiqué. Neither do we intend to challenge Mr. Churchill's highly speculative assertion that the use of the bomb saved the lives of more than one million American and 250,000 British soldiers. We believe, however, that these lives could have been saved had our government followed a different course, more honorable and more humane. Our leaders seem not to have weighed the moral considerations involved. No sooner was the bomb ready than it was rushed to the front and dropped on two helpless cities, destroying more lives than the United States has lost in the entire war.

Perhaps it was inevitable that the bomb would ultimately be employed to bring Japan to the point of surrender. (This, however, is contradicted by the astonishing report of the past few days that General MacArthur conveyed to President Roosevelt last January, and that the President summarily rejected, peace terms essentially the same as those finally accepted.) But there was no military advantage in hurling the bomb upon Japan without warning. The least we might have done was to announce to our foe that we possessed the atomic bomb; that its destructive power was beyond anything known in warfare; and that its terrible effectiveness had been experimentally demonstrated in this country. We would thus have warned Japan of what was in store for her unless she surrendered immediately. If she doubted the good faith of our representation, it would have been a simple matter to select a demonstrative target in the enemy's own country at a place where the loss of human life would be at a minimum.

If, despite such warning, Japan had still held out, we would have been in a far less questionable position had we then dropped the bombs on Hiroshima and Nagasaki. At least our record of deliberation and ample warning would have been clear. Instead, with brutal disregard of any principle of humanity we "demonstrated" the bomb on two great cities, utterly extinguishing them. This course has placed the United States in a bad light throughout the world. What the use of poison gas did to the reputation of Germany in World War I, the use of the atomic bomb has done for the reputation of the United States in World War II. Our future security is menaced by our own act, and our influence for justice and humanity in international affairs has been sadly crippled.

We have not heard the last of this in Japan itself. There a psychological situation is rapidly developing which will make the pacification of that land by our occupying forces—infinitely delicate and precarious at best—still more difficult and dubious. In these last days before the occupation by American forces, Japanese leaders are using their final hours of freedom of access to the radio to fix in the mind of their countrymen a psychological pattern which they hope will persist into an indefinite future. They reiterate that Japan has won a moral victory by not stooping as low as her enemies, that a lost war is regrettable but not necessarily irreparable, that the United States has been morally defeated because she has been driven to use unconscionable methods of fighting. They denounce the atomic bomb as the climax of barbarity and cite its use to prove how thin the veneer of Christian civilization is. They declare that Japan must bow to the conqueror at the emperor's command, but insist that she must devote all her available energies to scientific research. That of course can mean only one thing—research in methods of scientific destruction. Some officials have openly admonished the people to discipline themselves until the day of their revenge shall come.

Vengeance as a motive suffers from no moral or religious stigma in Japanese life. In the patriotic folklore of that land, no story is more popular than that of the Forty-Seven Ronin. It is a tale of revenge taken at the cost of their lives by the retainers of a feudal lord on an enemy who had treacherously killed their master. Every Japanese child knows that story. Until 1931, when Japan took Manchuria, the sacred obligation of retaliation was directed against the nations which had prevented Japanese expansion in that area and then had expanded their own holdings. After that it was aimed at white imperialism which was held to be the enemy of all people of color in the world, and particularly those in east Asia. In each case the justification of revenge was found in a real weakness in the moral position of the adversary. Our widespread use of the diabolic flame-thrower in combat, our scattering of millions of pounds of blazing jellied gasoline over wood and paper cities, and finally our employment of the atomic bomb give Japan the only justification she will require for once more seeking what she regards as justified revenge.

But there will be others. The terms of the surrender rightly strip from Japan the empire which she has acquired by force in the past half-century. But the British, French, Dutch, Belgian and Portuguese empires, each created by the same methods Japan has attempted to employ, stand intact. Undoubtedly, Russia will recover some of the rich concessions in the Asiatic mainland which Japan gives up, and it appears likely that China will return to the condition of civil strife which made Japanese economic relations with her a constant source of intolerable confusion. American might, it will seem to the Japanese, is re-establishing this state of affairs in the interest of white imperialism. From that view it is not a long jump to the conclusion that any people which plots successful revenge against a nation that uses such methods to serve such ends is rendering Asiatic humanity a service.

The Japanese leaders are now in the act of creating a new myth as the carrier of the spirit of revenge. The myth will have much plausible ground in fact to support it. But its central core will be the story of the atomic bomb, hurled by the nation most reputed for its humanitarianism. Myths are hard to deal with. They lie embedded in the subconscious mind of a people, and reappear with vigor in periods of crisis. The story of the bomb will gather to itself the whole body of remembered and resented inconsistencies and false pretensions of the conquerors. The problem of spiritual rapprochement between the West and the Japanese will thus baffle the most wise and sensitive efforts of our occupying forces to find a solution. Yet our theory of occupation leaves us with no chance ever to let go of our vanquished foe until the roots of revenge have been extirpated. The outlook for the reconciliation of Germany with world civilization is ominous enough, but the outlook for the reconciliation of Japan is far more ominous.

The future is further complicated by the fact that the Christian Church, which holds in its hands the only power of radical reconciliation, has also suffered a heavy blow. The atomic bomb can fairly be said to have struck Christianity itself. Only Christianity has the required resources for the problem of reconciliation at the deep spiritual level where it must finally be resolved. The Christian people of this country have been looking forward to the revival of their mission in Japan on an unprecedented scale, and on a broader and more co-operative basis than in the past. The same bomb that extinguished Hiroshima and Nagasaki struck this missionary enterprise. It will take endless explaining to the Japanese to dissociate Christianity, the Christian Church and the Christian mission from the act of the American government in unleashing the atomic bomb. This act which has put the United States on the moral defensive has also put the Christian Church on the defensive throughout the world and especially in Japan.

For this reason the churches of America must dissociate themselves and their faith from this inhuman and reckless act of the American government. There is much that they can do, and it should be done speedily. They can give voice to the shame the American people feel concerning the barbaric methods used in their name in this war. In particular, in pulpits and conventions and other assemblies they can dissociate themselves from the government's use of the atomic bomb as an offensive weapon. They can demonstrate that the American people did not even know of the existence of such a weapon until it had been unleashed against an already beaten foe. By a ground-swell of prompt protest expressing their outraged moral sense, the churches may enable the Japanese people, when the record is presented to them, to divorce the Christian community from any responsibility for America's atomic atrocity.

Without in the least condoning Pearl Harbor or the aggressive policy of Japan's war lords, such action will go far toward restoring the spiritual basis of community between the Christian Church and the Japanese people. Assuredly it will save the Japanese Christian community from the alienation which otherwise they are certain to feel toward their American brethren. It will save them from the embarrassment which they are bound to suffer in the face of their non-Christian neighbors as they maintain their loyalty to the Christian faith. It will thus assure a welcome in the hearts of Japanese Christians to the new missioners from the American church who will follow close upon the heels of the occupying forces.

Beyond all this the churches can take immediate steps to share the burden of suffering which now lies heavily on the Japanese people. The place to begin might well be to provide as many as possible of the surviving children and their mothers with food, medicine and clothes. It is now known that our fire bombs killed and burned out over eight million people. Every ship that goes out to the western Pacific to bring American soldiers home should carry relief supplies. Christian people will voluntarily fill the first of such ships if they are given the opportunity to do so. The American church is thinking in bold terms of its responsibility to Japan. It has no less a goal than the re-creation of Japan as a peaceful and democratic state through the regenerative power of the Christian gospel. It must not allow itself to condone any of the atrocities of the war or to seem to have been a party to the war itself.

With the ending of the war the time has now come for the Christian Church in this country to gather the fruit of its dissociation from the conflict. In no previous war has the church so boldly and generally seized the opportunity to be the church, and not a trailer behind the war chariot of the state. The widespread adoption of the concept that the church was not at war, and the almost universal conformity of its utterances and practice to this concept, should now come to fruition in the opening of the channels of ecumenical fellowship with the churches in all enemy countries, and particularly in Japan. But a church which condemns war and will not be a party to it has a peculiar responsibility to condemn those acts of war which trespass the limits beyond which the Christian conscience, though distressed by all the frightful dilemmas in which it is placed by war itself, will not knowingly go.

The destruction of Hiroshima and Nagasaki was such an act. The writers of the letters which appear in this paper have been profoundly shocked that their government was capable of such wantonness. Their protest will, we believe, be taken up by Christian people throughout the nation. And this protest will swell in volume until it reaches the shores and the people of Japan.

August 3, 1960

Fifteen Years in Hell Is Enough

AN EDITORIAL

Fifteen years after Hiroshima, we have not caught up with the tide of evil loosed upon the world by the first atomic bomb. No treaty exists for curbing the use of nuclear weapons, none even for control of testing. Four nations now qualify for admission to the nuclear club, and China may soon join them. Others press close behind, and with each addition the problem of nuclear disarmament moves closer to insolubility. To date, the peaceable uses of atomic energy which have been discovered or which are in likely prospect do not begin to balance or cancel out the threat to human existence contained in its military uses.

The American people and those of other countries were not prepared for the responsibilities of living in the new atomic age. The scientists who developed this awesome new dimension of energy had misgivings, but they operated under a cover of wartime secrecy and did not share their qualms. At the crucial point of their own involvement, they abdicated moral responsibility and deferred to supposed military necessity. The later regret of some of them has not helped much. Military leaders passed responsibility on to President Harry S. Truman, who had learned of the existence of the atomic bomb project only a short time before, when he became President. Mr. Truman, who in other respects freely confessed he was unprepared for his presidential duties, accepted responsibility for use of the bomb without hesitation and has ever since insisted he has no regrets. We can have regrets on his behalf and on our own. We now know that the presumed military necessity did not exist, that the Japanese were trying to surrender before the bomb was dropped on Hiroshima.

The unpreparedness of our political leaders for dealing with the consequences of the release of nuclear energy went far beyond the original decision to drop the bombs. It extended to steps for atomic disarmament. The Baruch proposal, as it was called, was that atomic arms should be a monopoly of the United Nations. The United States agreed to forego the use of its closely held knowledge concerning methods of manufacturing and assembling atomic arms. In retrospect it is not difficult to see why Russia, being the kind of state it is, rejected an arrangement which placed her in a position of permanent inferiority. Since we had and insisted on keeping "the secret," Russia determined to possess it before entering into any commitment. By espionage and by employment of German scientists the Russians got the secret and exploded a bomb within three years. Shortly afterward the Communists started the Korean war—and disarmament hopes went glimmering for a decade.

Also unprepared for the new age were religious leaders in this and other countries. Neither the Roman Catholic nor the

Eastern Orthodox churches have contributed anything substantial to Christian thought on the problem. Ecumenical leadership in this country and in the World Council of Churches has hardly moved past the recognition that devices releasing nuclear energy have to be accepted as weapons of war, and that their use is governed by the same considerations which apply to other weapons. Commissions of churchmen which have studied the matter say nuclear war may be condoned by the Christian if its cause is just, if the gains to be attained are greater than the losses which appear likely, if restraint is practiced in actions which endanger noncombatants, particularly women and children. Since nuclear weapons are particularly powerful, the commissions say they should be used with greater reluctance and more regret than other weapons.

This position is weak and deceptive. It fails to take sufficient account of the realities of the new human situation. The ancient theory of the just war breaks down when victory is impossible, when the weapons are so undiscriminating as to destroy both sides. What objective justifies the extermination of a whole nation or of the human race to attain it? How is it possible to practice restraint or selectivity with a weapon which wipes out cities with one blow and which creates fallout destroying all life within hundreds of miles? What is right about preparing for a nuclear war which could poison the atmosphere and make the earth uninhabitable?

The military answer is that only by making such preparations can we maintain the balance of terror, and so avert war. It is not an adequate answer, even though it provides the rationale under which the United States, the United Kingdom and now France on our side, and the U.S.S.R. and China on the other side, are spending on nuclear weapons a good share of their military budgets, which total nearly $100 billion annually. But the balance of terror is breaking down. For example, who in the United States was terrified by Khrushchev's recent threats to bombard the U. S. with rockets if we invade Cuba? Nobody. The main reason was not that we have no intention of invading Cuba, but rather that we simply do not believe Khrushchev intends to carry out his threats. Similarly, a few years ago John

Foster Dulles' warning of "massive retaliation" failed to scare the Russians. The balance of terror is already a waning and uncertain factor in international affairs and is certainly not an adequate basis for policy.

In such a situation religious leadership in the Western world has an obligation of conscience. It is to remove the religious sanction for the use of nuclear arms which is implied so long as religious people maintain silence about their use. The manufacture, testing and stockpiling of nuclear weapons proceeds on the assumption that under some circumstances they may be used. Religious people have no right to permit that assumption to stand unchallenged. The use of these weapons would loose indiscriminate destruction on the world and thereby violate the essential human right to life.

Why have Christian leaders a particular responsibility in this matter? Because the existence of man on earth is at stake. Christians are supposed to know God's purpose for man's existence on earth and to be concerned that God's will be done. The God we know through Christ intends the salvation of man; that purpose surely would be defeated by the extermination of man. Christian faith has always taught that self-destruction by an individual is wrong. It surely could not agree that a course of action which would probably lead to collective suicide can be right.

But some realist is likely to object by saying: "We do these things to live. Some of us may die, but the Russians know that if such is the case many more of them will perish. Their leaders should know we now have means to destroy every man, woman and child behind the iron curtain." This is true. We do have this power. But we cannot use it. We could not live with ourselves if we used it. We would earn the hatred and loathing of mankind if we used it. We should be honest and remove a threat we could not bring ourselves to carry out.

Looking at the gloomy side, suppose our side scuttled or scattered its nuclear weapons, and the Communists attacked and destroyed us. The situation would still not be so bad as it would if we and the Russians were to destroy each other. Two-thirds of the human race would still survive. The laws of God would still operate and the human community would rise up and destroy a system capable of a hundred Hiroshimas. Suppose the Communists did not destroy us, but tried to enslave us. We could organize non-violent resistance, as Catholics are doing in Cuba and as Indians did in Kerala, and tell the world what was happening. In the end we could conquer the Communist world by moral force. But if we fight the war for which we are preparing, neither side can win and neither is likely to survive.

The removal of the threat from our side by unilateral nuclear disarmament would very likely result in the lessening of the threat from the Communist side. We should continue to try to get an agreement to permit inspection, but we should not wait for that to declare our intention to turn over our nuclear armaments to the United Nations if that body would accept them, or to abandon them if it would not. Fifteen years of suspension over the fires of nuclear hell is long enough. It is time for a change. Let us say straight out that we are not going to destroy our enemies and menace our friends by nuclear war. Let us demonstrate our good faith by getting rid of the means for these purposes. Then we may be able to confront the central question of the nuclear age: What did God intend by permitting men to learn how to release the energy of the atom at this moment in history?

V

Some Areas of Concern

EARLY COMMENT on stirrings of the social conscience.
December 26, 1908

Labor and the Federal Council of Churches

AN EDITORIAL

A little noted but significant action taken by the Federal Council of Churches at Philadelphia was that relating to the church and labor as set forth in the enthusiastically received report of the Committee on the Church and Modern Industry. It declares for a living wage and protection of women and children against sweatshops, and pledges the church to assert the law of right for all who toil and to preach the gospel of social righteousness and industrial justice. It sends greetings to all those "who by organized effort are seeking to reduce the hardships and uphold the dignity of labor." The report is a notable document and sounds the tocsin for a sentiment that together with the missionary movement will be much more productive of church unity than ententes cordiales over the creeds, and arguments pro and con over their merits and demerits, or than even any specific organic effort for union that can be immediately put forth. Give us enthusiasm for Christianity's greatest causes and we will battle together for them.

March 21, 1912

The Sacred Rights of Property

AN EDITORIAL

We are still in that primitive period in human development when the rights of property tower up above the right of the person. Crimes against property are punished with the utmost speed and stringency, especially crimes against corporation property. The forger of a check goes to the penitentiary much more certainly than does the murderer, for the banks are organized to punish this kind of evil effectively. The brick hurled through the window of a factory in the time of a strike becomes the occasion of serious trouble for the offender. We are less concerned that the factory declares dividends upon the fruits of child labor and that its deadly machinery for the lack of safety devices takes its monthly toll of human life. Great is Mammon, God of the Americans!

THE DEPRESSION: *days of misery recalled in one noonday scene.*

November 9, 1932

Hunger on the March

PAUL HUTCHINSON

Randolph Street pierces the Northwestern Railway terminal in Chicago by means of a tunneled passage almost a block long. There, to get out of the pouring rain, I took my stand. The motorcycle police, barely keeping their machines in motion, had just reached the western entrance. Behind them, filling the street from curb to curb, an indiscriminate mass of people holding aloft a thousand jerking placards and banners, came the hunger marchers.

Out of the downpour they moved into the dry passageway in which I stood, and with them came the low, long roar that accompanies great masses on the march. Here and there squads made an attempt at a sort of regular chant: "We want bread!" "We want food!" Or more often: "Keep on fighting! Keep on fighting!" Some Communist locals took advantage of the enclosed space to sing the Internationale. But most of the roar was without form or words—the noise of thousands who paraded through the rain not because they had much idea of what might be accomplished by so doing, but because they were hungry and must do something.

There were no bands. There was no quickstep. But rank after rank of sodden men, their worn coat-collars turned up, their caps—most of them seemed to be wearing caps—pulled down to give as much protection as possible. Here and there women and a few children, but not a great many. If it had been a clear day the number of these would have been multiplied many times. But marching under such conditions was no business for women. A man's parade. Eight abreast. Closely massed. Stretching as far down the street as the eye could see through the rain. The biggest parade, the newspapers were to say, that Chicago had seen in years.

A heavily built man of sixty or so, trembling with excitement, came rushing up and grabbed my arm. "What do you think of that?" he shouted. "Give that bunch just a little dynamite and they could blow this city to hell! There's enough of them to do it!" Before I could answer, he was running on down the sidewalk. The police sergeant standing a few feet away looked at me and smiled; the marchers next to the curb, who also had heard, grinned as they plodded ahead. Some of them were carrying placards inscribed "Don't starve; fight!" But it wasn't a dynamiters' parade.

Police arrangements were perfect. There had been some stipulations about police censorship over the inscriptions on banners, but a wise police chief had evidently given orders to subordinate everything else to getting the marchers along their route with as little delay and as little cause for wrangling as possible. Hundreds of uniformed and plain-clothes police were on duty, for there is always the chance that some unbalanced individual may turn such a demonstration into a tragedy. But the police were there to protect and not to pummel the marchers. They brought the converging columns from the various sections of the city into Chicago's Loop in a perfectly timed order; they escorted the procession past the city hall and across the Loop to the lake-front park at the height of the noon rush hour without a delay or a disturbance; they provided a place for the mass meeting of paraders (in ankle-deep mud, to be sure, but that could hardly be charged up to the police) where the bitterness in their minds could have full and free expression. It was intelligent policing, as well carried out as it had been conceived.

The delegation that waited for the mayor as the parade was passing the city hall expected nothing and got nothing. It did get a chance, to be sure, to present a list of demands which, printed in the evening papers, must have made comfortable citizens mutter: cash relief on the basis of $7.50 per week for a family of two, with additional amounts for each dependent; no more evictions; free gas, water, electricity and coal; free hot lunches; clothing, textbooks and carfare for school children; free dental and medical care; no foreclosures; exemption from taxes; immediate release of all in jail as a result of unemployment clashes with the police; immediate inauguration of a local program of public works; no discriminations in relief work against Negroes or foreign-born; all unemployment funds to be administered by elected representatives of organizations of the unemployed. The mayor said that he had nothing to do with these matters; let them be put before the relief organizations, or the Reconstruction Finance Corporation. The committee filed out. It had put its demands, by means of the listening reporters, where it wanted them to go —before that part of the public that even in today's misery has no idea how the other half is living, or what he is thinking.

Still that sodden line of marchers. By this time I was on Michigan Boulevard, that proud and beautiful street which Chicago boasts will match in splendor any other in the world. As the bedraggled paraders, with their defiant banners, came swinging out of the narrow defile of the Loop street into this broad esplanade I found myself paying more attention to the onlookers than to the marchers. It was past noon now; the office population of the city lined the curb many rows deep. There was none of that thoughtless laughter that might have been expected at the sight of such a tatterdemalion crew. These stenographers, these clerks, these well-dressed men accustomed to push buttons and reach for the long-distance phone were obviously puzzled by many of the banners. What was the meaning of this talk about "restore the 50 per cent rations cut?" Who was the Joe Sposob whose last words were said to have been "They gave me lead instead of bread"? The crowd on the sidewalk did not know what most of this was about. But it did not laugh or mock. Twenty thousand people, plodding through the rain, shouting "we want bread" is nothing to laugh at in these days.

I suppose that this particular parade really achieved its objective in that puzzled crowd along the sidewalks. If there were 20,000 marchers there must have been ten times that many onlookers. And the tragic truth is that, except in the vaguest sort of way, these onlookers had no idea of the state of misery in which the unemployed are living. In Chicago, for example, where there are now about 700,000 people dependent on relief, the basis of relief has been such that a typical family—say, a man, wife and two children—would receive food orders worth $5.02 a week and a "county box" valued at $1.25; and during a large part of October shortage of funds, as the parade banners testified, forced a reduction of even this allowance by one-half. Think of trying to support a family of four on $3.15 worth of food a week! Yet as these words are written there is no one connected with either the city's government or its relief agencies who knows how even this provision is to be continued through the winter.

There was one aspect of this parade whose significance I

suppose escaped practically all the watchers. But in these ranks there plodded representatives of Communist organizations, of socialist clubs, of church and social settlements, of local community bodies, and of groups that the unemployed themselves have formed. It was a "united front" demonstration. To those who know the depth and width of the chasm that has divided the Communists from the rest of the community, the fact that a "united front" has been reached in Chicago, under the pressure of slackening relief, carries immense meaning. Will the present union in demands for such relief objectives as I have listed lead to union on the political front? It is not beyond the realm of possibility; certainly the Communists know how to capitalize such outbursts to their fullest possible political value.

This parade, it should be noted, came before the opening of winter. The hard months are yet to come. Already, however, there has been this cutting in half of the food rations; already there has been practical acknowledgment that the only hope for continued relief rests in continued grants from the federal RFC. No such parade had ever been permitted in Chicago before. When permission was asked for this one it was refused. But the pressure was too heavy; the city administration wisely decided that there was less danger of trouble in permitting than in forbidding the demonstration. So we have had these 20,000 marchers tramping through the October rain, marching at the very time when the cables tell of other marchers in London. There will be more marchers in more cities before spring. Will they be content with marching?

After I had made my way from the crowd wallowing about in the mud at the end of their march to a stool in a near-by coffee shop, I found one of Chicago's long-time radicals at my elbow. "Twenty-five years ago, I tried to lead a march of the unemployed down Michigan Avenue," he said. "We managed to get almost three blocks before we were arrested. It's different this year." A long pause. "Even the clergy are calling for socialism—some kind of socialism. It makes me feel like saying, 'Lord, now lettest thou thy servant depart in peace.'" (He twisted an amused glance at me from under his bushy eyebrows; evidently he was wondering whether I would be impressed by his ability to quote Scripture.) A longer pause. Then, suddenly, vibrantly, with his hand gripping my arm: "But there was something that you didn't hear out there today, although it was there. You read and you heard the slogans—'We want work!' 'We want bread!' Did you hear that other slogan they were not shouting, only thinking: 'We want revenge'? These people have lost their homes. They have lost their savings. They have lost their jobs. And they are beginning to march, through the rain, by the thousands, because they want revenge."

IN RECENT YEARS the sorry state of relations between the original Americans on and off the reservations and their later-come neighbors has been aired in a number of firsthand reports and extended studies by Harold E. Fey, the Century's present editor. Herewith, a brief editorial sets the scene as of 1913, while in overtones of an editor's requiem for an Indian hero, written almost a half-century later, are to be seen evidences that some social ills are a long time righting.

January 31, 1913

Another "Century of Dishonor"?
AN EDITORIAL

A sad story of neglect and exploitation is revealed in the recent report of the committee on expenditures in the Interior Department. Chairman Graham, of Illinois, asserts that the Chippewa Indians of the White Earth Reservation in Minnesota have been robbed of millions of dollars' worth of pine timber by lumber companies operating under favorable legislation and administration of Indian affairs. Through a Senate "rider" on an Indian appropriation bill in 1904, Indians of mixed blood were allowed to sell the timber on past and prospective allotments of land. At the same time an act originating in the House provided for the allotment of valuable pine lands, with the results that the best and most valuable pine allotments fell into the hands of those who were intended in advance to receive them. After it was all over, it was found that practically all the pine on the reservation had been sold to three lumber companies, almost as if by prearranged divisions. Not more than 5 per cent of the sales proved beneficial to the allotees. These are not gray wolves, but white wolves that howl around the miserable huts of these unsophisticated and helpless wards of the nation. In one desolate shack the committee found three women who, though blind, were about to be ejected by mortgage foreclosure, and this case is typical of others. In one part of the reservation where some 500 Indians live nearly every man, woman and child is afflicted with trachoma, many are blind, and 25 per cent have tuberculosis. Squalor and misery abound. If the statements of the report are well founded, a more serious indictment against our Indian service could hardly be imagined.

February 9, 1955

Ira Hayes—Our Accuser

EDITORIAL CORRESPONDENCE

Phoenix, January 28

Today thousands of whites and a few Indians filed through the Arizona state capitol past the flag-draped casket of Ira Hayes, hero of Iwo Jima. Yesterday thousands of Indians and a few whites, of whom I was one, attended his funeral in the Presbyterian church at Sacaton, fifty miles to the southeast. On February 2 this Pima Indian will be given a military funeral in Washington, and will be buried in Arlington National Cemetery near the huge bronze statue celebrating the raising of the flag on Iwo Jima, in which he shared. Veterans' organizations here have collected money so that Hayes' parents and three brothers will be able to make the long journey to the national capital. There they will see where Ira was once received by President Truman and decorated with the Medal of Honor. They may see the sights he once saw in a tour personally conducted by an Arizona member of Congress. They may recall how he was honored there when a film commemorating Iwo Jima, with him as one of its principal actors, had its premiere showing. They will stand where he stood less than three months ago when the Iwo Jima statue was unveiled.

The statue was completed in the nick of time, so far as Ira Hayes was concerned. Before he was able to make the trip to Washington for its dedication, he was given a course of treatment to relieve him sufficiently of his addiction to liquor so that he could carry out the role to which he was assigned in the unveiling. He was an alcoholic, and far gone. A year ago —November 12, 1953—the *Arizona Republic* of Phoenix reported that Hayes had spent the previous night in jail on a drunk and disorderly charge. The story said this was the 42nd time he had been arrested since 1941. With one exception— escaping from the prisoners' work gang—all these arrests were on the same charge. The library of the Phoenix paper has clippings on eight arrests subsequent to November 12, 1953, for drunkenness.

Once Ira Hayes was picked up on skid row in Chicago, dirty and shoeless, and sent to jail. The *Chicago Sun-Times* discovered who he was, got him out of jail, raised a fund for his rehabilitation, secured him a job in Los Angeles. Many organizations, including church groups, tried to help. Hayes thanked everybody and said, "I know I'm cured of drinking." But in less than a week he was arrested by Los Angeles police on the old charge. When he returned to Phoenix he received no hero's welcome. He told a reporter: "I guess I'm just no good. I've had a lot of chances but just when things start looking good I get that craving for whisky and foul up. I'm going back home for a while first. Maybe after I'm around my family

I'll be able to figure things out." He talked of joining
Alcoholics Anonymous, and was later placed in their custody
by a court, but to no avail. A few days ago drink overtook him
for the last time and stretched him all night on the ground
in the cold. By morning he was dead.

Yesterday in the big bare Sacaton church, crowded to
the doors with Indians of the Pima tribe and a few whites,
surrounded by hundreds who were unable to obtain entrance,
more than one worshiper felt that the tables had turned and
Ira Hayes was the accuser, not the defendant. He accused the
liquor industry—the distillers, the advertisers, the sellers, and
more than anybody else the "friends" who were always offering to buy the drinks for a picturesque public figure. In death
he accused everybody whose standard of hospitality requires
liquor to create the simulation of fellowship when its reality
is lacking. His still form, lying in a flag-draped casket before
the pulpit of the church, rebuked the lying advertising which
tries to make the drinker seem a man of distinction, but which
will never present the picture of Ira Hayes in that role, or
carry as a testimonial the epitaph of this national hero: "I've
had a lot of chances but just when things start looking good I
get that craving for whisky and foul up."

Judgment began at the house of God yesterday, and before
it ended it cut a wide swath through our whole social order.
The words of Esau Joseph, pastor of the Sacaton church, and
Roe B. Lewis, pastor of the Phoenix Indian Presbyterian
Church—both members of the Pima tribe—were gentle, but
the truth implicit in the situation was terrible to bear. An
American Legionnaire with whom I talked outside the church
put it bluntly: "That boy was killed by our government and
our people." After the war, he said, Ira Hayes was constantly
sent here and there for bond drives, Red Cross drives, patriotic
celebrations. He hated public displays and was irritated at
being made over as a hero. Drinks were pushed toward him on
every occasion, and he took them. Everybody was pulling at
him—patriotic groups, welfare groups, service groups, the
church, even his own tribe—seeking to "honor" him, forgetting
all the time that underneath the veneer of Ira Hayes the

symbol was the reality of Ira Hayes the man. That he was a desperate and dying man nobody except a few seemed to know or care. What they cared about was the symbol, the hero who helped raise the flag, and the gain they or their cause stood to make by exploiting their nearness to him. Toward the end he returned to his family in the little Pima village of Bapchule, near Sacaton, hoping to "be able to figure things out." Instinctively he sought here the saving love he could find nowhere else, and struggled to find in their presence the answers which eluded him.

What bothered him? Ira Hayes knew he owed his fame to the fact that Joe Rosenthal, an Associated Press photographer, snapped the dramatic picture of the flag-raising on Iwo Jima which caught the imagination of the country. The photographer did not secure the names of the six marines—an oversight understandable in the circumstances of battle. The marine corps supplied the names later. Up until the end of 1946 Hayes insisted that one of the six was his buddy, Corporal Harlan Block of Weslaco, Texas. Block, who was killed in that battle, was not named as one of the flag-raisers. Hayes tried again and again to right what he believed to be an error and an injustice, but without success. He lapsed into silence after the marine corps "rechecked" and stuck to its story. But it is not impossible that one of the things that disturbed him was his experience of conflict between official truth and his own knowledge.

Another factor that came to the surface more than once was his sense of grievance over the poverty and neglect of his own people, the Pima Indians. In 1950, according to press report, he took to the Bureau of Indian Affairs "his plea for freedom for the Pima Indians. . . . They want to manage their own affairs and cease being wards of the federal government." Behind such words lay a deeper resentment, which flashed to the surface in 1953 when he was asked to speak on Phoenix's KOY broadcast for Flag Day. He was then in Chicago. "I was out in Arizona for eight years and nobody paid any attention to me," he said. "They might ask me what I think of the way they treat Indians out there, compared to how we are treated in Chicago. I'd tell them the truth and Arizona would not like it."

Ira Hayes did not speak for KOY, but Phoenix did not hold it against him. Some weeks later the *Gazette* editorialized: "Hayes feels bitter about his failure to find a job in Arizona when he returned as a hero from World War II. We don't know who was to blame and it isn't particularly important. . . . Certainly there should be a place for such a man in Arizona . . ." There was. Just before he died, Ira Hayes was earning $3 a hundred pounds picking cotton. What would he have said about an attitude which hastily tries to cover with charity the plight of a typical Indian family when the death of its hero-son brings its poverty into embarrassing public view, but will not lift a finger to remove the obstacles of racial prejudice and economic discrimination which make charity necessary in an emergency, not only for a family but for a race?

When one thinks of it, it is astonishing how many elements in American life might have helped Ira Hayes but did not. The government of the United States, as represented by the marine corps and then by the bond-selling treasury, had its chance and failed. When he was a boy the little Presbyterian church in Bapchule could not reach him, although his parents are members. Neither could the Roman Catholic church, although he associated with young people of that church. The schools did not bring him the kind of teaching which produces stability of character, although they did prepare him to risk his life in battle for his country. The voluntary organizations which were so eager for his services after he became famous "used" him and left him hungry. The motion picture industry got what it wanted from him but left him unchanged. Television caught him in its bright light, then passed on. The patriotic societies only speeded his downfall. So it went. Ira Hayes passed up and down in our society, knocked on the doors of all our institutions—and found nobody who could save him from himself.

Even the Indian family of which he was a part, and the tribe to which it belonged, had lost their old capacity to heal their own. And America, whose manifold pressures are grinding and shattering the economic and spiritual substance of Indian tribal and family life, finds itself less than half-willing to share its own social and economic heritage, and only half-certain that its inner resources are adequate for living together as equals in multiracial nationhood.

The accusing memory of Ira Hayes is stronger because he was never bitter and never blamed anybody except himself. On the day before he reached his 32nd birthday on January 12 he wrote a man who had offered to help him find work: "Just a short letter this early morning before we go out to the cotton fields to pick cotton. You asked me once if I was ever in need of a job to come to see you. Well it seems I'm in that position, that is very soon, as the cotton season will be finished in a week or two. I feel I will make it this time. My folks are all in back of me."

He did not make it, and a great many Arizona people are sincerely sorry. One of them, Senator William A. Sullivan, has introduced a bill proposing immediate creation of a state commission to treat alcoholic victims before it is too late. He estimates that there are 12,000 alcoholics in Maricopa county alone. It is to be called the "Ira H. Hayes bill."

Harold E. Fey

AGAIN, THE PERSISTENCE of social ills is demonstrated by selections in tandem; in 1914, optimistic predictions of an end to intemperance; in 1961, objective analysis of a continuing problem. The modern-day report is from a professor of philosophy at Cornell College in Iowa, who through the years has contributed frequent articles on the temperance movement.

March 19, 1914

The Triumph of Temperance

AN EDITORIAL

Nothing is more cheering than the steady progress which the temperance movement is making throughout the nation. A few years since it was only the most persistent optimist who felt confident that the saloon would be driven from American life. Today the average man sees the signs of a fulfilment to that hope, the temperance workers are confident of early victory, and the supporters of the liquor traffic are fighting desperately against the advancing wave which threatens soon to sweep them out of business.

The triumph of temperance during the past ten years has been astonishing. With now and then a defeat, the march of the cause of sobriety under temperance, anti-saloon and prohibition leaders has been majestic and heartening. Formerly it was a question of winning here and there a spot of dry territory in the midst of a surrounding wet district. Now the movement spreads by townships, counties and states.

But most significant of all is the introduction into Congress of a bill for nation-wide prohibition.

It is not presumed that this bill will be passed without a desperate struggle on the part of the retreating and enraged friends of the saloon. But the very contest itself, thus carried to the supreme forum of the nation, will have very great educational value and in the end is bound to win. Men now living will survive to see a saloonless nation.

March 8, 1961

The Temperance Movement Today

ALBION R. KING

Temperance activity in the United States is still very much a matter of "drys" talking to themselves. This is not the case in Canada. In the series of institutes held across the Dominion each summer, Catholics, Anglicans, Lutherans, and moderationists among the other churches are numerous and vocal. Their presence makes for a more exciting discussion, to say the least. But some concerned persons feel that the drys and the moderationists should seek greater rapport and find ways of working together, and not merely contend with one another. For example, William Potoroka, executive secretary of the Manitoba Temperance Alliance, not long ago in an address before the Maritime Baptist convention called for a united front in the campaign for sobriety between churchmen who take the total abstinence position and those of the moderation tradition. His plea has met with varied response. The purpose of this article is to assess the requirements for attaining such a united front.

The first datum to be recognized is the fact that the drys no longer have a monopoly on concern about temperance. The dry temperance movement is more than a century old and has made notable achievements in our culture in spite of the failure of prohibition. There has never been a genuine moderation movement, although one seems to be in the making at present. During the prohibition era in the United States a powerful organization known as the Moderation League had as its propaganda objective the repeal of prohibition, and when that goal was accomplished the league folded. John A. Linton, head of the Canadian Temperance Federation, has observed that conditions today might be quite different if such a well-financed organization as the Moderation League had persisted and had sought to keep the flood of drinkers moderate. The nature and scope of the new moderation movement need not be detailed here. But I would like to call attention to one of its components: the joint commission on alcoholism of the Protestant Episcopal Church. A report this commission has made, titled "Alcohol, Alcoholism, and Social Drinking," is a solid example of the kind of thinking which must be done in regard to the problems confronting a moderation culture.

People in the temperance churches are going to be confronted more and more by the question of what attitude to take toward the moderation movement. So long as the moderation movement was an advertising device designed to sell more liquor, it could be bracketed with the enemy, but that cannot be done when it becomes thoughtful and sincere. Persistence in such an attitude toward moderates signifies self-righteousness—and in the long run is self-defeating. What are the possibilities and conditions for making common cause in the interest of sobriety?

The first need is semantic criticism and clarification of the philosophical and theological traditions which divide us. Many of the great temperance leaders of the past were assiduous in avoiding all such questions in their singleness of purpose—that of uniting all Christians in prohibition reform. Consequently, misunderstandings are great. Most often disputed is the meaning of temperance itself. The word has been a problem for definition since the time of the Greek moralists. Its ambiguity today, if recognized and respected, may be a basis for the collaboration desired. So long as we glare at each other from behind semantic absolutes there is no ground for understanding. In the orthodox tradition which stems from the ethics of Aristotle and the theology of Augustine, temperance means "moderation in all things." Augustine faced the question in a dispute with the Aquarians, whose repudiation of wine led them to use water in holy communion. This attitude, Augustine thought, violated the doctrine of creation and constituted a type of dualistic asceticism; he held that wine is one of "God's good creatures." In the scholastic tradition asceticism came to be not the repudiation of pleasure as sin but the voluntary sur-render of some pleasure for a higher good or the avoidance of an evil which outweighs the good. This is the doctrinal ground for the total abstinence groups among Roman Catholics, such as the Pioneers in Ireland and La Cordaire in French Canada.

The WCTU definition of temperance is "moderation in things beneficial, abstinence from things harmful." Actually the two definitions are not appreciably different, for when one gets into scholastic ethics he finds that the "all things" in the tra-ditional definition has to be qualified with the adjective "bene-ficial." And the assertion that wine is one of God's good crea-tures—or the opposite, that alcohol is of the devil—is a value judgment which in the final analysis must rest on criticized human experience. Appeal to dogma or tradition settles nothing. All parties must recognize that the alcohol problem which con-fronts us today is radically different from that reflected in He-brew or Greek literature and faced by St. Augustine. We need to understand each other in regard to our divergent use of terms and our differences in moral tradition, but nothing is more futile than bogging down in disputes about the teachings of the Bible or Aristotle and St. Thomas, or the efficacy of unfermented wine in holy communion. Our main effort must be to see clearly the situation in American culture today.

The modern temperance movement began as a moderation movement in the whisky-drinking culture of early nineteenth-century America. It was a flat failure before the Civil War and up to the time the movement became a total-abstinence pledge-signing campaign and a drive for prohibition. Harry Elmer Barnes had a point when he described prohibition as a product of the semibarbarism of the American frontier. A moderation culture involves a high state of civilization, as does a dry cul-ture. This fact is one of the points which moderation people must recognize. Most moderation sentiment is on the level of "I can take it or leave it." Or, worse still: "I don't care what happens to Jones. If he drinks himself to death that takes him out of competition." Study of moderation cultures—such as the Jewish and the Italian—reveals that genuine moderation is based on a closely knit security within the social group and a set of powerful taboos and sanctions against excess. These are very hard to achieve in our society—for instance, in a college fraternity where there is glib talk about moderation and the supposed deviation of alcoholics while the objective of party drinking is to "get high."

While the moderation group must realize the enormity of the problem of keeping drinkers moderate, the dry contingent must give up the idea of a simple solution to the alcohol problem. I do not mean to imply that prohibition is wrong, nor do I anticipate achievement of agreement on the nature and extent of legal controls, but the simple notion that legal coercions can solve the problem is an illusion which has been and continues to be divisive in the forces for sobriety.

There is also a theological question to be considered. Can man do anything about the human situation? A certain kind of current "orthodoxy" criticizes the social gospel and reaches for another beer. We must wait for God, it contends. Salvation is by faith alone. This "orthodox" stance is little different from the secular determinism which says you can't change human nature. Its reasoning seems to be: Men have always used alcohol and always will; I am not my brother's keeper.

The temperance movement probably cannot make common cause with theological or secular determinism. It was born in the utopian dreams of the nineteenth century after the Civil War and the abolition of slavery, and it was part and parcel of the social gospel movement. No responsible temperance movement of either the moderation or total abstinence variety can repudiate the social gospel; accepting it implies acceptance of moral and social responsibility along with the faith that God works through the institutions of men.

The modern temperance movement is often regarded as a failure, in view of the repeal of the prohibition amendment to the Constitution. But this judgment lacks discrimination. In the perspective of history it seems quite an achievement that nearly half the adult population in America does not partake of alcoholic beverages, and given the present popularity of drink this is chiefly a matter of moral judgment. The people who sell intoxicating beverages pay the temperance movement a tribute by spending billions on Madison Avenue schemes in an effort to sway the non-imbibing half of the adult population. Another point of necessary discrimination is to distinguish between a sincere moderation movement and the liquor industry's moderation talk, which is designed to sell more liquor to more people.

The basis for all co-operation must be humility; both the wets and the drys have a residue of pride to get rid of. Within the temperance movement there is a self-righteousness which in part stems from adherence to an absolutist moral position and in part is a residue of the utopianism of the last century. But nothing can match the pride of moderate drinkers who are sure they can handle their liquor. It is seen particularly in the common attitude they take toward the problem drinker, the cocksureness with which they assert that the alcoholic is some sort of abnormal person. In my opinion there is today much more understanding and concern for alcoholics among abstaining Christians than among the respectable denizens of cocktail bars.

Both sides should realize, without pride in past achievements or in personal attitudes, that the alcohol problem confronts us today with one of the worst evils of our sensate culture. No form of human suffering is more tragic and none involves more people. I am not suggesting that temperance societies should scrap their charters and start over on a new basis. But there are possibilities for co-operation without agreement.

I think we should promote more opportunities to talk to one another. Such opportunities are developing in the schools and seminars sponsored by committees on alcoholism and state-directed programs of research and rehabilitation, although the program-makers usually avoid any injection of wet-dry controversy if they can. Yale University's summer institute in alcohol studies started out with frank discussion of these issues; it was a pioneer in getting opposing sides to face each other. But in recent years this kind of confrontation has been dropped from the program, and even in the seminars a frank statement of dry sentiment now tends to be suppressed. Institutes and seminars set up by the temperance churches and leagues might well invite free expression of the moderation position in a dialectical situation. On one occasion in which that was done I witnessed a threatened cancellation of support, but I believe that that spirit is rapidly fading.

In many people there exists a real hunger for frank discussion of basic ethics; such people are not interested in loaded propaganda for a preconceived position. At a church seminar where I developed a thesis for abstinence along with a tolerant statement of the moderation position a layman took me aside and said "You are the only person who speaks my language." I urged him to state his convictions in the forum, but he never did—and not from any lack of articulateness. The whole atmosphere of the place was against it. I have also been in situations where the witness to an abstinence conviction was frustrated by wet sentiment and assumption. In some circles this orientation is so strong that to refuse a drink is a daring act indeed.

Aside from the question of "To drink or not to drink" there are three areas of current interest and activity which call for all the understanding and collaboration we can muster: (1) the support of the variety of programs of research and rehabilitation for alcoholics, (2) the research and work for better highway safety where alcohol is involved, (3) the support of programs of objective education through the schools. These should be vital concerns of all groups. And we should use these and other activities as opportunities to co-operate without suppression of personal witness. In the first of these one may find himself rubbing elbows with representatives of the Brewers Foundation and the Distilled Spirits Institute. Highway safety is everybody's business, and there are signs of a new popular understanding which may bring public policy on intoxicated driving into line with scientific realities —for example, requiring blood tests. But such measures must have the support of all if they are to be enacted. Objective education is the most difficult task of all. Everyone concerned about the future of our society wants to control the young through education, hence the propaganda approach. A basic understanding of alcohol should be a part of the thinking of all people no matter what decision or practice they adopt. This understanding must come about primarily through the work of educators trained in objective methods of dealing with controversial issues.

> ITS THEORY and practice in race relations has become a gauge by which the church tests the validity of its profession. Three men whose active involvement in the issue gives them the right to speak do so here: a world-famous South African novelist and opposition political leader who is also a layman active in Anglican and World Council of Churches affairs; a white professor-farmer, now retired, who writes from his South Carolina home; and a Negro clergyman, exponent of non-violent resistance as a tool for the obtaining of racial justice.

March 31, 1954

The Church Amid Racial Tensions

ALAN PATON

Not only is the church set amid racial tensions, but there are racial tensions in the church, too. These racial tensions we bring in with us; they are the evidence of our unregenerateness. We do not like the thought that it may be our own unconvertedness, our own unregenerateness, that causes racial tension within the church. Therefore we sometimes choose to think it possible that God likes racial tension, that it is part of his creative plan. In the story of the Tower of Babel we find support.

Or, alternately, we choose to think that although God does not like racial tension, he knows how inevitable it is, and therefore he thinks that the races ought to stay away from one another. We can go a step further, too, and think that God thinks that if the races cannot be reasonable then they must be made to keep away from one another. And we can go yet another step and make a law to keep the races away from one another; and not only law, but a whole array of regulations, social arrangements, customs, traditions, to keep them away from one another.

One thing we can be grateful for—it is getting very hard indeed for a Christian to think that God likes his race better than other races. A Christian may still like his own race better than others, but it is getting very hard to think that God agrees with him. And even if he does think that God agrees with him, it is getting very hard, almost impossible, to say it out loud.

Now what happens if you lose faith in these arguments, which when seen in darkness appear to the credulous to be dressed in God's majesty? They are like kings in invisible clothes, and once laughed at can never again be revered. What happens next?

This is what happens next. You can say that you yourself personally have no race prejudice, that you personally have Jewish friends, and that you see no reason why Asia should not belong to the Asians. But in your own country you can't go too fast. You have to consider local customs, local prejudices and last but by no means least the power of the state. You accept racial equality in theory, but you accept racial inequality in practice. In a thousand years things may be different.

You also have two other powerful arguments. These are geography and culture. Colored people often live in areas distinct from white areas; therefore geographically it would be difficult to have colored people in your church. Further, they are culturally different. They use different languages and have different customs. They like to have services lasting three hours, and you like services lasting one hour. You must not force them to do what they would not like to do.

Some Christians think that it is love that is impelling them to seek for a greater, more tangible, more visible unity among the races. But there are other Christians who doubt this, and who think that this "love" is really anything but love; it is guilt, it is busybodyism, it is patronage come back in a new and more subtle guise. Above all it is sentimentality, and what is worse, it is sentimentality that will actually defeat the ends of that true love that is so wise, so gracious, so intensely practical, so well controlled.

These are powerful arguments. So powerful are they that one may be pardoned for supposing that their strength often comes from somewhere else, from deeper motives whose existence we deny. These motives are fear and pride, seldom encountered in their pure state (though that can happen), but usually in compounds. And these compounds are at their most powerful when to them has been added a good dollop of love and consideration for others.

It is very difficult to counter these arguments; it is always very difficult to counter arguments that conceal emotional attitudes. You are very much in the position of a man who must comment on all the points of his friend's sheep, when all the time he knows that inside it is a wolf. Nor does it help very much to know that it is quite a decent wolf.

Let us be honest: it is often not the inadvisability, the impracticability, of going faster that deters us, but the fear of it. This fear is of two distinct kinds. One is the fear we feel because we ourselves are unregenerate; the other is the fear we feel of the unregenerateness of others, especially of an unregenerate state.

All these attitudes are intensely human, but they are not noble, courageous or generous. They are cautious, calculating and cold. They rule out of court any possibility that God may be calling us to transcend differences of race and culture and calling us to assert our common sonship. In a race-ridden world, but more especially in a race-ridden country, God may be calling us to proclaim something far more ineffable, far more Christian, than race difference.

If the Lord of our faith and church, the Savior of mankind, if Robert Herrick's "darling of the world" were to come to our state or country, what would he make of our laws and our arrangements? If people of every race and color flocked to see him, longed to touch him, would he be bound by our arrangements? Would he accept our segregated churches? Or could we suspend our arrangements while he was with us in person? Or would we beseech him to leave our coasts? Or would we crucify him?

Christians cannot ignore the problems created by racial tensions in their society, nor problems of geography and culture. There is not much danger that they will. The danger is that they will use the existence of these problems to excuse them from action, that they will use the unregenerateness of the world to excuse their own. The danger is that the church may consent to be used as an instrument to delay or prevent regeneration. It may, by overestimating the gravity of racial tensions, and by planning its course accordingly, help to entrench them.

One does not find that the church as a whole is enough concerned about the evil and unjust results of race discrimination and the color bar. It is not so concerned as its Lord in person would have been. One may condemn the evil results, but it is the color bar itself that needs our condemnation. And the best way for the church to condemn the color bar is to show that it has not got one. Now the church often says it has not got one. By this it often means that there is no physical color bar inside the physical church building; it means that Mrs. Jones will sit next to a black man in a church even though she wouldn't in a cinema. I suppose that's something, but it doesn't seem to be much.

To remove the color bar from the heart is a much more difficult matter. It would truly be difficult to imagine an unsegregated church in a segregated community. But even in a highly segregated community, the church should be moving away from segregation. Alas, in many places this movement is hardly to be discerned.

The problems of race within any state or country are paralleled by problems of race and nationality in the world itself. About this great area of task and opportunity I know very little, except to know that world leaders of the churches feel the weight of their responsibilities. But of one thing I am certain—the Christian churches of the world will face their task and their opportunity with a new authority, I dare to say with the divine authority, when they have faced squarely their own national tasks and opportunities. In some countries there is a danger that the churches, by having too great a respect for the prejudices of their own members, and for the prejudices of nonmembers, will make these difficulties greater than they are.

This seeking for a visible unity of Christians I believe to be good and right. I am not impressed by arguments for a spiritual unity which will not be visibly expressed. Much argument about the inadvisability and impracticability seems to me to conceal a reluctance to move. What I mean is, when I personally am too much aware of the impracticability, then I know that I personally am too reluctant to move. I also believe that when Christians are too reluctant to move it is mostly out of fear, to a lesser extent out of pride. On the other hand, that which moves them to move, I believe to be love; I do not believe it to be guilt, patronage or sentimentality. Because it is love it must be obeyed. In all simplicity and humility we must as Christians show our unity to the world; it is our witness to our Lord's claim, and to ours, that he is truly the hope of the world.

September 19, 1956

What Does the South Want?

JAMES McBRIDE DABBS

"Idealists are all right in their place, but this is a job for practical men." So runs a common thought in the South today. Accompanying this thought is the attack, open or veiled, upon preachers and intellectual leaders, upon theorists.

The practical men and their advocates couldn't be further wrong. What we face is a job primarily for theorists. For what are practical men? They are the men who, given the ends, figure out the means. They know how to manipulate things and people to attain a desired result. The city, partly because it desires greater cleanliness and greener lawns, desires more water. The practical men did not, as practical men, create these desires; but, given the desires, they go to work to obtain an additional supply of water. The community desires more education. The practical men are called in to determine how to attain and pay for this desire.

But when the desires of a community become confused and conflict with one another, when accepted ends begin to grow either undesirable or impracticable, or both, then the typical practical man, who is a master of means, is most at sea. What is needed then is a theorist in the root meaning of that word: a man who can see the whole picture and clarify for the community its conflicting desires. When the community again decides what it wants the practical men are called in to obtain it.

The South is now confused as to what it wants, especially in the realm of interracial relations. A large proportion of the white South will deny this and will maintain that it knows exactly what it wants: the continuation of the old pattern of segregation. But we shall see as we examine this claim that the matter is not so simple.

What did the white South want interracially during the heyday of segregation? In the first place, it wanted to use the Negro for its own advancement. In spite of all the talk about the sacredness of race, I am convinced, as I have argued elsewhere, that the chief desire of the white South was to maintain its position of economic and social advantage vis-à-vis the Negro. It wished to use the Negro for its own advantage.

Overlying this desire, however, was a second, which served to soften and even to a degree to ennoble the brute selfishness of the first. The white South desired to take care of the Negro. The utilitarian motive here is perfectly clear: we wish to take care of those objects, animals and people which lend themselves to our use. But the white South also desired to care for the Negro as one cares for a dependent, that is, paternalistically. If the individual in question is really dependent, this is a praiseworthy desire. Anyway, it served to surround the white man's basic selfishness with an aura of goodness.

What of the Negroes? Since they compose such a large part of the population of the South we must also ask what they wanted during the heyday of segregation. By and large they took their cue from the dominant race. Since the whites wanted to use them, they wanted to avoid being used or, if they were lucky, to use the whites. Since the whites wanted to take care of them, in the several senses we have noted, they wanted to be taken care of. Their chief desire was to get along with the whites; they satisfied this desire by letting the whites take care of them as much as possible and use them as little as possible. Of course they had other, independent, desires— for freedom, equality, economic advancement, education. But they subordinated them to the desire to get along with the whites.

Since the whites held most of the power, it was their desires which really mattered. So long as this state of affairs continued, the whites did not have to ask what the Negroes wanted. The South wanted what the whites wanted. So long as these wants were clear and practicable, practical men could obtain them.

Seeking to use the Negroes as they did, the white people of the South built up a stereotyped picture of the Negro. This was supposed to contain the truth about any Negro, that is, about the Negro race. One of the main results of segregation is that it has pretty effectively prevented white people from seeing the Negro as a person or even as an individual, and has trained them to see Negroes in the mass. Now, it can be admitted that Negroes generally, having been for a long time conditioned by a limited and enforced social environment, did and do show certain common characteristics. But no informed man today will argue that these characteristics are racial. Some of them may prove to be. However, there is already available considerable proof that they are environmental.

With the aid of segregation, the white people of the South were able to believe that all Negroes have certain racial characteristics. They naturally believed in those characteristics which justified their use of the Negro. I give here a picture of what they generally saw. The fact that this picture is of a creature who never was on sea or land or even in the wild blue yonder merely indicates that, when you control a people, you can tell all kinds of lies about them and get away with it.

This is the picture: The Negro is lazy, inefficient, irresponsible and licentious. He is satisfied with present conditions; yet he wishes to merge racially with the whites; and yet again he wishes to retaliate against the whites. He lacks the typical American drives toward freedom and economic advancement; yet he is also unaffected by the color revolution sweeping the world today (his is a race therefore without relationships); yet, strangely enough, he is a seedbed for the spread of communism.

Anybody who can believe all this can believe anything. Anybody who is defending a privileged position unjustly maintained has to believe anything that will justify his privileges. If the white man is to justify his controlling the Negro, it aids him to believe that the Negro is lazy, inefficient, irresponsible and licentious. (Insofar as these beliefs have any basis in fact, the fact is largely the result of environment: the Negro is lazy and inefficient to outwit the whites, irresponsible because he is denied responsibility, licentious because of economic and social conditions forced upon him by the whites.) Again, the Negro's satisfaction with present conditions justifies our keeping him there; his desire to merge with the white race or to retaliate against it justifies our fear of him. That he is neither a true American citizen nor yet a foreigner merely bespeaks our own confused ignorance.

With the mention of communism, I have brought this picture up to date. And this is the picture, the stereotype, in which generally the white South still believes. For all its absurdity it worked in the past because, as I said, the whites held the power and the picture served mainly to justify their use of it. But it's not working now, and the practical men who once succeeded have now become highly impractical. For the ends of southern society have changed, and the practical men no longer know what we want.

The change has taken place among both the whites and the Negroes. The whites have changed—as, according to Whitehead, we always do—through both the pressure of events and the lure of ideals. As regards the pressure of events, the Negro has become a powerful and growing economic force. The white

South, in one corner of its heart, still wants to control him. Indeed the recently organized white citizens' councils are trying economic pressure to bring him to heel. But that pressure is already backfiring, and whites are suffering because of retaliatory economic boycott. Such events will make the white South still more keenly aware that the Negroes have become economically a power to be conciliated, not controlled.

Furthermore, the white South is increasingly aware of the importance of the racial issue on the world scene. The world is in part pressing the South toward reform, in part luring it. We selfishly desire to protect ourselves by protecting our country; we unselfishly desire that our country should be worthy of protection.

World politics aside, the white South is undergoing a change of heart. Its conscience has never been entirely dead in regard to its treatment of the Negro; and the growing concern in the world for equality, for justice, for the rights of minorities, has touched the white South also. Southern religious leaders, in recent months, have taken stands against segregation which they would never have taken in the past. The happy days of exploitation are over; the heart of the white South is sadly divided.

The Negroes too are beginning to have and to express desires of their own. They have not participated in two world wars and the Korean action for nothing. While fighting for democracy abroad they steeled their hearts to have more of it at home. No longer are they willing to be a subservient race. Once they were willing, being helpless, to desire for themselves what the white South desired for them. Aware now of their growing strength, they desire for themselves what the white South desires for itself, no more and no less: first class citizenship.

Practical men, as such, are not concerned with these changing ends. Their business is to get for the people what the people want. When the wants of the people change it is necessary that theorists, philosophers, idealists—though I hold no brief for the starry-eyed variety—should come forward to clarify the change and state the new desires. For the practical man, claiming to handle facts, really shuffles shadows. Life, however, is not composed of shadows; it is composed of three-dimensional facts; and the ends it seeks are complex, manifold and changing, and suited to such solid creatures. The practical man abstracts from the complete fact just that aspect which can serve as means to a particular and accepted end. The living tree is for him five hundred feet of number two common. The tall pine sighing in the twilight, the poplar in whose shade I rested as a boy—the tree which stands in nature or in my heart simply is not there. The practical man shuffles the shadow and passes on.

But when people begin to question whether they want more houses of wood or more acres of woodland park, then the practical man must stand aside until they make up their minds. And that is the situation in the South today. We can't have what we did want; and partly, but not solely, for that reason we don't want it. But what do we want? Only those who know the complete man, white or black, only those who know the solid human being, alive in a manifold and living world, can answer. And these are the theorists, the philosophers —best of all, the poets.

February 6, 1957

Non-Violence and Racial Justice

MARTIN LUTHER KING, JR.

It is commonly observed that the crisis in race relations dominates the arena of American life. This crisis has been precipitated by two factors: the determined resistance of reactionary elements in the South to the Supreme Court's momentous decision outlawing segregation in the public schools, and the radical change in the Negro's evaluation of himself. While southern legislative halls ring with open defiance through "interposition" and "nullification," while a modern version of the Ku Klux Klan has arisen in the form of "respectable" white citizens' councils, a revolutionary change has taken place in the Negro's conception of his own nature and destiny. Once he thought of himself as an inferior and patiently accepted injustice and exploitation. Those days are gone.

The first Negroes landed on the shores of this nation in 1619, one year ahead of the Pilgrim Fathers. They were brought here from Africa and, unlike the Pilgrims, they were brought against their will, as slaves. Throughout the era of slavery the Negro was treated in inhuman fashion. He was considered a thing to be used, not a person to be respected. He was merely a depersonalized cog in a vast plantation machine. The famous Dred Scott decision of 1857 well illustrates his status during slavery. In this decision the Supreme Court of the United States said, in substance, that the Negro is not a citizen of the United States; he is merely property subject to the dictates of his owner.

After his emancipation in 1863, the Negro still confronted oppression and inequality. It is true that for a time, while the army of occupation remained in the South and Reconstruction ruled, he had a brief period of eminence and political power. But he was quickly overwhelmed by the white majority. Then in 1896, through the Plessy v. Ferguson decision, a new kind of slavery came into being. In this decision the Supreme Court of the nation established the doctrine of "separate but equal" as the law of the land. Very soon it was discovered that the concrete result of this doctrine was strict enforcement of the "separate," without the slightest intention to abide by the "equal." So the Plessy doctrine ended up plunging the Negro into the abyss of exploitation where he experienced the bleakness of nagging injustice.

Living under these conditions, many Negroes lost faith in themselves. They came to feel that perhaps they were less than human. So long as the Negro maintained this subservient attitude and accepted the "place" assigned him, a sort of racial peace existed. But it was an uneasy peace in which the Negro was forced patiently to submit to insult, injustice and exploitation. It was a negative peace. True peace is not merely the absence of some negative force—tension, confusion or war; it is the presence of some positive force—justice, good will and brotherhood.

Then circumstances made it necessary for the Negro to travel more. From the rural plantation he migrated to the urban industrial community. His economic life began gradually to rise, his crippling illiteracy gradually to decline. A myriad of factors came together to cause the Negro to take a new look at himself. Individually and as a group, he began to re-evaluate himself. And so he came to feel that he was somebody. His religion revealed to him that God loves all his children and that the important thing about a man is "not his specificity but his fundamentum," not the texture of his hair or the color of his skin but the quality of his soul.

This new self-respect and sense of dignity on the part of the Negro undermined the South's negative peace, since the white man refused to accept the change. The tension we are witnessing in race relations today can be explained in part by this revolutionary change in the Negro's evaluation of himself and his determination to struggle and sacrifice until the walls of segregation have been finally crushed by the battering rams of justice.

The determination of Negro Americans to win freedom from every form of oppression springs from the same profound longing for freedom that motivates oppressed peoples all over the world. The rhythmic beat of deep discontent in Africa and Asia is at bottom a quest for freedom and human dignity on the part of people who have long been victims of colonialism. The struggle for freedom on the part of oppressed people in general and of the American Negro in particular has developed slowly and is not going to end suddenly. Privileged groups rarely give up their privileges without strong resistance. But when oppressed people rise up against oppression there is no stopping point short of full freedom. Realism compels us to admit that the struggle will continue until freedom is a reality for all the oppressed peoples of the world.

Hence the basic question which confronts the world's oppressed is: How is the struggle against the forces of injustice to be waged? There are two possible answers. One is resort to the all too prevalent method of physical violence and corroding hatred. The danger of this method is its futility. Violence solves no social problems; it merely creates new and more complicated ones. Through the vistas of time a voice still cries to every potential Peter, "Put up your sword!" The shores of history are white with the bleached bones of nations and communities that failed to follow this command. If the American Negro and other victims of oppression succumb to the temptation of using violence in the struggle for justice, unborn generations will live in a desolate night of bitterness, and their chief legacy will be an endless reign of chaos.

The alternative to violence is non-violent resistance. This method was made famous in our generation by Mohandas K. Gandhi, who used it to free India from the domination of the British empire. Five points can be made concerning non-violence as a method in bringing about better racial conditions.

First, this is not a method for cowards; it does resist. The non-violent resister is just as strongly opposed to the evil against which he protests as is the person who uses violence. His method is passive or non-aggressive in the sense that he is not physically aggressive toward his opponent. But his mind and emotions are always active, constantly seeking to persuade the opponent that he is mistaken. This method is passive physically but strongly active spiritually; it is non-aggressive physically but dynamically aggressive spiritually.

A second point is that non-violent resistance does not seek to defeat or humiliate the opponent, but to win his friendship and understanding. The non-violent resister must often express his protest through non-co-operation or boycotts, but he realizes that non-co-operation and boycotts are not ends themselves; they are merely means to awaken a sense of moral shame in the opponent. The end is redemption and reconciliation. The aftermath of non-violence is the creation of the beloved community, while the aftermath of violence is tragic bitterness.

A third characteristic of this method is that the attack is directed against forces of evil rather than against persons who are caught in those forces. It is evil we are seeking to defeat, not the persons victimized by evil. Those of us who struggle against racial injustice must come to see that the basic tension is not between races. As I like to say to the people in Montgomery, Alabama: "The tension in this city is not between white people and Negro people. The tension is at bottom between justice and injustice, between the forces of light and the forces of darkness. And if there is a victory it will be a victory not merely for 50,000 Negroes, but a victory for justice and the forces of light. We are out to defeat injustice and not white persons who may happen to be unjust."

A fourth point that must be brought out concerning non-violent resistance is that it avoids not only external physical violence but also internal violence of spirit. At the center of non-violence stands the principle of love. In struggling for human dignity the oppressed people of the world must not allow themselves to become bitter or indulge in hate campaigns. To retaliate with hate and bitterness would do nothing but intensify the hate in the world. Along the way of life, someone must have sense enough and morality enough to cut off the chain of hate. This can be done only by projecting the ethics of love to the center of our lives.

In speaking of love at this point, we are not referring to some sentimental emotion. It would be nonsense to urge men to love their oppressors in an affectionate sense. "Love" in this connection means understanding good will. There are three words for love in the Greek New Testament. First, there is *eros*. In Platonic philosophy *eros* meant the yearning of the soul for the realm of the divine. It has come now to mean a sort of aesthetic or romantic love. Second, there is *philia*. It meant intimate affectionateness between friends. *Philia* denotes a sort of reciprocal love: the person loves because he is loved. When we speak of loving those who oppose us we refer to neither *eros* nor *philia*; we speak of a love which is expressed in the Greek word *agape*. *Agape* means nothing sentimental or basically affectionate; it means understanding, redeeming good will for all men, an overflowing love which seeks nothing in return. It is the love of God working in the lives of men. When we love on the *agape* level we love men not because we like them, not because their attitudes and ways appeal to us, but because God loves them. Here we rise to the position of loving the person who does the evil deed while hating the deed he does.

Finally, the method of non-violence is based on the conviction that the universe is on the side of justice. It is this deep faith in the future that causes the non-violent resister to accept suffering without retaliation. He knows that in his struggle for justice he has cosmic companionship. This belief that God is on the side of truth and justice comes down to us from the long tradition of our Christian faith. There is something at the very center of our faith which reminds us that Good Friday may reign for a day, but ultimately it must give way to the triumphant beat of the Easter drums. Evil may so shape events that Caesar will occupy a palace and Christ a cross, but one day that same Christ will rise up and split history into A.D. and B.C., so that even the life of Caesar must be dated by his name. So in Montgomery we can walk and never get weary, because we know that there will be a great camp meeting in the promised land of freedom and justice.

This, in brief, is the method of non-violent resistance. It is a method that challenges all people struggling for justice and freedom. God grant that we wage the struggle with dignity and discipline. May all who suffer oppression in this world reject the self-defeating method of retaliatory violence and choose the method that seeks to redeem. Through using this method wisely and courageously we will emerge from the bleak and desolate midnight of man's inhumanity to man into the bright daybreak of freedom and justice.

VI

National Scene

A QUAKER PHILOSOPHER questions the validity of a widely held assumption.

July 7, 1954

In God We Trust

HENRY J. CADBURY

In God we trust, proclaim our coins, and if the quality of our trust has seemed dubious to some, at least the claim was circulated only among ourselves at home. But now the motto on our coins has been put on a stamp whose widest use will be to carry letters abroad. It is estimated that 200 million of the 8-cent "trust" stamps will be used annually, and we have been advised by a high authority that in using them we are sending overseas a message saying that ours is a land of liberty and one in which there is respect for the almighty truths. We may thereby feel that we have done "something definite and constructive."

At the same time that we are expected to publicize our trust in God abroad, I find that many of my domestic letters come bearing a message that it is on NATO we are to rely, or that it is General Patton and the armed forces of the United States whom we are to honor.

The use of the words "in God we trust" as an American motto does not go back, as I first imagined, to the Founding Fathers, but is less than a hundred years old. It was first put on our coins in the closing years of the Civil War.

That was a time when, in spite of other moods, many Americans were religiously moved, perhaps just because of the tragedy and the inner distrust of the rightness of the method, if not of the aims, of the fratricidal conflict. Abraham Lincoln was among those who felt the contradiction of war and freedom and in his unconventional piety often recalled the people to trust in God.

Circulating among ourselves, the motto on our coins might be considered a reminder to us that it is in God we should trust. But the words have long served to fuel those who challenge us that we trust far more in the almighty dollar than in the Being whom the coins proclaim.

Unlike our coins, these new stamps are not issued as reminders to ourselves but are intended to fall into the hands of other people. Each is meant to be a little beam of propaganda. In the face of our anxious reliance on military strength, to send out 200 million messages a year affirming our trust in God would be ridiculous were it not so serious.

In terms of government policy, our proclaimed trust is simply untrue, and there could hardly be a more inappropriate time for flaunting a trust which must seem even to our best friends abroad hypocrisy and sham. Even our friends are impressed by the strength of our very different kind of trust—in multiplied air bases, in striking power, in ever more destructive bombs, and in our boasted capacity to deter or at least to retaliate by the use of force.

If there was ever a time when actions belied words it is when we profess to trust in God while we are thus engaged. And in this war, hot or cold, our policy expresses very little of those qualities which one associates with religion—penitence, forgiveness, humility.

If it be true of our nation that "in God we trust," then either the trust is weak or the God is false. Are we adopting a god of war who appears as a nationalistic deity directing the bombs and bullets into the hearts of enemies? And what of the God of our opponents, who has also been beseeched for victory? In both world wars, Americans and Germans prayed to the same God for victory against each other. During the First World War, while American coins proclaimed "in God we trust," the buckles of German soldiers carried the inscription *"Gott mit uns."*

Is it not in finding our way back to a trust in God which is expressed in actions and in constructive attitudes, rather than in circulating hypocrisies abroad, that our only hope lies? The urge of most Americans to do "something definite and constructive" can perhaps find a more wholesome outlet in reaching neighbors at home and abroad with messages and acts that express not the counterfeit but the true piety of our motto. Is it not the duty of every one of us to practice the real trust in God that leads from fear and anxious dependence on weapons outside ourselves to love and peace?

Recurring Rumpus.
June 5, 1946

Why Is the DAR?

AN EDITORIAL

Again the Daughters of the American Revolution have been in the headlines. Every annual convention of this organization seems to provide the press with a field day—a phenomenon which has become so familiar that a good friend of ours, who had held high office in its ranks, always referred to it as the "Daughters of the Annual Rumpus." Most of the issues which have provided such sensational newspaper copy have been about on a level with the one which so upset this year's gathering. The excitement swirled this time about the efforts of an unofficial committee of seventeen members to change the rental terms for use of Constitution Hall, the large auditorium which the DAR owns in the national capital. Led by their president-general, the Daughters proceeded to pin back the ears of the upstart committee. Constitution Hall will continue to be available, except under extraordinary circumstances, only to Caucasian performers. The matter might be dismissed as a tea-pot tempest, except for the symbolic significance which it acquires from the name of the organization which thus upholds this color-bar policy. But the whole episode, so vividly and widely reported, raises the question: Why is the DAR? What

does it do? What useful purposes does it serve? Does it stand
for the perpetuation of the bold innovating spirit which produced the American revolution? Does it further the study of
the nation's history, and if so how, and what sort of history?
Does it take any importantly helpful part in any of the nation's
activities? Or is it simply a proof that the human animal is still
incorrigible in his (or her) desire to build tombs for the prophets whose spirit he (or she) utterly rejects?

The McCarthy blend.
June 10, 1953

We Shall Not Sign
AN EDITORIAL

Four weeks ago we published a letter from a gentleman in
Texas who ordered a trial subscription to The Christian Century and sent his check to pay for that subscription. The subscription, however, was conditional. It was not to be entered
until the editor had signed a pledge denying membership in the
Communist party or sympathy with its ideas. This pledge was
to be taken not only on behalf of the editor but of all employees
of The Christian Century.

We feel a sense of humiliation that anybody could ask us
to sign such a pledge. The contents of The Christian Century should have made that impossible. Anybody can examine
our record. It is found in a series of annual volumes reaching
back for many years that are available in nearly all the libraries
in the country. Chagrin over our own failure to make our views
plain is compounded by misgiving that the general climate of
opinion has become so baleful. For a request of this kind, unusual as it is, is instantly recognizable as a product of the character of our times.

Part of what is involved here is the question of credibility. We have been asked to sign an oath so that we may be believed. If our readers cannot believe us without an oath, they could not trust our word if it were given on a stack of Bibles (RSV) as high as the San Jacinto Monument. We are ready to state, and do now state, that we are Christians, not Communists; that our understanding of what it means to be a Christian makes it impossible for us to be a Communist; that nobody having anything to do with the publication of this paper is or has been a Communist. That statement stands, exactly as everything we publish stands, on our honor. We shall not sign this oath.

Would an oath establish credibility when it did not exist otherwise? Of course not. Would it mean anything if we printed an oath on the cover of each paper, all in legal form and properly notarized, in which the editor solemnly swore that to the best of his knowledge and belief the entire contents of the issue were the truth, the whole truth and nothing but the truth, so help him God? Absurd. Should the editor ask each member of the staff to sign, at the end of each day's work, a notarized statement swearing before the Almighty that on this day he or she had (knowingly) told no lies? Or have each take an oath every time a piece of copy is handed in? How silly can this stupidity become?

Have we come to the point where it is necessary to remind ourselves that we take integrity and truthfulness for granted? This oath-taking business, which is now being carried to such ridiculous extremes, calls all that into question and gains nothing. The Communists, whom it is allegedly the purpose of the oath-demanders to trap, do not hesitate to lie if it serves the purpose of the party line. Honest men and women, and journals which have built their reputation on their search for truth, refuse to believe that years of integrity and openness of conduct count for nothing.

Why do you read The Christian Century? Your promotion does not depend on it. You get no premium, no credit in meeting a quota, no guarantee that it will increase your salary. The main reason, we hope, is that you think that the matters this paper discusses or reports are important, that its editors and

writers honestly intend to place before you the truth about issues
that we are in fact as well as in name openly committed to a
of success in doing so. You know and we know that we sometimes err, because the paper makes a practice of publicly acknowledging error. But when we err it is not because the paper
is influenced by a hierarchy or other hidden and entrenched interest to misrepresent the truth. It is not because we are afraid
of retaliation, for our independent position to some extent pro-
tects us from that. And it is not because we can be bought off or
otherwise made to serve some subversive interest.

What then is the real ground of your confidence—if you have
confidence—that we try to tell the truth, that we are not serving
any hidden interest, Communist or otherwise? Basically it is
that we are in fact as well as in name openly committed to a
Christian witness. To the degree that we live up to that high
calling, we attain the highest level of civic loyalty and responsibility. There are times when it seems to us that the Christian
witness requires acknowledgment that the behavior of men has
fallen short of righteousness and the law of the land has fallen
short of the law of God.

But when we say so, we speak with a consciousness that we
could be, as we sometimes have been, mistaken. We are not
God. You, the reader, have to decide, also before God, whether
our margin of error is so wide that you are wasting your time in
reading our pages. But you do not question the assumption that
commitment to Christ is basic to right human relations, including the relationship with other people in our national life. This
is the assumption that underlies every issue of The Christian
Century. We believe profoundly that it fosters a dependable
sense of civic responsibility and an unwavering commitment to
the search for truth.

But there is more involved in the letter from our prospective
subscriber than its imputation of a lack of editorial integrity.
We are a part of these times, and we refuse to try to escape from
them by flights into yesterday or tomorrow. Once that demand
for our pledge was received, we had to publish it because we
share the life of contemporary America. It casts a strong light on
that life. It told us much about the position in which we now

stand. We benefit from America's wide-ranging good, and we also suffer from its evil. Its social neuroses, its seizures of suspicion, its black moods of fear and despair do not exempt us. We would not have it otherwise. We recognize the cross lurking in these evils for independent Christian journalism, but we would rather go down fighting for freedom than live having betrayed it by holding aloof when it suffers.

Our freedom is part of the general liberty of the press, but it also has a Christian dimension which makes an important difference. We share the general obligation to witness to the truth, with the added responsibility that we have to find ways to confess that we find the center of truth in Christ. Our freedom is the liberty that upholds the dignity of man in a democracy, plus the liberty that is in Christ. It is the latter which takes away fear, for Christ conquered fear. We believe that no human order is secure which is not defended by men whose final trust is outside that order, in God. We believe that no man can really call his soul his own who does not entrust the keeping of its integrity to God, to whom he is finally responsible.

Being a part of these times requires us to recognize that there is a Communist conspiracy against freedom in the world and in our country, and to do all we can to oppose it. Because of it a few errant professors are being exposed and driven from their posts. But because of it many honest scholars in colleges, universities and theological seminaries are being pilloried for their refusal to surrender their intellectual freedom, so precious in the history of Western thought, so essential to the future of our country and all mankind. We also refuse to submit to thought-control; so we take our place beside these honest and thoughtful men, aware that the glare of public suspicion often bedazzles discrimination between the innocent and guilty.

We know that communism has exploited for gain in its struggle for power the rightful resentment of men of color against racial discrimination and segregation, and we have tried to warn against this maneuver. We also know that all over this land Christian employers, pastors, labor leaders and churchwomen are held up to derision because they preach and practice the gospel of Christian brotherhood as it applies to relations be-

tween the races. Those who spit on them must also spit on us.
Here again the attack on communism by some of its opponents
sometimes betrays them into attacks against men and women
whose Christian conviction compels them to stand for what
they believe to be racial justice.

For our anxious friend in Texas it can all be summed up by
saying that The Christian Century's first loyalty is to Christ and
his cause, that our encompassing devotion as a venture in Christian journalism is to the search for truth and the service of
liberty, and that we mean to stand fast in such freedom as we
possess, since freedom unused is freedom denied and dying. We
shall not sign the pledge which he has concocted. But we shall
invite him to increase his acquaintance with our paper, confident that if he does so he will find that his fears were ground-
less.

March 15, 1961

High, Wide and Ugly

AN EDITORIAL

Two recent decisions made at the highest levels of government
weaken still further the fragile restraints under which the House
Un-American Activities Committee functions. In the same week
that the Supreme Court upheld the committee's power to require witnesses to say whether they are members of the Communist party, the House of Representatives approved HUAC's
full budget for another year. On the surface it would appear that
the committee has been given renewed sanction and funds to
ride high, wide and ugly over the liberties of citizens. But a
closer look at these developments indicates that the committee's
victory is something less than absolute. While the two bodies
which alone have power to curb the committee have declined to

use that power at this time, each has provided indications that its forbearance is not unlimited.

On February 27 the Supreme Court upheld the convictions of Frank Wilkinson and Carl Braden on charges that they stood in contempt of Congress for refusing to answer questions asked by a HUAC subcommittee member. The questions had to do with whether they were members of the Communist party. In a 1958 hearing in Atlanta, they declined to answer on grounds of conscience. Wilkinson challenged the legality of the HUAC mandate, arguing that "Congress cannot investigate into an area where it cannot legislate, and this committee tends, by its mandate and its practices, to investigate into precisely those areas of free speech, religion, peaceful assembly and the press wherein it cannot legislate and therefore cannot investigate." He then refused to answer the question "Are you now a member of the Communist party?"

The Supreme Court majority opinion holds that the House committee is properly constituted, that the specific hearing at which the interrogation took place was duly authorized, that, as the court had held in the earlier Barenblatt decision, it is proper for the committee to investigate communism. It holds that Wilkinson's plea that the committee was persecuting him because he was working for the abolition of the committee did not exempt him from action by the committee. It declares that the fact that a witness in a hearing in California had charged that Wilkinson is a Communist was sufficient ground for the House committee to ask the question and to insist on an answer.

The four-man minority opposing this view consisted of Chief Justice Earl Warren, Justices Hugo L. Black, William O. Douglas and William J. Brennan, Jr. The minority opinion, written by Justice Black, does not mince words: "In my view, the majority by its decision today places the stamp of approval upon a practice as clearly inconsistent with the Constitution, and indeed with every ideal of individual freedom for which this country has so long stood, as any that has ever come before this court. For, like Mr. Justice Douglas, I think it is clear that this case involves nothing more nor less than an attempt by the Un-American Activities Committee to use the contempt power of the

House of Representatives as a weapon against those who dare to criticize it." He accuses the majority of a "sweeping abdication of judicial power" and asserts that the meaning of its ruling is that "the committee may continue to harass its opponents with absolute impunity so long as the 'protections' of Barenblatt are observed."

Two days after the Supreme Court handed down its 5 to 4 decision, the House of Representatives voted 412 to 6 to approve the Un-American Activities Committee's request for $331,000 to finance this year's budget.

So now the stage is set. The House Un-American Activities Committee, in its zeal to save America from totalitarians of the left, is pushing it toward the totalitarians of the right. It sets the stage for the fearful to rob Americans of their liberties, for the powerful to demand uniformity of thought from a free people, for agencies of government to ride roughshod over individual rights even though those rights are guaranteed by the Constitution. When one legislative committee is permitted to violate the separation of powers provided by the Constitution, is permitted to take over the judicial power and try people without giving them the protections tested by time and provided by our courts, and to take over the executive power and punish people by "exposure" and harassment without conviction after a fair trial, other branches of government and other committees are tempted to overrun the bounds of their authority. So free government is disrupted, public discussion is silenced and fear stalks the land.

At present the House Committee on Un-American Activities has both money and authority. As Justice Black puts it, " . . . the only real limitation upon the committee's power to harass its opponents is the committee's own self-restraint, a characteristic which probably has not been predominant in the committee's work for the past few years." The committee should be encouraged to use that self-restraint. It will be so encouraged if citizens of unquestioned convictions and status insist that the committee stick to its proper legislative function and object when it steps over its proper bounds.

Further, a great many people are going to have to do their

bit to change the present repressive political climate by openly resisting intimidation. This can be done in connection with *Operation Abolition*, the HUAC-sponsored film now being used to brainwash the country. Wherever the film is shown, supporters of HUAC are ready to attack anybody who raises a question as to the truthfulness of representations the film makes. So let questions be raised! We are free to question a presidential speech or a Supreme Court decision, and we are free to question a film.

The House committee is now equipped with great power. It should remember that "all power corrupts, and absolute power corrupts absolutely." The committee's power is not absolute; it can misuse the law of the land, but it cannot repeal moral law. Let it read the warnings deeply imbedded in both the majority and the minority decisions of the Supreme Court to avoid the absolute corruption which is associated with absolute power. And let it remember what happened to one U.S. senator who seemed capable, only a few years ago, of bringing down anybody who opposed him. Let it remember Senator Joseph McCarthy.

IN NO PHASE of the "church and world" confrontation has the Century taken a more all-out and consistent stand over the years than that demonstrated in these selections, which incorporate the editors' insistence that the line of separation between church and state must remain clear cut and inviolate.

November 26, 1947

The Meaning of "Separation"

AN EDITORIAL

What do we mean by the separation of state and church? The subject is clouded with much confused thinking among Protestants as well as among Roman Catholics. This, as we pointed out, is largely caused by the fact that writers on both sides do not check their use of the formula with the Constitution.

Let us take a good look at the Constitution. The opening words of the First amendment dealing with this question read: "Congress shall make no law respecting an establishment of religion, or prohibiting the free exercise thereof." It is this double limitation upon the state that gave rise to the formula, "separation of church and state," in the American system of government. What does the First amendment mean? First note certain things that it does not mean.

It does not mean the separation of *religion* and the state. The state, through its representatives, can act from religious motives as well as from economic or political or other motives. In a word, there is nothing in the Constitution that forbids the state to perform a religious act. And it does perform such acts.

Nor does it mean the separation of the church and politics. The church has full liberty to engage in political action, either as a body or through its members in the discharge of their democratic responsibility as citizens. The church has the same right in this respect as a labor union, or the National Association of Manufacturers, or a political party or any other group of citizens. The only inhibition on the church at this point arises from its own conception of itself as a church.

Nor yet does the First amendment mean the separation of *religion* and *politics*. As Dean Weigle well says: "The religious freedom of the citizen includes his right to hold the state itself responsible to the moral law and to God, and the right to labor to this end through appropriate judgments, witness and constructive participation in the activities of citizenship."

The separation of church and state does not mean that the state must be indifferent to religion; that it must be impervious to the considerations which religion may bring to bear upon its policies; that church and state must exist in watertight compartments and can have no contact with each other; that the church may not bring its influence to bear upon the state in behalf of just laws and their righteous administration; that the church may not criticize the state, its laws or their administration. There is not a word in the Constitution which indicates or implies any of these limitations.

Nor, on the other side, does "separation" mean that the state must be strictly secular, that it may not recognize the Deity, or open the sessions of its legislatures with prayer, or include the study of religion as an integral part of the curriculum of state-supported education, or confess the dependence of the state upon the guidance of Providence.

The First amendment is precise in what it does: it separates —sharply separates—*church* and *state*, a concept wholly different from any of those referred to above. The church is the organized institution of religion, as the state is the organized institution of political life. It is these two institutions that are to be kept separate. But it is a separation which leaves room for moral and spiritual and political interaction and responsiveness. In what respect, then, are these two institutions to be kept separate? They are to be kept separate—completely separate— in their institutional or official functioning. The official functioning of the state must be kept separate from the official functioning of the organized church. There must be no interlocking of their respective institutional processes by law or the administration of law. This is the constitutional basis of religious liberty.

Look again at the Constitution. It does two things. It forbids Congress to make any law (1) respecting an establishment of religion or (2) prohibiting the free exercise thereof. The first clause is sharply specific; the second states a general principle. Consider the second clause first. "Congress shall make no law prohibiting the free exercise of religion." No religion is to be put under a ban by the state. No religion, on the other hand, may be given a special recognition by the state, for this obviously would have the negative effect of hampering all other religions; they would have to take a subordinate place in the shadow and operate against the prestige of the religion that was given special recognition. The plain design of this clause is to set all forms of religion free, to let them stand on their own feet and flourish or perish by the strength or weakness of their own faith. This is religious liberty.

But the first clause is more specific than the second. It implements the second. It specifically forbids Congress to make any law "respecting an establishment of religion." We must examine this carefully. What did the drafters of the First amendment have in mind when they used the words "establishment of religion"? Clearly, they had in mind the union of church and state, a system which had existed through many centuries of European history, and which even existed at that moment in some of the thirteen states of the young republic.

The founding fathers were determined that this system should not be taken over by the democratic republic they were engaged in setting up. With penetrating insight they saw that the root principle of this union or establishment consisted of the interlocking of the institutional processes of church and state by law which enabled the state to intervene in the affairs of the church and vice versa. They therefore struck at the root of this system and forbade Congress to make any law that would allow this system to get so much as a foothold in their new republic. This single stroke completely severed the official functioning of the state from that of the church. It placed the church, as church, outside the jurisdiction of the state, in the broad domain of freedom which the Bill of Rights as a whole forbade the state to invade. This the fathers did by providing in the First amendment that Congress should make no law "respecting an establishment of religion."

Two distinguishing features characterize an establishment of religion. One is the power of control over the church by the state, or by the church over the state. This may be a limited control, but insofar as it exists and is exercised at all by one over the other, it is potentially unlimited. The other feature inherent in an establishment of religion is that the church derives its institutional or temporal support, in whole or in part, from taxes levied on all citizens. This is in contrast to a church which is self-supporting, that is, which derives its total support from the voluntary gifts and services of its members, or by other means than government aid. When the fathers drafted the First amendment they had in mind this concept of an establishment of religion.

At first glance it seems that the fathers chose a rather awkward way of phrasing the prohibition of a religious establishment. Why did they not say merely, and more forth-rightly, "Congress shall not establish any religion by law"? The key to the answer is in the word "respecting." "Congress shall make no law *respecting* an establishment of religion." This word means something. It meant something to the draft-ers of the First amendment. It means "pertaining to," or "tending toward," an establishment of religion.

The First amendment is more sweeping and radical than would have been the case had it merely prohibited the establish-ment of religion. The formula as adopted takes account of the possibility that a religion might come to be established by a gradual process: a law might be enacted which, though it fell far short of establishing a religion, nevertheless would con-tain the principle of such an establishment. Such a law would become a precedent for the enactment of further legislation pointing in the same direction, thus gradually creeping up to the goal of a full and complete establishment of religion.

The First amendment strikes at the root of the matter. It forbids the making of any law *"respecting"* such an establish-ment, that is, pertaining to, or tending toward, such an establishment. Congress is thus put on the alert against the making of any law in which the *principle* of union of church and state is implicit.

There is a notion in some quarters that the situation we confront today calls for a new amendment to the Constitution which shall restate the principle of separation of church and state in terms specifically applicable to present-day attempts to subvert and nullify it. A bill for this purpose was recently introduced in Congress. We hold that such an effort is most unwise and entirely unnecessary. No form of words could im-prove upon the language used in the Constitution, nor apply more sharply to the specific issues now at the fore.

We set out in the present writing to formulate a definition of separation of church and state. Such a definition has al-ready appeared in our exposition of the Constitution. It should, however, be stated once more and in full. *By the separation of church and state is meant the constitutional provision which forbids the making of any law, and therefore the taking of any executive action, that involves the interlocking of the official functions of the state with the official or institutional functions of any church.* The all-inclusive function of the state is to make and administer law. And the Constitution forbids the making of any law the effect of which is to establish an interlocking relationship between the two institutions of church and state. Such an interlocking relationship is what is meant by the establishment of religion, in principle or in full actuality.

This severance of the institutional processes of organized religion from the official processes of the state is sometimes described by the formula, "a free church in a free state." But this is an inaccurate and dangerous formula. In the American system the church is not "in" the state. So to conceive it is to go over to totalitarianism. In totalitarian countries the church is indeed "in" the state, for the state embraces the whole social order. But in America the state does not embrace the whole social order. The American state is not totalitarian. It specifically leaves broad areas of intellectual, aesthetic, moral, cultural and religious life outside its jurisdiction. The state may not invade these areas. (Unless, of course, a church offends public law or morality or health by committing acts of nuisance or indecency or crime.) The true conception of the relation of church and state in America is that of a free church *side by side* with a free state, both of them *in* a free society.

This uniquely American solution of an age-old problem has been hailed by historians and political philosophers as marking the most significant and fruitful advance in this realm since the beginning of the Christian era.

Unrecognized by the law, except as voluntary associations of citizens—this is the meaning of separation of church and state in America. The Constitution prescribes for the state a "hands off" policy toward all forms of religion, forbidding any interlocking relation between church and state by law or the administration of law.

Let Protestants and Roman Catholics apply this definition to any of the numerous measures or practices that have caused this issue to be raised anew in our time. If a particular measure involves an interlocking of the official functions or processes of the state with those of any church by the use of tax funds for the benefit of any church, or by the meshing of the diplomatic processes of the state with those of any church, or by any other entanglement of their respective functions, it is unconstitutional. If it does not, the principle of separation of church and state is irrelevant to its consideration.

April 9, 1947

Churches Should Pay Taxes!

AN EDITORIAL

At other times, The Christian Century has expressed the strong opinion that the present system of tax exemption for churches is wrong. The decision of the Supreme Court in the bus transportation case inevitably brings other questions besides the bus issue to the fore. It is an opportune moment, therefore, for Protestants to re-examine the position in which their churches stand in relation to the state. We hold that churches should pay taxes on their church property and that Protestants should lead in demanding the enactment of a law abolishing for all churches the subsidy the state now gives them.

It will, of course, be a formidable undertaking, politically, to bring about the enactment of legislation to annul this long-established privilege. The opposition that will arise from the churches themselves whose vested interests are enormous can probably be overcome only by a long process of education and agitation. This, however, is no reason why the issue should not be clearly defined and the agitation begun. A sufficient number of the churches will have to be brought to the point where they are willing to put aside short-range, selfish considerations in the interest of unselfish principle and long-range religious and social good. The principle, stated simply, is that churches should pay their own way.

The legislation required for the annulment of this privilege would have to make a distinction between strictly church property and what might be called human service property owned and operated by churches. But this distinction would not be too difficult to make. Church buildings proper and auxiliary buildings (manses and houses for the clergy), unimproved real estate and parochial schools are plainly church property, used or to be used for religious purposes. These should not be exempt from taxation. On the other hand, hospitals and other eleemosynary institutions owned and operated by a church are in essentially the same category as similar institutions owned and operated not for profit by secular corporations. The humanitarian ends served by these institutions are the same, and their exemption from tax does not violate the principle of separation of church and state.

The case stands otherwise with respect to the exemption of strictly church property. The accumulation of such property has now become so great and is increasing so rapidly that its removal from the tax rolls adds an unjust and increasingly felt burden upon every taxpayer. Obviously, the taxpayer pays more because the church pays nothing. This means that every taxpayer pays for the support of all churches of whatever kind. The Protestant citizen pays for the support of the Roman Catholic Church, and vice versa. Both Catholics and Protestants help to maintain the innumerable sects which have sprung up in American society.

For the state to use its taxing power to compel the citizen, willy-nilly, to support churches is a violation of the First amendment of the Constitution which forbids the making of any law respecting the establishment of religion. It encourages the churches to aggrandize their property holdings and so increase their political power on the secular plane. The Roman Catholic Church has taken full advantage of its exemption from taxation by systematically accumulating enormous properties, especially in the large cities. In some cities, the burden of this exemption has become so acute that it is beginning to define itself as a conscious resentment against the churches. The resentment does not find expression in the press—of course not!—nor in political platforms or candidacies —again, of course not! But it becomes increasingly vocal in the conversation of citizen with citizen who resent the fact that their property tax goes to aid a church against their will, and that removal of these huge properties from the tax roll adds a substantial increase to their own tax burden.

Government tolerance of the widest diversity and variety in the field of religion is of the essence of political democracy. Indeed, this is the meaning of religious liberty. But the institutions embodying these diversities should pay their own way. They should be as nearly absolutely self-maintaining as it is possible to be in a society which grants them the great boon of religious liberty. This means that their property should be held subject to the same obligations that the law lays upon other property. It should be considered just as immoral for a church not to pay taxes as not to pay its ordinary debts.

The churches cannot hide behind the argument that they, too, are working for the general good of the community and therefore, like hospitals and nonsectarian schools, deserve to be tax-exempt. It is, of course, their belief that they are working for the common good, but taxpayers are by no means agreed that their influence is good for the community. Even those citizens who profess a religious faith do not agree, and they are entitled to choose what religious faith they desire to support. To compel them to support all religious faiths, among which are many they would definitely repudiate, is both confiscatory and a denial of their religious liberty.

From every angle, therefore, it appears that this long-established practice which, in basic theory, is contrary to the Constitution, should be abolished. The churches themselves should lead in bringing this to pass. No support for such a movement will come from the Roman Catholic Church, whose theory of the relation of church and state is incompatible with the American concept of democracy. But Protestantism has a vital stake in effectuating its own conception that church and state must be kept separate if society is to be kept free. The acceptance of a privileged position in the economy of the state, even though this same privilege is accorded all churches, puts Protestantism at a disadvantage. It is handicapped in its resistance to the encroachments of the Roman church upon the public treasury for the support of its parochial schools.

In principle, and in strict logic, there is little difference between the acceptance of a subsidy by tax exemption and subsidy from public funds for free textbooks and bus transportation to parochial schools. What difference there is lies in the fact that one is an immemorial custom whose undemocratic implications did not appear at the time our nation was founded. The issue was not raised. It was assumed without challenge that churches, inasmuch as they operated not for profit, should be lumped together in the same category with all such non-profit corporations and made tax-exempt. The fact that in the case of churches this practice created a bond between church and state, that it actually constituted a subsidy to the church by the state and was therefore legislation "respecting an establishment of religion," was not perceived.

It remained for the true nature of this practice to become apparent only when additional encroachments further threatened the constitutional principle of separation of church and state. Sponsored by a powerful church whose emergence has become formidable only in our time, whose theory of the relation of church and state is itself incompatible with the American theory, these new encroachments have brought the whole question of church-state relations under review. These new violations must be condemned and resisted and any law sanctioning them repealed. But this is not enough. Thoughtful Protestants have now to examine their own position in relation to the state. And when they do, they will find that they, too, are being subsidized by the state through tax exemption.

Therefore, as Protestants mobilize their citizen forces in opposition to further encroachments, they should not undertake to defend their own exemption from property tax. On the contrary, they should concede the fact that their own and all other churches are the beneficiaries of an ancient rule in violation of the Constitution which provides for the complete separation of church and state. Not only should this point be conceded, but Protestants who oppose Roman aggression have no alternative save to condemn this anomalous benefit and labor for its abrogation.

For Protestants to concede this on their own behalf would greatly strengthen their cause in resisting the step-by-step strategy of the Roman church in America. For this strategy embraces much more than the gaining of state support for its parochial schools, ominous as this is. Protestantism can be aroused from its complacency with respect to today's encroachments only by recognizing how radical is the incompatibility of Roman theory with American institutions. The ultimate end sought under its theory is nothing short of the attainment of state support for its entire ecclesiastical institution. Wherever the Roman church gains ascendancy in a state, its acknowledged theory calls for tax exemption for "the true church" and the imposition of a tax on all other religious faiths.

No principle is more important in a society now as never before threatened with totalitarianism than to affirm and demonstrate the absolute independence of the Christian Church—its autonomous life and its total responsibility for its own maintenance. What the future may have in store by way of suffering for those who steadfastly bear witness to the Christian faith, only God knows. But if a crisis comes to us like that which came to other countries gripped by totalitarian tyranny, the strength of the church will be determined by the degree in which it has become conscious of itself as solely dependent upon the devotion and loyalty of its own members and as absolutely independent, under God, as the state itself.

VII

People and Places

ONE OF A NUMBER *of articles and editorials reporting and discussing the "monkey trial" in Tennessee and the principals in the "show."*

July 30, 1925

Amateur Dramatics at Dayton

AN EDITORIAL

The curtain has fallen over the little stage in the Tennessee town which sprung into a sudden notoriety as the scene of a curious trial. The nearest approach to this rapid publicity achieved by Dayton was the meteor-like emergence of Shelby, Montana, to the fame of a prize fight arena, and its equally swift oblivion. Both towns have succeeded in securing a place in local annals, if only for a nine-day period. There was a difference, however. Shelby got only a trifle for its heavy investment. Dayton, with better business judgment, spent much less in preparation and rather wearied of the pageant before it was over. It was fortunate that the so-called trial lasted no longer than it did, for the public was growing as weary of its futility.

Few people cared for the legal issue that formed the only ground for the case. The question as to whether a teacher may have freedom to teach the ordinary principles of science as they are everywhere recognized by educators was not a matter to be settled in a country court and before a partisan judge and jury. At best it might serve as the means for bringing the familiar theme of scholastic liberty to settlement before some court of adequate jurisdiction and competent character. But the real interest of the occasion lay in the meeting in forensic contest of two well-known verbal pugilists. Therein once more the scene resembled in some degree the recent spectacle at Shelby. The chief difference lay in the fact that the prize fighters who met in the Montana town were chosen for their supposed fitness to settle the matter in controversy, were selected by promoters, and the choice was approved by a measure of public opinion. In the case at Dayton neither of the leading figures was selected and no suitable selection for the parts was made. Each volunteered in a manner to make any declination of his services rather difficult. Each was an embarrassment to the cause he insisted on championing. It was from the first a foregone conclusion that any real value the trial might have would be secured in spite of rather than by the help of the leading counsel.

In the case of Mr. Bryan it proved, as might have been expected, that he and his opinions on religion were on trial, rather than the young man, Mr. Scopes, who was the technical accused. The most valuable result of the case was that Mr. Bryan was given the opportunity, or was forced, to make clear some of his views on the Bible and the Christian religion. Confessing with naïve frankness that he had made no study of the problems raised by the contact of science with religion, he affirmed with the utmost candor a body of opinions regarding the Bible which Christian scholars as reverent as he, and actually informed upon the matters at issue, have ceased to hold this many a day. There is a scholarly and convincing argument to be made for the conservative position generally held by the church in the last generation, and still maintained by many who can give a reason for the faith that is within them. But Mr. Bryan is manifestly unable to make this argument, for he has neither the mind nor the temper for the task. His views of the Bible are those held generally by the generation to which Robert Ingersoll spoke, a generation that was shocked and baffled by his attacks upon the Bible because it had no adequate judgment upon the nature of the book it reverenced but did not understand. Mr. Ingersoll's platform success lay in the fact that he was assaulting the theory of a level Bible, all portions of which were divinely and inerrantly inspired, and whose statements on matters of history and nature were indisputable. To people without acquaintance with the critical and historical studies that have enriched the church during the past two decades, the diatribes on the mistakes of Moses were blasphemous but unanswerable. Today such lectures would fall completely flat, for that view of the Bible which they assumed as valid is as dead as Caesar.

It is the work of Christian scholars in the fields of textual and historical criticism, archaeology and the entire area of science that has made the Bible a fresh and vital book to those who care to avail themselves of the results of such scholarship. And these results are the commonplaces of the leading pulpits, the competent Sunday schools, the great majority of Christian colleges and every university. It is these materials of biblical interpretation which are conserving the faith of thousands of young people in the schools and colleges of the land, whose religious convictions would have been wrecked by such crudities of biblical teaching as those avowed by Mr. Bryan. It is this combination of genuine religious conviction and great ability as a public speaker which makes Mr. Bryan such a menace to the religious life of the nation. If the youth of the land must choose between an amiable but uninformed piety on the one hand and loyalty to the facts of science and the truths of history on the other, it is not difficult to perceive where the choice will fall.

The appearance of Mr. Darrow on the side of the defense was an embarrassment and a misfortune which threw still further discredit on a so-called trial where the essential evidence was excluded, and where everybody had a chance to hear the facts except the jury. At the best Mr. Darrow's agnostic views completely disqualify him to represent any but the most extreme antagonists of the Bible and the Christian faith. Clever as a criminal lawyer and highly gifted as a master of judicial procedure, he has neither the disposition nor the training to conduct such a case as he assumed to defend. If he had possessed any adequate knowledge of the Bible and the processes by which it is interpreted today, he could have set Mr. Bryan some real questions, rather than the stale inquiries that were the stock in trade of skeptical argument a generation ago. It was inevitable that the impression made by the conduct of the defense should be that of hostility to the Bible and the church. Mr. Bryan made an effort to capitalize this sentiment prevalent among the listeners. That he failed was due to the fact that even the prejudiced courtroom crowd understood something of the incompetence of the lawyer to assume the role of defender of that freedom with which the truth makes men free. Any one of the other members of Mr. Scopes' counsel could have made a far abler presentation of the case, as was proved when Mr. Malone brought even his unwilling audience to the highest level of interest reached during the entire hearing. The controversy at Dayton was not over the truth or authority of the Bible, or the validity of the Christian religion. The prosecution and the defense were of one mind on these themes, with the exception of the brilliant but unsuitable leader of Mr. Scopes' staff.

Next to the opportunity to discover the actual baldness and crudity of Mr. Bryan's conception of the Bible was the value of the testimony of the scholars who were not permitted by the court to present their evidence, but whose statements on the leading features of evolution, religion and the Bible were read into the record, and were published widely for the information of the public. Never has there been such a chance for information on the subject which has thus by accident been brought to attention. Hitherto evolution has been a word for the classroom and the laboratory. Now it is familiar and to some degree understood. The possibility of discovering a simian ancestry or kinship for humanity has no longer any terrors. In fact the whole ape involvement in the problem of evolution is one of the minor items in the discussion. Between the view that man has come from lower orders of life and is on the way upward and the opposite contention that he has come from above and is still going downward, it is not difficult to choose. At all events, the name of evolution is no longer likely to disturb the informed people of the present generation. If, as it seems, it is the theory that best accords with the facts as we know them, then it proves to be merely God's way of working. And if it is but a theory, so is gravitation, or molecular attraction, or radioactivity. They are theories which appear best to explain the phenomena of nature. No theory is final. New facts will amplify or limit it. But back to yesterday's conceptions of nature and the Bible we shall never go. And the men who are best prepared to comprehend the new truth as it breaks out from nature and the word of God in every generation are those who have made most adequate use of the emerging truths of their own time.

> *ELMER GANTRY was yet to appear, but the groundwork for his entrance was being laid.*

July 29, 1926

Sinclair Lewis' Sunday School Class

SAMUEL HARKNESS

A casual estimate of Sinclair Lewis would depict him as the bad boy of the literary world who flings novels, instead of stones, at the hornets' nests of prejudice and provincialism, and occasionally breaks large windows of good taste. This estimate is confirmed by two incidents in his recent visit to Kansas City: he stood in one of the pulpits on a Sunday evening and, before two thousand people, invited the God of all the fundamentalists to strike him dead; and a few days later, he rejected the Pulitzer prize. In spite of those confirmations, conclusive to so many, the casual estimate is wrong. Lewis is a humble, friendly man, unspoiled by his success and possessed of an uncanny genius that not only sees life, but sees straight through it. He does not see all of life, but what he sees, he tells with photographic accuracy. He does no "retouching"; he "leaves the warts on." He is the archenemy of bunk, intolerance and stupidity. He is a destructionist. He has no substitute for Gopher Prairie; no suggestions for Babbitt; and he feels no necessity to replace the preachers against whom he is now leveling the guns of his next novel. He is an iconoclast—the Jim Reed of novelists.

He came to Kansas City to do the preliminary fashioning of a missile intended for a bulging hornets' nest. He was perfectly frank about it. He gathered a group of preachers of all shades of theological opinion to meet in a series of weekly luncheon-conferences. He demanded that the ministers call him "Red"; he had their first names at his tongue's tip; and graduates of the greatest schools of religion in the old and new worlds, who preach to some of the largest congregations in the city, liked the experience so well that his suite became a rendezvous for the strangest "Sunday school class" in the history of the Christian Church. These ministers lent him books with such titles as *Aids to Sermon Building, How to Promote a Successful Revival* and *Why I Am a Presbyterian,* and gave him samples of the crude and incredibly silly songbooks used by evangelists. He attended tent revivals, read church papers and church yearbooks, listened to radiocast denunciations of himself, and then went on a two weeks' trip, motoring through Iowa and Minnesota with a former national chaplain of the American Legion that he might call on small-town preachers as a book agent and get their unguarded views. If he should use the data he has gathered thus far, he would be more verbose than Theodore Dreiser.

I was a train companion recently of a man who said: "I am writing a novel with a Presbyterian preacher as the hero. Will you give me a little information about the Presbyterian church?" A "little" satisfied him, and he made no notes. Lewis would learn the shorter catechism and dissect the "form of government" into shreds. He gets everything knowable together and feels it to the bone. He writes from the "inside."

He shakes words as a terrier worries a rat. In the meetings of the "Sunday school class" he probed through the vague and platitudinous words that preachers too often use: "What is religion?" "The art of living!" The other pupils smile approvingly—but not "Red." "What do you mean by 'art' and 'life'?" and soon he has one of the "class" floundering in a descriptive morass. He demands an exactitude of definition for new conceptions of religion without remembering that exactitude of definition is a cause of sectarian division and doctrinal controversy. Teacher trips once in a while, and the "class" laughs.

Soul-shaking moments come when Lewis speaks with the passion of an Old Testament prophet, demanding: "What sacrifices do you make? What risks will you take to end these paralyzing influences which you tell me are creeping over your church? Who will give up his wife and children, house and bank account? Who will literally follow Jesus into loneliness, ridicule and death?" Lewis has been reading the New Testament, and its iron and flame have gotten into his blood. "Why do you men stay in pulpits and use terms that mean nothing to you, and repeat creeds you have denied to me?" In vain he is told that the cause of religious freedom is best served from within the walls of orthodoxy.

There is a sophistry in the ministerial attitude that he scorns, and to which he attributes the fading distinction between the church and the world. "Why don't you tell your congregations that you are agnostics?" he storms. "The conventional Christ is sheer myth. Your Jesus is the hatrack on which men have hung their prejudices through the ages. Do you not realize that organized Christianity has had two thousand years to conquer the mind—and has failed? What other idea has ever had a like chance? Don't you see that no man can be a successful preacher unless he is a fundamentalist, because dogmatic denunciation is the intellectual gait of the people in your pews?" So he flings verbal grenades into the theological dugouts. There is nothing flippant about him now, and there is an uneasy hush. Instantly he feels that his words have given pain: "I am sorry for you—you are caught in a dilemma, but you must face it like Luthers and Wesleys."

There is something Lincolnesque about Lewis, tall, awkward and rustic. Yale and Europe cannot erase Sauk Center. If someone offers a prize for the homeliest novelist, he will have to take it. He is a strange mixture of sophistication and simplicity, but his sophistication is incidental and his simplicity is elemental. Nervous and volatile, he burns up enough energy to slay the average man. To the young writers who lick their lips while he reads their manuscripts, he is gracious and candid. To the affected and curious, he is harsh and abrupt. The fire in him is not pale and smoldering, but bright and intense. He can be with people, but is never quite of them. He is a wistful and lonely man whose contentment lies only in his dreams. He so lives in the grasp of the thing that he has not yet done that he hardly feels the touch of his past achievements. There is humor in him, clear and silvery like the humor of Voltaire. He is a voice crying in the wilderness.

And like all prophets he is doomed to failure. Sauk Center has a "Gopher Prairie Inn" and a "Main Street Garage"; the Rotarians have made him a life member; and when his preacher-novel appears the pulpits will buzz with invective, and all the hornets will be on the wing. A long-legged, red-haired man will stand off and grin, but his grin will fade when some denominational school tries to confer on him the degree of doctor of divinity, "with all the rights and dignities appertaining thereto," for branding the untypical preacher.

Lewis squirms under this analysis, but he is essentially a preacher. One day an employer of many young girls drifted into the "class." The talk was frank and a little facetious. The business man interrupted it by saying ponderously, "And what must I do to be saved?" To which Lewis answered in his shrill, breathless way, "Go, sell that thou hast and give to the poor." The rapier was sticking out of his back before he had felt it entering his chest—he did not come again. Lewis is a preacher, but his congregations would shrink and the offering plates might contain an occasional infernal machine or box of poisoned candy.

The last session of the "class" was gay and sad. The Sage of Emporia and the Buddha of Kansas City newspaperdom were guests of honor. Every man present had been stabbed and shocked into new realizations, and the author of *Arrowsmith* sheathed his stiletto with these words: "Boys, I'm going up to Minnesota, and write a novel about you. I'm going to give you hell, but I love every one of you." And as the "class" disbanded, the man who had called himself an atheist flung his arm about each one in turn and said, "Good-by, old man; God bless you!"

ON WHAT HE SAW *in the course of several visits to pre-World War II Germany, Paul Hutchinson, then managing editor, based recurrent warnings of chaos to come. When this report was filed Albert Einstein was still an honored citizen of the Reich.*

August 28, 1929

Einstein and the Red Flag

EDITORIAL CORRESPONDENCE

Somewhere in Latvia
August 3

Berlin is a city of contrasts. And there fell to my lot there two experiences about as completely in contrast as could happen, but both sure to live in memory among the few crystal-clear recollections of my life.

The whole story falls within three hours. The first took place on a sheltered porch at the rear of one of the city's loveliest suburban homes, with the sunshine streaming down on flowered terraces that stretched away from our feet to the sparkling waters of the Wannsee. It was as secluded and as beautiful a spot as I have wandered into on this trip; as we sat there drinking our tea, the bees hummed lazily among the bowls of flowers. The second part took place in a great city square. On all sides there were cold piles of granite architecture. People were packed in against each other. Bands blared. Orators shouted. Police kept careful watch. In near-by streets, lorries loaded with armed soldiers waited. The whole atmosphere was surcharged with tensity, doubt, a certain grimness.

It happened this way. Arnold Wolfers had an invitation to meet Professor Albert Einstein. Dr. Wolfers is a brilliant Swiss-German economist who teaches at the Berlin Hochschule für Politik, and who has a major part in making the annual visits of the Sherwood Eddy party to Germany such memo-

rable affairs. Einstein is Einstein. Dr. Wolfers had wished to
take the entire party to meet the famous mathematician, but
the delicate state of Einstein's health made that impossible.
So only five of us were invited, and I was one of the lucky
ones. We motored out to the home that a Berlin family had
made available—one of those lovely places that the wealthy
have built about the shores of the Wannsee—and Professor
Einstein, who lives in a miniature cottage somewhere west of
Potsdam, came in an equal distance to meet us.

He came onto the porch without announcement of any kind.
There was no momentary pause at the door, no attempt at
proper staging. We had been looking at the beauty of the garden
and the lake; there was a slight stir, and we looked up to find
him standing there with outstretched hand and simple greeting.
He is a man of medium height, whose stocky body filled out
his suit of red-brown rough-spun cloth. The head sits solidly
on the body. It is a large head, crowned with waving hair which
once was black and now shades from deep black at the roots
to clear white at the ends. It blows about like the mane of a
musician. Dr. Wolfers had warned us, "He looks like a
magician," and the phrase is not a bad one.

The man's skin is dark brown—browner than the sun-
burned tint which the summer girl of 1929 has sought to cultivate. Whether he has been thus deeply tanned by constant
living in the sunshine or whether it is his normal pigmentation
one cannot decide. But the brown face, which might be
shadowed and somber, is brought to life, kept vibrant, by the
large and glowing eyes. The eyes have deep wrinkles at their
corners. They are the wrinkles of a man who laughs often.
There are no creases cut by tensity or by frowns, not even by
the frowns that are supposed to be the natural possession of
the thinker. There is a mobile, full mouth, but it is the eyes to
which attention constantly returns. They are very gentle and
very kind.

After one has become acquainted with the degree of consideration which is ordinarily expected for the learned men of
Europe—and especially for those of Germany—the simplicity
of Einstein comes with startling effect. The man is wholly

without affectation. He does not expect to be treated like a demigod. There is nothing whatever in his manner that suggests the great man affably consenting to receive the homage of the herd. Instead, with all the directness and friendliness of a child, he answered our questions and developed the topics that we suggested. He let us lead the conversation wherever we desired; he never drew away from any of the subjects that were broached. When he wished to take exception to any of the views advanced he did so unhesitatingly, but generally with a smile. He forgot to remind us that he was the father of the theory of relativity.

So there we sat in a circle—Sherwood Eddy with Dr. Wolfers beside him. Then Dr. William J. Hutchins, the president of Berea who wrote that prize-winning "American Creed" a dozen years or so ago. Then Dean William Scarlett of St. Louis. Then me. Then Professor Jesse H. Holmes of Swarthmore. And then Einstein. The conversation went forward in a sort of mixture of German and English. Professor Einstein understands English, but prefers to answer in German. Once in a while he would appeal to Dr. Wolfers for a precise German translation for some phrase in one of our questions; throughout the interview Dr. Wolfers—who is the finest interpreter I have ever seen in action—kept up a running flow of interpretation to be sure that we were understanding what was being said.

We started with Russia, to which our party is bound. Russia suggested Italy. Einstein has no use for dictatorship anywhere, but he paid Russia the compliment of saying that at least its present dictatorship was set up by men whose motives were pure. And if—with accent on the if—it can finally establish its economic ideas in a permanent order, it will have an effect on world history beyond that of the French Revolution.

In some way it came out that Mr. Eddy is on his way to India, where he will meet Gandhi. Immediately, Einstein was eager to express his admiration for the mahatma. He doubts the wisdom of certain of the economic policies which Gandhi has avowed—probably because he believes the machine irresistible when it comes to providing the necessities of life—

but the spiritual power of the Indian leader he acknowledges. India's true road, according to Einstein, is the way of non-violence; let her win her soul spiritually and culturally, and freedom in other realms will eventually follow.

Out of this talk of India and the teaching of Gandhi came Einstein's avowal of his own pacifism. "I am an absolute pacifist," he said, and put it as one of the main purposes of his life to oppose at every turning the ancient European tradition of warfare. He believes in the taking of what the hundred per-centers of Germany must call a slacker's oath (a "holy oath" he called it) never to take part, either directly or indirectly, in any act of violence. Einstein has no illusions as to the forces which oppose the cause of peace. He is quite aware of the tradition of "honor" which has constantly driven Europe to war, and he knows that that tradition still retains power. But that does not at all discourage him nor affect him in his pacifism.

One of us tried to find out whether his pacifism is the result of his philosophical thinking or is a reaction against the events of the past few years. "Oh, it is an instinctive feeling," he told us. "It is a feeling that possesses me, because the murder of men is disgusting. I might go on to rationalize this reaction, but that would really be *a posteriori* thinking."

Sherwood Eddy was eager to draw him out on religion, and took Sir Arthur Stanley Eddington as a means of doing it. At the first mention of Eddington's name Einstein's face lit up, and he became animated to a far greater extent than before. The German adjectives which he bestowed on the Cambridge physicist indicated a deep-seated admiration. But when Mr. Eddy, seeking to suggest that leeway for an interpretation of the universe in terms of personal freedom which certain scientists see in recent developments in physics, asked whether the great German agrees with Eddington in thinking that the veil of the unknown falls in the center of the atom, the answer was instant: "*Das glaube ich nicht.*" There is no freedom in Einstein's universe; he left no room for doubt as to his absolute determinism. With the scientist's caution he frankly admitted that the present state of physics admits of reasonable doubt in this matter. "I only say, 'I think,'" he reminded us. "Nobody can say 'I know.' We know nothing about life." But as for himself: "I am an absolute determinist."

Religion? Of course there is a place left for religion in life; as long the human spirit preserves its sense of the greatness and harmony of the universe there will always be religion. And in that sense, "How can the religious feeling be disturbed by science?" To be sure, the idea of an anthropomorphic father-god, from whom people may expect to obtain things, is impossible for those with scientific knowledge. But the sense of awe before what Einstein called "the spirit shown in existence" is common to all great thinkers. That, I should take it, to him is religion.

It was at this point that Professor Holmes intervened. Professor Holmes is a Quaker, and apparently was not content to let the religious implications of the ideas of his fellow Quaker, Professor Eddington, be dropped quite so quickly. Eddington has pointed out that some of the so-called laws of physics are really only what he calls "statistical laws." That is, while certain actions of, let us say, atoms may be true when considered in terms of millions and quadrillions of atoms, it does not necessarily follow that these actions are always uniform for individual atoms. I cannot take space to try to interpret Eddington here; he is in print and can speak for himself. But it is plain that Eddington's statistical theory, if accepted, has devastating implications for a complete determinism. Did Professor Einstein accept it?

No; at this point, too, he disagrees with Eddington. It is unnatural to believe that there are statistical laws which are not real laws. He could imagine a God who leaves his system absolutely free; he could imagine a God who holds his world under law in every respect; but a God who establishes a world and then plays dice with it as though its laws were not established—"Das glaube ich nicht."

But, objected Professor Holmes, might it not be possible to take the total set of values that we see making for the progress of humanity and call that God? Instantly the laughing wrinkles at the corners of Einstein's eyes crinkled. "That is an

American sort of an idea," he laughed. What if tomorrow we awaken to find the world cold, mankind gone? If, then, God is only the sum of certain experiences of men, with man's extinction God will be extinct too.

So the conversation went on, getting back into political fields before we were done. Einstein does not see how America can let Europe pay the debts, unless the entire American population is to quit work and live on the receipts from Europe. (Perhaps I should label this a German mathematician's joke, but it is a joke with meaning.) He is interested in the work of the committee on intellectual co-operation of the League of Nations, of which he is a member. He believes that it may do something eventually to rout chauvinism out of the elementary schoolbooks of Europe. He is even more interested in a committee on which he is serving which is seeking to unite German Protestants, Catholics and Jews in working for world peace—first effort of the kind in Germany.

It was with an indelible impression of a kindly man, with a giant's brain and a child's heart, that we left at the end of our hour. To find a man of that kind so wrapped up in the cause of peace was to feel a new hope for Europe. But almost immediately we were plunged into a peace demonstration of a different sort, one that left us wondering how far, after all, Europe is from bloodshed. Our chauffeur hurried us from the quiet villa in which we had met Einstein across Berlin to the great square which lies beyond the university and the Spree, bordered on one side by the palace of the kaisers, on another by one of the great museums, and across its broadest front by the gigantic pile of the Dom—the kaiser's cathedral.

The square was jammed. Marching bands had centered here from all over the city. Above their heads waved red flags, red banners, crude cartoons. At eight points about the square orators waved their arms and shouted with all the lung power they could command. When they could shout no longer, hats came off and arms were raised while voices lifted three strident "hochs" for the Soviet Republic, and from one point after another there rose the deep-throated strains of the "Internationale."

The crowd did not look bloodthirsty. It was massed about as tightly as was humanly possible, and if trouble had started it might have spread quickly from one to the next. But for the most part these demonstrators looked like very peaceful, somewhat tired and disillusioned workingmen, with a large proportion of women. Almost a third must have been youngsters still in their teens or early twenties. Yet there was tenseness. Only three months before—on the first of May—the Communists had attempted to demonstrate, with resulting riots during which fourteen were killed by the police. Now there were police in every point of vantage, with reinforcing troops, mounted and in motor lorries, massed only two or three blocks distant.

It was supposed to be a peace demonstration. That is, it was a Communist peace demonstration, and there is a difference between that and the sort of peace that most of us are seeking. The badges worn by the marchers showed a Soviet soldier—a most ferocious person—apparently howling out the motto of the occasion: "War against imperialistic war." And the Communist peace idea is just that: first conquer the imperialist (i.e., the non-Communist) states, and then Communist peace will reign. The banners carried all sorts of threats to the established order. One, in particular, I remember: "The only way to peace is over the barricades."

So, in one afternoon, I listened to the expression of two different—and completely opposed—peace ideals. You will find both today in Europe. There is the horror of the man of science, of the thinker and the philosopher, at any continuation of the bloodshed which would turn the Continent into a shambles. Out of this revulsion comes absolute pacifism. And there is the revolt against all the old orders and systems that have ground down large portions of the populace and sacrificed them to ruthless and needless imperialistic ends. Out of this comes communism. Somewhere between the two must lie the way to peace. Will Europe find it in time?

Paul Hutchinson

February 11, 1948

Gandhi

AN EDITORIAL

Mahatma Gandhi's death at the hand of a Hindu assassin shakes the soul with its shocking reminder of the power of evil. More than any other man of this century, Gandhi returned good for evil, blessing for cursing, love for hatred. When he was reviled, he reviled not again. He prayed for those who persecuted him. He turned the other cheek again and again. He made no effort to save his life by surrounding it with the protections usually considered necessary by the great. He knew the risks he ran, for several attempts had previously been made to kill him. But he went freely among the people, received everybody who wanted to see him, and finally was shot at one of the public prayer meetings which he held daily.

If anyone could be said to have tried to overcome evil with good, Gandhi made that attempt. But he is dead. The good has been overcome. Gandhi did not seek to save his life, and he did not save it. The apostle of non-violence is dead, a victim of violence. The champion of truth has perished, laid low by treachery. The man who loved even his enemies died at the hand of an enemy. Evil has done its worst. Has it triumphed over good?

Gandhi was the greatest man in our world. Standing beside him Roosevelt, Stalin, Hitler, Churchill, or even Wilson, Sun Yat-sen and Lenin, all his contemporaries, lose stature. His greatness did not lie in the fact that more than any other man he must be given credit for winning independence for India. Neither did it reside in his recent amazing achievement by which, through "soul-force," he brought a truce between the warring religious communities of India. Rather it was in his

recognition that the supreme struggle of the modern world is
not in politics but is the battle between good and evil in the
soul of man. This insight on Gandhi's part often confused and
dismayed his political associates. Nehru's books are full of
confessions of his inability to understand the saint whom he
nevertheless loved and to whose wisdom he generally deferred.

But Gandhi was right, as his own death reveals. The outcome of all political arrangements depends in the last analysis
on the issue of the spiritual struggle. The final boundary is the
inner frontier of the soul, and modern man is being pushed
back to that ultimate outpost. Gandhi was murdered because
he relentlessly drove his fellow Hindus back to that frontier.
He undertook his recent fast because he could not endure seeing India destroy itself in communal strife without doing something about it. When people of all parties came to plead with
him to state on what terms he would consent to give up his
self-imposed suffering, he laid down conditions only for his own
religious community. He asked no pledges of Moslems or Sikhs,
but he asked a great deal of the Hindus.

In effect, Gandhi brought his fellow Hindus to pledge that
they would take upon themselves the humiliation and pain of
walking through the fire of suffering. They agreed to invite
the millions of Moslems who have been forced to emigrate to
Pakistan back to their homes in India. Hindus, who had themselves suffered frightful atrocities at the hands of Moslems,
agreed to assure safe conduct for all who accepted. Moslem
mosques were to be reopened and restored to their owners, and
all social and economic discriminations were to cease. As a
pledge of good faith and an act of penance, Hindus agreed to
visit their Moslem friends on the first feast day and to take
them gifts, as they did before communal strife began a generation ago. On top of all this, Gandhi insisted that India release
$166 million of Pakistan funds, impounded because Indians
had every reason for believing it would be used to finance the
Moslem attack on Kashmir. The money was turned over.

Can an American even faintly grasp what this meant? Imagine California's landed interests apologizing to the dispossessed
Japanese-Americans! Imagine the American Legion seeking

amnesty and indemnification for imprisoned conscientious objectors! Imagine white Protestant churches opening their membership to Negroes, or Roman Catholics holding out the hand of fellowship to Communists! If the United States were now freely to welcome all homeless Germans, and if we had lost twice as many dead at German hands as we did in the recent war, we would be doing something comparable to what the Hindus agreed to do to save Gandhi's life. It is not surprising that a considerable number of people in India took the view Gandhi's assassin took—that forgiveness under these circumstances, on such a scale and at such a price, was madness.

So Gandhi is dead, murdered by a Hindu because other Hindus had been moved to repent and to forgive their enemies. But being dead, Gandhi yet speaks. He has sealed with his life the covenant made between himself and the Hindu leaders, binding them to its fulfillment more strongly than any pledge made to the living. And his sacrifice will do more to soften the attitude of the Moslems toward the people of Hindu India than anything that has yet happened. One refuses to contemplate what might have happened had Gandhi's murderer been a Moslem, but the fact that Gandhi was killed by one of his own brethren dramatizes the inner and spiritual nature of the Indian problem in a way which will bring it home to the members of all India's communities.

Gandhi is dead, yet paradoxically he lives more powerfully than ever. He lives in the common people of India, whom he lifted to self-respect for the first time in modern history. He lives in Nehru and the other leaders of India, Hindus and Moslems alike, who have pledged themselves to return good for evil. He lives in the Christian community around the world, which has been forced to recognize in him a more compelling embodiment of Christian practice in political relationships than it has been able to produce from its own ranks. And he lives in history as one more proof that our conflicts in the inner and outer worlds, our spiritual and our political struggles, are really one and must be decided together.

Having said all this, it must be admitted that unless something more can be affirmed, Gandhi's life ended in failure. So far as his seventy-eight years were concerned, his attempt to overcome evil with good was smashed by the bullet of a killer. Unless there is a life beyond this, then injustice, hatred and violence won the day over the most Christlike life this century has known. The persistence of a man's influence, even the healing influence of Gandhi, is not an adequate answer to the problem of evil as embodied in the murder of this good man.

Gandhi believed with the Christian Church that death is not the end of a good life, but that the soul lives on. Long ago he said some words which bear remembrance now: "I do perceive that whilst everything around me is ever-changing and ever-dying, there is, underlying all that change, a living power that is changeless, that holds all together, that creates, dissolves and re-creates. That informing power and spirit is God. I see it as purely benevolent, for I can see that, in the midst of death, life persists; in the midst of untruth, truth persists; in the midst of darkness, light persists. Hence I gather that God is life, truth and light. He is love. He is the supreme good." In that faith Gandhi lives on. In that faith, and in it alone, the cross of Christ has meaning for our day, and forever.

OBSCURE AND UNSUNG, *a notable human being is lifted up for admiration by one whose path chanced to cross his.*

January 15, 1958

The Sage of Ballard Vale

PHILIP M. KELSEY

Readers of this journal who through the years have noted in its columns the frequent piquant and perceptive "letters to the editor" from Steven T. Byington may be interested in knowing something of the life of this great man who lived in relative obscurity and died last September in his rural New England home.

Steven Byington was born in a Vermont parsonage 88 years ago. Early in life he revealed a very unusual mind and, as frequently happened with such children, his parents steered him toward the ministry. He was graduated from Union Theological Seminary and academically would seem to have been destined for greatness. However, he had a speech impediment which he was not able to overcome and shortly had to resign the only pastorate he ever held.

This frustration sent him back into the world of books, in which he remained throughout his long life. Although he never traveled, he became an accomplished linguist in both ancient and modern languages. Because of his greater avocational accomplishments, the field in which he earned his living deserves only passing mention. He was chief proofreader for Ginn & Co. In his work he translated and read proof. I remember his translating into Spanish a book on higher mathematics. His remarkable mind seemed to retain just about everything that ever passed before his eyes, for he was a veritable encyclopedia not only of facts but of ideas and issues and movements.

While still a young man Byington began what was to become his life work: translating the Bible from the original tongues into modern English while retaining its full flavor. This task took the patient devotion of forty years, during which time Moffatt, Goodspeed and other translations were published. Possibly Byington's Psalms have been printed in pamphlet form, but that is all. One copy of his manuscript is in the parsonage at Ballard Vale, Massachusetts; the original is in his estate. During the years he was working on the Bible, he would daily board the commuter train to Boston with satchel and typewriter and work as he rode. Conspicuous as he was with these impedimenta plus the flourishing beard he always wore, he aroused the curiosity of many of his fellow riders. One day a reporter from the *Boston Globe* followed him as he left North Station and walked across the bridge to Ginn & Co. Soon thereafter there appeared in the *Globe* a feature article in which he received the title by which he was known to the *Globe* readers for years, the "Sage of Ballard Vale."

When I was a senior in seminary I was called to be pastor

of the little church in Ballard Vale. Like many old churches
in this part of the country, this one has a few pews at the front
which face the side of the pulpit. There sat Steve Byington. It
was good discipline for a young minister to have Mr. Byington
there. No carelessness with facts, biblical or otherwise, could
be risked, for Mr. Byington always waited until the rest of the
people had left, then came up and, without malice, offered
his corrections to the morning message. His fellow parishioners
would apologize for Mr. Byington to each new minister. They
didn't need to. Steve Byington liked the ministers and there
was no sting to his criticisms.

In the spring of 1954 I stopped to visit him and discovered
that he was wanting company on his annual climb up Mount
Mansfield in Vermont. This was five years after I had left
Ballard Vale. I expressed an interest, and, following an exchange of letters, I met him in August for the trip. He was
then 85 years of age and still able to set a steady pace on the
steep mountain trails. What was more amazing was the keen-
ness of his eye as he identified birds and trees with ease. Second
to his intellect, what amazed people most was the perfect vision
of this man who had read proof for a living and done extensive
research as a hobby.

I have always cherished the two days spent in the wilds with
a man who, though eccentric in many ways, had a depth of
feeling that he seldom allowed to come to the surface. His voice
broke as he told the story of fugitives from religious persecution
who had fled over just such wilderness trails as we were travel-
ing. That evening as I cooked supper in the mountain cabin in
which we spent the night, he pulled out of his pocket some
reading he had brought along. I glanced over his shoulder to
see what philosopher he was reading and saw that it was a
detective story.

My sadness is that a man of such true greatness was not
better known. He could have wasted his life away in resentment
at the poor portion that was his. He could have inflated his ego
by humiliating each young minister of humbler intellect who
came to serve the church. Yet this man whose handicap prevented his occupying an academic chair, chose to toil for forty

years at the work he loved. His translation was too late, but he continued doing research even when it was clear that there would be no publisher for his work. Many neighbors jeered, but some appreciated the greatness of his intellect and his soul. So did a few people who knew him only through his communications. And among them, I am sure, are many readers of the Century.

DEATH—and life—in Rome and Assisi.

October 29, 1958

Italy and the Pope

EDITORIAL CORRESPONDENCE

Rome, October 10

As the bus from Assisi came into Rome last night workmen were hastily plastering city walls and buildings with huge white posters bordered top and bottom with broad black bands. "Pio XII é Morte," they proclaimed, and they called on Romans to observe the prescribed nine days of mourning appropriately, with decorum. The Vatican, they announced, would be closed to visitors—except for St. Peter's where, after an uncertain interval, mourners would be able to view the body of the late pontiff.

Life in the teeming city seemed to be proceeding as usual. The sidewalk cafés were jammed to capacity; lovers strolled, embraced in the parks; traffic roared by at breakneck pace; until the wee hours the frantic put-put of the ubiquitous motor scooters deafened ears and shattered nerves. (Whoso would be blessed in Italy would be he who could find some way to muffle those raucous beasts without at the same time doing irreparable harm to the ego of their exuberant, headlong masters!)

The city continued busy through the morning hours today: people thronged the shops and markets; workmen pegged away at the never-ending task of street repair; the screeching scooters roared on in disregard of narrow curve and stranded pedestrian; at the travel agencies would-be pilgrims to Vatican City complained bitterly at alterations in plans for sightseeing itineraries.

It had been announced that Pius XII's body would be borne from Castel Gandolfo eighteen miles south in the Alban hills, where death occurred, to the Basilica of St. John Lateran (Rome's cathedral) for absolution and blessing, then taken to St. Peter's within the walls of Vatican City. So when the shops closed for the usual 12 to 2 P.M. siesta, the streets leading south from the center of the city toward that church and the near-by gate of St. John opening from the Appian Way were suddenly thronged with slowly moving crowds, while southbound trams were unable to take on any more riders. Gradually the great square before the basilica filled with the people of Rome. Through their ranks scurried priests, monks, friars, in robes black, brown, white and red—surplices under arm, sometimes donned hastily as their bearers neared the side door of the cathedral. On the broad steps before the façade, unadorned except for black and gold draperies around the main door, a group of dignitaries garbed in black, white and red assembled. Then, from positions at the right of the basilica, military detachments, companies of Roman police augmented by squads of resplendent *carbonieri* marched into the square, clearing a broad path to St. John's portal, forming two solid lines behind which the thronged thousands milled restlessly in the hot, hazy sunlight.

It was a casual, decorous crowd, intent on minor distractions: the play of children, the wisecracking of a seedy young man promptly squelched by an irate elderly woman in black, the activities of the truck-mounted television cameramen. There were few evidences of deep grief. The feeling seemed to be that this was but another event—one not unexpected—in the very satisfactory career of "Il Papa," and they wanted to be on hand for it, as they had for the events which had preceded it. When the funeral party finally appeared in St. John's portal—an hour later than scheduled—there was a silent surging forward, on tiptoe, in an effort to snatch a glimpse of the gold crowned, red draped funeral car, followed by the sleek black limousines of official-dom. Quickly the small procession entered the towering basilica, and the doors were closed. The ranks of military and police guards held their positions as the thousands moved away in con-versational groups, circling the surrounding blocks to take up new positions along the broad avenue behind the basilica lead-ing to the Coliseum and thence to St. Peter's down which the procession would pass after the preliminary ceremony. Through-out, strangely, there had been no music, no tolling of bells.

News of Pope Pius' death had come early yesterday morning to tranquil Assisi, whose St. Francis is now proclaimed the pa-tron saint of all Italy. Twists of black cloth appeared above the two banners outside the door to the bastion-like monastery below the mammoth hilltop church of San Francesco, but other-wise the simple rhythm of life on the towering cliffside con-tinued undisturbed. The deep-toned bells tolled the passing of the hours; tourist buses arrived; their passengers were guided through the crypt, the lower and upper churches, shown the saint's tomb, the faded frescoes from centuries long past.

Many hairpin curves above the walled town, beyond sight of its towers and domes, plunges the oak-rimmed gorge where St. Francis and his companions retired to meditate and pray. In the pregnant stillness, the young brown-robed friar's voice scarcely rose above a whisper as he pointed out to us—two slender Ital-ian nuns and a lone American visitor—the bare stone grotto, the tiny hewed-out chapel and refectory, the great live oak under which tradition has it St. Francis was wont to converse with his "little bird friends." All was quiet, dignified, peaceful—no en-trance fee, no religious gewgaws for sale.

Beyond the gorge, on the lower slopes of Mount Subasio, farmers plodded between the rows of ancient olive trees, scatter-ing grain from sacks held loosely beneath their arms, returning at the end of each furrow to guide over the seeded ground the clumsy harrows pulled by the milk-white oxen of the region. Across the broad, flat valley with its intricate patchwork of olive rows and vineyards, toward the softly rounded Perugian hills, lay a soft, dreamy haze. Little changed, surely, from the scene as St. Francis must have known it over seven centuries ago. And far, indeed, from the crowds, the pomp and spectacle of Rome. From here, from the eternal silence of Mount Subasio, from the simple rhythm of seedtime and harvest, from the perspective of one who meditated here on the eternal truths of man's relation to God and the universe—from here the death of a pontiff, the ending of *any* man's bodily existence, could hardly be seen as other than of small moment in a far mightier whole.

Margaret Frakes

LIVES THERE AN EDITOR who has not long since ceased to count the missives that have arrived at his desk recounting "a day with Albert Schweitzer"? This one's authorship gives it unique relevance.

March 18, 1931

Sunday at Lambaréné

ALBERT SCHWEITZER

The old hospital was at the mission station. So the sick and those who came with them had the opportunity of attending divine service. The new hospital lies two miles upstream from the mission. There is no path along the riverbank, and it is impossible to make one because of the numerous swamps. Anyone who wants to go from the hospital to the service at the mission must go in a boat. But most patients have neither boat nor rowers. It is true they come in a boat. But the people who have brought them have paddled off home again, leaving them here alone, or with an attendant, to be fetched away later.

If, therefore, the inmates of the hospital are to get to know the gospel, a service must be held for them here. So I preach every Sunday morning in the hospital.

Among my sick people there are many who know nothing whatever of Christianity, and have scarcely had an opportunity

of hearing a missionary. They are young men who do not belong
to this district, but only live here for a time. Coming from hundreds of miles away in the interior, they have let themselves be
recruited for two or three years as timber-workers, and they live
far in the forest amid swamps at lumber camps never reached
by the missionaries, when making visits to the indigenous population in the villages. After two or three years these natives return home with their earnings, if these have not been given in
pledge for the purchase of a wife. If they hear the news of the
gospel in the hospital, they carry it back first to the lumber
camp and later to their distant homes, where as yet there are no
missionaries. So to preach to my patients and those who ac-
company them is to sow seed which may be resown far away.

On a Sunday morning at 9 o'clock a hospital orderly with a
bell goes round the separate wards to call the people together
for "prayers," as he calls the service. Slowly they make their
way to the place between the two wards on the side of the hill
and sit down under the wide roofs in order to be in the shade.

A good half-hour goes by before they are all together. Mrs.
Russell's gramophone plays a record of solemn music, and as
soon as it is finished, the sermon begins. My parishioners cannot sing hymns, for they are almost exclusively heathens, and
what is more, they speak six different languages. To begin with
prayer is almost impossible, because the many new people who
every Sunday are at the service for the first time would not
know what it means and would cause a disturbance. So they
must be prepared for prayer by means of the address.

During the address I have two interpreters at my side, one on
the right and one on the left, who repeat each of my sentences.
The one on my right translates them into the Pahouin language, the other on my left into that of the Bendjabis, which
most people from the interior understand more or less. The interpreter on the right is either the hospital tailor, Sombunaga,
who is a Christian, or the hospital orderly, Mendoume, who is
not yet one. On the left the orderlies Boulingui and Dominique,
who are both in the same position as Mendoume, take it in
turns to act as interpreter.

I cannot demand of my hearers that they should sit as stiff as the faithful in an Alsatian church. I overlook the fact that those who have their fireplaces between these two wards cook their dinners while they are listening, that a mother washes and combs her baby's hair, that a man mends his fishing net, which he has hung up under the roof of the ward, and that many similar things take place. Even when a savage makes use of the time to lay his head on a comrade's lap and let him go on a sporting expedition through his hair, I do not stop it. For there are always new people there, and if I were continually to keep on admonishing them during the service, its solemnity would be much more disturbed; so I leave things alone. Nor do I take any notice of the sheep and goats who come and go among my congregation, or of the numerous weaver-birds which have nests in the trees nearby, and make a noise that forces me to raise my voice.

Not even Mrs. Russell's two monkeys are regarded as a disturbance. They are allowed to run about free on Sundays, and during the service they either practice gymnastics in the branches of the nearest palm tree or jump about on the corrugated iron roofs, and finally, when their energy is spent, settle down on their mistress' shoulder.

In spite of all this movement, the service in the open air has an impressive solemnity from the fact that the word of God comes to men and women who hear it for the first time.

While preaching, I must take pains to be as simple as possible. I must assume nothing. My listeners know nothing of Adam and Eve, of the ancient fathers, of the people of Israel, of Moses and the prophets, of the law, of the Pharisees, of the messiah, of the apostles. And as my congregation is in a constant state of renewal, I cannot think of attempting to teach even the most elementary of those historical ideas with which we have been familiar from infancy. I must let the word of God speak to them almost without reference to time. Since I must avoid so much when I am speaking, I feel as if I were playing the piano without being allowed to touch the black keys.

If I utter the word "messiah" I explain it at once as "king of our hearts, who was sent by God."

Once having accustomed oneself to preaching on this assumption that nothing is known already, the task is comparatively simple. The difficulties that have to be overcome are more than compensated for by the permission of writing the words of Scripture on the hearts of men to whom they are something entirely new. Every Sunday this is to me a fresh and a beautiful experience which "almost passeth understanding."

As text I choose a saying to which I add some Scripture story or one or two parables which explain it. At the end I repeat this saying several times, until I think that my hearers have got it by heart and will remember it. If anybody after a stay at the hospital takes away with him even but three or four such sayings, which give him something to think about, it is already a great thing for all his life.

As much as possible I try to resist the temptation to which everyone who addresses heathens is exposed, of "preaching the law." One's first thought, of course, is to keep on holding up the Ten Commandments to people who take lying, stealing and immorality for granted—and in this way to try to prepare them for the gospel. Naturally, too, I often preach about some one commandment or another. But in addition to that I try to awake in their hearts the longing for peace with God. When I speak of the difference between the heart that knows no peace and the heart that is full of peace, the most savage of *mes sauvages* know what I mean. And when I describe Jesus as he who brings peace with God into the hearts of men and women, they understand him.

Thus my sermon endeavors in a quite elementary way to be concerned with what the hearers have already themselves experienced, and with what they may experience if they have the will to let Jesus have power in their hearts. Whatever I make my starting point, I always lead on to the innermost fact involved in becoming a Christian, namely, the being led captive by Christ, so even the man who is only present at one service can get an inkling of what it really is to be a Christian.

In order to be understood, I must diligently endeavor to speak as much as possible to the point. Thus, for example, I must not leave Peter's question to Jesus whether it is enough to forgive one's brother seven times as a general proposition, but with examples from real life must show my natives what it may mean for one of them, as it did for Peter, to forgive seven times in one day. In one of my last addresses I described this to them in the following way:

"Scarcely are you up in the morning and standing in front of your hut when somebody whom all know to be a bad man comes and insults you. Because the Lord Jesus says that one ought to forgive you keep silent instead of beginning a palaver. Later on your neighbor's goat eats the bananas you were relying on for your dinner. Instead of starting a quarrel with the neighbor, you merely tell him that it was his goat, and that it would be the right thing if he would make it up to you in bananas. But when he contradicts you and maintains that the goat was not his, you quietly go off and reflect that God causes so many bananas to grow in your plantation that there is no need for you to begin a quarrel on this account.

"A little later comes the man to whom you gave ten bunches of bananas in order that he might sell them for you at the market along with his own. He brings the money for only nine. You say, 'That's too little.' But he retorts, 'You made a mistake in counting, and only gave me nine bunches.' You are about to shout in his face that he is a liar. But then you can't help thinking about many lies, of which you alone know, for which God must forgive you, and you go quietly into your hut.

"When you want to light your fire, you discover that somebody has carried off the wood that you fetched out of the forest yesterday, intending it to serve you for a week's cooking. Yet again you compel your heart to forgive, and refrain from making a search round all your neighbors' huts to see who can possibly have taken your wood so that you may bring an accusation against the thief before the headman.

"In the afternoon, when you are about to go and work in your plantation, you discover that somebody has taken away your good bush-knife and left you in its place his old one, which has a jagged edge. You know who it is, for you recognize the bush-knife. But then you consider that you have forgiven four times and that you want to manage to forgive even a fifth time. Although it is a day on which you have experienced much unpleasantness, you feel as jolly as if it had been one of the happiest. Why? Because your heart is happy in having obeyed the will of the Lord Jesus.

"In the evening you want to go out fishing. You put out your hand to take the torch which ought to be standing in the corner of your hut. But it isn't there. Then you are overcome by anger, and you think that you have forgiven enough in one day, and that you will now lie in wait for the man who has gone fishing with your torch. But once more the Lord Jesus becomes master of your heart. You go to the shore with a torch borrowed from a neighbor.

"There you discover that your boat is missing. Another man has gone fishing in it. Angrily you hide behind a tree in order to wait for him who has done you this wrong, and when he comes back you mean to take all his fish away from him and accuse him before the district officer, so that he will have to pay you just compensation. But while you are waiting, your heart begins to speak. It keeps on repeating the saying of Jesus that God cannot forgive us our sins if we do not forgive each other. You have to wait so long that the Lord Jesus yet again gains the mastery over you. Instead of going for the other fellow with your fists, when at last in the grey of the morning he returns and tumbles down in a fright as you step out from behind a tree, you tell him that the Lord Jesus compels you to forgive him, and you let him go in peace. You don't even ask him to give up the fish, when he does not leave them to you of his own accord. But I believe that he does give them to you from sheer amazement that you don't start a quarrel with him.

"Now you go home happy and proud that you have succeeded in making yourself forgive seven times. But if the Lord Jesus were to come in your village on that day, and you were to step in front of him and think he would praise you for it before all people, then he would say to you, as to Peter, that seven times is not enough, but that you must forgive yet seven times, and yet again, and yet again, and yet many more times before God can forgive you your many sins. . . ."

So far as is possible, in every sermon I find an opportunity of speaking of the nothingness of idols and fetishes, and then at the same time I attack the mad delusion that there are evil spirits, and that fetishes and magicians are in possession of supernatural powers. All my savages live with these ideas. It is possible that the words he has heard in a single sermon at the hospital may bring liberation to a man who is under the spell of these horrible ideas. In the course of our medical work, how much do we learn of ill treatment and murder as the result of the pronouncement of a fetishist carried out against people to whose magic he refers as illness or death! Again and again I get a shock when I see this misery of superstition.

I need not complain of any want of attentiveness among my hearers. One can see in their faces how their minds are occupied with what they have heard. I often break off in order to ask them whether their hearts and thoughts agree that what they have heard of the word of God is right, or whether anyone has anything to say to the contrary. Then, in a loud chorus, they all reply that what I have said is true.

A black evangelist who, as a patient, attended the hospital services related at the mission station that the doctor preaches just as if he had studied theology, like a missionary.

At the end of the sermon I give a short explanation of what prayer is. Then I tell them all to fold their hands. Those who don't yet know how learn by looking at the others. When at last all the hands are folded, I say very slowly an extempore prayer in five or six sentences, and it is repeated equally slowly by the interpreters in both languages. After the Amen, heads are bent long over the hands. Only when the soft music of the gramophone begins do they raise them. Then after I have said thank you to the two interpreters and have taken my leave, the listeners begin to rise.

IN THE COURSE of a round-the-world reporting tour in 1956, Dr. Gill, then managing editor, recorded vivid impressions of the situation in turbulent lands from Hungary to Hong Kong.

Ocober 10, 1956

The Sometime Holy Land

EDITORIAL CORRESPONDENCE

Jerusalem, Jordan
September 13

Only one good thing can be said about the Israeli-Arab impasse: it forces Air Jordan to fly one of the most absorbing routes in the world between Cairo and Jerusalem. Because neither side dares trespass on the other's air, the plane flies due east from Cairo, over drifting desert to the Suez canal, across the tortured terrain of the Sinai peninsula, jogging a bit to bring the Mount of the Law into view, thence north in much less than forty minutes over forty years' worth of Wilderness. At the head of the Gulf of Aqaba the pilot bisects the distance between the Israeli and Jordanian forts glowering at each other across a short stretch of sand, and flies straight up the terribly arbitrary, terribly embattled boundary between the little states. The south half of the Dead Sea is in Israel, so the plane veers over the hills of Moab, cutting west at Mount Nebo to cross the Jordan and land in Jerusalem.

This is my first visit to the sometime holy land, and my reactions and impressions are more dialectical than the early Barth. In the space of one typewritten line I can exult in being here and wish I had never come.

The land itself is reason enough for exultation. Don't ever think that those Old Testament panegyrics on the Promised Land are the ancient enthusiasms of parochial patriarchs who didn't have anything to judge by and so thought Palestine just

about perfect. Scenically and atmospherically it really is. After
the sultry vapors of Egypt, at any rate, the sweet, clear, dry, cool
winds of Jerusalem were unction and balm, full of grace. And
the hills: where does any land rise and fall more gloriously? Apparently it is impossible for a Palestinian hill to assume anything
but a beautiful line. Be it a low swell covered with a white-walled, flat-topped village, or a higher rise veined every which
way by rocky terraces and vined all over with grapes, or a fat-sided mound silver-gray with olive orchards, or the templed
Mount Zion itself, or the tortured, tumbling mountain spurs
falling in stark grandeur to the deep valley of the Dead Sea—
comfortable or splendid, all are beautiful. It was not, as I used to
think, a dubious compliment to compare the beloved's hair to
goats streaming down out of Gilead. There is a fluid loveliness
to the Bedouin's black flock leaping down a deep ravine at
dusk. I shall be everlastingly grateful for the few days' visit
which will let me hereafter read from the inside the love song
the Bible sings throughout to a particular land.

All that—and dear friends met in Jerusalem, and spacious,
spotless, peaceful quarters at the American Colony where a tiled
fountain laughs in a tiled court all night—I hope never to forget. But I shall hope very earnestly that time will blot out
shortly other memories of the storied city. If it does not, then I
can only wish that I had never seen some of the holy places of
the church. Where have I been all my life that I was so unprepared for the dead, clammy weight of the temples and churches
built over the traditional sites? It would be ungracious and impolite to branches of the church which have guarded the spots
for centuries to say what I thought between successive shocks.
After all, the tons of ornamentation that so oppressed this Protestant American are the treasured marks of generations of another devotion. But I do not want to go again to many of those
places. Coming out of each dim reek, feeling bludgeoned by the
irrelevant baubles, I sought in haste the land itself, trying to
press other memories out of mind by printing more strongly still
the serene silhouette of hills that must have stood the same then
as now, the sight and feel of living rock and living water.

Far more to be forgotten, yet even more unforgettable, is the turmoil that torments the ancient city and the tensions that tear up the very air. You can taste the bitterness even in these sweet breezes, and the clearest of them are stained with hatred. That is not callow impressionism, however much it sounds so. You look and you listen and you cannot miss the fact that crisscrossed antagonisms are the tissue of life here. Right now it is the British whose name and fame are withered in blasts of hot fury. Held responsible in large part for the triumphs of Zionism, blamed for their military bluster against Nasser and the intensely popular nationalization of the Suez canal, reviled as the most recent colonial masters of Jordan, the English are despised out loud and hated out of hand. Such extreme emotions are not limited to the unlettered and unsophisticated. A brilliant British-trained doctor at the Victoria Augusta hospital, sipping tea one afternoon, observed very matter-of-factly that if he were to suggest any sympathy with England, in any line or on any matter, he would expect to live only until the next night.

Some of this animosity, of course, rubs off on Americans. They have long been identified by the very active Communist agitators as the arch villains, who share the blame for encouraging Zionism and are not too solid on the Suez question. So far, though, our withholding new arms from Israel and our restraining influence in the Suez crisis have kept us off the active hate-list. Some Americans even claim to have noticed a slight improvement in their stock with Jordan since the expulsion of Glubb Pasha. Apparently that doughty major domo was regularly suspicious of American intent and activity in Jordan, and kept it, like everything else, under close scrutiny. His banishment seems to have eased that surveillance at least.

But of course the fires of invective still leap highest around Israel. Wherever you go in the Middle East this sense of outrage is the deepest diapason in the unison indignation. By now no one needs to be told how the offense was given. However reasonable the Israeli spokesman manages to make his country's cause sound, from this side of the line there is seen only injustice, fraud and collusion in high places. A little land was brutally divided, terror was instituted, property was stolen, a million residents of ancient landholdings were driven into the wretchedness and squalor of refugee camps around the rim of their former

homeland. The argument of Israel and of much of the rest of
the world that Jewish suffering had to be assuaged somehow
quickly lost force here when Israeli policy produced not incom-
parable Arabian suffering. And no Arab will ever admit—and
who will say that he should?—that *fait accompli* outweighs justice in any scales.

From Chicago the Israel-Arab problem looks like one of those
occasional insoluble ones that give the lie to any left-over Enlightenment notion that every question has an answer express-
ible in clear and distinct ideas. From Jerusalem the problem
looks just the same, only more so. Certainly the complexities
inhibit conclusions in a four-day visitor. But in the best manner
of recent ecumenical pronouncements, there are some questions
that can be asked on the basis of the briefest look-see. First, and
above all and in a kind of helpless fury, one must ask where the
alleged minds of the alleged statesmen were who ever dreamed
that a country as little as Palestine could be divided so arbitrar-
ily and exist. Fly in or out of this region and from a very low
altitude you can see from border to border. Yet this scant area
is savagely chopped in two by the craziest boundaries imaginable, zigzagging this way and that to divide villages, to separate
homes from fields, to leave roads leading to nowhere, and to
lay each side's flanks everywhere exposed to the other side.
Whatever the issues of justice, whatever the subterranean pressures, is not this partition political, economic and military nonsense, insanity, suicide? When supposedly wise, obviously powerful nations accede to such a monstrous arrangement is it any
wonder that intelligent men caught in the wreck should give
credence to rumors of dark plot and illicit coercion that make
the old Protocols of Zion canards look tame? And then there are
those wretched refugees living into their ninth year in caves,
tents and tin-can huts. What of them? Whence and whither?
Why do they sit in squalor while newcomers from abroad usurp
their apartments, their houses, their ancestral homesteads? I
hope no one seriously seeks biblical texts to justify any of this.
The verse that could definitely be construed to approve this
mess, far from rationalizing the situation would qualify the
whole biblical witness.

And let no one ask whether Arabian political leaders are not now using the refugees' plight for their own purposes, as if that question answered the whole question about why the refugees have not long since been resettled around in the Middle East with the proffered American aid. Of course the leaders are using conditions within the camps to their own ends, both in shaping the opinions of the refugees and in seeking to affect the opinion of the world. But who gave those leaders the chance and the material in the first place? And who will say that it is obstructionist leaders alone who force the refugees to their futureless vigil? Is it not imaginable that great numbers of these dispossessed want no new possessions but will hold out for repossession of what is rightfully still their own? I for one got the distinct impression that the refugees themselves by and large are not interested in finding new homes. They want to go *home*. And a people adept at waiting will not jeopardize its claim to what is back there by moving on to they know not what. At least, far from getting ready to go, they are now settling down more solidly than they have in nine years. Beyond Bethlehem a big camp is just now transferring itself from its shacks and rags into little cement block houses. There still is nothing for them to do there. They are still just going to wait. But they will be dry now, even if it is for another nine years.

A parenthetical word probably ought to be said at this point about the Western friends of the Arabian cause in this continuing crisis. Short of a visit to this area, it is impossible to assess highly enough the role that sheer principle must play in their concern. For the Arabs whom they seek to help, at least the vast numbers of village and country folk, are a singularly graceless people. Though those who try to help can hardly be accused of participating in the original offense, most of the Arabs seem to take completely for granted every assistance given as if they had it coming in expiation for the donor's crime. An editor's skin thickens quickly, but it is tissue-thin compared to the hide the patient Americans must develop who persist in their efforts to help the Arabs and to plead their cause. Motives are always mixed, but there is not much room here for ulterior ones.

The question, of course, is what can be done to resolve the issue, or at least to move in the direction of resolution. The deeply disquieting fact at this point is that an alarming gap is fast opening between the responsible leaders and the great bulk of the people. This is not the only place in the Middle East, nor is it the only subject, where the wise and experienced leaders are falling back of the mass. But the widening gap is perhaps most apparent here. Conversation with everybody from the tall, elegant governor of Jerusalem to taxi drivers and shopkeepers confirms that. In most cases, at the top you still have the hope that if Israel will permit the return of those Arabs who want to go back to their homes and lands, will compensate those who do not choose to return for whatever property has been commandeered, will buy out those who now want to come away from Israel and allow them to leave—that then fruitful negotiations and even resolutions can be essayed. Up in Lebanon, Statesman Charles Malik writing in the July *Foreign Affairs* holds out much the same hope.

The revealing fact, though, is that no one but Dr. Malik is willing to be quoted on this point. Other leaders still express the hope in private, but always the proviso is "not for publication." Can there be any explanation except that public identity with such views is now dangerous, if not fatal, politically? Certainly there is not the faintest echo of such moderation in the people's conversation, either at a pleasant tea in a garden or in the babel of the bazaar. Far closer to their mood and mind is the cry of the Algerian nationalist who called for his country to solve its problem by "driving the French into the sea." The cultivated Jordanians, most Arab Christians, try hard not to be vindictive, try to keep the line clear between anti-Zionism and anti-Jewishness, but ultimate expulsion has now replaced whatever more moderate solution might once have satisfied the populace. It remains to be seen whether finger-crossed leaders can overhaul the people and redirect their ambitions more realistically.

Another place where the gap between leaders and led shows up is in the Jordanian attitude toward Abdul Gamel Nasser. The people here, as everywhere in the Middle East, are bewitched by this dynamic and daring new leader. He is hailed, in so many words, as a savior. His picture is everywhere—the same badly colored portrait in the back window of all cabs, in most shop windows, plastered on walls, on many magazine covers, carried around by children and by soldiers. You don't have to understand Arabic to hear the name studding all talk: Nasser, Nasser, Nasser. There is fascination with the man himself, and leaping enthusiasm for his abrupt action.

Yet the leaders refuse to admit that Nasser himself has fast become more important to the people than anything he is, does or stands for. It is quite obvious that the governments of the countries around Egypt would like to harness to their local purposes the great nationalistic energies generated by the Egyptian president and his action. But they have no joy at all in seeing Nasser dominate the political affections and allegiances of the home constituency. They try to persuade themselves, therefore, that there is no such danger. Under questioning on this point, they remind you that Nasser is not really important even in Egypt as an individual: that he is only the visible agent of a committee, that his personal significance is in the very structure of things subordinate to a program. They quite manifestly deceive themselves. At the moment, Nasser could chuck his whole committee and stand higher with the people of the Middle East than ever before. The mystique has coalesced around this single personality. Local leaders may be suspicious of the new hero, but there is precious little they can do about it right now. In the present mood, to try to save their own prestige and authority by qualifying Nasser's in any way would be to lose all of their own. However often the surrounding kings and presidents meet to consider ways and means to clip the Egyptian's high-flying wings, they may well have to keep their doubts and suspicions to themselves. This is why it will not do for Western governments to bank too much on dynastic jealousies in the Middle East to keep Nasser's personal aggrandizement under check. Outside of Saudi Arabia and Lebanon, perhaps, I doubt that any government could long stand which mitigated in the slightest its public appreciation and support of President Nasser.

Finally, no leader around here has yet shown much sign of realizing how far and fast the Communist influence is spreading in this area. Maybe they know, but no one is admitting any-

thing; so the impression persists that once again developments
are well ahead of the leaders. For communism is not spreading
here; it is rampaging. Refugee camps which Harold Fey visited
two years ago are now virtually off limits to Western visitors.
Whatever the UN authority over the camps, real control is with
Communist ringleaders. Earlier this year under Communist
direction some of the camps rioted, destroying church mission
supplies intended for the refugees, threatening missionaries,
stoning the American consulate. The Jericho camp is a powder
keg. Around Hebron the Communists are in such control that
missions of every kind are closing up under fantastic charges
about how they abuse and endanger even the children they
serve.

On Sunday morning, while tracing the Via Dolorosa in old
Jerusalem, I was myself caught in the first Communist demonstration to dare tear through the town: bull-voiced bull sergeant
running backwards before a hundred young huskies, shouting a
line about the Suez, having it roared back by the mob, the hate-
ful antiphon going over and over again; banners stretched from
one side of the street to the other, bitterness twisting every
straining red face. There were no police in sight. Leaders, when
told about the demonstration, commented that it was quite
illegal. It was. But it happened and is happening, and no one
can seem to move fast enough to keep up with the development,
much less keep on top of it.

So this is the sometime holy land, a deadly stew of rancors
and hatreds. Everything that is going on is ominous, and what is
worse, pell-mell. If ever there was a place where outsiders might
better have imposed a solution in time, this is it. The imposing
nations have not been notably squeamish about taking firm steps
in other cases, but here drift was unaccountably encouraged.
Well, there is no drift any more, and action that might have
been proper once would probably be pointless now.

The situation is so netted and knotted that no one in it can
back off far enough to see it whole. Mount Zion itself is not
high enough to give any perspective on it. There is a hole in
Jericho, though, that might help. It is a deep cleft driven down
this summer by archaeologists through the mighty mound of

ancient Jerichos. I came to it at dusk the other day. Far below, in the depths of the cut, the last light showed a great stone wall and a massive round tower. Even in the gloom and at the distance the mysterious structures asked their question. For they stand in strata that date them *thousands* of years before human society is supposed to have been organized in the way necessary for such ponderous construction. Six thousand years or more they have stood there. The pyramids are babies beside that wall and tower. Who built them? When? No need to ask why, though. That wall and that tower in the dark depths were not built for fun. Somewhere there was division and from somewhere there was danger. And who won? Up on top of the mound, looking from the shadowy ruins below to the fading sunset above, you really wonder: Who won?

Theodore A. Gill

AN ASSOCIATE EDITOR visits the Valley of the Fallen, re-flects on what it reveals about Spain and her dictator.

August 23, 1961

The Tomb of the Chosen One

EDITORIAL CORRESPONDENCE

Madrid

Francisco Franco Bahamonde is a very religious man. Each night Franco and his wife kneel and say their beads together; each night, reverently relates one biographer, Franco thanks God for having chosen him to be the forger of Spain's destiny and asks that he may return Spain to God with the purity of its Catholicism unsullied. In the subservient Spanish press Franco is reputed to carry in his pocket a cherished reliquary containing a mummified hand of St. Teresa of Ávila. Spanish coins bear his profile and are inscribed "*Francisco Franco Caudillo de España por la G. de Dios"* ("Francisco Franco, Leader of Spain by the Grace of God").

When a new concordat was signed between Spain and the Vatican on August 27, 1953, the devout Caudillo was made a canon of the Basilica of Santa Maria Maggiore in Rome. On February 25, 1954, he was awarded "in recognition of his service to Catholicism" the papacy's highest decoration, the Supreme Order of Christ, bestowed by Cardinal Pla y Deniel, primate of Spain; the significance of the occasion was properly noted by the celebration of a pontifical mass. At his own insistence the Roman church has granted Franco the privilege of nominating candidates for vacant bishoprics. Also at his own insistence, a canopy is borne above him on all churchly special occasions at which he is present. And how pleased he was when his first grandchild, at her christening at his palace, El Pardo, was given the name "Maria del Carmen Esperanza Alejandra *de la Santísima Trinidad y Todos los Santos"* (". . . of the Holy Trinity and All the Saints"). Francisco Franco is indeed a remarkably religious man.

But the crowning glory, so to speak, of Generalissimo Franco's religious ardor (for that matter, of his entire career) is the incredible monument he has built to himself—and, of course, to God. Lauded in the Francoist press as "the great spiritualization of the Hispanic feelings of the twentieth century" and "the solemn recognition that the victory in our last war came from God," the monument has received similar praise from the lips of the Chosen One himself. At the monument's inauguration on April 1, 1959, he glowingly spoke of it as "a great temple raised to our Lord" in thanksgiving for his having granted victory to "Spain" (the general and his rebels, substantially aided by troops and arms from fascist Italy and nazi Germany) against "anti-Spain" (the weak but legally constituted republican government that Franco had sworn to defend) in the "true Crusade" of 1936-39 (a tragic, fratricidal holocaust in which one million were killed and from which Spain has yet fully to recover). Franco went on to insist that his "Crusade" was accorded "providential and miraculous" assistance, including shipments of arms seemingly from nowhere. And all the important battles were won, it seems, on feast days of "our Holy Church." But miracles could hardly be alien to "the Savior of Spain"—for so his newly formed Burgos government proclaimed him, with a capital "S," on February 7, 1938.

Franco's Pharaonic monument, which has been given the name *Santa Cruz del Valle de los Caídos* (Holy Cross of the Valley of the Fallen), stands on rocky, romantic terrain in a valley high up in the Guadarrama mountains, at the crossroads called Cuelgamuros, about thirty-five miles north of Madrid and only four miles from the edifice Franco wanted to rival and, if possible, to surpass: Philip II's somber, massive palace-monastery-pantheon El Escorial. The official guidebook credits Franco with being the "architect in spirit of the whole monument," the scheme of which "gradually took shape in his mind." Moreover, "his advice has been sought continually, and no part, however small, has escaped his eye." This, one can readily believe.

Dominating the Valley of the Fallen, which encompasses almost 46,000 acres, is a huge granite cross about 500 feet high, rising from the crest of the mountain called El Risco de la Nava. Something of the size of the cross is perhaps conveyed by the fact that its arms are wide enough inside for two automobiles to pass each other, and by the fact that the cross (described as a "lighthouse of faith") contains an elevator. On the cross's lower base are statues of the four Evangelists (each one 60 feet high); on its smaller, higher base from which its shaft springs are still larger statues of the four cardinal virtues. Comments the guidebook: "Only a deep understanding of the part played by nature in the making of the monument, together with a sense of the tortured flame-like quality of the crags of El Risco, could succeed in creating harmony, through sculpture, between rock and Cross." ("Harmony" and "unity" are favorite words of the guidebook, as of Franco's regime itself.)

Below the lofty cross is the Valley's second major unit: the subterranean basilica, "the largest ever built in the history of mankind." Hollowed out of El Risco, it is 850 feet long and at the nave crossing almost 200 feet high. Leading up to the basilica's esplanade is a landscaped drive lined with the Stations of the Cross in sculptured marble. The esplanade, which can accommodate 250,000 people, is reached from the road by a stair-way "in two flights, of ten steps each, symbolizing the Ten Commandments, or the ascent to moral perfection inspired by faith." Above the entrance to the basilica-mausoleum is a mammoth Pietà. One enters through ponderous bronze doors "decorated with panels in relief depicting the fifteen mysteries of the Rosary," and in the vestibule one encounters two gargantuan archangels, watchfully resting on their swords. Passing through a florid wrought-iron screen crested with angels, one comes to the long, gray-walled, vaulted "great nave" itself, its grim heaviness somewhat softened, if questionably so, by shallow side chapels, each nestling a sentimental Virgin in alabaster relief and dedicated to a division of Franco's civil war forces. More palatable respites from the gloom are some remarkably fine Flemish tapestries, *circa* 1540, illustrating the Book of Revelation—destined to be replaced, I understand, by new ones from Segovia portraying civil war scenes.

To the accompaniment of piped-in music one proceeds to the altar area. Dazzlingly bright compared with the nave corridor, it boasts a colorful mosaic-encrusted cupola with a pseudo-Byzantine Christ the Pantocrator and "groups of Saints, heroes and martyrs, doctors, Popes, prelates and peasants" floating toward him, "on their way to the glory of the Lord." On the high altar, which is directly in line with the towering cross outside, is a carving of Christ crucified, "made of ebony specially chosen and cut by General Franco himself from a tree in the woods of Riofrío." In the paving in front of the altar is a tablet honoring José Antonio Primo de Rivera, founder of the Falange, Spain's only legal political party; supposedly he is buried beneath it. (I say "supposedly" because informed people, including Miss Victoria Kent, editor of the distinguished journal *Ibérica*, contend that when José Antonio's body was removed from the Escorial it was taken not to the Valley of the Fallen but to a family crypt in Andalusia. This has never been denied by the Franco regime.) Speculation varies as to the precise location of Franco's final resting place: some say it will be beside the presumed remains of José Antonio, others say in a chapel to the right of the altar.

Also uncertain is the number of soldiers' bodies transferred to Franco's necropolis. The ossuaries that parallel the main sanctuary have room for the bones of 150,000 men, but it is doubtful that that number will ever be reached. Ostensibly departing from his original intention of a memorial only to the rebel dead, General Franco in a politically motivated token gesture has sought to include a few republican corpses in his tomb —provided they are also Catholic corpses. But republican families have refused to give their consent. The president of the Spanish republic in exile, Don Emilio Herrera, with whom I talked in Paris, and Miss Kent both maintain that there are no republican bones at all in Franco's crypt. Furthermore, many families of soldiers fallen on the Franco side have also refused to have their sons' bones moved to the megalomaniac monument. Not sharing the Caudillo's preoccupation with the past, the Spanish people prefer to leave the remains of their loved ones undisturbed.

The monument's third major unit, located behind the cross and connected to it by a tunnel, is a spacious Benedictine monastery, replete with the latest electrical appliances. According to the noted *New York Times* correspondent Herbert L. Matthews in his survey of Spain titled *The Yoke and the Arrows*, the monastery was first offered to Franciscans but was turned down by them as being much too luxurious. Opposite the monastery is a building housing a hostel and a center of social studies, the latter "an institution with the object of obtaining a maximum of social justice and peace for Spain." ("Social justice," a phrase much bandied about by the Falangists, has a rather ironic ring for Spanish peasants, whose average monthly incomes range from $8 to $15; for Spain's industrial workers, who average about $18 a month; for the regime's hundreds of political victims, imprisoned under appalling conditions for daring to engage in the kinds of criticism and dissent which in democratic countries are considered normal and healthy.)

The guidebook, at no point grudging in its use of superlatives, extols the Valley as one of "the great architectural and artistic creations of all time." Given the grandiose dimensions of the undertaking, one cannot help being impressed by it—at least for a time. But it is oppressive as well as impressive, and there is nothing particularly creative or imaginative, certainly nothing modern, about it. Taking more than fifteen years to complete, the monument is more of an engineering feat than an aesthetic achievement. (Much of the initial excavation was done by prisoners, who in exchange for a day of work received a three-day reduction in sentence.) Some of the statuary has a certain slick competence, but no one with taste would call it art. Apart from the tapestries, which apparently are only temporary, the whole enterprise smacks of sham. The monument is, in a word, *Kitsch*.

No official figure has been disclosed, but estimates of the cost of Franco's pet project—curiously characterized by the guidebook as "in keeping with the simple piety of the Spanish people"—run as high as $300 million. Spain's economy has seen some improvement in recent years, thanks largely to U.S. aid (now a main prop of the regime, along with the army, the church, and the wealthy landowners and businessmen). The country still, however, has a very low standard of living, and the "historic" Spanish hunger remains. Illiterates number almost 20 per cent of those over fifteen. Somehow one gets the idea that the money for the memorial could have been better spent. But the monument is not only colossal in size but sturdy in structure, and, barring atomic destruction, no doubt both the monument and the memory of Francisco Franco will endure for a long, long time—which is precisely the Chosen One's wish. Though he considers himself responsible not to men but only "to God and to History," he nevertheless wants to be remembered.

Dean Peerman

VIII

Other Voices

NEED "RELIGIOUS" POETRY *be so labeled?*

January 2, 1909

On the Religious Significance of Poetry

MARIETTA NEFF

The fundamental objection to didacticism in literature is not,
one may venture to suggest, any subjective criterion of taste,
but the simplest of logical principles—that life is larger than
anything one can say about it, experience more complex than
any formula, the test of the ways of the spirit of man more
subtly wonderful than the power of any gloss to define. Things
that are generally accepted are generally wrong; truths that can
be reduced to a proposition have lost their vitality. It is the failure to remember just these truisms—themselves only half-truths,
to be sure, by virtue of their formulation—that is in large measure responsible for the inability of the world to understand the
religious significance of poetry. Men and women content themselves with the dry bones of moralizing and didacticism such as
they read in hymns and other types of second-grade poetry, finding religious values in what is often neither true nor artistic,
while the whole body of that great literature which has in it the
breath of life awaits their acceptance.

No poetry, it is true, can give us life as it actually is, even the
comedy of the street and of the drawing room; no poetry can
give us the chivalrous grace of young romance or the strength
and quietness and breathless certitude of a maturer love; no poetry can give us the bugle blast of battle, the horror of carnage,
the tramp of victorious armies. But if the function of poetry be
after all the religious function of stirring high passion, of making the heart sensitive to the finer issues of life, of speaking to
the listening soul with voices that are not heard on earth forever
save in dreams—if these appeals constitute the function of

poetry, then indeed its essence must be not a ponderous didacticism, but even so frail and fleeting a thing as beauty like the poignant fairness of moonlight waters, or of silvery pools under the sun of early winter, or of blue lakes at peace with the blue sky; even, moreover, beauty as vast and terrible as the surge and thunder of multitudinous seas.

It is at rare intervals happily true that this beauty may be closely associated with what is conventionally looked upon as a religious idea.

As for all great poetry, then, one may repeat in slightly different terms the truth about the religious value of tragedy—that poetry is to preserve one from a facile orthodoxy, from any tendency to compress life into neat formulae, from any danger of too great respect for the wisdom of schools. Poetry is to be a cordial to one's heart, a light to one's eyes, music to one's ears —even a thorn in one's flesh, or a bitter wind to dispel one's drowsiness; any influence, in truth, which will produce that spiritual hyperaesthesia without which one can maintain no ecstasy in life.

EN ROUTE FROM HIS NATIVE INDIA to a teaching assignment at Boston University, Mr. Chakravarty stopped off in Russia to confer with the Nobel prize winner who rejected his prize, and there gained insights into the soul of a great-minded champion of soul freedom.

July 6, 1960

Pasternak: Poet of Humanity

AMIYA CHAKRAVARTY

December 28, 1959, is a day that will long remain in my memory. For it was on that day, in the wintry village of Peredelkino, that I came to know Boris Pasternak as a man who found peace through suffering, whose victory lay in his being conquered by the goodness of life.

My snowbound journey from Moscow ended at the gate of Pasternak's modest *dacha*. On the door was an inscription admonishing in several languages: "No interviews, no exceptions, no preferences." But it opened at my knock. A maid, busy at her dishpan, looked up as I, somehow unable to remember a single word of Russian, hesitated in the doorway. Then a face peered out from an inner room. It was that of Boris Pasternak, the poet whose integrity of spirit has fired the world's imagination. In his blue eyes, set in a noble, sensitive face, I sensed a background of vast suffering—and something greater. Though he knew German best of all languages except Russian, we conversed in English, which he spoke fluently.

The details of our conversation in that warm and pleasant room are woven together with inner reflections into a pattern illumined by impressions of the physical surroundings: the piano in the corner, the lemon-colored curtain, the snowy scene outside the window. But memory of our conversation comes back to me vividly, as it did the other day when I read that the sensitive poet's life had ended.

Pasternak was anguished at thoughts of how his novel *Doctor Zhivago* had been made a tool in the cold war. There were many reasons for his rejection of the Nobel prize, he told me, and it was under no outside dictation that he determined on that rejection. His firm refusal to be identified with a nation-state, he explained, went wide and deep; it would apply to *any* organized government, monolithic or otherwise. But he was devoted to the Russian people, his people, and could not bear the thought of separation from them. The excited children playing with snowballs, the good neighbors hard at work—how could the glare of publicity hide them from him? He complained that because of publicity he now found it hard to attain that obscurity which an artist needs if he is to be creative.

We talked of Pasternak's startling use of imagery, particularly apparent in his earlier poems but present also in his prose. He agreed that in his poetry there are traces of Rimbaud, of Rilke, of the strange clarity of the symbolist world, along with insights observable in Russian authors of the past who looked on the steppes and prairies and peopled their novels with thousands of characters. But the Pasternak blend, he pointed out, was his own. He insisted that he had no philosophy of art except that gained from stark experience. I reminded him of his "escape" from a philosopher's degree at Marburg, of how his curiosity about "secondary thoughts" had made his primary thesis slip from his mind. Perhaps it was his growing into his own concept of art and otherness, his immersion in a complex interior world of his own, that in his youth protected him from collective indoctrination but at the same time separated him from direct encounter with historical change.

Pasternak explained that *Doctor Zhivago* was written "with his heart's blood." In it he was neither "proving nor attacking." His words and images were the result of "the reaction of a life to Life." His unforgettable characters depicted many types of people, with different political ideas and different personal tastes, but the drama was humanity's. Though the novel, many times rewritten, was to a great extent autobiographical, because it was art it transcended any narrow mirroring of self. In his book Pasternak had tried to trace the design in which wholeness becomes holy, in which love leads to the mountain top—a design which emerges through personal involvement. He had blended terror and triumph, loneliness and human goodness; but through it all he had, as a believer in God, "sought the greater revelation."

Pasternak made it plain that he opposed violence, at no matter whose hands. Militarism is no answer to evil, he said, nor can it ever be an ally of goodness. But he found it difficult to use the word "peace" in relation to a movement of people. When I suggested that he devise a qualifying term or a clearer frame of reference, he promised to "think further" on the matter.

We sat quietly for a while, looking out at the tall, dark trees now partly obscured by heavily falling snow. There were certain events, Pasternak said, that he could not forget or forgive. Deeply spiritual men have to decide what proportion judgment, remembrance and charity must be accorded in the full concept of redemptive faith. Evil, we know, is not to be evaded or tolerated; but the issue lies deeper.

The problem for a man like Pasternak, I realized, is greater in view of the historical changes which have occurred in his country. Green lawns now cover village areas where terrible injustices once were perpetrated. Though the violence of a more recent past strikes us with horror, children of a kindlier generation now play in kindergartens, and the atmosphere around them is brighter.

Essentially, men like Boris Pasternak are sustained by tenderness. I felt it in his voice, in his firm yet gentle movements. At 70, he retained an eager wistfulness of manner and facial expression. As he spoke of the "insanity" that has swept through so many lands, including his own, where he knew it beyond measure, he again pointed out that his novel "lived beyond all that," and that it ends with light spreading over his beloved city. In the new play which he was writing, he said, he was dealing with a blind girl who regains her sight.

Then, dwelling on the agony of his age, Pasternak said quietly: "I could not have endured it without my discovery of Jesus, the Christ." And he added: "He came to me." I knew that his parents were of the Jewish faith—his mother a gifted musician, his father a famous painter and friend of Tolstoy. As a youth Boris Pasternak absorbed the religion of his parents, but later, on his own, he turned toward the Christ. Thereafter his outlook changed, a change revealed particularly in his later poems.

Together we read an essay by Dean Walter Mueder of Boston University that I had brought with me: "The Idea of the Responsible Society." Pasternak was struck with its reference to the eternal testimony of the community of Christ. He wrote a note for me to send to Dean Muelder: "Your splendid essay . . . touches me closely and intimately. I thank you for this honor and joy. I also believe that men are united by love to God and to each other. I wish for your theological school, students and faculty alike, all that is good—success and discoveries."

THE CHAIRMAN of Baylor University's graduate studies in music examines a contemporary phenomenon about which strong differences of opinion have swirled.

March 23, 1960

Jazz at the Altar?

ELWYN A. WIENANDT

There is a new sound in the sanctuary. Where once stately hymns and anthems were unchallenged and the organ reigned as the proper and suitable medium of instrumental music, the harmonies and rhythms of jazz groups can now be heard. True, these have not supplanted the traditional types of music for worship, but they have been used in several lands with the approval of various denominations, and the experiments in their use are continuing. The reactions of the public have been varied, ranging from alarm, tolerance or amusement, to enthusiastic acceptance of this "new" approach to sacred music. So long as these differences of opinion exist and so long as there is interest in the jazz idiom, some consideration of its probable success or failure is in order.

If the idea of intruding a contemporary and popular musical style into Christian worship were truly new and without precedent there might be cause for alarm, but the fact is that the practice is strongly founded on historical patterns. A review of the previous appearances of this phenomenon should help place the current practice in perspective—and also demonstrate, I think, that traditions are not in such immediate danger that we churchmen must man the ramparts against the jazz combo or its vocal counterpart.

The earliest great assault upon sacred music came in the thirteenth century, a time that marked the developmental peak of a musical form called the motet, a polyphonic piece usually per-

formed at vespers in the Roman Catholic service. This motet
was usually an extremely involved three-voiced composition.
Each of the voice-parts had a different poem to sing, and sometimes more than one language was being sung at one time; yet
the meanings of the texts were related in that two of them
served to comment on the basic set of words. By the end of the
century the situation had become far more complex—and
worldly as well. Dance tunes, vendors' street cries, love songs and
even lascivious subjects had made their way into the previously
decorous settings. Even after the secular elements had made
their way into the motet form, one of the voices in every case
clung firmly to the Gregorian melody (the necessary liturgical
basis of sacred music of the period), thereby presenting a union
of sacred and secular music and text.

There are apologists who justify the apparent incongruity of
the amalgam as an expression of the Thomist doctrine of theological universalism. It is probable that the mixture of sacred and
secular ideas was more readily accepted in that century than in
ours, for it is a rare student of music history who discovers this
pairing of expressions without showing some degree of surprise.
In the fourteenth century the motet dropped all secular devices and concerned itself solely with structural complexities
which were of interest to composers but apparently disturbed
neither the clergy nor the public.

During the fifteenth and sixteenth centuries polyphonic mass-
settings were often based on borrowed material—tunes taken
from sacred or secular compositions that already had a successful, independent existence. The resulting work was called a
parody mass, the descriptive term denoting the borrowing of
material without implying the term's present-day meaning of
comic mimicry. The melodies whose original functions lay in
the church might be those of motets (now based entirely on
sacred texts) or hymns; those lifted from secular sources were
often borrowed from well-known chansons or madrigals. In
either case the idea was to base the mass-setting on a tune that
had achieved wide currency.

These settings of the Renaissance differed sharply from the
medieval motets in the degree of musical sophistication they

displayed. Whereas the earlier motet used song material from secular life in a straightforward manner, the later musical forms were usually based on modifications of the popular tunes. Commonly known melodies, including "*L'Homme armé*," "*Fors seulement*," "*Je suis déshéritée*" and (in England) "The Western Wynde," were altered by expansion of note-values, subjected to a fragmentation process by the insertion of originally composed music between the quoted sections, or dealt with in such subtle ways that the ear did not readily perceive the use of secular elements. In every instance the original connotations were minimized because the text now was that of the appropriate section of the mass—the Kyrie, Gloria and so on—rather than something concerning the mighty man at arms or the lover grown pale and wan through loneliness. Actually, then, the degree of recognition of this secular intrusion depended on the musical background of the listener. The person who had never heard "*Je suis déshéritée*" would not be able to recognize it when Palestrina employed it as material in one of his masses and would consequently have to accept it simply as a part of a complete sacred work. The process of borrowing secular ideas for parody masses disappeared because of pressure from the clergy who saw its continued use as a threat to the dignity of worship.

The use of popular elements in Protestant music is equally distinguishable—and far more enduring. The chorale, developed by Luther as a means of encouraging congregational participation, relied on secular tunes just as parody masses had. In the case of the chorale however there was a broadening of the area from which the material was taken, for it included many folk songs and popular tunes of the day in addition to chants borrowed from the Roman Catholic tradition and the melodies especially composed for the new service. It is perhaps sufficient to point out that the famous Passion chorale, "O Sacred Head Now Wounded," was originally a love song entitled "My Peace of Mind Is Shattered by the Charms of a Tender Maiden" and that its employment represented a normal appropriation of current material consciously brought from secular to sacred environment for the purpose of including familiar material in the church service. One great point of difference was apparent between the popular tunes and the chorales derived from them: while the popular material was lively and exciting, the chorale was rhythmically inert by comparison. The principal feature that identified it with secular activity had been removed, in much the same way that the popular element had been disguised when used in the parody masses.

The intermingling of the secular and sacred has been a continuing feature in the musical products of the generations following the Reformation. Both of the principal vocal forms common to almost all of Protestantism, the hymn and the anthem, have been greatly affected by the extremely thin line between secular and sacred that has existed at various times.

Anthems that derive from secular music have been so numerous and varied that they beggar both description and inventory. Their employment has been more frequent in some denominations than in others, but their presence has not been gauged entirely by their musical value. Often a choice has been contingent upon local standards of taste, presence of the material in the choir library, or even upon a mistaken idea that such music is more readily within the range of capabilities of a volunteer choir. From the many examples that might be cited, sufficient illustration can be made by recalling the use of such gems of an earlier decade as "Danny Boy" and "The Old Refrain," supplied of course with texts that permit them to be used in church without suspicion of sacrilege. The application of this same treatment to instrumental works of wide appeal has produced anthems based on the "Agnus Dei" from Bizet's *L'Arlésienne*, the chorale from *Finlandia*, the "Pilgrims' Chorus" from *Tannhäuser*, and has moved much other operatic and instrumental literature from the concert hall into the church.

Twentieth-century hymnals generally show the same wide range of borrowed material as is found in the Lutheran chorales. National hymns are drawn into use, along with borrowings from the patriotic music of Russia and Austria, and folk melodies are still abundantly employed. Opera is still drawn upon, as in "My Jesus, as Thou Wilt," from Weber's *Der Freischütz*, and the sentimental literature for piano solo is paraphrased in "Holy

Spirit, Truth Divine," taken from Gottschalk's "The Last Hope." An enduring tune from the earlier English tradition is found in the ballad "Greensleeves," best known to us in its sacred function under the title "What Child Is This."

Finally, a kind of music that derives its style directly from the barbershop quartet, with added elements of ragtime, was immensely popular in some parts of the country a decade or two ago and is still highly esteemed by large numbers of people. Coupled with a rhythmically active and melodically elaborated piano accompaniment, this kind of music has served to stimulate many listeners, both at group meetings and by means of radio. It should be noted however that the new hymnals of the denominations that were most closely associated with this music have either begun to give it less importance or have excluded it entirely from their official music publications.

Even within this last type of hymn material there is variety. Some of the examples are patterned after the gay-nineties ballad and feature a solo or duet with a chorus (refrain). At the other end of the scale is "When the Saints Go Marching In," borrowed from the early jazz idiom and now gradually returning to that sphere because of its continued identification with the field of entertainment.

Superficially it would seem that the use of the jazz idiom in a worship service of our time should be no less acceptable than most of the foregoing examples were in their own; however, the close identification of jazz, in the eyes of many observers, with exuberant forms of secular entertainment and, at least in its early years, with establishments that can in no way receive even the tacit sanction of the church has made of it an intruder that is already guilty by association. It is largely this identification of the style with the night life of the thirties and earlier that has led many people to view its appearance in its new surroundings with a suspicion bordering on revulsion.

By the second decade of our century the jazz idiom had already begun to penetrate the areas of serious music, and its presence in the concert hall is now a common occurrence calling for little or no comment. However, this development provides no a priori justification for including it in religious worship.

There are numerous examples of musical works of unquestioned artistic worth that are by common consent performed in concert halls rather than in places of worship, even though they are intended to convey religious sentiments and do not overtly employ musical material that is objectionable to church authorities or congregations.

The point of justification that is foremost in the attempt to provide a place for jazz in the church service may be stated as follows: The church serves the people of our time, and jazz is a (some ardent supporters of the idiom say "the") musical style that represents contemporary life. Unfortunately, we can become entangled in an undergrowth of terminology here, for in the minds of most people jazz exists on only one of several planes. The term is used more often than not to signify all types of music associated with light entertainment and dancing, unless the user can place these activities in the equally broad category of folk music.

At the other extreme there exists a group, small only by comparison, that sees jazz as a leading style in the art of music, a group that analyzes, compares and discusses the idiom as a type of concert-hall art now utterly divorced from its dance function. (The concert hall is now smaller, and its audience may be found seated at tables rather than in rows of seats.) The jazz that has been moving into the precincts of the church is largely of this latter type. It seeks admission on its own merits and at its own level of maturity as an art form; it strives to shed the former associations with dance, drink and debauchery.

It is on such a basis, then, that the decisions will be made. If the musical style of jazz can be assimilated into an area of our lives that is marked by dignity, tradition and solemnity (or at least restrained enthusiasm), it stands a chance of being recognized as an enduring feature. Many of the groups and individuals to whom it is being presented do not recognize it as having strong roots even as a secular style; therefore its chance of a successful assimilation into church functions by these people is small indeed. Just as each of the earlier secular intrusions was successful in proportion to its early loss of identification with secularism, so will jazz have to face this problem. At the moment it achieves such a release of identification it will very likely have lost its vitality, for the very thing that makes it exciting, vital and readily identifiable outside the church stands as the greatest barrier to its acceptance within.

THOSE 'RELIGIOUS' MOVIES: *How gullible can we be?*
October 28, 1959

The Bible Against Itself

AN EDITORIAL

After years of relative quiet, the movies are once again making noisy news. No longer does the film industry desire compatibility with the nation's mores and co-operation with its religious impulses and organization; it has declared its independence from both. In fact, the industry has recently been acting like an irresponsible boy who runs away from home. Over the years Protestants have become so accustomed to decrying censorship against the mass media that they have created the impression of being imperceptive about the quality of films. Roman Catholicism, in the two decades since its last major clashes with this particular medium, has had, in the public eye, a virtual monopoly as guardian of religious standards in movies. In the process a significant change in our national life has come into play; as Daniel W. Brogan has observed, "legal Puritanism" has moved from rural Protestantism to urban Catholicism.

The movies have always presented unique problems. A mature theatergoer sees a Broadway play after he has read reviews, has discussed the play with others, and after considerable hardship has secured tickets. He is not likely to find his imagination or his conscience compromised. But the promotion of movies is geared to frontland *and* hinterland and, in our drive-in theater era, particularly to the teen-age and family trade. Thus what the movies portray becomes a part of young people's lives. The Catholic-sponsored Legion of Decency has recognized this influence, even if it has not always acted responsibly. Hollywood cannot complain that Protestants have interfered. But moviemakers have misused their freedom.

Recently Protestants have begun to ask, What can we do? How can we bring about a change without ourselves undertaking coercion and censorship incompatible with Protestant principles? Following an initial and tentative attack against the film industry by George Heimrich of the National Council of Churches, Hollywood has remained rather sensitive about Protestant reaction—to the surprise of Mr. Heimrich and all of us. The national stir his charges provoked should give us courage to look for things that Protestants *can* do to set new moral and artistic standards in the mass media.

We have a specific suggestion for a specific first step. Protestant churches have in recent years become the unwitting and gullible promoters of some of Hollywood's worst movies. They have been sending families and Sunday school classes and youth groups to the least artistic and least edifying examples of film fare. We are speaking of the free publicity given in church periodicals and Sunday bulletins to the anti-biblical biblical extravaganzas. These films are the culmination of what Mr. de Mille was the first to discover: that Bible and bubble-bath make an unbeatable box-office combination. We are sure that, since he deserted the bald-head row for the saw-dust trail, father has not seen as much to excite him elsewhere as he has at movies which the churches tell him to see: *The Prodigal, David and Bathsheba, Samson and Delilah, The Ten Commandments,* and now and soon *The Big Fisherman, Solomon and Sheba,* and *Ben-Hur.* Mother enjoys a dinner-to-midnight epic not realizing that it is undercutting biblical religion. And the kiddies think it great fun: all this world and heaven too. We cannot remedy everything about Hollywood (and there is much about it that is good and does not need remedying), but Protestants can at least begin to challenge the promotion of lurid distortions of the Bible. Protestants need not subsidize these vulgar efforts to use the Bible against itself. Let us now explore in the light of certain biblical realities the ballyhoo for the three newest and biggest Bible films.

We may as well deal with the most obvious example first. Biblical religion grew up in protest against the fertility cults of the ancient Near East. Could it have coped with the subtler perversion of our Far West? One need not be prudish to blanch at the thought of Sunday schools trucking off piously to see *Solomon and Sheba*, a film which *Esquire* and *Pageant* have termed an "unblushing rewrite of the Bible" in which Gina Lollobrigida "twists and twirls in one of the screen's wildest orgies." Recently we received a hard-bound glossy book promoting *The Big Fisherman*. Its most dramatic full-page color picture could have been taken from one of the 50-cent pornography magazines: Martha Hyer as "Herodias, one of history's most wicked women," in a non-flannel nightgown, suggestively extending an invitation into a veiled-and-satined bedroom.

Biblical religion set itself in opposition to the modest materialism of the ancient Babels. Must its heirs subsidize modern grossness? The promotion for both films proudly concentrates on the idol of Mammon—the huge cost of sets that were destroyed a day after use. Vastness and waste are thus equated with cinematographic excellence. One of these films must gross $20 million to break even. Much of the money will come from church people whose religious leaders have urged them to attend. *The Big Fisherman*'s promoter boasts that the Tetrarch's garden set, which cost weeks of labor and $125,000, was "completely destroyed by a howling tempest during a bacchanalian party"—filmed, no doubt, for Sunday school children. *Ben-Hur* makes the others look like pikers in this perverse transvaluation which would replace art with gaudy but costly superficialities.

Biblical religion finds its center in God's revelation in Jesus Christ. Promoters of biblical films want to have their cake and eat it too. They want the distant voice of the Master, with sound effects via echo chamber (we don't really allow for the Incarnation—a man among men, a servant of his brothers), but

they don't want it or him to offend anyone, either. The eva-
sions and euphemisms used in *The Big Fisherman* ballyhoo
("the Nazarene," "the Master," "an exalted faith") are for-
tunately unnecessary in the Old Testament plot of *Solomon
and Sheba*. In deference to the known wishes of General Lew
Wallace, the fine print of *Ben-Hur*, say its promoters, will carry
the subtitle "A Tale of the Christ." In the chariot race there is
no question as to where this tale is left.

Biblical religion has consistently pointed beyond externalities
to the human person. The promotion of most of the spectacular
pseudo-Bible films suggests boundless preoccupation with the
minutiae of technical perfection, with *ersatz* authenticity (e.g.,
rebuilding Palestine in southern California) and with the mere
piling up of detail upon detail. *Ben-Hur* leads the thundering
herd in this particular chariot race also.

Religiosity is the greatest enemy of biblical religion. *Solomon
and Sheba*'s promoters make little effort at piety, but *Ben-Hur*'s
men have the nerve to say, after crawling out from under their
carload of statistics, that "the picture will emphasize the human
story rather than the mere eye-filling pomp and splendor."
The Big Fisherman's promotion propaganda is the phoniest of
all; twice it hints that providence interfered, that the macro-
cosm responded to the microcosm's pietizing. For example,
when an Arab-tent scene was disrupted by California desert
winds, new cloud formations "urgently essential for other
scenes" appeared—"as if in compensation."

Inch by inch and second by second one does not always perceive how the Bible is used against itself in this promotion and
in these films. When the record as a whole is studied, however,
one sees the need for a large-scale indictment. Not the least
element in this indictment is that the promoters of anti-
biblical biblicism in the movies use trophies, awards or orders
of thousands of extra copies of publications which advance their
game to subvert the sources of information of church people.
Protestants need not waste their time in indiscriminate condemnation of the movies. The beginning of a program on which
Protestants can act is that they can, first of all, stop letting
themselves be used.

Positively, Protestants can support Hollywood at its best. Christianity does not run from the world, does not turn its back on it. But having confronted the world of fertility deities, materialism, evasion of Christ, gadget worship and religiosity, and having exposed its bankruptcy, Christianity points beyond these to the real world, the one God created, in which He was incarnate and in which His Son was crucified and arose. This means that the Christian's relation to the cultural world of man's devising is always in tension. The Christian can, however, respond to Hollywood's non-religious but mature films with serious and even Christian interest. After the passing of this season's three big-budget Bible travesties, we can hope for the clearing of air and the chasing away of phonies with the coming film version of *Elmer Gantry*, Sinclair Lewis' stinging study of hypocrisy.

REFLECTIONS *by a New Zealander who contemplated our "westerns" while a member of Stanford University's religion and humanities program. The author's untimely death deprived Christendom of an able interpreter of theological aspects of the cultural scene in which the church has its being.*

November 27, 1957

The "Western"—A Theological Note

ALEXANDER MILLER

A while ago I had a week-end visit from a fellow theologian who made it clear early on the Saturday that he would accept no engagements that clashed with "Gunsmoke" on TV. Since I watch "Gunsmoke" myself, come hell or high water, I knew I had a kindred spirit as well as a fellow apostle. So we spent the early part of the evening analyzing the appeal of the show, which was not wholly to be explained by its undeniable quality. For not only do I find myself maneuvering to watch TV westerns of lesser quality than "Gunsmoke," but I discover that through the long years I retain an unabated zest for every kind of western yarn, in print or in picture. And while I'm glad of quality when I can find it, a western has to be pretty bad before I find it intolerable. Enough for me if the hero runs to type, if there is the scent of sage and the squeak of saddle-leather, if the high hills are high enough.

At one level the attraction of the thing is obvious. I am professionally involved with the high matters of speculation and the deep matters of theology; and nothing is more relaxing after a bout with Hegel or Niebuhr than a vicarious ride into the sage. And there is the practical advantage that this particular escape mechanism costs but twenty-five cents in paperback (plus one cent sales tax in some states). It's rarely necessary even to buy a new one. An old one will do equally well, since nothing of it sticks in the mind, and the formula is constant.

My friend wanted to go deeper. "If just once," said he, "I could stand in the dust of the frontier main street, facing an indubitably bad man who really deserved extermination, and with smoking six-gun actually exterminate him—shoot once and see him drop. Just once to face real and unqualified evil, plug it and see it drop . . ." None of this complex business of separating the sin from the sinner, of tempering justice with mercy, of remembering our own complicity in evil. To blow, just once, an actual and visible hole in the wall of evil, instead of beating the air with vain exhortation and the nicely calculated less and more of moral discrimination and doleful casuistry. To see something actually drop, as the gospel says Satan once fell as lightning from heaven.

Yet there must be more to it than that, and there is more to it than that. Another theologian friend of mine, whose specialty is Christian ethics, makes a point of reading the *Saturday Evening Post* from cover to cover, since, he says, it is a transcript of American folkways; and if the gospel is to be taken into all the world, the contemporary world into which it has to be taken is between the covers of the *Satevepost*. (I know other professional colleagues who find the same illumination in the funnies, but I don't read the funnies. I can't find time to master Pogo and Kingaroo, which appear to be theological staples;

and in any event, when I'm worn out with Hegel everything is too strenuous except the westerns.) The western serial is standard in the *Post*, for the good and trite reason that it is *par excellence* the American folk tale.

The quality of "western" writing varies endlessly. Eugene Manlove Rhodes was a literary artist of high caliber. Ernest Haycox could and did write as well as the next man and better than most, but was apparently content to be, for the most part, the best of western hackwriters. He is only one of a number of highly competent operators. Then the stream runs out into a drab flatland of pedestrian writing (odd phrase for the horse opera!) which yet—at least for me—is never dull.

The so-called formula western is compact and predictable. It runs like this: Over the ridge of the high hills (or it may be against the backdrop of the desert) appears the maverick rider; he of the lean flanks, the taut, long-planed face, the lips stern yet capable of smiling, the dust of the trail in his clothes and on his horse. A single colt, its butt hand-polished, hangs low on one hip (only lesser men carry two guns). His eyes miss nothing. As he drops over the last ridge, there on the flat or in the valley is the cattle town, a one-street town of clapboard —saloon, livery stable, store and sheriff's office, with a coffee-and-steak house in which the heroine (unless she is a cattleman's daughter) can be located handily, yet outside the saloon.

There is no reason why the rider should stop longer than to find vittles for himself and his cayuse. He is headed nowhere in particular, except that somewhere in the long distance lies the "spread" of his dreams. But he doubts that he will find it, or that he could settle if he did find it, for towns stifle him (he needs "a land where a man can breathe") and he knows no peace except under the stars. Yet his horse has no sooner cat-footed it into town than he feels the tension in the place, "a full dozen pairs of eyes watching him from odd coverts." A shooting, the sight of a gratuitous beating, and he is hip-deep in the range war that is tearing the community apart.

Now there is nothing for it but to see it through, and see it through he does, surviving a half-dozen knock-down-drag-outs that would finish any normal man, snaking out the gun which is his pride and torment with a speed no man can match, and finally outdrawing the hired gunman brought in by the wicked cattle baron with the unsatisfied land-hunger. The ending is open: he may either marry the baron's daughter (or the local caterer who has feminine merits lacking in the baron's daughter) and find that "spread" on an unclaimed piece of bottom land; or he may take to the road again. In the first case he puts his gun away, as he had always longed to do. In the second case it stays strapped to his thigh, since in a world like this one there is always need for the law outside the law, the law embodied only in the strength of soul and speed of hand of the incorruptible man.

He is a philosopher after his fashion, but at no time does he understand the whys and the wherefores. Why not keep going? It's not his fight. And yet he cannot pass it up and "go on living with himself." "A man has to play the hand he's dealt." Yet now and then he takes time out to try to make sense of it all. But he's in a world that doesn't add up.

Men were not meant for peace. Their minds, so filled with incessant wonder, would never let them alone, and their bodies were racked by feelings that eventually destroyed them; there was a form and a substance and a meaning somewhere, no doubt, but men died before they knew what any of it was.—Ernest Haycox, *Long Storm* (Boston: Little, Brown & Co.)

The pattern is worth analysis, if only because the flood of formula westerns grows greater all the time. I'm pretty sure that they now outnumber the sexy and salacious items on the pocket-book stands, and this is no doubt to the good. The TV channels are choked with them this fall, and this too is O.K. by me, both for their own sake and in view of the alternatives. But without being too heavy-handed about it, I would say that there must be some cultural symptoms here. It is not only the bulk of the phenomenon that requires explanation, but the pervasiveness of the appeal. My ten-year-old and I are radically unequal, I pride myself, in sophistication; yet we watch "Gunsmoke" or "Cheyenne" with equal absorption, and dang-bust it if I don't join him from time to time for "The Range-Rider." Relaxing? Sure; and the sight of good horses against the skyline alone is worth the low price of admission. But one can, I think, without forcing it, find more in it than that: can find, in fact and in simplicity, most of the working philosophy, the bothersome confusions and the perplexed yearnings of the average twentieth-century American—maybe the average twentieth-century man, since you can find the same items in Charing Cross station as in Grand Central, and I myself am no American, but an amiable alien.

There is, for one thing, the eternal dialectic of pilgrimage and rest. The hero of this tale seeks his Shangri-la—which for him is a place of good grass and free water: but he doubts if the world holds such a place; if it does, he doubts if he could bed down there in peace; and if his restlessness would let him stay, sure as shootin' the bad men wouldn't. This side of that six feet of earth which is the end of everything, he will keep moving or be kept moving, though he will never quite give up his dream. A longing for the home spread does battle with what T. S. Eliot calls a "distaste for beatitude" in a fashion which is of great Christian and theological interest.

There is a dialectic too of justice and mercy, of war and peace, and of war for the sake of peace. The gun is cruel but the gun is necessary. Good women hate it while good men wear it. A man wants nothing better than to hang it on the hook, but if he does then evil rides rampant, and the good things—including the good women—are not safe.

So a man does what he has to do, though never clear why he has to do it. "A man has to play the hand he's dealt." And since the things he has to do make curiously for a bad conscience, he uses the two human and perennial and contemporary "outs"—which are fatalism and moralism. The gunman has to die. But in the heart of the "good" man who smokes him down there is no real enmity, for even the bad man "does what he has to do."

About all he could make out of it was that a man was meant for motion; he was meant to hope and to struggle, to be wrestling always with some sort of chains binding him. It was true of . . . Ringrose [the villain in this piece]; it was true of himself.— Ernest Haycox (*Ibid.*)

So each explosion of violence has about it an inevitability which is in a way its justification. Or if it is not justified in this fatalistic fashion, we pass over into moralism. The issues are so unambiguous, the good so firmly fixed, the evil so clearly embodied, that the bad man may be stamped out "like a sidewinder," without compunction and without regret.

Burro Yandle! The rusty-haired, rodent-faced destroyer. Dirty inside and out, but gifted with a malignant touch that ruined men and killed them. How long before . . . fundamental justice caught up with him?—L. P. Holmes, *High Starlight* (Pennant Books, Doubleday & Co., Inc.)

The range war becomes a Holy War.

"A man has to play the hand he's dealt." A man does what he has to do, and justifies it one way or another. His is the incorrigible yearning after virtue, the inevitable implication in sin, the irrepressible inclination to self-justification. Every theological theme is here, except the final theme, the deep and healing dimension of guilt and grace.

Talking of self-justification, I have to ask myself, in respect of westerns, whether I pretend to analyze them to have an excuse for reading them, as a man might justify a visit to a burlesque house. Could be. Anything could be, human nature being what it is, in theologians as in other men. I can only protest unconvincingly that I do read westerns and I don't go to burlesque houses—I *think* because the former have more to offer.

INTERESTINGLY, this 1960 estimate of Oberammergau and its world-famous passion play, by the Century's drama critic and Union Theological Seminary faculty member, echoes a note sounded in the magazine's pages three decades earlier by the late Edward A. Steiner. In "The Fashion Play of 1930" (August 13, 1930) Mr. Steiner was, like Mr. Driver thirty years later, disturbed by signs of commercialism in the village, by the cardboard-figure interpretations on the huge stage. And a week later an editorial called attention to evidences of anti-Semitism similar to those noted by Mr. Driver in 1960.

September 7, 1960

The Play that Carries a Plague

TOM F. DRIVER

Oberammergau, July 27

P. T. Barnum, who reputedly said that you can't fool all of the people all of the time, but you can fool some of the people some of the time, would have admired Oberammergau. The gullibility of the general public is always great, but when the credulity of the religious is added it becomes immense. The Passion Play at Oberammergau is surely one of the biggest pieces of falderal ever palmed off on the innocent masses.

Masses they are. A million requests for seats were received; half had to be refused. Whether the masses are innocent is, of course, not a matter that can be documented, but I have observed in conversation with many spectators tenacious conviction that the Passion Play is (a) a great work of religious art or (b) the work of sincere peasant folk bent only on fulfilling an ancient vow. To the spectator who comes with eyes accustomed to the ways of the world, it is neither. If some hold that the play is not for such eyes but for the eyes of faith, I reply that in matters of religious art, as in other matters, we have the injunction to be harmless as doves but wise as serpents. The village of Oberammergau itself is not lacking in the wisdom of the world.

The first criteria to be applied to the play are those of theatri-

cal art. These criteria cannot be excluded by the argument that
the play is a piece of folk craft for which the criteria of formal
art are irrelevant. After all, the play is advertised throughout the
world and thousands of people pay enormous sums of money to
come and see it. It is a profit-making venture not only for the
village but for the several travel agencies that hold a monopoly
on the tickets and for countless other agencies which profit from
it indirectly. These tangible benefits and the organized publicity
that produces them cannot be reconciled with claims put forward in behalf of folk art.

Moreover, the form of presentation of the play has changed
many times since the vow to perform it every ten years was
taken in the seventeenth century. The present text dates only
from 1860. The costumes and scenery have been altered frequently, as has the theater itself, which now accommodates
some 6,000 spectators. Many elements from the professional
theater have entered. The actors are indeed amateurs, but the
officials are anything but simple peasant folk; they go about
their work with great self-consciousness. There is therefore no
question but that the play must be judged according to the
same standards as any other work offered to the general public
in a commercial theater.

The criteria applied to any work of theater art are these: Does
it have vitality? Is it faithful to some respectable idea of
reality? Are the artisans in control of their medium? Does it
exhibit good taste? On any or all of these counts the Passion
Play at Oberammergau falls down miserably. Its lugubrious,
plodding manner kills all vitality, except perhaps for a few
moments in some of the Judas scenes. Imagine a play lasting
over seven hours with no humor and no irony, and you have a
notion of how much vitality this work possesses. As for reality,
I think it safe to say there is hardly a moment of truth in it. I
do not refer at this point to theological truth, but to the ways by
which art represents the truth of life.

What can it mean, after all, to see Jesus and the disciples
wearing pastel gowns and gloomy looks, climbing over card-
board rocks beside painted two-dimensional trees in front of a
blue canvas sky that trembles in the wind? How can it move
us to be told that Jesus gave his body as a feast "truly from

heaven come down," and then to be treated to a *tableau vivant* showing the children of Israel in the desert, in the style, colors and postures of bad Sunday school illustrations, with manna falling from the sky in the form of bits of fluttering paper? The twenty *tableaux vivants* are atrocious beyond my power to describe; they are all scenes from the Old Testament and Apocrypha, linked by dubious typology to incidents in the Passion of Christ. For instance, when the chorus tells us that Judaism has been rejected by God in favor of the Christian community, we are shown a mournful picture of "Vashti rejected and Esther chosen Queen."

The chorus, on stage a great deal of the time, is unbelievably stilted. Its forty-eight singers plus a leader called the "Prologue" plod in single file from the two sides of the stage like so many resigned workhorses. Never once in seven-and-a-half hours did any one of the forty-nine smile; they obviously enjoyed it as little as did I. The crowd scenes are from the worst Hollywood tradition—the participants not untrained, but trained in a manner that suggests the lavishness of the production more than the reality of the historical moment. The individual performances I saw were not too bad for amateurs, especially that by the Judas; but the Christ was wooden when not irate. The crucifixion scene was real at two points: where the cross was raised and Jesus groaned from the pain of his own sagging weight, and when his side was pierced and blood flowed from the wound. But two or three credible moments cannot redeem a performance that lasts all day. The music, which might be described as inferior Mozart, was not bad, though it had nothing whatever in common with the script and the staging. Let's face it: the Oberammergau play is *Kitsch*.

My bristling thoughts about the lack of quality and integrity in the Oberammergau Passion Play were softened somewhat by words I found in the official guide to the play which indicate that the village itself is not devoid of agitation for reform. In an article entitled "Some Notes on the Question of a New Version of the Text," Dr. Alois Fink expresses the argument clearly and with pertinent attention to the central point:

The greatness and inviolability of a subject have never yet exempted those who endeavor to find expression for it from the effort of giving their very best from the artistic point of view; and to fail to fulfill this demand when a religious subject of such a sublime nature as the story of Our Lord is involved, is not merely an aesthetic sin. There is every danger of a piously suppressed smile at artistic faults in the performance of the text engendering doubts of the true religious feeling and faith of the actors, danger also of misinterpretation of the . . . motives of the community in performing the Play.

It must be said to the people of Oberammergau that this danger has become a reality, and that the play as it is now performed is not merely worthless but positively harmful to the curious and the faithful who journey to see it.

As for the motives of the actors and the community, it is admittedly dangerous to speculate. But there are many disturbing signs over and above the falsity and ineptness of the play itself. The commercialization of the village has often been remarked upon. It is perhaps as natural as it is disturbing. It would not be disturbing, of course, if there were not so many protestations about the religious intentions of the villagers. Even more serious, however, is the question of the sale of tickets and accommodations. These are made available by the Oberammergau authorities only to certain travel agencies. I have first-hand knowledge that at least one agency with which Oberammergau co-operates has been misrepresenting to its customers the so-called "hotel" space it has for sale, and has been engaged in other unethical practices. There has been a notorious black market in Oberammergau tickets.

The authorities in the village are naturally quite eager to dissociate themselves from all such practices, but if they are to be successful in doing so they will have to adopt firmer policies. Since they have absolute control over the supply of tickets and since they deal only with their own selected list of agencies, it would seem to be within their power to correct the abuses now prevalent. If they do not do so, the character of the enterprise will be blackened by the cloud of suspicion now gathering.

This year the Oberammergau Passion Play has been the object of much controversy arising from allegations that it is anti-Semitic. The discussion was triggered by an article by Robert Gorham Davis in the March 1960 issue of *Commentary*. In Germany the discussion was intensified by the fact that the opening of the play coincided with a meeting of the Society for Christian-Jewish Co-operation, which issued statements criticizing the play and suggested that a committee consisting of a Catholic, a Protestant and a Jew be formed to advise on revisions of the text.

I inquired in the village for someone who could tell me about the official reaction to this controversy and was referred to Karl Bauer, director of the Office of Arrangements. I obtained an interview with Herr Bauer. He informed me that Professor Davis' article had been read in the village, but that there had been no particular reaction to it other than regret at its publication, since its charges of anti-Semitism were patently false. He said that since the play was written by monks in a seventeenth-century monastery, it was inconceivable that the authors could have harbored anti-Semitic feelings, and he pointed out that the text has not been revised since 1860. As for the suggestion by the Society for Christian-Jewish Co-operation that an interfaith committee advise on revisions, he referred me to a statement by the burgomaster of Oberammergau dated May 13, 1960, which asserted that all matters pertaining to the play are entirely the business of the community of Oberammergau, that the Society for Christian-Jewish Co-operation had overstepped its bounds, and that if revisions became necessary Oberammergau would consult only the church, the poets and the experts in theater practice. The burgomaster pointed out that the play is performed under the protection of the church and the laws of the land.

There is no need for me to restate the points made by Professor Davis; his article may be consulted by anyone interested in the subject. His conclusions are based on examination of the Daisenberger text of 1860, the one now being performed.

After seeing the play and perusing the text, I can only conclude that Professor Davis is right. The play *is* decidedly anti-Semitic, and its interpretation of the crucifixion and the events leading to it is harmful not only to Christian-Jewish relations but to proper understanding of the Christian gospel.

Two major points are to be made in support of my conclusion. The most important has to do with the structure of the play, which turns the story of the Passion into a melodramatic clash between on the one hand the good Christ and his followers (including by implication the entire Christian Church), and on the other the evil Sanhedrin and its followers. The first action shown is the expulsion of the money-changers from the temple, an act which stirs up the merchants against Christ. They in turn agitate the Sanhedrin to action, and the play proceeds as an unequal struggle between the good guys and the bad guys. Judas' role is central, and the motivation for his treachery is entirely that of monetary greed.

I see it now, there is nothing in prospect but to live in continual poverty and misery. . . . I have always been prudent and careful, and, now and then, have laid aside a little for myself out of the general purse, in case of need—I can use that now until I find other means. I must provide myself for a long time.

Self-preservation, monetary gain and preservation of the status quo—these are the motivations the play gives for the crucifixion. And they are portrayed as the traits of a particular race; the many ugly scenes in the Sanhedrin make this clear.

The second point has to do with the play's statements, most of them spoken or sung by the Prologue and chorus, which portray the Jews as a people rejected by God in favor of the Christian community. I cite one passage from among many that might be adduced:

> But blind and deaf remains poor Jerusalem,
> Thrusting away the hand lovingly held out to her.
> Therefore the Highest from her His face hath turned.
> So He leaveth her to sink down to destruction.

> Queen Vashti once disdaining to attend the royal feast
> Enraged thereby the king, who swore to banish her
> From his presence and to choose
> A gentler soul for his consort.

> Thus too will the synagogue be thrust away,
> From her will the kingdom of God be taken and entrusted
> To another people who shall bring forth
> The fruits of righteousness.

One has only to compare these lines with the statements of St. Paul regarding the destiny of the Jews to see that the biblical thought has been drastically reduced in a way that is decidedly prejudicial. The Christian spectators of the play are flattered as members of a "gentler" people, while the Jews are left "to destruction."

It would be a mistake to suppose that the anti-Semitic elements of the Oberammergau Passion Play are the result of nazism. Though the village was the site of an elite Nazi *Kaserne* and though many of the villagers were members of the party, there seems to be no evidence that Nazi sentiments led to any changes in the text. What is present is something older and deeper than nazism—a Bavarian if not a German racial consciousness supported by a conservative religious culture. The pity is that the Bavarian seems hardly able to distinguish between his religious feelings, his anti-Jewish prejudices, and his racial and cultural pride. This is why he is but little affected by charges that he is anti-Semitic.

As a matter of fact, the ability to recognize anti-Semitism as such is chiefly a modern capacity fostered by democratic ideals and sharpened by the reaction of civilized consciences to the racial atrocities of nazism. For this reason we probably ought to distinguish between anti-Semitism and anti-Jewish thought—the former being that modern phenomenon all democratic persons are eager to combat; the latter the expressions of hostility or dislike found in earlier periods as a result of the specific religious and historical role the Jews and their antagonists have played. Thus Egypt and Assyria in Old Testament times were anti-Jewish or anti-Hebrew, though it would be foolish to call them anti-Semitic. The Arabs today are not anti-Semitic, since they are Semites themselves. What nazism did was to turn the anti-Jewish feelings of the German people into anti-Semitism. The same phenomenon occurs in other Christian countries on a less systematically organized basis. What Oberammergau should realize, but probably will not, is that its anti-Jewish play today serves to propagate anti-Semitism, a modern disease as loathsome as the seventeenth-century plague which struck such fear into the hearts of the Oberammergau forefathers. Delivered from one plague, they have, unwittingly or not, become the carriers of another.

I have said that the play leads to misinterpretation of the Christian gospel. It is sometimes argued that the play is no more anti-Jewish than the New Testament itself. It might be fairly held that the play is no more anti-Jewish than *certain passages* of the New Testament, but the point is that the play distorts the New Testament story of the Passion primarily by selection and emphasis. I have already referred to the way in which Paul's discussion of the destiny of the Jews is reduced and thus misrepresented. There are numerous anti-Jewish references in the Gospel of John, but that is the only one of the four Gospels that has them. Moreover, none of the four Gospels tells the story of the Passion in such a way as to make it a simple tale of injustice done by the bad Sanhedrin to the good Christians.

The intent of the Gospels is to show that Christ was crucified by mankind, as he is crucified daily by our sins. When the story is made to flatter the Christian Church at the expense of the Jews (or when, as in the play, Pilate, a non-Jew, is made to appear noble in contrast to the scheming Sanhedrin) the true import of the Christian gospel is corrupted. That the Roman Catholic Church blesses such a representation and that Protestants, beguiled by romantic publicity, countenance it is evidence of a shocking weakness in religious and moral sensitivity.

My travels this summer have taken me now to three large festival plays in which the crucifixion of Christ is portrayed: the York Mystery Plays in England, the Passion Play at Tegelen in Holland and the Oberammergau Play in Germany. The plays at York and Tegelen are not subject to the anti-Semitic charges one must level at Oberammergau. Nevertheless, these plays have convinced me that when the crucifixion story is played out by amateurs for mass audiences distortions of one kind or another are inevitable. The playing of the Passion as a spectacle for vast audiences is in itself an offense, since it leads to detachment. The plays tend to become big shows more or less in the manner of De Mille. Even a sensitive director like David Giles at York is impelled in that direction by the nature of his play and the size of his audience.

If religious drama is to be judged by this sort of activity, it has patently already failed. We must move away from the big spectacle or pageant easily understood. We must move toward the subtleties of thought and nuances of feeling that belong to authentic art and which alone are capable of expressing the inner qualities of religious faith.

IX

Along the Way

IT WAS HARD to choose which to settle on among the dozens of heart-warming, heart-disturbing autobiographical pieces contributed during the twenties by the versatile professor of applied Christianity at Grinnell College, the Jewish boy who arrived penniless in New York from an immigrant ship, and in later years was to devote his pen to interpreting vividly to his fellow Americans the plight of immigrants less fortunate than he.

February 21, 1924

My First Communion

EDWARD A. STEINER

It was spring in town and we knew it, only because the Passover had been celebrated, the air was less chill and the swallows were nesting under the straw thatches.

No blades of grass, no flowers, no leaves nor blossoms; yet in me a strange yearning for them, as if in the long ago I had walked in gardens, had breathed the odor of lilacs every day, and dreamed young dreams beneath scented cherry trees.

Somewhere, I knew, there must be lilacs and cherry trees, and I wandered out one Saturday afternoon, leaving the Sabbath stillness of the ghetto street, the stifling smells, ages old, the dust and the grime, the spirit's prison.

I walked as in a dream, beyond the sight of the lone church tower, beyond the toll gate which marked the farthest I had ever walked away from town, and on, to a little shrine buried beneath huge beeches, where some saint who blessed harvests awaited adoration when harvests were in peril of hail swept from the near-by mountain or of the pitiless drought, when the peaks drew all the clouds and left the plain to suffer.

Beyond the beeches a path led through the fields and into the distant woods. On either side were lilacs in full bloom, meadow-larks were rising full-throated from the sweet carpeted earth, and I walked amid all this splendor as if in my fathers' gardens somewhere in Palestine, where once they dwelt before they were immured forever in towns.

I was a stranger here, yet never more at home. It was as if I picked up the threads of life which were broken in me thousands of years before. They say (wise men or fools) that we shall never die; nor living, live in some other sphere, but here on earth again—the soul the same, but in some other form encased.

I felt newborn, so like a child I was, yet never could be; for I was born old, born in the travail of a woman mourning for her mate, slain by the pestilence which always follows war, and even now lays its foul poison in men's minds and souls, though driven from their veins.

My first cry, my mother said, echoed her woe, for well she knew that I was born to a heritage of sorrow, fear and hate. Born with a fatal gift of seeing what others cannot see, feeling the things which left dullards dull; a gift, a fatal gift of saying what men least desire to hear or, hearing, will not heed.

There beneath the lilacs I felt myself for once a child, the only childhood which I really ever knew, so sweet that I taste it to this day and renew the thought of it whenever I am with children.

The wind blew gently on my cheeks, the birds sang sweetly their familiar lullabies—not as my mother sang; but my soul knew there were such melodies somewhere in God's world.

I buried my head in lilacs, I broke off heavy branches of the rich perfume, and then a man's harsh voice cried: "Jew boy!" The flowers grew heavy in my arms and dropped to the ground, the birds seemed silent, I smelled the foul, familiar ghetto air, and I was old again.

I had broken lilacs, he said. They were his, his father's. He himself was studying to be a priest, a holy man, and now was for a time at home, because even in monasteries it was spring.

My punishment he said should be that I must kiss the cross, a cross of brass which hung upon his girdle of white stout rope, round about a seamless robe such as he wore whom he called Lord, whose image he was pressing to my lips and whom he loved so much that he must hate the little Jew who was breathing lilacs and washing off the ghetto stains, in dews of May.

I would not kiss the cross; instead I struck it, and it fell into

in the afternoon: what kind of released-time program
s this? And the thousands of adults: were they all so
hy that they didn't need to work today, or has the recession
so far that they had been laid off and were using this as
be? Whatever the reason, crowds were there, but with less
rest in transportation than in adoration.

he Chicago Auto Show is in its fiftieth year, which puts
us a special weight of responsibility in coverage as it gives
bit of perspective on the progress of this magazine. It is help-
ul to see who else is fifty years old when we are. So far I have
ounted the *Christian Science Monitor*, General Motors, the
Progressive, and now the Chicago Auto Show. From the
glimpses I have had of The Christian Century's first volume and
the reminiscent snatches of the first auto show displayed at
the amphitheater, I must admit that the show has changed
more than the magazine in this half-century. So deeply sunk in
the bedrock of our national mores is the automobile show that
—remember, culture is the form of religion—it has become an
excellent opportunity to find America at worship. While the
churches go about their quiet business, the really relevant activities, we are told, go on elsewhere. J. Paul Williams and the
late A. Powell Davies argued eloquently that America's *real* religion is its elevation of democracy to the level of religious ul-
timacy. Morris Cohen contended that to see America at worship
one must observe it in a grandstand watching baseball or football (I forget which). But he was wrong. If we were once inclined to agree with him, that faith was shaken last summer
when we noted the relative ease with which the major deities
were dismissed by once-fanatic cultists from Ebbets Field and
the Polo Grounds to seek new Olympuses in the west.

To suggest that there is a broad idolization of automobilia is
of course not original, but the familiarity of the observation does
not relieve us of the responsibility of surveying this idolatry in
its massive, institutionalized form. The major automobile
shows in all our cities attract pilgrims of every race, caste and
color—no question of the universality of this religion. They
congregate here at the International Amphitheater in greater
numbers, with greater determination and certainly with greater
reverence than do the politicos who quadrennially while away

the dust. I spat upon it thrice,
cleanse myself of that hated tou

The age-long rage of Gentile
smote me with the rope, he beat m
it to my bleeding lips to kiss; then t
grew sweet upon my lips, my tears
lying prostrate there I grew young a
breathed more deeply the scent of lilacs,
Presence which I could not touch, or nan
It, had I known. I did not know that so
height, which men call depth, where length
forms a cross—we two should meet again.

AN ASSOCIATE EDITOR *meets new gods fresh*
sembly line.

January 22, 1958

The Altar of Automobility

EDITORIAL CORRESPONDENCE

International Amphitheater, Chicago
Our nation's most revered theologue has argued that religion
is the substance of culture and culture is the form of religion.
If this is true in any sense, why confine editorial correspondence
to ecclesiastical affairs? Why not report those assemblies where
the Really Important Things of our culture are taking place?
With this rationalization I hied myself off to have a good time
with a clerical friend at the annual Chicago Auto Show at the
International Amphitheater. Rationalization was necessary because, being of the old school, we still find enough of the compulsion of the Protestant ethic laid upon us to necessitate ex-
cuses for enjoying ourselves on a weekday afternoon. We were
puzzled on arrival, by the way, at the numbers of children there

a week in the same arena nominating presidential candidates. This year devotees were confronted by the lowest, longest, sleekest, chromiest and most expensive motorcars ever assembled. The highest price tag was $73,756 (for a truck), but there were many autos costing much more than one-tenth that. One salesman affronted us by detracting from the *mysterium tremendum* of the atmosphere when he suggested that a $5,379 station wagon was a good buy because station wagons are "so practical."

Comparative religionists may be missing something by confining their dealings to "high" religions. Everything we have been told to look for is here. Joachim Wach used to underscore certain elements common to world religions: they provide objects of ultimate concern, have universal potential, offer practical expression (what is more practical than hundreds of horsepower at your disposal in 10-mile-per-hour Loop traffic?), need metaphysical sanction. The argument today was: Buy an auto, dispose of last year's obsolete model, because the auto is the barometer of our economy and you must buy to have prosperity. In this case the sanction is doubly worthy because singly true.

Religion also needs ceremonial reinforcement. That the auto show provides in spectacular dimensions. We paused, for instance, at the holy of holies—a black Crown Imperial mounted on a red-carpeted dais against a backdrop of silver cloth. One visitor intuitively removed his hat. Even stouthearted William Penn would have been put to it to assert the Protestant principle at such an altar. There is room here too for fetishism, for totemism, for tactile sensation—these are deities that we are allowed to caress. (Someone is always standing by to remove the traces with a waxed rag.) Half a million people at a ten-day show will not wear tail-fins away as toes are worn on much-kissed statues. What is more, these are deities that blossom with the cycle of the seasons. At the close of these mysteries new gods will spring forth full-grown from the womb whence these issued at Detroit. Most assuredly there will again be special revelation in 1959, and there will be new initiation rites.

Wherever we wandered there were ushers with flowers in

lapels or, better, temple priestesses in low-cut chasubles. Enticingly they invited passers-by to participate in acts of devotion ("Observe the convenience and luxury of this television set installed in the rear seat. You can remove it should you ever wish to get out of the car"). They explained features of the engine about which they knew less than most of us, if that is possible. Revivalists fairly shrieked the virtues of the models which caused a lot of backsliding last year. If this clash of competing kerygmas became too deafening, one could always retire to the interior of the station wagons, designed to foster family fellowship. Even in such a haven, however, one could not escape the evidences of steely will to power and the gadget-filled models that bred a feeling of absolute dependence.

And there is corporate worship at the show too. Twice a day devotees move from their wanderings in the outer courts to do homage at the high altar. Here liturgists of at least two genders dance before the procession of Baalim to the accompaniment of a commentary lush with competing superlatives. Goddesses elevated from the prose of secretarial desks and modeling agencies detract only momentarily from the business at hand. This rite commanded more attention than most religious processions we have seen. By now all are initiates, all are involved. True, as with other religions there are cultured despisers, scoffers, dilettantes; just as with Christian Sunday schools, some only come "to bring the children." But most are converts; and agents are there to help us translate reverence into purchase, that we may show our faith by our works. This involves a pitch for stewardship and for sacrifice. All is very serious. "Don't Squash Me—I Eat Harmful Insects" said a sign mounted on the windshield of a buglike deity, the capricious little Isetta. This was the only humor we noted, and you can't get much mileage out of that.

This is a historical religion. The flivvers of 1908 were paraded, but only briefly. As with popular Christianity, the past seems to be used largely to suggest the enlightened glory of the present. There was even that familiar phenomenon the athlete of the gods, the virtuoso of holiness: a 1958 Plymouth that had weathered 58,000 miles. Above its dashboard the evidences of

travel, a pack of cigarettes and a candy bar, were placed as carefully and phonily as the tattoo on the hand of a Marlboro
man. The demythologizers would realize distressfully how far
they miscalculate Modern Man's capacity for fantasy if they
saw the auto mounted on foam-like clouds while in the background a movie of continued wafting through space suggested
Il Paradiso. There it floated, just beyond the reach of most
mechanics and ministers. And there was the El Dorado, attainable only by the elect. One eschatological note interfered—a
gigantic Jupiter missile at the rear of the main auditorium. But
we didn't let it bother us very long.

All in all it was an enjoyable afternoon, if terrifying in a
minor sort of way. There seems to be a fatal fascination in all
this, visible in the faces of both those who contemplate the
leap of faith and those who are already knights of infinite
resignation. The triumph of our technology, our obsession with
gadgetry, our preoccupation with externals—all are flamboyantly
spread out here. Do you recall the cartoon that brought two
events together last autumn: a woman reading the newspaper
to her husband and commenting that "they" and "we" had
both progressed last week—they had the I.C.B.M. and we had
the Edsel? The human predicament, I suppose, is portrayed
in full here for those who go deeper than journalists need to.

But the point of this correspondence will be missed by
those who seek in it a note of absolute detachment and complete condescension. No one, I imagine, escapes authentic involvement with this glittering symbol of our pervasive materialism. But the 50th Annual Auto Show, it seems to me, gives
the lie to surveys in *etc* magazine and to motivation researchers
who suggest that at the root of America's disproportionate
reverence for automobility there is something profoundly sexual. Few people give ultimate devotion to sex; their really
ultimate devotion goes to religions like this one.

Incidentally, we paid admission, assuming that the guard at
the gate would not buy the religion-and-culture connection
that would have made a Century press card meaningful. And
we certainly received our money's worth. After the corporate
worship we returned once more to the private cubicles of con-

templation and paid last respects at the shrine of a foreign
deity, our strictly wistful choice: the Mercedes-Benz. Outside
it was snowing. Fortunately, I didn't have my 1957 station
wagon there to burden my conscience further (it was planned
for "togetherness"). We climbed into my friend's 1950 Plymouth, and in it we felt somehow shriven. And it carried us
safely home.

Martin E. Marty

THREE COLUMNISTS

WEEK IN, WEEK OUT, from 1915 through 1960, many a reader turned first to relish the latest witty, incisive comment on life and letters by the Century's currently reigning columnist. The magazine's pages through those forty-five years were enriched by a type of writing difficult and becoming ever more rare—the contributions of three men, each man's column ceasing only on his death. William E. Barton of Oak Park, Illinois, was Safed the Sage (1915-30); Edward Shillito of London, Quintus Quiz (1931-48); Halford E. Luccock of Hamden, Connecticut, Simeon Stylites (1948-60).

March 10, 1927

The Sins I Have Saved

A PARABLE OF SAFED THE SAGE

There came unto me a man who desired my Advice, and he did not come Any Too Soon. And I said unto him, Thou hast acted Unwisely.

And he said, I am afraid that what thou sayest is true. Tell me wherein my Fault Lieth. And I told him the best I could.

And he said, I verily believe thou art right. I will amend my ways.

Then we talked of other things, and he spake as one who was free from Care. And when he left me, he seemed Happy.

And I got to thinking it over, and I said, I did not Rub It in enough. I should have been more Severe.

And I sate down and wrote him an Epistle, and said unto him, Forget not that thou hast much whereof to Repent, and I told him again Two or Three things.

Now I had other letters to Mail, and it chanced when I picked them up that I overlooked that one. And I returned to mine home and saw it still unmailed. And I said, Let me look again at that Letter.

And when I read it over, I said, How will that sound when he readeth it, and peradventure handeth it across the Table to his Wife?

And I said, Verily, it was of the Lord and not of mine own wisdom that this Letter had not gone out in the Mail.

And I tore it across, and then again across, and threw it into the Fire.

And I said, I have rarely repented of a harsh word that I left unspoken or a harsh letter that I did not mail.

And when I next met that man, he said unto me, I thank thee for what thou didst say, and I thank thee yet more for what thou mightest have said that would have been true, but which I was in the Mood to Resent. And because thou wast kind to me, and didst hurt me no more than was Necessary, behold I have resolved to be a Better Man.

And I went unto my home, and I said, O my God, I have much to thank Thee for, but just now I thank Thee for the times when I stopped just short of Making a Fool of Myself. For surely it is no Credit to me that having done that man a Good Turn I did not Ruin it all by Overdoing it.

September 29, 1937

The Perfect Ending

Editor The Christian Century

Sir: In a book of essays I once read these wise words: "The perfect ending is generally to be found about seven minutes before the real end of a sermon, and about a page before the end of a book." I think you will agree, though I should not be surprised if you moved an amendment to the words "seven minutes"; seven, as you say, is a very generous estimate. But I am not concerned with that first judgment. I will only add that you can never measure a sermon by clock-time; no sermon is too long if the hearer at the end wishes it were longer. But he may want no more of it at the end of five minutes.

However, it is the endings of books of which I am thinking, and here it is not easy to set down any law. The essayist from whom I have quoted says that Bunyan should have ended his Pilgrim's Progress with "All the trumpets sounded for him on the other side." As it is he ends with a quiet and even commonplace note about Christian's children: "Also since I came away, I heard one say that they were yet alive, and so would be for the increase of the church in that place where they were for a time. Shall it be my lot to go that way again, I may give those that desire it an account of what I here am silent about. Meantime, I bid my reader, Adieu."

Which ending would you prefer? For my own part I am all for Bunyan's own modulation to a quieter key. But I must admit that modern taste is against me. It is generally preferred that a writer should end on some note of high emotion. The orator keeps his noblest flight of imagination to the end. In spite of everything, there are still perorations.

But I think the Greeks, whose judgment no man can reject without serious reason, would have been with Bunyan. They did not end on the climax; they loved to provide for the reader or hearer a way back to his common life. The guide did not leave him on the summit, but quietly led him back to the foothills within sight of his home in the valley.

There is no more moving passage in literature than the end of the Phaedo, where Socrates drinks the hemlock. When the end had come Crito "closed his mouth and eyes." "Such was the end, Echecrates, of our friend, who was, as we may say, of all those of his time whom we have known, the best and wisest and most righteous man." They said that Plato wrote eighteen drafts of the first sentence of the Republic; how many did he write of this last sentence of the Phaedo? How subdued it is! How satisfying! How like a bridge back to life in the city of Athens!

There is no rule in this matter of endings. Sometimes it may be right to leave the reader stunned and almost gasping for breath. At other times—I think more often—it is best to lead him gently out of the realm into which he has been admitted for a time, back to earth on which if anywhere he must win his soul.

I think they do well who end as Milton did in his *Samson Agonistes,* where he tells how God his servants

> With peace and consolation hath dismist
> And calm of mind, all passion spent.

Milton was indeed in the great classical tradition as he made his perfect endings. Is there in all literature a nobler end than this:

> They hand in hand with wandering steps and slow
> Through Eden took their solitary way.

But there too he has modulated back to subdued and tender music, so that we may be helped in our departure.

We know that the Bible is not a book but a literature, and the order is not always easy to explain. But I find the end of it perfect. That it is the end is the work of the editors. But editors too may have inspiration; and when I read "Even so, come, Lord Jesus," I know that no other ending could have closed the Book so fitly.

Yours bidding adieu,
Quintus Quiz

April 30, 1958

Appointment for the Prophet Amos

Editor The Christian Century

Sir: The pastor of St. John's-by-the-Gas-Station was having a morning coffee break at the drug store across the street. "You are getting to be quite a barfly," I said deferentially, hoping to start a fight. No use; I was beneath notice. Then all of a sudden he asked, "How long will a tape taken by a tape recorder last?" "Longer than you will," I answered. "Perhaps fifty years." "I wish it had been invented some centuries ago," he said. "I would like to have a tape recording of Socrates' speech before taking his last brimming cup of hemlock. I would like to have one of Martin Luther's defiance of the Diet of Worms. And of Lincoln's Inaugural address."

Then he went on: "I would also like to have recordings of some things I have heard myself. One I would like most is the recording of an informal speech given at a meeting several years ago by Methodist Bishop Francis J. McConnell. He was called on to sum up the proceedings. He did that—and then he generously wandered off on a fascinating detour as a bonus gift. Believe me, it was a *big* bonus. His subject was what would happen if the prophet Amos came up for appointment at a Methodist annual conference. The bishop really went to town. He staged for our imagination a conference cabinet meeting with the district superintendents facing the question, 'What shall we do for the prophet Amos?' One by one they shed bitter tears, vowing undying admiration for the prophet Amos, and explaining why they could not give him a church in their districts.

"The superintendent of the North district said in a faltering voice (they were all utterly sincere, no doubt about that): 'You all know how I love and admire Brother Amos. He is one of the finest men in the church since John Wesley, one of God's gifts to our time. But he doesn't have enough tact for Grace Church. He just blurts out his ideas with no suavity at all, and Grace Church folks need a lot of suavity. They are in a building campaign. If only Brother Amos would raise fewer controversial issues and more money he would get on better. He went to an anniversary celebration at Grace Church and had no more judgment than to denounce some of the members as being at ease in Zion. So obviously he is not the man for Grace.'

"Then the superintendent of the West district opened up. 'I too have loved Brother Amos,' he said. 'I have been deeply moved by many of his sermons. I would love to put him at

Trinity Church. But he is just not eloquent enough. It has been a great preaching place. You remember the crowds that Dr. Demosthenes drew, and Dr. Webster. But Brother Amos is a plain blunt man who speaks straight on. He doesn't have the literary touch or the oratorical lift the people of Trinity are used to. I'm sorry.'

"The superintendent of the South district was perplexed, too. 'I wish that Brother Amos was more interested in matters of organization,' he said. 'I would like to put him at Wesley Memorial. But it has been the leading church in the conference. It is used to men who take places of leadership. Its last three pastors have all gone to General Conference. The church will want a man who takes a sharper interest in leadership and does not spend all his time on his prophecies and on people—some of them, not the outstanding ones.'

"After careful consideration, the superintendents agreed to give the prophet Amos a sabbatical year.

"I wish I had a tape recording. It would be a good one to play at the first session of the cabinet in every annual conference, or at a presbytery or state association."

Yours,

Simeon Stylites

POEMS

A FAMOUS POET once characterized poetry as the "antennae of the race." Through some such conviction Century editors have over the years seen to it that the magazine's pages afforded a generous sampling of contemporary verse—poems speaking in new and memorable ways about old and enduring themes: God and man, life and death, peace and war, joy and despair, eternity and time.

November 8, 1923

God's Dreams

THOMAS CURTIS CLARK

Dreams are they—but they are God's dreams!
Shall we decry them and scorn them?
That men shall love one another,
That white shall call black man brother,
That greed shall pass from the market place,
That lust shall yield to love for the race,
That men shall meet with God face to face—
Dreams are they all,
  But shall we despise them—
  God's dreams!

Dreams are they—to become man's dreams!
Can we say nay as they claim us?
That men shall cease from their hating,
That war shall soon be abating,
That the glory of kings and lords shall pale,
That the pride of dominion and power shall fail,
That the love of humanity shall prevail—

Dreams are they all,
  But shall we despise them—
  God's dreams!

October 16, 1929

Non-Employment in Heaven

ELINOR LENNEN

Lord, what will heaven be like,
That rich folks talk about?
To strut eternally
Before the down-and-out
Who never do find work
While walking streets of gold?
O Lord, for ice when hot,
Or heat, just once, when cold!
No land of rest for us,
Nor harps—a whistle, bell;
Lord, promise heaven has work,
Or leave us here in hell.

July 24, 1935

Prayer

AMOS N. WILDER

The invisible world with thee hath sympathized;
Be thy affections raised and solemnized.—Wordsworth, "Laodamia"

Omnipotent confederate of all good,
Inexorable foe of all our ill,
Extirpate these bold motions of self-will,
Mortify these strange slips, the unblushing brood
Of vanities, and be thy surgery rude,
Until we wake to thee alone, until
All mild and disabused and meek and still
We pass in awe into thy plenitude.
So in an hour we have seen the face
Of nature change, and with our garish eyes
As though anointed with some lymph of grace
Seen common day grow solemn, as the skies
Foaming above with sable panoplies
Made of the world a hushed transfigured place.

November 9, 1938

War Relics

TERTIUS VAN DYKE

What shall we do with the battle flags
    After they're churched with a loud Te Deum?
Label them carefully, glassed from dust,
    For all to see in the great museum.

What shall we do with outmoded guns
    Brought from their place in the bloody fray?
Set them up on the village green
    To trouble the children in their play.

What shall we do with the wounded men
    Battered and torn in the fearful fight?
Quick, take them up and put them away;
    Hide them, hide them, out of our sight.

March 27, 1940

Spring Offensive

EDWIN McNEILL POTEAT

Why must the Spring come hither where the white
And deathly silence of the Winter lingers?
Must it advance with stout and busy fingers
Kneading the earth to softness and delight?
Should it report with quick, ecstatic breathing
To endless ranks of regimental pines
Rumors of insubordination seething
In the soft sunshine, just behind the lines?

Were it not wiser that the season dally,
Stifle its passion, abdicate its hour,
Lest in the fields where hate and fury rally
Crosses invade where crocuses should flower?
Were it not better, numbed with cold to lie
Than stir a moment in the sun, and die?

October 2, 1940

Luther*

W. H. AUDEN

With conscience cocked to listen for the thunder
He saw the Devil busy in the wind
Over the chimney steeples and then under
The doors of nuns and doctors who had sinned.

What apparatus could stave off disaster
Or cut the brambles of man's error down?
Flesh was a silent dog that bites its master,
World a still pond in which its children drown.

The fuse of Judgment spluttered in his head:
"Lord, smoke these honeyed insects from their hives;
All Works and all Societies are bad;
The Just shall live by Faith," he cried in dread.

And men and women of the world were glad
Who never trembled in their useful lives.

* Reprinted from *The Collected Poetry of W. H. Auden*. Copyright 1945 by W. H. Auden. This poem originally appeared in The Christian Century.

January 30, 1946

To a Japanese Warrior

(Written in Kure, Hiroshima Perfecturate)

HARGIS WESTERFIELD

Rest at the crossroads, homecoming
Jap in the khaki and queer peaked cap,
Tired under your heavy pack. I'll accept
Your gift of an orange; you deserve my
Cigarette (I'll not forget the vile Nippo
Tobacco I took from your corpses on Wake).
This is *bushido* American, *bushido* Japanese,
The Way of the Warrior. Brothers in battle,
We can grin and understand. The war's
Done, like a football game. Leave bitterness
To the old and vengeful, to the stay-at-homes.
What are typhus and malaria and New Guinea's
Nights in the jungle, when two fighting men
Find the grin in each other's eyes?

February 22, 1956

Towards Gethsemane

WARREN LANE MOLTON

When you have pitied Self enough
And wept the bitter gulf
Of tears, walled especially for this seeming ruin
Of mine, *I will come again.*

Together we shall take
Up the new life and shake
Off the grave with impavid speech
Beyond the cross's reach.

In the honesty that comes of long wait
I *will come again,* late
In your grief, early in your harsh abuse
Of death. I shall carry a bruised reed to reduce
The scepter's cry for thrones, and a growing stone
To fill the cold night. These alone
I shall bring in wounded hands; you shall not fear
Death, for I shall hold its globe-tear
In satisfied fingers. You shall not forget me
For I go in the hour of your grief and of my victory.

       September 4, 1957

Portrait of a High Court Judge

WINIFRED RAWLINS

You see, I am quite alone.
You cannot know, because you have not felt
The gray tide of separateness that laps around me.
Here in the courtroom
People believe it is the accused
Who is cut off from all others,
But that is an illusion.
Even though the cold handcuffs
Embrace his flesh alone,
Yet all men secretly feel themselves
Standing beside him.
There are indeed a few

Who imagine they sit with me here;
But they know in fact they will never do so,
And that comes between us.

After the verdict, as I leave the courthouse,
I touch the rough bark of a tree;
Will it still give back to me
A neutral uncritical caress?
I have just deprived a man's hands
Of the comforting touch of all natural surfaces
For twenty years.

In truth it is I who stand
Continually accused.
What man or god can invest me
With this terrible kingship?
Yet if I refuse, if I abdicate,
I shall have to commit humanity
To the judgments and mercy of life itself.
And for that I am not yet ready.

July 16, 1958

Ruach

PIERRE HENRI DELATTRE

Lazarus, you have been touched,
Lazarus, His good friend, word made flesh,
Lazarus, you have been loved so lavishly the crippled
        dance,
Lazarus, O Lazarus, rise from your trance!

Why should I rise, why should I unwind
These rags that reunite my bones

With dust and wind
And all the sweetness of a dying mind?

The assembly of the wicked and the wise
Draw up their cloaks of doubt and of disdain.
Think of their shock, oh think of their surprise
To see your whiteness walk before their eyes!

Leave me to dream about the rain
Rushing across my rock tomb, never again
Shall I be born, for we are born to die.
Seek me in streams, look for me in the sky.

We seek you in the world where, wanting you,
The Christ Himself has trespassed into death.
Who breathes His Spirit breathes a living breath,
We fishermen invite you to the feast!

A raucous wind breathes fear into all flesh.
Who saves me suffers thorn and lash.
But that you may believe, I shall awake
And walk a little longer for His sake.

December 23, 1959

Journey to the Holy Land
EDITH LOVEJOY PIERCE

But even if you go you are not there.
For too much rubble has defaced the land,
For too much gunsmoke has obscured the air,
And wire and walls impede. On every hand
Pretentious buildings do but give the lie—
Signposts thrown down, their lettering all awry.

Open the Book and learn the ancient Greek,
See, as it were for the first time, the land.
Follow and let the changeless pages speak.
Here at the lakeside walk. Here on the mountain
    stand.
Now once again the field flowers are in bloom.
Here is the street, here is the upper room.

The vineyard and the boat, the ox, the plow,
Simple and unselfconscious as they broke
The past, are vivid in the shimmering now,
Transfixed upon the truth by One who spoke.
Oh, make it real, this world without frontier.
Open the door. The Holy Land is *here.*

May 11, 1960

Atonement

TONY STONEBURNER

Within the drone drowse hum and monotone
Of the unmoving summer afternoon,
Full leaf hangs slack and wilted from its poise
On sap-siphoning stem, as I turn off
The rural road and park at the rest home.

I visit the old woman—with the head
That always shakes No/No for she lacks nerve
On her left side either to lift limp hand
Or to relax cold cramping foot—and serve
The dice of bread and thimbles of grapejuice.
(*We water down the blood and mince the word*)

Next morning, nearer noon than dawn, more shrill
Than the cicada, equally without
Cessation, I ram the lawnmower over
The backyard turf and leave behind crushed mint,
Halved apples, and sliced pinkrooted rhubarb.

Beside the doorsill are neat extra cubes
From the same loaf, rasp crisp with staleness, white
As hard crapshooting upon baize, discarded
To mourning doves, quails, crows and even starlings
To satisfy their stomachs to the guts.

But my son David, diaper-wadded, gathers
Up crumbs and eats them garnished with grass-
    clippings
In ignorant communion with the joy
In flight of wind-exulted fowl and with
The agony of the sick aged female.
(*Our only nourishment is such a myth*)

November 2, 1960

Afternoon Coming

BETSY FEAGAN COLQUITT

We were not prepared for this. In the summering afternoon
dizzying with bottomless skies, all heaven broke loose.
Lounging in the comfortable chaise, sipping some cool nectar,
bantering an inconsequential novel, thinking far from eternity,
we were not prepared for holy splendor.
Brightness of birds nosing wilting flowers was enough
of dazzle, buzzing of bees ample trumpeting,
mirages patterned against our made surfaces sufficient angels.
Yet importunate, impervious, intervening in our welcomed time,
eternity came.

On some fall morning of sabbath feeling we could have greeted
holiness appropriately perhaps, our needs shaping due courtesy
and our hopes not so comfortably earthward.
But in our spring-summer afternoon, earth was miracle enough,
and in the afternoon of this showing forth,
we turned mute eyes back to unholy books,
greeted angelic songs as unneeded noise
as we lay in comfortable body and uneager spirit
while all heaven sang hymns to him who came
in bright beauty seeking recognition, whom we
in the indifferent afternoon could not rise
even to crucify or offer nectar to assuage thirst.

December 21, 1960

Tautology

WILLIAM I. ELLIOTT

Cradle and Cross are of wood,
    Rock-rough and chill.

Out of the hard landscape,
Out of the flint of the earth,

For men, a Cradle and a Cross—
The tautology of Grace.

March 29, 1961

At a Grave on Easter

STANLEY J. ROWLAND, JR.

Earth wayfares through the spangled void,
Drifts like stars and the strewn birds
That curve in the long throbs of instinct,
Turning to the lucid instant of God—
He is

Transfixing dirt and senseless rain
That rattles on my child's grave,
Age three and slain with cancer. He was
Projected like a star from me,
A quickened body swirled to flesh
And shred, like Jesus' screaming sides.
Nor can the world's gravel tears
Return his flesh or cancel life—
He is gone

And women sorrow to the tomb
To find the linen thrown aside,
The stench of death replaced, the grave
Still like the held breath of God—
He is gone

They stole his broken flesh, and only
The strange gardener walks the morning:
Mary, why are you weeping now?
Mary, whom seek you in a grave?
And lightning splits to her nerve ends—
Yet he lives

Mary ragtimes through the streets,
The bonnet ladies peer and fluster,
And even the fool fly can hear
Her cry that stones the firmament,
That rolls the dawn into a ball
And hurls it flaming down the wind—
He is risen

At Emmaus breaking bread
And smashing through the doors of time,
He strides the nights and sandy days,
Born before the world congealed,
A quickened body swirled to blood
And killed for being flesh and God,
Slain into a new dimension—
He is risen, and here

Walking in the dawn of cool rain.
The body lives in different forms;
If flesh can rise, then fleshless body
As time is cracked for newer time
And bursting suns must keep his pace:
I shall not judge the galaxy.
The Lord is risen; it is enough.
I go in peace. The child lives.

Index

Academic freedom, 317, 335
Africa, 145-46, 191, 359-65
Ainslie, Peter, 156, 178
Alcoholism, 281-82, 285, 288, 290, 291, 292
Amsterdam Assembly, World Council of Churches, 185-89
Amos, 426-28
Anglicans, 150, 156, 157, 162, 174, 178, 182, 184
Animism, 145-46, 364-65
Anti-Semitism, 175, 407-11
Arab refugees, 369-71, 373
Assisi, 358-59
Auden, W. H., 433
Augustine, 288-89
Auto show, Chicago, 417-22

Balfour, Lord, 141, 152
Ballard Vale, Massachusetts, 354-56
Barnes, Harry Elmer, 289
Barth, Karl, 96-105, 108, 109, 129, 130, 190
Barton, William E., 423
Bauer, Karl, 408
Ben Hur, 395, 396, 397
Bennett, John C., 47
Bible, 54, 82, 88, 127, 306, 336-39, 354, 394-97, 406, 409-11, 426
Big Fisherman, The, 395, 396, 397
Birth control, 153
Black, Hugo L., 319, 320
Braden, Carl, 319
Brent, Charles H., 141, 154, 159, 180
Bryan, William J., 142, 336-38
Bultmann, Rudolf, 120
Bunyan, John, 94, 425
Byington, Steven T., 353-56

Cadbury, Henry J., 311
Calhoun, Robert L., 113
Canada, temperance movements in, 287-88
Capitalism, 32, 33, 60-65, 118, 157
Carnell, Edward John, 110
Cavert, Samuel McCrea, 164
Censorship, 394
Chakko, Sarah, 190
Chakravarty, Amiya, 384
Chatterji, K., 146
Chiang Kai-shek, 208, 209, 240
Chicago, hunger march in, 274-79; Auto show, 417-22
China, 146-47, 159, 170, 208-11, 216, 218, 222, 243, 265, 267
Christian faith and society, 21-22, 23-70, 74-77, 93, 99-100, 117-120, 124, 148-55, 165-70, 172-178, 193-94, 198-201, 207-11, 216-21, 258-59, 263-65, 266-69, 273, 288-91, 293-97, 307, 311-12, 314-17
Church and state, 31, 49-53, 168-169, 174-77, 231-39, 311-13, 321-331, 374-79
Churchill, Winston, 240, 241, 243, 260, 350
Church unity, 33, 66-70, 133, 139-194, 273, 297
Citizenship, 251-55, 301, 322
Civil liberties, 125, 251-55, 301, 317, 318-21, 323
Clark, Thomas Curtis, 429
Coffin, Henry Sloane, 199
Coins, 311
Colquitt, Betsy Feagan, 439
Commentary, 407-08

Communism, 32, 33, 37, 49-50, 119-20, 125, 207-11, 218-20, 226, 240, 243, 268-69, 275, 278, 300, 314-18, 319, 345, 348-49, 368, 372-73

Concentration camps, 251, 254, 256-59

Confessing Church (Germany), 233, 236-39

Congregational Churches (U.S.), 180

Congress, U.S., 172, 173, 212-13, 286, 318-21, 322-25

Constitution, 202, 206, 251-53, 320, 321-26, 329, 330

Cuba, 267, 269

Dabbs, James McBride, 297

Dante, 93, 94

Darrow, Clarence, 337-38

Darwin, Charles, 83, 84

Daughters of the American Revolution, 313-14

Davis, Robert Gorham, 407-08

Dayton, Tennessee, 335-39

Declaration of Independence, 253, 255

Delattre, Pierre Henri, 436

Depression, economic, 214, 274-79

Disarmament, 266

Disciples of Christ, 83, 179

Doctor Zhivago, 385-86

Douglas, William O., 319

Drama, 404-12

Driver, Tom F., 404

Drummond, Henry, 81-86

Dulles, John Foster, 190, 268

Eckardt, A. Roy, 53

Economic Consequence of the Peace, by John Maynard Keynes, 119

Economics, 23, 32-33, 43, 46, 50, 60-64, 117, 118-19, 154, 166-67, 209-11, 214, 248, 273, 274-79, 298, 301, 345, 378

Ecumenical movement; *see* Church unity

Eddington, Arthur Stanley, 346-47

Eddy, Sherwood, 142, 343, 345, 346

Edinburgh Conferences: World

Missionary (1910), 139-47, 156, 166; Faith and Order (1937), 178-84, 199

Editorial Correspondence, 42, 74, 280, 343, 356, 366, 374, 417

Editorials, 21, 66, 70, 88, 105, 185, 189, 197, 198, 199, 201, 204, 207, 245, 251, 256, 259, 265, 272, 274, 279, 286, 313, 314, 318, 321, 327, 335, 350, 394

Einstein, Albert, 343-48

Eliot, T. S., 129, 402

Elliott, William I., 440

Elmer Gantry, 339, 398

England, 74-77, 171

Ethics, 23-28, 29-30, 38-41, 92-94, 99-100, 111, 119, 124, 146, 202-203, 216-21, 244, 256-59, 260-65, 274, 279-80, 282-85, 293-97, 298-302, 305-07, 350-53, 362-65, 368-71

Evangelism, 42-47, 70-77

Evanston Assembly, World Council of Churches, 189-94

Evolution, 25, 83-86, 106, 108, 110, 336-38

Existentialism, 125-26

Federal Council of Churches, 231, 273

Fey, Harold E., viii, 139, 231, 285, 373

Fink, Alois, 406-07

Finland, 241-42

Fosdick, Harry Emerson, 90, 231

Frakes, Margaret, 356

France, 150-52, 213, 262, 267

Francis of Assisi, 358-59

Franco, Francisco, 374-79

Fundamentalism, 26-28, 70-77, 82-86, 88, 89, 107-09, 109-12, 121, 336-39, 341

Gandhi, Mohandas K., 305, 345-46, 350-53

Garrison, Winfred Ernest, 171

Germany, 97, 98, 101, 102, 123-25, 150-51, 153, 175-76, 200-01, 213, 231-39, 240, 243, 255, 256-59, 261, 343-49, 404-12

Gill, Theodore A., 366, 374

Great Britain, 43-47, 74-77, 81-82, 139-41, 152-53, 171, 213, 241-243, 246, 267, 368
Graham, Billy, 74-77
'Gunsmoke,' 398

Harkness, Samuel, 339
Haycox, Ernest, 400, 401, 402
Hayes, Ira, 280-85
Herrera, Emilio, 378
High Starlight, 403
Hindus, 145, 146, 350-52
Hiroshima, 259-66, 269
Hitler, Adolf, 244, 255, 257, 350
Holmes, Jesse H., 345, 347
Holmes, John Haynes, 240
Holmes, L. P., 403
Holy Land, 366-74
Horton, Douglas, 96
Hough, Lynn Harold, 148
House Un-American Activities Committee, 318-21
Hutchinson, Paul, viii, 47, 274, 349

India, 145, 146, 147, 170, 269, 305, 345-46, 360-62
Indians, American, 254, 279-85
Ingersoll, Robert, 336
International Missionary Council, 164-70
Iona Community, 42-47
Israel, 366, 368-71
Italy, 345, 356

Japan, 170, 208, 216-18, 221, 222-223, 227, 246-48, 259-66
Japanese-Americans, 251-55
Jazz, 388-94
Jerusalem, 164, 366-67, 371, 373
Jerusalem Conference, International Missionary Council, 30, 164-70
Jews, 27, 175, 236, 255, 294, 368-369, 371, 387, 407-11, 415-17
Jones, E. Stanley, 169
Jordan, 366-74
Jowett, J. H., 198-99

Kagawa, Toyohiko, 31
Kansas City, Sinclair Lewis in, 339-342
Keats, John, 91

Kelsey, Philip M., 353
Kent, Victoria, 377, 378
Keynes, John Maynard, 119
Khrushchev, Nikita, 267
King, Albion R., 287
King, Martin Luther, Jr., 302

Laity, 30, 42-47, 59-65, 193
Lambaréné, 359-65
Lausanne Conference on Faith and Order, 156-64, 180
Laymen's Foreign Missions Inquiry, 30, 210-11
League of Nations, 90, 92, 201-04
Lennen, Elinor, 430
Levinson, Salmon O., 204-07
Lewis, Sinclair, 339-42, 398
Liberalism in theology, 25-26, 84-86, 87, 99, 105-10, 113-22, 127, 129-35, 341
Lincoln, Abraham, 93
Liquor, 153-54, 281-82, 285, 286, 289-93
Literature, 91, 93, 94, 339-42, 383-384, 385-87, 399-403
Long Storm, The, 401, 402
Loyalty oaths, 314-18
Luccock, Halford E., 423
Lutherans, 150, 175, 390-91

MacArthur, Douglas, 260
McCarthyism, 49-52, 314-21
McConnell, Francis J., 169
McLeod, George, 43-47
Malik, Charles, 371
'Man Upstairs' cult, 56, 57
Marty, Martin E., 422
Matthews, Herbert L., 378
Melle, F. H. Otto, 176
Micklem, Nathaniel, 45
Middle East, 366-74
Miller, Alexander, 398
Milton, John, 426
Ministry, 42-47, 52, 71-76, 82-86, 161, 193, 339-42
Missions, foreign, 29-35, 139-47, 156, 159, 163-70, 210-11, 263, 359-65
Molton, Warren Lane, 434
Morrison, Charles Clayton, viii, 81, 113, 139, 178, 204

Moslems, 351-52
Motion pictures, 321, 394-98
Mott, John R., 141, 144, 147, 170, 173, 179
Muelder, Walter, 387
Music, 388-94

Nagasaki, 259-65
Nasser, Abdul Gamel, 368, 371, 372
National Council of Churches, 66-70, 395
Nationalism, 23, 24, 31-32, 40-41, 49-52, 57-58, 151-52, 223, 261-262, 311-13, 314-16, 348
Neff, Marietta, 383
Nazism, 232-39, 256-59, 410
New York Times, 52, 378
Niebuhr, H. Richard, 120, 216, 228
Niebuhr, Reinhold, 22, 109, 130, 222
Niemöller, Martin, 232-38
Non-Christian faiths, 29-31, 144-47, 165, 264
Nonviolent resistance, 302, 305-07, 346, 350-53
Norris, George W., 212
Northcott, Cecil, 77
Nuclear warfare, 193, 259-69

Oberammergau, 404-12
Oldham, J. H., 173
Operation Abolition, 321
Orthodox churches, 67, 157, 160, 171, 174, 184, 190, 267
Outler, Albert C., 128
Oxford Conference on Life and Work, 171-78, 179, 181

Pacifism, 117, 118, 124, 176-77, 216-31, 305-07, 346, 349, 350-352
Pact of Paris, 204-06
Pakistan, 351
Passion Play, Oberammergau, 404-412
Passion plays in Britain, Netherlands, 411
Pasternak, Boris, 384-87
Paton, Alan, 293
Peace-of-mind religion, 47, 54-56, 58

Peerman, Dean, 379
Pierce, Edith Lovejoy, 437
Pius XII, 356-58
Plato, 114, 116, 117, 306, 425
Poetry, 383-84, 385
Poland, 242
Poll tax, 253
Poteat, Edwin McNeill, 432
Presbyterian Church in the U.S.A., 52
Prohibition, 153-54, 286, 287-91
Protestant Episcopal Church, 156, 179-80, 288
Protestantism, 26-28, 31, 66-70, 97-102, 133, 139-94, 201, 211, 321, 326, 327-31, 390-91, 394-98, 411

Quakers, 28, 179, 347
Quintus Quiz, 423, 426

Race relations, 26, 27, 166, 167-69, 175, 182, 252-54, 293-307, 313, 317-18, 410, 416-17
Rankin, Jeannette, 249-50
Rawlins, Winifred, 435
Religiosity, 28, 53-58, 63, 397
Religious education, 337, 361-66
Revivalism, 27, 28, 70-77, 340
Roman Catholic Church, 27, 67, 156-57, 266, 289, 321, 326, 328-331, 356-59, 374-79, 389-90, 394-95, 411, 416-17
Roosevelt, Franklin D., 240, 241, 243, 245, 260, 350
Rowland, Stanley J., Jr., 441
Russia, 209, 213, 240-44, 257, 266, 267-68, 345, 384-87

Sacraments, 45, 46, 161-63, 178, 182, 190, 191
Safed the Sage, 423
Salveson, Lord, 153-54
Santayana, George, 25
Saturday Evening Post, 399-400
Schools, parochial, 328, 330
Schools, public, 302
Schweitzer, Albert, 359
Science, 24-26, 83-86, 114-16, 335-339, 346-48
Scopes, John T., 336, 338

Scotland, 43-47, 81-86, 139-41, 178
Secularism, 23-28, 59-65, 76, 180
Shelby, Montana, 335
Sheppard, Dick, 177
Shillito, Edward, 173, 423
Simeon Stylites, 423, 428
Sino-Japanese war, 208-11, 216-31, 247-48
Sockman, Ralph, 53
Solomon and Sheba, 395, 396, 397
South Africa, 175
Spain, 374-79
Speer, Robert, 87, 142, 147
Stalin, Josef, 209, 240-44, 350
Stamps, postage, 311-13
Steiner, Edward A., 404, 415
Stockholm conference on Life and Work, 148-55, 180, 220
Stoneburner, Tony, 438
Suburbia, 59-65
Supreme Court, 302, 303, 318-21, 327
Sweden, 148-49, 175
Switzerland, 97, 99, 102

Tax exemption for churches, 327-331
Television, 398, 401
Temperance movement, 286, 287-293
Temple, William, 179, 182
Theology, 25, 26, 30, 33-34, 39, 41, 46, 48, 54-58, 63, 83-135, 146, 160-63, 173-74, 183-84, 192, 219-221, 225-28, 288-89, 290, 293-97, 307, 347-48, 353, 399, 402-03
Tillich, Paul, 109, 123, 129, 130
Toynbee, Arnold J., 36
Truman, Harry S., 266, 281

Unitarians, 85
United Nations, 266, 269, 373

Valley of the Fallen, 375-79
Van Dyke, Tertius, 431
Vatican, 156, 356-58, 375

War, attitudes toward, 92, 117-20, 124, 150-53, 154, 176-77, 193, 198-207, 212-31, 245-51, 259-269, 312, 346, 348-49, 386
Webster, Daniel, 206
Weigle, Luther A., 322
Westerfield, Hargis, 433
'Westerns,' 398-403
White citizens' councils, 301, 303
White, Hugh Vernon, 29
Whitehead, Albert, 26, 116
Wienandt, Elwyn A., 388
Wilder, Amos N., 431
Wilkinson, Frank, 319
Wilson, Woodrow, 200, 241, 350
Winter, Gibson, 59
Wolfers, Arnold, 343, 344, 345
WCTU, 289
Wordsworth, William, 91
World Council of Churches, 66, 185-94, 258-59
World War I, 97, 101, 176, 199-203, 212-15, 241, 261, 312
World War II, 240-49, 280-84, 312
Worship, 28, 40, 45-46, 91-96, 100-101, 134, 172, 178, 388-94

Yoke and the Arrow, The, 378

Zeppelin, Count, 197
Zionism, 368, 371